John M. Ingham reviews recent developments in psychological anthropology and argues for an inclusive approach that finds room for psychoanalytic, dialogical, and social perspectives on personality and culture. The argument is developed with special reference to human nature, child development, personality, and mental disorder, and it draws on studies set in many different cultures. He also shows the relevance of some recent work in psychoanalysis and child development to current concerns in anthropology with agency and rhetoric.

Publications of the Society for Psychological Anthropology 8

Psychological anthropology reconsidered

Publications of the Society for Psychological Anthropology

Publications of the Society for Psychological Anthropology is a joint initiative of Cambridge University Press and the Society for Psychological Anthropology, a unit of the American Anthropological Association. The series has been established to publish books in psychological anthropology and related fields of cognitive anthropology, ethnopsychology, and cultural psychology. It includes works of original theory, empirical research, and edited collections that address current issues. The creation of this series reflects a renewed interest among culture theorists in ideas about the self, mind–body interaction, social cognition, mental models, processes of cultural acquisition, motivation and agency, gender, and emotions.

1 Roy G. D'Andrade and Claudia Strauss (eds.): *Human motives and cultural models*

2 Nancy Rosenberger (ed.): *Japanese sense of self*

3 Theodore Schwartz, Geoffrey M. White and Catherine A. Lutz (eds.): *New directions in psychological anthropology*

4 Barbara Diane Miller (ed.): *Sex and gender hierarchies*

5 Peter G. Stromberg: *Language and self-transformation*

6 Eleanor Hollenberg Chasdi (ed.): *Culture and human development*

7 Robert L. Winzeler: *Latah in Southeast Asia: the history and ethnography of a culture-bound syndrome*

Psychological anthropology reconsidered

John M. Ingham

University of Minnesota

CAMBRIDGE
UNIVERSITY PRESS

Published by the Press Syndicate of the University of Cambridge
The Pitt Building, Trumpington Street, Cambridge CB2 1RP
40 West 20th Street, New York, NY 10011-4211, USA
10 Stamford Road, Oakleigh, Melbourne 3166, Australia

First published 1996

Printed in Great Britain at the University Press, Cambridge

A catalogue record for this book is available from the British Library

Library of Congress cataloguing in publication data

Ingham, John M., 1940–
    Psychological anthropology reconsidered/John
M. Ingham.
        p.   cm. – (Publications of the Society for Psychological
Anthropology; 8)
    Includes bibliographical references.
    ISBN 0 521 55107 2 (hardcover). – ISBN 0 521 55918 9 (pbk.)
    1. Ethnopsychology.   2. Personality and culture.   3. Social
psychology.   I. Title.   II. Series.
GN502.I55   1996
155.8–dc20   95-39730   CIP

ISBN 0 521 55 107 2 hardback
ISBN 0 521 55 918 9 paperback

SE

Contents

Figures

Preface

In this book I review work in contemporary psychological anthropology. I also consider psychoanalysis and the social analysis of cultural forms, among other things. As I see it, psychological anthropology is a good deal more than a branch of cultural anthropology that studies the individual; it is the place where we can begin to reimagine a holistic understanding of human beings and the human condition.

Throughout this book I resist theoretical extremes, reductionism, and one-sided formulations and hold instead that human behavior is complex, dialectical, dialogical, even paradoxical. Rather than emphasizing either the psychological determination of culture or, what is now more common, cultural influences on the individual, I look for tension and interplay between individual subjectivity and collective thought and behavior.

The notion of dialogue captures some of this sense of complexity, dialectic, and interplay. In dialogism, human subjects are subjects as well as objects; they speak as well as listen, and they influence each other. There is dialogue within persons as well as between them. Internal dialogues may result in various sorts of compromise formations, while interpersonal dialogues may move toward provisional social contracts and shared symbols and values. Alternatively, internal and interpersonal dialogues may end in unresolved tension and conflict. In either event, they influence each other; the conversations that go on within the person can influence communicative interaction and discursive practices. These interpersonal conversations can, in turn, influence internal conversations.

Another notion here is that classical and post-Freudian psychoanalysis offers the most comprehensive and anthropologically useful framework for thinking about personality. Implicitly dialogical, it can accommodate the observations of other dialogical perspectives. It is also more suggestive than other psychologies when it comes to interpreting and theorizing about the motivational underpinnings of social relations and the symbolic content of myth, ritual, folklore, and other cultural practices.

Admittedly, this favorable assessment of psychoanalysis runs counter to commonly expressed opinions. Psychoanalysis is often said to be reductionistic and antisocial and to lack scientific credibility. Throughout this book I challenge these reservations. I show that psychoanalysis describes a social creature, one who lives in society and takes shape through social experience, and I argue that classical and post-Freudian psychoanalysis are surprisingly consistent not only with ethnographic observations but also with what is now known about human nature. To be sure, some psychoanalytic ideas and propositions are questionable or outmoded (e.g., Freud's ideas about female psychology). But it is important to realize that psychoanalysis is a loose and evolving collection of ideas and observations, not a timeless, rigidly integrated theory; a few erroneous ideas do not impugn the whole enterprise.

Yet another theme here is an emphasis on social relations and social practice. Culture in my view is always and everywhere socially grounded. Social relations underlie expressive culture because social relationships are emotional matters for human beings. Since drive and emotion are important features of personality, social relations are where we are apt to find connections between personality and culture.

Here again I recommend a dialogical framework. Culture is not simply an expression of childhood experience or fantasy, as some psychoanalytically oriented writers once implied. Unconscious fantasies and desires are often too idiosyncratic or too generic to account for the peculiar characteristics of particular cultures in any case. What actually seems to happen is that the expression of the individual unconscious is mediated by internal dialogical processes and again in dialogue between individuals. Unconscious desire is modulated by common sense and moral reasoning. As individuals interact, they may further temper their thoughts and desires, consciously and unconsciously, to fit social expectations, and they may appeal to emotion or to unconscious fantasy in their interlocutors in order to strengthen the rhetorical effects of their discursive practices. These discursive practices may rekindle or strengthen unconscious fears, wishes, and fantasies. Over time, they may gradually restructure or retranscribe the unconscious residues of childhood experience and fantasy. In the social psychoanalytic perspective I formulate here childhood experience is still important, but it does not offer the reductionistic explanation for culture and cultural differences it seemed to promise in the earlier culture and personality studies.

Acknowledgments

This book developed while I taught psychological anthropology at the University of Minnesota. I am grateful to the many students who stimulated my thinking and alerted me to relevant contributions in the scholarly literature. I am indebted especially to Mary Larson, Cynthia Rudolph, and Bjørn Westgard for reading the manuscript and offering incisive comments.

Many friends and colleagues have been helpful. Robert Butler, Mary M. Grove, Robert A. Paul, David H. Spain, and Melford E. Spiro read entire drafts. Tom Conley commented on an earlier version of the Introduction, and L. Alan Sroufe read the chapter on childhood. Gloria Goodwin Raheja and Tullio Maranhão read earlier versions of the section on Hindu India. The thoughtful comments of two anonymous reviewers for the Society of Psychological Anthropology and Cambridge University Press prompted many improvements. Deborah Schoenholz drew the figures. I am grateful to Sylvia Rosen for editorial assistance. Anthony Braus's encouragement was crucial. I also wish to thank Jessica Kuper and Sandy Anthony at Cambridge University Press for editorial assistance. I owe many thanks as well to my wife Mary and to our children, Sean and Anika; their love and patience made all the difference.

I am thankful to Kathleen Barlow for providing me with a copy of her dissertation and an unpublished paper on cognitive development among the Murik Lakes people of Papua New Guinea, and to David H. Lipset for allowing me to draw on his description and analysis of Murik myth and ritual in his work, to be published later in 1996 by Cambridge University Press as *Mangrove man: The embodiment of society in the Sepik estuary*. Other acknowledgments are the following:

> Figure 2: The trinue brain. *The triune brain in evolution: Role in paleocerebral functions*, by Paul D. MacLean. Copyright © 1990 by Plenum Publishing Company. Reprinted with permission of author and publisher.
>
> The dialogue between Billy and Mother. Kurt W. Fischer and Malcolm W. Watson. "Explaining the Oedipus conflict," p. 84.

In K.W. Fischer (ed.), Cognitive development. *New directions for child development* 12 (1981): 79–92.

The passage on depression. *Black sun: Depression and melancholia*, by Julia Kristeva. Copyright © 1989 by Columbia University Press. Reprinted with permission of the publisher.

Part of the section on Hindu India. John M. Ingham, "Oedipality in pragmatic discourse: The Trobriands and Hindu India." *Ethos* (in press). Reprinted with permission of the American Anthropological Association.

1   Introduction

Common experience provides a glimpse of what psychological anthropology is about. We are individuals who have feelings, desires, thoughts, and memories. We are, in effect, psychological beings. Yet we are social and cultural creatures also. We live in communities and in moral worlds of shared (and contested) symbols, beliefs, and values.

Ordinary experience also suggests that these subjective and social worlds affect each other. Our feelings register our successes and disappointments in social life. We often think with the words, meanings, and images of our cultures. Even our dreams and daydreams reflect our social experiences and cultural surroundings. It is perhaps less apparent that this relation between personality and culture is reciprocal, that culture reflects intrapsychic states and processes. Even so, with a little effort we can notice that we bring feelings, desires, thoughts, and purposes to social relations and cultural activities.

Psychological anthropology is concerned with these subjective and sociocultural worlds and with the interplay between them. Scholars in psychological anthropology examine social and cultural influences on individual psychology and the psychological foundations of social behavior and shared culture. As individuals, we have a great deal of intuitive knowledge about personality and culture. Still, such knowledge is constrained by our cultural and social horizons and, perhaps, by the fact that meanings and motives can be unconscious. In psychological anthropology scholars try to go beyond these limits by studying personality in other cultures and by entering into an ongoing discussion about ethnographic observations and interpretive perspectives.

I take a position in this discussion by arguing for a broadly psychoanalytic view of personality and a socially grounded view of culture. Personality and culture, it seems to me, are complicated phenomena. I prefer psychoanalytic and dialogical perspectives on personality because they recognize this complexity. Together, they imply that human beings are embodied, desiring, willful, anxious creatures as well as thoughtful, moral, speaking subjects.

1

Psychoanalytic and dialogical views of personality also afford a more interesting view than other theories of the social entanglements of personality and culture. Whatever else it may be, culture is a social phenomenon. Cultural beliefs and practices symbolize and sanctify social relations or, alternatively, they are used to call social relations into question. Expressive culture in particular reflects and informs sociality in these ways. People use cultural symbols, idioms, and rituals to mark social boundaries, to affirm social positions, and to negotiate (and renegotiate) the social contract. While informing culture in these ways, social relations also involve emotion and motivation. Thus, social relations are important for understanding the connection between personality and culture. We will see that many of these connections involve dialogue or discourse about power, eroticism, attachment, and anxieties about self-preservation, that is, issues that figure prominently in psychoanalytic thinking about motivation.

Human beings are power-seeking creatures. Hobbes and Nietzsche made this observation, as have various twentieth-century writers. Social theorists recognize power as a ubiquitous dimension in social relations. It can involve not merely an ability to coerce but also authority, prestige, and wealth. Psychoanalysts refer to the power-seeking impulse as narcissism – the person's striving for and experience of social and moral superiority. Eroticism informs courtship, art, ritual, humor, folklore, carnival and saturnalia and, in more subtle forms, many other activities as well. Attachment appears in parent–child relationships, kinship, friendship, and other social ties. Eroticism and attachment occur together in passionate attachments, marriage, and zealous loyalty to charismatic religious and political leaders. Many individual and collective beliefs and practices can be seen as attempts to allay anxiety by ensuring a safe and predictable environment.

I also stress that the interconnectedness of subjectivity and sociocultural milieu involves discursive interaction and individual agency. Subjects interact with one another and take turns influencing each other. Subjects are shaped by social and cultural expectations; they listen and accede to what others are saying, learn the rules, and internalize the norms. They follow political leaders, respect the knowledge and expertise of elders and authorities, model themselves after cultural heroes and exemplars. Yet subjects not only listen, they also speak. They become authorities and leaders. They argue and negotiate with one another about values and about the meaning, form, and salience of cultural practices. They produce things and create culture. Even when working within existing institutions and genres, subjects are constantly experimenting and inventing. They may conform to the canons of accepted usage, but what they say is often original. It may also prove persuasive, thus modifying the body of received opinion and understanding.

Culture and personality studies

The social dialogical-psychoanalytic approach I favor and develop here differs from the earlier culture and personality studies. It also differs from contemporary forms of cultural determinism. The psychological approaches in culture and personality studies were too reductionistic and, at the same time, too preoccupied with accounting for differences between cultures. The culturalist versions and their contemporary successors, on the other hand, put too much emphasis on the cultural shaping of the individual while giving too little thought to human nature and the general psychological foundations of culture.

Between 1930 and 1960 or so the working hypothesis was that personality and culture are mutually congruent elements of a society. One version of this thinking tried to account for cultural differences in terms of group differences in personality. The neo-Freudian psychoanalyst Abram Kardiner (1939) argued that the "primary institutions" (family organization, childcare and rearing practices, patterns of neglect, etc.) of a society produce a shared "basic personality structure." This set of shared, core features of personality, in turn, affects the projective style of individuals and thus the "secondary institutions" of a culture (e.g., art, religion, folklore, politics). According to this view, the effect of one set of cultural institutions on another is mediated through shared personality.

Studies were undertaken to support the group personality idea with ethnographic description and personality tests, particularly the Rorschach Ink Blot Test and the Thematic Apperception Test (TAT). Other researchers attempted to document childhood determinism of culture with the cross-cultural method. Correlations between child-rearing practices and secondary institutions in large samples of the world's cultures were seen as indicating the influence of formative experiences and shared personality (Whiting and Child 1953).

Generally speaking, the efforts to explain cultural differences psychologically were not very successful. For one thing, it was found that the people of different societies could have similar psychological characteristics even though they had very different cultures (Kaplan 1954). Studies also revealed considerable psychological variation in human groups, even when the people of a group seemed to share a homogeneous culture. Shared psychological traits were often abstractions that subsumed actual individual differences (Devereux 1961).

Childhood determinism of personality was another questionable postulate. Culture and personality theory assumed that socialization practices have highly predictable consequences for adult personality. The findings from child development, however, were ambiguous on this point, and cross-cultural correlations between child-rearing practices and adult customs varied from modest to nonexistent. In an important review of the field, Anthony F.C. Wallace (1970) concluded that "organization of diversity" probably better describes the relation between personality and society than "replication of uniformity."[1]

Another approach in culture and personality studies emphasized the role of culture in shaping subjective experience. In *Coming of age in Samoa*, Margaret Mead (1928) contended that adolescent emotional turmoil is a by-product of culture; while it may be commonplace in the west, it is largely absent in Samoa. In *Patterns of culture*, Ruth Benedict (1934) suggested that different cultures form distinct configurations, much like individual personalities, and she emphasized that culture shapes the thought patterns, attitudes, and moods of entire peoples.

Cultural interpretivism, postmodernism, and cultural psychology

Many scholars find in the shortcomings of psychological explanation an argument for the cultural determinism of Ruth Benedict and the early Margaret Mead, that is, for focusing on how culture or discourse shapes individual subjectivity. Current versions of this approach reflect the influence of cultural interpretivism and postmodernism.[2]

Clifford Geertz, the leading advocate of cultural interpretivism, was influenced by the sociologist Talcott Parsons. Parsons viewed culture as a system of symbols and meanings and as a powerful influence on the individual. Drawing on Durkheim and Freud, he understood this influence in moral terms. Durkheim saw symbolic orders as collective representations that reinforce social solidarity and moral order while suppressing the egoistic inclinations of individuals. Parsons supplemented this insight into the role of collective representations in shaping the moral behavior of the individual with Freud's concept of the superego. For Parsons, the notion of the superego helped to explain at a psychological level how a collective moral order actually shapes the moral behavior of the individual.

Building on Parsons's view of culture as a system of symbols, Geertz (1973, 1983) reasoned that understanding culture requires interpretation, not explanation. To Geertz, cultures are exemplified in public symbols and meanings. The self, emotion, and subjective experience are shaped in different ways by local cultures.

Postmodernism has roots in both Durkheim's emphasis on the collective nature of culture and the linguistics of Ferdinand de Saussure. Saussure distinguished between speech and language. Speech is a novel concatenation of signifiers that affirms something, often something about the world. Language, in contrast, is a system of shared and arbitrary conventions involving relations between signifiers. Saussure's concept of language, in other words, drew attention to relations between units within language and away from the ways in which intentional subjects use signifiers to represent the world (Harland 1987).

This inclination to emphasize group and language was taken further by Lévi-Strauss, Lacan, Althusser, and, more recently, Foucault, Barthes, and Derrida. Lévi-Strauss argued that cultures are constructed on frameworks of symbolic oppositions, mediations, and analogies. He assumed that such structures are shared and unconscious, and he paid little regard to intentional individuals or actual sociality.

Jacques Lacan asserted that language and culture are part of the very structure of the mind. For Lacan, Freud's early work on hysteria suggested that the "unconscious is structured like a language" (1978: 20). The unconscious minds of Freud's patients seemed to Lacan to incorporate the voices of social others. In effect, the unconscious is the language and culture of the group. Language, the signifying chain (the Other), is held together by moral authority, by what Lacan called "The-Law-of-the-Father" or the "Phallus." In effect, Lacan tended to merge the superego with the id, the seat of unconscious desire, and to expand the superego-id at the expense of the ego, which he viewed as a fiction of western society. The neo-Marxist Althusser equated the symbolic with ideology. Thus it was the dominant ideology, the "Law of Culture," that constructed the subject (see Smith 1988: 19–20).

Postmodernism retains structuralism's emphasis on the group and on the relations between signifiers, but it no longer portrays cultures as coherent systems. It questions the representational functions of language and even the existence of a conscious, intentional subject. Skepticism is expressed about the power of signs or signifiers to represent meanings or the objective world, and attention is turned to the "play of signifiers," to how signifiers refer to other signifiers. The individual subject ceases to be a locus of intention who speaks about the world and becomes instead a decentered artifact of the symbolic system. Lacking depth, continuity, coherence, moral center, agency, or – it seems – contact with reality, the individual is little more than a relay in the semiotic circuitry (see Colapietro 1990). According to Kenneth J. Gergen, "The question 'why' is answered not with a psychological state or process but with consideration of persons in relationship" (1985: 271). Meaning is unstable and displaced; there is never a fixed meaning or purpose in any human activity. Structures are critiqued or deconstructed in terms of what they exclude or take for granted (Sampson

1989). Postmodernism, then, disregards underlying motives, meanings, or structures. The emphasis falls instead on the way in which social and cultural context shape various subjective positions, experiences, and modes of living.

Richard A. Shweder (1991) has been a forceful advocate of culturalist and postmodernist thinking in psychological anthropology. Shweder (ibid.: 88) opines that "psychological anthropology" is a misguided search for the "transcendental" in a world of mere "appearances," and for universals where there are only local, cultural psychologies. Shweder urges us to avoid assumptions about psychic unity or underlying mechanisms in human psychology and to consider instead the ways in which individual psychology is culturally constituted and culturally variable. Shweder and others who share his culturalist orientation attempt to show that emotions, intentions, the self, and moral reasoning vary from one culture to another.

Intentional individuals and intentional worlds, according to Shweder, create and recreate each other through dialectical interaction. "The breath of psyche is the stuff of intentional states, of beliefs and desires, of fears and fancies, of values and visions about this or that" (Shweder 1991: 101). "Culture," meanwhile, "refers to the intentional world" (ibid.). The distinction between intentional selves and intentional worlds seems to allow some separation between psyche and culture, and even seems to leave the door slightly ajar for a motivated subject; on closer inspection, however, we see that "the breath of psyche" reflects cultural conceptions about "self, society, and nature" (ibid.: 102). The breath of the individual, that is, comes from the surrounding atmosphere. In effect, the metaphor downplays the embodied, stable nature of personality and construes personality as a transient effect of culturally patterned discourse.

In cultural psychology the emphasis falls on language and intellect.[3] Cultures consist of cultural values, principles, or schemas, particularly as they are expressed in language. Moral beliefs are especially important for understanding behavior. Thus, the superego is the one concept from psychoanalysis Shweder finds useful (Shweder 1980). This, of course, is the same theme we see in Durkheim, Parsons, and Lacan.

Each culture, according to Shweder, defines a distinct reality. The origins or reasons for cultural beliefs do not seem especially problematic for Shweder. Sociological, pragmatic, and psychoanalytic strategies of interpretation are dismissed as "Nietzschean" because they treat the "reality posits" of other peoples (e.g., their beliefs about gods, ghosts, spirits, demons, etc.) as manifestations of underlying forces or structures rather than as self-sufficient propositions.

There is much that is appealing in interpretivism, postmodernism, and cultural psychology. The contention that cultures shape thought, emotion, moral orientation, and the self is well-documented and unexceptionable. Human behavior is meaningful, and understanding it requires interpretation. Memory and perception are structured by cultural assumptions and preconceptions, and signifiers can have multiple, shifting, and contextual meanings. A good deal of human behavior makes sense in terms of culturally constituted situations.

Culturalism, postmodernism, and cultural psychology, however, reify and overemphasize the group and culture. In this respect, they recall Parsons's sociology. In a trenchant but now largely overlooked paper, Dennis Wrong (1961) observed that Parsons assumed that human beings are more socialized than they actually are. Wrong pointed out that Parsons's use of the superego concept disregarded Freud's understanding of intrapsychic conflict, and he questioned the inclination of his colleagues in sociology to overemphasize needs for social approval. "Sociologists," Wrong noted, "have appropriated the superego concept, but have separated it from the Freudian id" (ibid.: 187). These trends, he suggested, were corollaries of a tendency to exaggerate stability and integration in social formations. Sociology in Wrong's view had settled uncritically for a "disembodied, conscience-driven, status-seeking" caricature of real individuals (ibid.: 193). Melford E. Spiro (1984, 1986, 1993a) expresses similar reservations about culturalism and postmodernism.[4] He doubts that self and emotion are simply or primarily socially constructed or culturally formed, and, like Wrong, he wonders what happened to the id.

Desire and thought are influenced by discourse and expressed in words. And words figure prominently in the organization and expression of the self. It is too simplistic, however, to say that the unconscious is structured like a language. Images and emotion probably play a greater role in unconscious thought than language. Moreover, an emphasis on the linguistic structuring of the mind begs questions about the precultural and prelinguistic foundations of cultural schemas and linguistic structures. Culturalism and postmodernism have little to say, Spiro observes, about the enigmatic content of culture or about emotionality in human behavior.

Additionally, they underestimate human capacities for accurate observation and rational reasoning. In emphasizing how people make inferences from arbitrary "reality-posits" (i.e., beliefs about the world, natural and supernatural), culturalism and postmodernism tend to disregard the social and psychological foundations of collective beliefs and representations. They underestimate the ability of human beings to perceive and represent the world and thus to question and resist authoritative assertions and dominant ideologies. "Reality-posits," in other words, may be more or less rational than Shweder admits. The notion that cultural beliefs are valid in their own terms, moreover, disregards how beliefs are contested and negotiated in social life. It also blurs the differences between practical knowledge and ideology, reality testing and delusion, understanding and misunderstanding, and authenticity and artfulness. It thus glosses over variations in personality and many dialectical complexities and contradictions in social life.

My principal criticism of culturalism and postmodernism is that they simply have too little to say about the details of personality, society, and culture. They either ignore subjectivity or reduce it to culture or social context. And they tend to gloss over social structure and the symbolic content of culture. The two inclinations are interrelated. Social relations involve desire and emotion. In oversimplifying or ignoring desire and emotion, these perspectives also minimize or elide the subject's affective involvement in both mutually supportive relationships and competition for wealth and power.

Cultural psychology, it seems to me, is too postmodern insofar as it disregards the precultural origins of emotion and motivation. On the other hand it is not postmodern enough insofar as it ignores the political motivation of cultural constructions. Serious social theory involves concerns with power, agency, and pragmatics. Serious psychological anthropology, in turn, requires serious social theory. Psychological anthropology, in other words, must be Nietzschean to some extent.

Cultural psychologists may reply that they are interested in subjectivity, desire, or agency. Joan G. Miller (1994: 143–144), for example, avers that cultural psychology differs from cultural determinism and structuralism in this respect. If this is so, cultural psychology is more promising than one would have thought. In practice, however, cultural psychology has little to say about individual motivation or how, through social practice, motivation hooks up with social relations and culture. Cultural psychology clearly disavows human nature, and it reduces the psyche to internalized cultural ideas and propositions. In other words, cultural psychology lacks a compelling story about the intrapsychic, embodied foundations of will, desire, and agency.

Freudian subjects and dialogical selves

In this book, "personality" comprises the emotional and mental characteristics of the individual. It includes basic drives and needs, emotional capacities and dispositions, and ongoing wishes, desires, and purposes. It also involves representations of emotionally significant others, self-representations, cognitive style, attitudes and values, and patterns of moral reasoning.

Personality has various parts. In the psychoanalytic scheme, the *id* includes drives and impulses and primitive, poetic thought processes. The *ego* is the executive agency of personality, the seat of the person or subject and self-representations. The person or subject is animated by drive, need, and emotion, and self-representations reflect embodied experiences with social others. The *superego* is the seat of conscience and the ego-ideal. Each of these components has its own purpose and agenda. While they work together at times they also may work at cross purposes.

A basic assumption here is that wishes, desires, and thoughts are often unconscious. Individuals may be unaware of their personal desires, purposes, and fantasies and, at the same time, less than fully aware of the layered meanings of their cultural beliefs and practices. Such lack of conscious awareness can be habitual but, also, it can be intentional, a form of self-deception. Whether unconscious motives and meanings are personal or widely shared, they may be influential precisely because they escape conscious scrutiny.

Another notion is that the most influential unconscious desires and fantasies often develop in the early and middle years of childhood, especially in experiences with parents and siblings. These "nuclear fantasies" center on attachment, separation and loss, gender identity, and the self, or they involve erotic desire and needs for empowerment. Unconscious wishes and desires may conflict with the demands of objective reality and cultural rules. As a result, thinking and behavior are often mixtures of will and desire on the one hand and moral values and social aims on the other.

These ideas about the role of unconscious thought and conflict in mental life were first formulated in systematic fashion by Sigmund Freud. In his studies of hysteria, Freud discerned anxiety about repressed wishes and traumatic experiences. Obsessive-compulsive disorder, in contrast, seemed to involve guilt about illicit wishes. The hysterical patient expressed unconscious conflicts in a language of the body or splitting of consciousness, whereas the obsessive patient was caught in a cycle of forbidden wishes, guilt, and expiatory rituals. In both conditions, Freud found the beginnings of disorder in childhood traumas or fantasies. He also noticed, however, that constitutional factors, idiosyncratic perceptions of objective events, and creative revisions of memories in response to later experience make the consequences of childhood events and fantasies hard to predict.[5]

The study of hysteria and obsessive-compulsive neurosis and their childhood origins led Freud to a theory of personality and mental disorder. Sexual and aggressive drives were singled out as especially important. These were seen as regulated by the ego and superego. Distinct personality styles represented variations in emotional disposition and diverse compromises between desire and self-control. Dreams, humor, and the errors of everyday life also revealed intrapsychic tensions. Depression was a turning of anger against the self, and schizophrenia was a dreamlike state resulting from a major rupture in ego organization.

In psychoanalysis, these formulations have been emended and revised in various ways (see Eagle 1984; Pine 1990). Object-relations theory has drawn more attention to human needs for attachment and security and to the inherently social nature of all drives and emotions. Self psychology and clinical studies of personality disorders have brought narcissism, an affectively colored striving for perfection and "a felt quality of perfection" (Rothstein 1984: 17), to the fore of theoretical discussion (Kohut 1971).

A corollary of this increased attention to needs for love, attachment, and empowerment is more recognition of emotional vulnerability to loss and narcissistic injuries. Losses of love and blows to self-esteem are common sources of negative affect in human beings. Such traumas figure repeatedly in the etiology and onset of various emotional disorders. Early psychoanalysts were aware of this fact but it took self psychology and object-relations theory to refocus attention on objective events in childhood. The result is a clearer picture of the childhood experiences that are most apt to have important effects on the development of normal and abnormal personality.

In trauma, defenses are overwhelmed and the sense of safety is shattered. After trauma, people try to reestablish control and a feeling of security. To this end they may revisit or recreate traumatic scenes to try to transform victimization into security, agency, or triumph. They also may try to redress losses and blows to self-esteem with substitutive objects or ego-enhancing tokens of power and prestige.

Since its beginning, psychoanalysis has been interested in the way in which people use words to express desire and to defend themselves against anxiety. This interest in language is even greater in contemporary psychoanalytic thought, partly because of the influence of Lacan.

Lacan is controversial (the unconscious, contrary to his notion, is not simply or primarily linguistic), but there is an important sense in which the personality involves language. People express themselves in behavior but, also, and perhaps especially, in speech. They identify, define, and memorialize themselves in the stories they tell about themselves (Spence 1982, 1987). Symbolic interactionists similarly see the self as a narrative, as stories individuals tell about themselves (Sarbin 1986). This role of story telling in self-representation is not, it seems, merely a western phenomenon. Ethnographic reports show that in many cultures narratives are part of self-organization (Peacock and Holland 1993).

According to psychoanalysis, wishes, desires, anxieties, and fantasies develop in relationships, and self-representations reflect both identifications with others and the way in which others mirror the self back to the self. The individual's habitual modes of relating to and talking with others, then, develop in self–other relationships and dialogical interactions (Cantlie 1993; Daelemans and Maranhão 1990; Maranhão 1986).

The American pragmatists (Charles Sanders Peirce, William James, John Dewey, and George Herbert Mead) and the Russian literary theorist Mikhail Bahktin have also noticed that dialogical interaction is important for understanding personality and its expression. In their views, the individual exists in a community of speakers and constructs himself or herself with the signs and meanings that circulate within the community. At the same time, individuals express and assert themselves (Colapietro 1990). They "author" themselves through speech even as they work with the linguistic and cultural materials of their communities (Holquist 1990). They talk to each other but also to themselves (Hermans and Kempen 1993; Singer 1984).

Throughout his writings Freud tended to portray the relations between mental agencies as conversations or arguments. Similarly, D.W. Winnicott (1965), Christopher Bollas (1987), and other object-relations theorists construe intrapsychic object relations as intrapsychic dialogues. Julia Kristeva (1982, 1986) is an interesting thinker in this regard because she brings together semiotics, dialogism, and a more conventionally psychoanalytic understanding of drive than one finds in Lacan. She divides what Lacan called the "symbolic" into the semiotic chora and the thetic or symbolic proper. The semiotic is associated with drives, emotions, rhythms, and metaphor and metonymy. Developmentally, it is preoedipal and thus, for Kristeva, associated with the maternal. The symbolic is the discursive, rule-bound semantics of authority, language, and cultural rules. Her notion of the semiotic draws on Bakhtin's notion of carnival; the semiotic resists the symbolic but also transgresses it and merges with it, giving it vitality and force.

In fact, psychoanalysis and dialogism are complementary. Although psychoanalysis is more concerned with the deep-seated, enduring motivation in the subject, and dialogism gives more attention to language in self-expression and self-formation, both perspectives find will, desire, and an ability to speak in the individual subject. Like psychoanalysis, some versions of symbolic interactionism and dialogism see the subject as an embodied subject. For James, feeling and intention are core experiences of the self; and in the work of George Herbert Mead, the "I" of enunciation is closely associated with feelings and drives. Dewey also began with an embodied self (Colapietro 1990). For Bakhtin, the self is an embodied, situated self with a unique perspective (Holquist 1990). Bakhtin also recognized the bodily basis of the self through his notion of carnival, an evocation of the lustful body, ambiguity, creativity, humor, and spontaneity that resists dominant discourse (Bakhtin 1984).

There is, moreover, some agreement about the internal organization of the mind. Bakhtin translated the psychoanalytic opposition between conscious and unconscious into an intrapsychic opposition between private ideology and public ideology (Clark and Holquist 1984: 183). In psychoanalytic theory communication between parts of the mind resembles ideas about dialogue between internal voices in current versions of symbolic interactionism. Similarly, the psychoanalytic notion of repression can be reformulated in dialogism as the dominance of one internal voice and the suppression of another (Hermans et al. 1992; Hermans and Kempen 1993: 162–165).

Society, affect, and culture

Social relations, expressive culture, and feelings are interconnected. Social relations are everywhere matters of passion and affect, as are social symbols and meanings. Having power and fulfilling needs for love and security in social relations are associated with positive emotions, whereas loss of power, reputation, love, or security often triggers negative emotion. Mere references to social relations in ritual and discourse may stimulate will, desire, and emotion.

Power is expressed in and through language and symbols (Bourdieu 1991). When vying with one another for status and influence, social actors invoke truths, nostrums, and myths. Specialized knowledge and skills generally accompany higher social statuses and strata. In many cultures power is associated with fertility and sexuality. Men's secret organizations and fertility cults, for example, institutionalize the power of older men in relation to younger men and women, and higher-ranked clans often claim descent from illustrious ancestors. In complex societies, beliefs that rulers have mysterious, beneficent influences on animals, plants, or people may legitimize their positions and prerogatives.

Desire and needs for attachment and security inform social activity and social relations. We see their traces in courtship, marriage, kinship, friendship, youth gangs, godparenthood, or sacred covenants. In modern nations, social relations are predicated on shared citizenship and a common "motherland" or "fatherland." Emotional ties to leaders, elders, big men, chiefs, kings or queens, queen mothers, and patron deities and emotional investment in rituals of communion, which can include the sharing of festive meals, also bind groups together. Often leaders sponsor feasts, and the feasts themselves are apt to symbolize social solidarity and communion with the deity.

A common corollary of ingroup solidarity is hostility toward the outgroup. The ingroup ritualizes its cohesion in commensality whereas the outgroup represents danger and pollution. Leaders voice their concerns with dangerous others to reinforce ingroup solidarity and, especially, their own popularity within the group. Collective violence against scapegoats and war against the outgroup exemplify these tendencies.

Morality also figures in social relations and cultural discourse. Cultural beliefs and practices in many societies imply that social order depends on the regulation of wishes, needs, and desires. All societies have codes of conduct for sexual behavior that include prohibitions against incest. In many societies people relate the success of hunts, gardens, raiding parties, fertility rites, or religious ceremonies to sexual continence or the prevention of contamination from sexual fluids and emanations. High social status, in particular, may be thought to depend on asceticism although, sometimes, prodigious or risque sexual gratification is a special prerogative of royalty or aristocrats. Social rules and understandings regulate and constrain expressions of power and the acquisition of wealth. Unauthorized assertions of power are contested and censured. Mythic incest and parricide may represent a state of nature, the antithesis of affinal relationships between families and respect for authority.

In other words, moral values and cultural symbolism suggest that social order demands a shift from egoistic sexual interest to the sharing of food, exchanging women in marriage, or sublimating sexual concerns in fertility rituals. Cultural beliefs and practices are used in various ways to suppress disrespect for authority and subversive claims to power. Of course, valuation of authority and asceticism varies. In contrast to many pre-industrial societies and early capitalist society, there is less restraint and more skepticism about authority under the contemporary conditions of late modernity.

Even in traditional societies some idioms and practices are apt to express resistance to restraints on desire and will. People use conversation, humor, art, songs, laments, literature, saturnalia, and carnivals to express desire and to challenge or subvert political authority and received morality (Bakhtin 1984; de Certeau 1984; Scott 1990). Women dispute and contest patriarchal power and values in their stories, songs, and everyday speech. Moral positions and resistance are also affect laden. Moral positions may involve guilt, shame, or pride, while resistance may be motivated by desire, envy, resentment, and anger.

Agency, resistance, and the active subject

My contention is that a dialogical-psychoanalytic view of personality can illuminate these links between desire, emotion, and discursive practice in social life. I also think it can illuminate agency (and lack of agency) in the speaking subject. For many social theorists, the problem is no longer structure and stability but, rather, the interaction of structure and agency. Renato Rosaldo notes the manner in which agency raises questions about subjective states:

Insofar as it is concerned with how people's actions alter their forms of life, social analysis must attend to improvisation, muddling through, and contingent events. In this context, the study of consciousness becomes central because people always act (however imperfectly) relative to their desires, plans, whims, strategies, moods, goals, fantasies, intentions, impulses, purposes, visions, or gut feelings. (Rosaldo 1993: 103)

It is difficult to imagine how individuals assert themselves in social life without assuming that they have emotional and mental characteristics.

Various writers have noted that the turn in social theory toward concerns with agency, practice, and pragmatics needs a psychoanalytic view of the motivated subject or something close to it (Mahoney and Yngvesson 1992; Paul 1990). The psychoanalytic ideas illuminate not only the subjective foundations of agency and resistance but also how the individual can act against social expectations. They help to account, moreover, for lack of will – the failure of the individual subject to exert agency or resistance – as Freud ([1892–1893]1966) showed in a paper about a woman who could not nurse her babies although she wanted to (see also Moran 1993: 13–15).

The woman was in her twenties, of good health, and generally free of any indications of mental disorder. With her first baby, she did not produce milk well, had pains in her breasts, and lacked appetite. The baby was turned over to a wet-nurse. When the second baby arrived, the effort to nurse failed again. Freud was consulted after this second disappointment. He promptly hypnotized the woman suggesting that she would "make an excellent nurse" and that the baby was going to do just fine. The woman regained her appetite and began to produce milk. On the following day she over-ate and her difficulties returned. Freud then hypnotized her again and addressed her more firmly. He told her among other things that after he left she would become angry with her family for *not giving her enough to eat*. Then her symptoms disappeared and she nursed her baby for eight months. The hypnotherapy again proved necessary with her third baby, and again the treatment was entirely successful.

An unconscious, countervailing will seemed to work against the woman's conscious will, even at a physiological level. Freud theorized that intentions and expectations can prompt antithetical ideas and in this and other cases of hysteria, the antithetical ideas may take on a life of their own.

To be sure, there is less explicit attention to subjectivity and agency in Freud's later work. Agency became a quality of different components of the mind, and the subject and self were viewed as parts of the "mental apparatus" in Freud's later, more systematic theorizing about personality. Lacan is interesting in part precisely because he refocused attention on subjectivity, desire, and agency (Moran 1993).

According to Lacan, agency derives from words, from the Other, or culture, and operates unconsciously within a divided subject, although in places Lacan also seems to allow that the speaking subject makes meaning. Agency is a quality of the signifier and the subject is itself a by-product of the signifying process. To put it another way, desire reflects the voices of social others and, beyond them, the symbolic order. The origin of desire is the splitting of the relationship with the mother. It operates in a space between physiological need and a demand for love which the other may or may not be willing or able to fulfill. Once the child begins to speak, she may use "Mommy" as a symbolic substitute for the mother. The word fills the place where the mother once was, but because it is merely a word it installs the mother's absence in the unconscious. Through metonymy or metaphor, other words may replace "Mommy" as the representation of longing. Words thus generate a chain of unsatisfied desire.

Lacan can be read in different ways. One reading places him within the current of thinking that leads to postmodernism. By this reading, Lacan emphasizes the influence of the symbolic order on the individual subject and the way in which social influence produces a fragmented, divided subject.

Another reading gives a more complicated picture of the subject. In this picture the subject is divided by the internalization of external voices but also sutures together the parts of the self with signifiers. Moreover, the subject identifies with others in imagination to fashion a makeshift coherence of the self. The desiring, agentic subject participates in creating and recreating the very symbolic order that shapes the subject in the first place (Žižek 1989).

This second reading of Lacan is more useful for my purposes. Indeed, there will be some Lacanian nuances in my approach in this book. Still, it seems to me that Lacan overemphasized the linguistic and cultural determinants of subjectivity and desire. As we shall see, there are important precultural and prelinguistic sources of motivation and agency. I also think that Lacan and many of Lacan's followers have been too quick to dismiss the coherent, volitional subject. While every personality is fragmented to some degree, integration is also a feature of personality. Some measure of integration seems necessary for agency, as the example of the non-nursing mother suggests. The most divided and fragmented personalities (e.g., persons with hysteria, multiple personality disorder, and schizophrenia) are often the ones who have the greatest difficulties negotiating social relations and pursuing effective courses of action.[6]

Social conditions, pragmatic discourse, and motivational structures

I try to piece together a more complete view of what motivates the subject than we get from either Lacan or his post-structuralist successors. I draw on the study of human evolution, studies of primate social behavior, and neurobiology to sketch a view of human nature. Building on this view, I then explore psychoanalytic and dialogical perspectives on child development, personality, and mental disorder. I suggest that the stages of child development, formative developmental experiences, and the common features of human personality reflect our evolutionary heritage.

I show how human nature responds to objective conditions and actual events. Not all situations are culturally constructed. Some are contingent and unexpected, and some are simply awful and tragic. Nor must situations always have cultural meaning, or a great deal of it, to have emotional significance for individuals. Poverty, victimization, losses, and blows to self-esteem figure in mental disorder and the subjective foundations of religious cults, political extremism, and collective violence in widely different social and cultural settings. They can also be the impetus for constructive transformations of the self and social relations. In either event, the explanation for the powerful subjective effects of adverse conditions may lie not simply in any cultural meaning they may have. It may also have something to do with human nature.[7]

Yet, I also suggest that personal motives and social meanings become interconnected through discourse and dialogue (Crapanzano 1992). In dialogue, speaking subjects make assertions and counter-assertions about themselves, each other, and their worlds. They try to define or transform themselves, others, and social relationships; they affirm claims to social status, love, and privilege or, more modestly, they may merely seek a fair arrangement, an equitable social contract. A series of conversations may produce or reproduce understandings about mutual rights and obligations or at least a stable disagreement.

While trying to influence social others speakers may invoke common sense and conscious and unconscious cultural understandings. They may also try to appeal to emotions and unconscious fantasies. Allusions to unconscious desires, wishes, and fears may render objects of exchange more valuable, the symbols of power more impressive, and ideological constructions more persuasive. When individuals exchange one item for another, make claims to power and desiderata, entertain each other with stories, songs, or drama, or merely amuse each other with humor, they may employ figurative images and idioms (Crapanzano 1981; Ewing 1987). Discourse may be more persuasive and agreement more likely when speakers imbue their speech with semantic ambiguity and emotional appeals, including appeals to unconscious fantasies. That is, speakers buttress their claims and contentions with tacit appeals to the hidden thoughts, fantasies, and emotions of their interlocutors. This is how we begin to understand why nurturing and reproductive metaphors, sexual symbolism, and oedipal themes often figure in humor, myths, rituals, and cosmologies.

In order to develop this idea about the pragmatic functions of cultural practices, it is necessary to have some working hypotheses about motivational structures in human beings. I explore the question of motivational structures in the chapters on human nature and childhood. And I consider motivational structures further in discussions of personality disorders and mental illness. As Freud noted, obsessional disorder and hysteria are particularly suggestive for thinking about the motivational foundations of society and culture.

In *Totem and taboo*, Freud argued that incest taboos and rules of exogamy among "primitive" peoples imply a dread of incest. He suggested that taboos governing behavior toward the dead and leaders may reflect unconscious feelings of hostility and fears of retribution. And he theorized that people project their unconscious thoughts and desires into ideas about magic and the dead and they fear, like obsessional neurotics, the consequences of their own thoughts. Obsessional neurosis, in effect, suggested to Freud that culture might reflect unconscious guilt about illicit desire, and that it can be expected to involve various attempts at expiation and reparation (Paul 1991).

Social systems, according to Freud, resemble hysteria in that they depend on identification with social others. In hysteria, bodily symptoms may replace love objects through identification; the painful body part may represent an attempt to hold on to the absent parent. Similarly, identifications with peers and leaders may substitute for primary object relations or fulfill needs for emotional attachment. Society, like hysteria, also involves hypnoid mental processes; followers may succumb to the influence of leaders much as hypnotic subjects accede to the will of hypnotists (Freud [1927a]1961, [1930]1961).

Psychoanalysts applied these ideas in studies of many social and cultural phenomena. Folklore and religion became fertile fields for investigation (see Dundes 1985a). Initiation rites, reproductive rituals, and sacrifice received attention (Money-Kyrle [1929]1965; Reik 1931); so, too, did art and literature, group formation, political leadership, revolution, and war (see Hoffman 1981; van Ginnekin 1984).

These studies, in turn, stimulated several anthropologists to consider the psychodynamic foundations of culture. Géza Róheim was the first to do so. Others included John Layard, George Devereux, Weston La Barre, and, more recently, Melford E. Spiro.[8] These scholars sometimes tried to account for cultural differences in psychological terms in ways that now seem questionable, but they were also interested in individuals and the universal psychological foundations of culture.

Various social anthropologists also incorporated psychoanalysis into their work, or at least had passing interests in psychoanalysis (e.g., T.O. Beidelman, D. Freeman, K. Gough, E.R. Leach, B. Malinowski, R. Murphy, W.H.R. Rivers, C.G. Seligman, and V. Turner).[9] These anthropologists were primarily social anthropologists, but they realized that there is an emotional, subjective dimension to social relations, and they noticed the sometimes strikingly Freudian content of expressive culture. Freud, in their view, was interesting, not because his theories could explain the differences between cultures but because they seemed to delineate the psychological foundations of social relations and expressive culture.

The orientation in psychological anthropology I prefer recoups and builds on the work of these two groups of scholars. It combines psychoanalysis and social analysis. Theorizing about the psychological foundations of society and culture is more productive when it considers social motives and meanings and unconscious motivation. Biographical studies are more illuminating when they consider both the subjective and social dimensions of a person's life. Social analysis, for its part, becomes more insightful – and more compelling – when it makes subjectivity part of the story.

Pathological models

A final issue is the use of mental disorders as models for understanding "normal" personality and collective behavior. Culturalists and postmodernists often complain that psychoanalytic interpretations of nonwestern cultures are Eurocentric and denigrating because they are based on psychopathology in western culture.

We have some unfortunate examples of heavy-handed use of pathological terminology in psychological anthropology but they are misuses of psychoanalysis. The psychoanalytic understanding of personality suggests that the difference between normal and abnormal is one of degree; abnormal psychology is merely an exaggeration of what is observed in "normal" individuals. Psychoanalysts discern similarities between the mental processes in neuroses and serious mental illness and those that motivate and organize dreams, slips of the tongue, mental lapses, superstitions, and poetry. They also observe that the emotional and mental problems of patients are often variations on common themes in human life. Psychoanalysis, in other words, humanizes our view of mental and emotional disorder much more than it pathologizes the unusual. Writers who regard all psychoanalytically oriented thinking in anthropology as "pathologizing" may be assuming, incorrectly, that persons with mental and emotional disorders are radically Other.

The use of models of neurosis and psychosis to understand human behavior need not imply that the people or cultures under study are pathological. Like people everywhere, they may simply have patterns of thought and motivation that are more apparent in neurosis or psychosis. The real issue is whether mental disorder has anything to teach us about normal psychology and its relation to culture.

Since culturalists and social constructionists are reluctant to make judgments about what is normal or abnormal (or good or bad), they might still object to any comparison, however tempered, of mental disorder to sociocultural phenomena. Yet in this event we should perhaps ask which is the more positive view of human beings: one that divests people of their common humanity and reduces them to artifacts of social discourse or one that portrays them as intentional but conflicted moral agents?

The prevalence of mental and emotional disorder is another consideration for this issue of the role of mental disorder in the psychological foundations of society and culture. Mental and emotional problems in living are common in western societies, and many persons suffer major mental or emotional problems during their lifetimes. Epidemiological studies reveal similar statistics in other societies. These findings may imply that psychiatrists and psychotherapists overdiagnose but they may also imply that the boundary between mental health and mental disorder is fuzzy at best. This in turn suggests that disorder, however we view it, probably informs normal sociality and cultural practice, a possibility that is even more likely when we consider that many persons with emotional and mental problems continue to play effective and positive social roles. It is common knowledge that psychic pain can be the well-spring of creative cultural activity, and that many influential people in human history have had unusual psychological characteristics. In this book we explore this phenomenon in some detail. While mental disorder may, and often does, marginalize its victims, it can also move them into the center of the cultural process. In this event, an understanding of emotional and mental disorders may be a means of appreciating creativity and eccentricity.

Confronted with these observations, culturalists and social constructionists may respond that distress syndromes are culturally determined roles or socially constructed labels, not deep-seated expressions of emotional and mental organization. There may be a modicum of truth in this proposition but it is also an exaggeration.

I offer another view of mental illness and personality and social life generally. It is more complicated and, sometimes, more paradoxical. It also is considerably more interesting for anthropology.

Plan of the book

I begin with a discussion of human nature since the question of human nature is decisive for theoretical orientation. In Chapter 2, I lay a basis for much that follows with a review of current thinking about human nature. Evidence suggests that the mind/brain is plastic in some respects, but it is not simply a "tabula rasa." It everywhere has certain emotional and mental characteristics and potentialities.

Building on this discussion of human nature, chapters on child development, personality, and mental disorders round out the perspective on the individual subject. These chapters portray human beings as embodied, desiring, willful, emotional, thoughtful, speaking, morally oriented subjects. At the same time, these chapters also suggest that human beings have dialogical selves, that is, selves created – often through words, symbols, and meanings – in the give and take of social life. Together, Chapters 3 through 6 make a case for combining psychoanalytic and social interactionist approaches to understanding normal personality and mental and emotional disorder.

Chapters 7 through 9 explore the implications of human nature and personality for understanding social ties, social attitudes, and cultural beliefs and practices across a broad spectrum of human societies and cultures. Chapter 7 focuses on common psychological mechanisms and processes in social activity and cultural practice, and takes up a number of substantive ethnographic issues, such as marital and other social ties, ritual pollution, sacrifice, initiation rites, symbolic objects, and the subjective dimensions of charisma and leadership.

Chapters on collective violence and religion, two of the most enigmatic phenomena anthropologists study, complete the book. Collective violence (Chapter 8) is an unpleasant topic but it is one psychological anthropology cannot or should not avoid. War is not only commonplace but it often has a profound influence on social relations and culture also. Religion, the subject of Chapter 9, has always been a subject of great interest in psychological anthropology. Rich in metaphor and symbolism, religion seems to involve, more than other cultural activities, powerful emotions and unconscious fantasies. Both war and religion seem to involve a variety of emotions, needs, wishes, fantasies, and meanings and various social and political functions. Thus, the chapters on war and religion reiterate what I say throughout this book about the intrapsychic complexity and social entanglements of human subjectivity.

2   Human nature

Perspectives on human nature are critical for psychological anthropology and, indeed, for anthropology as a whole. Studies of societies and cultures, past and present, are in some sense attempts to clarify not only the human condition but also human nature. At the same time, thinking about human nature can have implications for field work and theory. In all sorts of ways it is apt to influence what is noticed – and not noticed – in individual and social behavior. And it can prefigure the answers to questions about how and why individuals and peoples behave the way they do.

Assumptions about human nature are unavoidable in any event. Even the inclination to dismiss human nature, common among proponents of cultural interpretivism and postmodernism, is a manner of making assumptions about human nature. This inclination is understandable and, up to a point, justifiable. It warrants the study of history and culture as decisive components in human behavior and resists simple-minded biological reductionism. Yet it can lead to simplifications of another sort, that is, to an overemphasis on social and cultural influences on the self and to a neglect of drive, emotion, and purpose in the active subject.

Often, assumptions about human nature are simply taken for granted. Given their ramifications, however, it may be instructive to assess their plausibility. Pertinent work on human nature is being carried out in neurobiology, paleoanthropology, and studies of primate social behavior. In my view, findings in these fields are, on the whole, more congruent with psychoanalytic and social-analytic perspectives on human behavior than with either cultural interpretivism or postmodernism.

The findings show that the mind is instinctual and emotional as well as mental, and that the mental characteristics of human beings involve a good deal more than a generalized capacity for learning language and culture. More particularly, they show that the mental endowments of human beings include capacities for self-organization and moral reasoning. They also suggest that language and culture are not *sui generis*. To an important degree, they presuppose drive, emotion, and embodied experience.

Freud, in other words, seems to have been on the right track in his view of mental agencies and of basic motivational systems.[1] I begin my discussion of human nature, therefore, with an overview of Freud's theories about drives and mental agencies and functions. This is not to say that Freud was on the right track in every respect. The drives in Freud's theory are too mechanistic and too unresponsive to intrapsychic imagination and external stimulation (Holt 1989). It can also be argued that Freud put too much emphasis on sexual and aggressive motives and too little on the drive for power and the need for attachment and intimacy. Still, Freud succeeded in pointing to much of what is interesting and problematic about human nature. In this chapter we will see how Freud's ideas can serve as an organizing framework for a contemporary discussion of human nature, but we will also see how current research on human nature in various fields points beyond classical psychoanalytic thinking toward themes in post-Freudian psychoanalysis and, to some extent, to themes in the writings of interpretivists and postmodernists.

Metapsychology

Intrapsychic conflict is a basic feature of Freud's view of drive and mental organization. Seemingly irrational thought and behavior, whether in neurotic symptoms, jokes, or dreams, are products of competing wishes, modes of thought, or mental agencies. Freud first formulated such conflicts in terms of conflict between the conscious and unconscious minds.[2] The primary process thinking of the unconscious system is illogical and impulsive. It uses poetic tropes and seeks immediate gratification with little regard for the past or future. Secondary process thinking, in contrast, is logical and aware of time. It also sustains commitments to persons, goals, and social and cultural values and ideals. While the primary process works toward motor discharge, the secondary process imposes delay and reason with the aim of adjusting impulses or desires to the real world.

Psychic energy is also part of the drive-conflict model. Following Darwin, Freud recognized two drive systems, reproduction and self-preservation or ego-instincts ([1910]1957: 214–215).[3] Recalling this view, Freud later wrote that the ego-instincts included "everything that had to do with the preservation, assertion and magnification of the individual" ([1933a]1964: 96). The libido (sexual energy) is polymorphous – given to seeking pleasure in various parts of the body – and bisexual or both active and passive. It can be invested in the self, love objects, and cultural symbols, images, and activities.

Consideration of narcissism (exaggerated self-love) complicated this neat scheme, however. Narcissism seems to link the libido with self-assertion and, thus, with the ego ([1914]1957: 87; [1923a]1961: 256–257).

Aggression poses another complication. Aggression, it seems, can be both libidinal and nonlibidinal (Stepansky 1977). Eventually Freud postulated a death drive, or aggressive drive, and a narcissistic, power-seeking component of the libido (Freud [1923a]1961). Anxiety, at first, was thought to be a transformation of the libido. Later, it was seen more aptly as a signal of danger and the cause of repression (Freud [1926]1959).

In his structural model, Freud ([1923a]1961) distinguished the agencies of id, ego, and superego. The id is the seat of drive energy and a locus of primary process thinking. The ego mediates the relation between the id and the external world, while the superego provides moral direction for controlling impulses and acting in the world. Freud saw the ego and superego developing from the id and drawing energy from it. The ego and superego are also closely related; at one point Freud described the superego as the "nucleus" of the ego ([1927b]1961: 164). The distinction between id and ego–superego was not quite the same as the topographic distinction between unconscious and conscious. The ego and superego include both conscious and unconscious perceptual and mental processes.

Phylogenetic heritage and the divided brain

Human nature is the product of a long history of biological evolution, a variation on ancient mammalian and primate patterns. More precisely, it represents the result of evolutionary processes in a line of advanced apes. Molecular and genetic comparisons and the fossil record suggest that the hominid and chimpanzee lines separated a mere five to six million years ago (Cronin 1986; Hasegawa et al. 1985). The protohominids, in other words, were probably chimpanzeelike. In particular, they may have resembled the living bonobos or pygmy chimpanzees (Zihlman et al. 1978; Zihlman 1984).

Mammals – and the higher apes in particular – have large brains relative to body size. This characteristic correlates with adaptation: mammals depend more on cunning and learning than on instinct and reflex. Slow maturation and a close relation between parent and offspring are also part of this pattern because infants must be born premature in order for their heads to pass through the birth canal; postpartum brain development and learning the basic behavioral repertoire of the species take many months, even years. During the period of postpartum dependency, breast-feeding nourishes the offspring and parental support provides a safe environment for physical maturation and learning.

Competition for reproductive success is another conspicuous feature of the mammalian–primate pattern. In many species, agonistic interaction and dominance competition among males precede mating. Dominant males tend to have more access to sexually receptive females. Among chimpanzees, this connection between male aggressiveness and sexuality appears in territoriality and an inclination toward polygyny, behaviors which persist in human behavior. Females also compete for power, apparently because dominance improves their access to valued resources. Competition for reproductive success may involve aggressive self-assertion in these ways, but it can also involve tactical and strategic uses of friendship and cooperation (Waal 1982; Ghiglieri 1987).

Intelligence and playfulness are part of this system of mother–offspring closeness and reproductive politics. Maternal behavior depends on learning and intelligence. Success in social competition hangs on intellectual abilities also, especially among the primates, where social relations are increasingly complex. Socially successful animals form and maintain friendships, calculate the likely behavior of social others, and make tactical uses of guile and deception. They also subordinate their impulses to long-run goals. These skills develop through childhood play and, perhaps, dreaming.

Emotion is another element in this behavioral configuration. Parent–offspring and male–female attachments and reproductive competition are critical to survival and reproductive success. They are also intensely emotional. Secure attachment and success in dominance competition involve positive affect, whereas unwanted separation and threats to social status evoke fear and anger.

In a number of respects human beings represent a further development of this mammalian–primate pattern. During hominid and human evolution, the brain expanded in size and intelligence increased. As a corollary of this brain expansion, infants were born even more premature, and they remained dependent even longer. Mothering became more critical than ever for the offspring's survival and so too did the child's attachment to the mother. At some point fathers began to do more parenting. Hominids also became more emotional. Although common prejudice suggests that emotion is lower and reason is higher on the evolutionary scale, in actuality the range and depth of emotional feeling and expression probably increased during hominid evolution along with advances in intelligence and the development of capacities for language and culture. The social relationships of human beings involve passion, pride, love, and hope, and also shame, sadness, and despair. The evolving hominids may have become more playful. Human beings are arguably more playful than other primates, and they have active and creative imaginations.

One way to characterize these features of human nature is to say that human beings are "neotenous." They preserve the characteristics of primate young; in addition to having relatively large heads for body size,

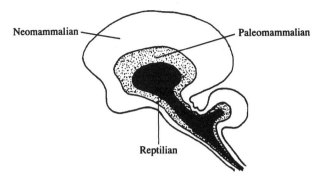

Figure 1 The triune brain (after MacLean 1990)

they are emotional, inquisitive, and playful (La Barre 1954, 1991). Yet human beings are not simply neotenous. While "infantile" in certain respects, they are also unusually sexual. After puberty, they develop conspicuous secondary sexual characteristics and, in comparison with other primates, their sexual impulses are less constrained by hormonal cycles.

What separates human beings most from the rest of nature, however, is reasoning and the capacity for spoken language and, hence, a capacity for culture. This capacity for symbolic communication and shared understandings is striking, but it is not the whole story so far as human cognitive abilities are concerned. The evolution of the human mind/brain also involved advances in social intelligence. Human beings are not only capable of reasoning and spoken language but, in contrast to other primates, they are also more aware of themselves and each other and more perceptive and thoughtful regarding social relations. In addition to being more playful and imaginative, they are more capable of deception and self-deception. They also can make moral and social commitments and anticipate the future in ways other primates cannot.

Human nature, in short, is a further elaboration of a primate pattern, itself an elaboration of a basic mammalian pattern. The old mammalian pattern was a revision of a still earlier reptilian pattern. The brain preserves many traces of this phylogenetic progression. According to Paul D. MacLean (1990), it includes a "reptilian" brain, a "paleomammalian" brain, and a "neomammalian" brain. These several "brains" compose what MacLean calls the "triune brain" (Fig. 1).

The "reptilian brain," the core of the triune brain, includes the brain stem, striatum, and related nuclei. The reptilian brain mediates neural activation systems and phylogenetic memory. It also may be the locus of territorial impulses and of compulsions to repeat certain behaviors.

Libidinal energy depends on dopaminergic neurons originating in the reptilian brain, particularly in the nucleus accumbens. The self-preservation system may depend on noradrenergic neurons projecting from the locus coeruleus.

The "paleomammalian" or emotional brain lies between the reptilian and neomammalian brains. Also known as the "limbic system," it figures in memory, emotion, and the organization of reproduction and self-preservation. The mature emotional brain has three components: (a) a system involving the amygdala that mediates irritable aggression, fear-induced aggression, fear, and recognition of inedible foods; (b) a system involving the septum, preoptic area, and corticomedial amygdala that, along with the nucleus accumbens, mediates reproductive behavior and reward; and (c) a more recent phylogenetic subdivision involving the anterior thalamus, cingulate gyrus, mammillary bodies, and mamillothalamic tract. This third subdivision, which reaches its greatest elaboration in human beings, may figure in sexuality, parenting, pair-bonding, play, and capacity for moral sentiment. It relies primarily on visual information and has elaborate connections with the prefrontal cortex (MacLean 1990).

The limbic system is probably a locus of object relations, of the process of linking emotion with memories of socially significant others. It seems to connect drive, emotion, and object through visual imagery with little or no direct supervision from the cerebral cortex (Halgren 1992). The amygdala in particular seems to be a key nucleus for recognizing and reacting to social others, especially those who pose dangers to the self (Kling and Brothers 1992). Subjective experience during temporal-lobe seizures and electrical stimulation of the human amygdala may include fear, other aversive emotions, feelings of familiarity (*déjà vu*), and visual hallucinations (Gloor 1992). Whereas the reptilian brain energizes the libido and aversive arousal, the limbic system supplies emotional coloring to motivation and begins a process of connecting drive and emotion with mental representations of social others.[4]

The increased range and subtlety of emotional experience in human beings no doubt reflects the greatly expanded powers of categorization in the cerebral cortex, but it may also reflect changes in the limbic system itself. The emotional brain expanded in size during hominid evolution along with the neocortex. The basolateral amygdala and the septum reach their largest dimensions in the human brain (Armstrong 1991; Richardson 1973).

The cerebral cortex or "neomammalian brain" forms the outer layer of the triune brain. In human beings it provides the biological underpinning for spoken language, memory, perception, reasoning, and social intelli-

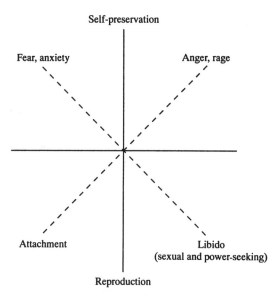

Figure 2 Drives and emotion

gence. Language function is concentrated in the dominant, usually the left, hemisphere. Social intelligence and many elements of the cognitive organization of personality depend on the prefrontal cortex of the frontal lobes.

Gerald L. Edelman (1992) suggests that the limbic–brain stem system supplies "values" (i.e., concerns with survival and reproduction), whereas the thalamocortical system (i.e., the neomammalian brain) is concerned with categorizing and adapting to the social and physical environment.

Drive

Research in neurobiology and child development suggests that there may be five motivational systems in human beings: (1) psychic regulation of physiological needs, (2) attachment–affiliation, (3) aversion (fight/flight), (4) exploration–assertion, and (5) sensuality–sexuality (Lichtenberg 1989). It is not difficult to see, however, that the last four of these systems fit comfortably within Freud's distinction between reproductive drives, on the one hand, and the principle of self-preservation, on the other. Attachment–affiliation and sensuality–sexuality belong to the reproductive system and, for reasons that will soon become apparent, so too does exploration–assertion. Aversion, of course, exemplifies self-preservation (see Fig. 2).

The libido and the erotogenic body

The ethnographic data leave little doubt about the importance of the libido in human behavior. Eroticism is a recurrent element in humor, insult, song, tales, drama, film, myths, and cosmology in many different cultures. It is often part of the drama – and melodrama – of everyday life.

Freud's observation that children have sexual impulses and interests has been confirmed by observations of childhood sexuality in many cultures. As we shall see later, cultural beliefs and practices in various societies reveal that erotic interest can focus on the mouth and anus as well as the genitals. They show that there is a potential in human eroticism for homoeroticism as well as heterosexual sexuality and that libidinal impulses are subject to displacement and symbolization.

Freud was also correct in discerning a narcissistic or power-seeking dimension to the libido. In many mammalian breeding systems inter-male competitition for dominance and social space precedes or accompanies mating. The pattern occurs among chimpanzees (Goodall 1986; Waal 1982). In various primate species mounting and sexual thrusting signal dominance, whereas affectionate grooming and genital touching may lay the emotive bases for political alliances and coalitions. After making threatening gestures, dominant male chimpanzees sometimes grab the penes of subordinate males. When a dominant male pygmy chimpanzee chases a subordinate male, the latter may display submission by crouching. The dominant male may then mount him; alternatively, the two animals may touch rumps, with the subordinate male screeching and either or both animals thrusting rapidly. The dominant male may develop an erection in the interaction (Kano 1980).

Circulating androgens seem to be an important part of the substrate of the libido in males and females along with pathways and nuclei in the brain stem and limbic system (Money and Ehrhardt 1972). This same physiology and neurobiology links the will-to-power with the libido. Androgen is associated with assertiveness or inter-male aggression in competition for social status (Mazur 1976). Monoamine neurons may also figure in this association between power-seeking and the libido. Dopamine agonists (chemicals that potentiate dopaminergic activity in the brain) increase sexual and aggressive behavior in animals and human beings. The major tranquilizers, which exert antipsychotic effects by blocking brain dopamine, inhibit sexual and aggressive impulses (Everett 1975). Persons with Parkinson's disease have reported sexual and power fantasies and upsurges of pleasure and self-esteem after taking L-Dopa, a dopamine substitute (Sacks [1973]1983). One patient on L-Dopa therapy imagined himself in dreams and fantasies to be "a burly caveman equipped with an invincible club and an invincible phallus; a Dionysiac [*sic*] god packed with virility and power; a wild, wonderful, ravening man-beast who combined kingly, artistic and genital omnipotence" (ibid.: 195). Increased dopamine turnover is a biochemical substrate of mania, a condition variously manifested in euphoria, grandiosity, increased sexual drive, assertiveness, and acquisitiveness (Post 1980).[5]

Attachment and parenting

Mutual attachment between mother and infant is the defining characteristic of mammalian adaptation. Mammalian infants cannot survive without at least some caregiving, and human infants are especially helpless and vulnerable. Infant attachment to caregivers and separation anxiety ensure the infant's survival. Smiling rewards the mother while crying and other forms of distress signal the child's need for the mother (Bowlby 1969). Subjectively, secure attachment is pleasant and unwanted separation is unpleasant.

The primate pattern includes sustained physical contact between mother and infant and nursing on demand. This pattern has apparently continued throughout hominid and human evolution. Maternal presence and indulgence of infants and young children have been reported for !Kung hunting and foraging peoples of the Kalahari desert of southern Africa (Konner 1976) and are common in many other societies also. Mothers breast-feed their babies for two to three years or longer in nearly 70 percent of the world's societies and, in many places, they nurse their babies on demand and are almost always close to them (Whiting and Child 1953: 69–71).

There is reason to think that the contribution of fathers to parenting has increased during the course of human evolution. The time fathers spend with offspring, however, varies with cultural expectations, social status, and economic and ecological factors.[6] In some cases, fathers may devote little or no time or effort to the care of offspring. Overall, though, human fathers are more paternal than the males of most primate species. Psychoanalysts have noted that the subjective meaning of parenthood for men may involve rich inner fantasies, and that motivations for parenting among men can be strong and highly emotional (Cath 1986; Diamond 1986).

Classic psychoanalytic theory offered a mechanistic view of attachment behavior, and had very little to say about paternal inclinations. It subsumed nursing and attachment under the libido. Oral gratification was viewed as the primary impetus for the infant's attachment to the mother. Similarly, affectionate social relations in adulthood were regarded simply as sublimations of the libido.

This formulation is now considered questionable (Weiss 1982). Bottle-fed babies attach to their mothers, and motherless children attach to fathers, surrogate mothers, peers, and other persons. Some married couples maintain loving relationships without sex, and many social ties seem to have little or no erotic element. Biological evidence also implies that the libido and attachment are separate systems. Surgical removal of endogenous sources of androgens in women diminishes sexual libido but not affection (Waxenberg 1969).

Human parenting probably has biological bases. Female hormones promote nurture, and androgens suppress it. Girls androgenized *in utero* show more masculinity and less interest in marriage and motherhood in their play and fantasy. Adult virilized women are less maternal than women with normal hormones (Money and Ehrhardt 1972: 96–105). Mothers respond to the smiling, crying, and clinging of infants. The milk letdown response in mothers is part of this response pattern. In the course of human evolution both female and male parental inclinations were probably supported by further elaboration of the basic biology of attachment. Recent studies suggest that oxytocin, a chemical that is synthesized in cells originating in the hypothalamus, may be part of this biology. Among rodents, at least, oxytocin is involved in various aspects of sexual response, bonding, and, especially, parenting (Insel 1992).[7]

Whatever the biological bases of parenting, social learning is clearly a major ingredient in parenting among the higher primates and, particularly, among human beings (Money 1988: 62). A comparison of ovariectomized and normal rhesus monkeys showed that previous mothering experience predicted mothering of foster infants better than did hormonal condition (Holman and Goy 1980). Despite the lack of gonadal hormones, girls with Turner's syndrome resemble matched controls in interest in dolls, nurturing, and fantasies about romance, marriage, pregnancy, and mothering (Money and Ehrhardt 1972: 105–108). Nancy J. Chodorow (1978) argued that a girl's developmental experience with her mother plays a greater role in the reproduction of maternal inclinations than does innate biology. In a study of infant neglect in the shanty towns of northeastern Brazil, Nancy Scheper-Hughes (1985) concludes that cultural expectations and economic conditions profoundly influence maternal inclinations.

Daniel Rancour-Laferriere (1985) adduces a variety of clinical and ethnographic data to show that for men paternity has subjective associations with motherhood. The male becomes a father, psychologically speaking, by identifying with his mate and, ultimately perhaps, with the already internalized image of his own mother. Rancour-Laferriere's argument is intriguing for, as we shall see, there are many intimations in the ethnographic literature that not only paternity but also male economic and political activities are often modeled on maternal behavior.

Passionate attachment

The libido and attachment systems, although separate, are closely related. Nursing is physically pleasurable for infants, and many mothers experience sexual pleasure while nursing their babies. Giving birth, lactation, and sexual intercourse and orgasm are similar physiologically, and some women report them as subjectively similar (Newton 1973). The mouth, breast, and skin figure in both nursing and adult sexuality.

Sexual passion and emotional attachment merge in romantic love. The elements of romantic love include infatuation, idealization of the partner, obsessive thinking, anticipation, ecstatic yearnings, and worry about loss and rejection. Romantic love in this sense is widespread in human cultures, if not universal, and seems to be a basis of the human proclivity for pair-bonding and monogamy (Fisher 1992; Jankowiak and Fischer 1992). It has been theorized that romantic love may be a mixture of the euphoria associated with sexual drive and the feelings of affection associated with the attachment system. According to this conception, intense infatuation is mediated by brain dopamine and perhaps other monoamines, including the monoamine agonist phenylethylamine (PEA). As passion gives way to attachment, brain endorphins may become more important in mediating feelings (Liebowitz 1983). Oxytocin may play a role in romantic attachment as well as parenting. A comparison of the montane and prairie voles is interesting in this connection. The montane vole is polygynous, not very parental, and asocial. The prairie vole, in contrast, is monogamous, very parental, and more social. Oxytocin is much more richly distributed in the limbic system of the prairie vole (Insel 1992).

To be sure, the notion of "romantic love" has peculiarly European meanings. "Passionate attachment," the phrase now in use in the psychoanalytic literature, is less culture-bound (see Gaylin and Person 1988). It alludes to the underlying biology of passionate relationships without making so many assumptions about cultural associations.[8]

Passionate attachment may be inherently short-lived; in many societies divorces are most common after about four to seven years of marriage. Helen E. Fisher (1992) has stirred controversy with the suggestion that these phenomena reflect a natural inability of the body to sustain PEA-mediated euphoria over a long period.

It is interesting to note that associations between sexuality and food are common in many cultures. Experiments with hypnosis in the early days of psychoanalysis revealed strong associative links between food and sex (Roffenstein [1924]1951).[9] Further evidence of this association is contained in the folklore of many cultures which uses oral and culinary metaphors for the genitalia and for sexual behavior.

This inclination to associate food with sex also appears in exchanges of food for sex in male–female relations. Among hunter-gatherers, for example, suitors and husbands often give food to their wives and parents-in-law. Thus marriage and sexual relations with the wife depend on sharing meat from the hunt. Janet Siskind (1973) observed that successful hunting implies virility in the interfluvial regions of Amazonia. The successful hunter may attract extra wives, whereas the unsuccessful hunter may be spurned by women. The basic idea is "an exchange of meat for sex" (ibid.: 234). Alluding to this understanding, a Sharanahua woman said, when men returned without game, "There is no meat, let's eat penises" (ibid.: 233). Thomas Gregor (1985) finds many associations between food and sex among the Mehinaku of central Brazil where sexual appetite is compared to hunger, and copulation to eating. Men offer fish – explicit phallic symbols for the Mehinaku – to women for sexual favors.

The sexual connotations of food and food-sharing may inform social avoidance practices. L.R. Hiatt (1984) noted that mother-in-law avoidance protects the sexual prerogatives of the father-in-law in aboriginal Australia. Because a son-in-law gives meat to both his wife and mother-in-law, and because there is an assumption that husbands provide meat in exchange for sexual favors in relations with their wives, the son-in-law's relation with his mother-in-law may have disturbing sexual nuances. These nuances become all the more worrisome because the mother-in-law is often close to her son-in-law in age (men marry younger women) and resentful of her husband's devotion to other wives.

C. Owen Lovejoy (1981) and Fisher (1982) have theorized that the trend toward a more humanlike sexuality – more cognitive control of sexuality – favored exchanges of food for sex, and, ultimately, the human family.[10] This line of thought finds support in observations of both chimpanzees and human beings. Common chimpanzee males are more apt to share food with estrus than anestrus females (Goodall 1986: 311). Among pygmy chimpanzees, food-sharing is common and often associated with eroticism. Males have been observed to share meat with females and their young after copulating with the females (Badrian and Badrian 1984; Badrian and Malenky 1984; Kano 1980: 256). Among caged pygmy chimpanzees, the arrival of food stimulates copulatory behavior. Dropping food in front of a partner and taking food prompt copulation. One animal may even take food from a partner's mouth during sexual intercourse. In one captive group of pygmy chimpanzees copulation was observed in more than 90 percent of 109 feeding situations. Pygmy chimpanzees also mix homoeroticism and food-sharing. Females engage in genital rubbing before or during feeding sessions (Kano 1980: 253; Kuroda 1980: 189; Savage-Rumbaugh and Wilkerson 1978: 338), and most instances of male–male mounting and rump contact also occurred in feeding situations (Kano 1980: 255). Some of this eroticism in feeding situations may occur simply to reduce anxiety associated with feeding, but some seems oriented toward bribing partners for food.

Self-preservation

In order for reproduction to occur, animals must first survive. They must take care of their needs for water, food, and protection from the elements, and they must be prepared to respond to threats to survival posed by other animals, whether of their own species or another. Flight, fight, and freezing (hypnoid immobilization) compose the three basic strategies in self-preservation. Animals may try to escape danger or they can struggle with aggressors. A third strategy is passivity; animals may remain motionless to conceal their presence or as a gesture of submission to a dominant animal. Also known as sham-death, cataplexy, or death-feint, this response may calm fears while fooling a predator or appeasing a same-species rival (Gellhorn 1967: 61–65).

Just as there is an affective dimension to reproduction, there is an affective dimension to self-preservation. Flight, struggle, and freezing are associated with the emotions of fear, anxiety, anger, and rage. Some evidence suggests that fear and anxiety are mediated in part by noradrenergic fibers arising in the locus coeruleus in the brain stem (Redmond 1979). Fear responses are also mediated by the basolateral amygdala and the posterior hypothalamus (Gellhorn 1967; Gloor 1975). The physiology of fear prepares the body for escape and self-defense. Anxiety or stress prepares it for protracted struggle. These states of alarm and stress – also known as ergotropic response – comprise reactivity in the sympathetic nervous system and increased muscle tone and cortical activity. They contrast with the trophotropic response which includes parasympathetic discharge, muscle relaxation, and decreased cortical activity (Gellhorn 1967).

Disgust must be counted as part of the emotional apparatus of defense. Disgust occurs in all cultures (Ekman 1980). The sense of disgust depends on smell and occurs readily in response to the thought of eating something inedible (Rozin and Nemeroff 1990). Since food, as we saw above, is easily associated with sex, illicit sex readily gets connected with items that are inedible and disgusting, including excrement. Associations between pollution, incest, and death occur in many cultures (Brain 1977). Although children may at first play with excrement, nasal mucous, dead skin, and the like, eventually they usually learn to regard anality with varying degrees of disgust. Anality also has associations with sadism and sexual submission. In western culture, some of these associations, and corresponding expressions of disgust, appear in folklore about rats and geese (Shengold 1988). Disgust becomes a central, orienting emotion for some people who are especially concerned with external dangers and self-defense; attitudes of disgust are particularly evident in some hysterical and obsessive person-alities (David-Ménard 1989; Straus 1948). On the other hand, what is digusting to others may become the focus of desire and pleasure in persons with sexual perversions (Chasseguet-Smirgel 1984).

Humans have hypnotized animals of many species, and animals some-times hypnotize each other (Volgyesi 1966). Freezing and hypnotic states may involve fear, relaxation, and pleasure in varying proportions. Human counterparts of freezing may include hypnotism, dissociative states, and psychotic catatonia. Kempf (1917) noted that persons in catatonic states sometimes experience mixtures of fear and erotic pleasure, and he sug-gested that catatonic stupor may be a human counterpart of defensive sexual submission and immobility among infrahuman primates. Maslow, Rand, and Newman (1960) proposed that the use of sexual gestures in ago-nistic interaction in primates may be the phylogenetic origin of sadism and masochistic submission in human beings. Engel and Schmale (1972) sug-gested that the freeze reaction may be a precursor of a syndrome they call "depression-withdrawal" or "conservation-withdrawal." The syndrome includes muscle collapse, a hangdog expression, loss of energy, apathy, withdrawal, helplessness, hopelessness, and depression. A hypnoid, freez-ing response, then, may lead from fright to euphoria or, alternatively, from fright to depression.

Current thinking about the biology of the emotions supports the distinc-tion Freud drew between libidinal and nonlibidinal aggression. Non-libidinal aggression is an aversive reaction to threat or frustration. It can become a learned response to frustration also, but it is basically reactive. Libidinal aggression is less destructive and more concerned with self-asser-tion and power-seeking. Whereas destructive aggression is reactive, libidi-nal aggression is more drivelike. The two forms of aggression often occur together, however. Although libidinal aggression is more narcissistic than destructive, destructive aggression can be a response to narcissistic injury or a mode of preserving narcissistic self-representation (Rochlin 1973).[11]

Reproductive drives and self-preservation are related in other ways as well. Freud thought that self-preservation and reproduction were mutually exclusive systems; one tended to prevail at the expense of the other. The relation between the two systems may be more complicated than Freud realized, however. On the one hand, anxiety can trigger activity in dopaminergic circuits of the brain and thus stimulate hunger and desire. Eating and sex, in turn, can have a calming effect for some people or in some situations (Antelman and Caggiula 1980). Intense anxiety and pro-

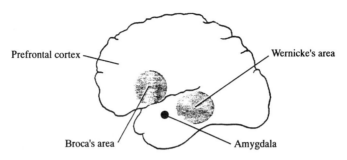

Figure 3 The dominant hemisphere

longed stress, on the other hand, tend to inhibit sexual arousal. In keeping with Freud's formulation, they can decrease blood testosterone and androgen levels in males, and they can cause birth defects and interfere with menstruation, conception, and lactation in women (Gray 1987).[12]

The thinking, speaking brain

The size of the brain increased more than threefold during hominid and human evolution.[13] While this encephalization was underway, the organization of the neocortex also changed. Selection pressures for handedness and, later, for speech, modified and accentuated a preexisting lateralization of the neocortex. The left hemisphere is usually dominant for speech, right handedness, and manual dexterity. Wernicke's area and related association areas in the left temporal and parietal regions mediate the understanding of denotative and connotative meanings (see Fig. 3). Broca's area of the frontal lobe seems to play a role in the production of speech and, therefore, in sound sequencing and syntactical construction. Similarly, an area of premotor cortex above Broca's area organizes sequential movements of the right hand (Falk 1987; Kosslyn and Koenig 1992).[14]

The capacity for symbol-making and symbol-using allows for the mapping of, and communication about, natural and social worlds. Signifier, meaning, and referent are linked together through words, and words convey information that can be transmitted or stored in memory for future use. The ability to connect words with meaning in an arbitrary fashion, meanwhile, permits metaphor, allegory, verbal modeling, and paradigmatic constructions. The signifier can slide away from its conventional meaning and relate to other more poetic significations.

I noted earlier that in the Lacanian reworking of Freud and in socioculturalist and postmodernist theorizing generally, the mind/brain is a semiotic machine, a site where signifiers are registered and reproduced.

While there is no doubting the very great importance of language in sociality and mental functioning in human beings, this view may overstate the matter. It is already clear from what has just been said about the drive/emotional components of human nature that language is not everything. But there is also reason to think that many of the more sophisticated or cognitive processes of the mind/brain are not linguistic in the first instance and that even language depends on nonlinguistic processes.

The work of Ronald W. Langacker (1990), George Lakoff (1987), and Mark Johnson (1987) suggests that preverbal processes of conceptualization may precede and underlie both language and thought. In Langacker's cognitive linguistics, spatial schemas involving "bases" and "profiles" subtend syntax and semantics. Johnson (1987) similarly theorizes that embodied developmental experiences with direction, balance, containment, and causality supply schemas for abstract thinking. Spatial-motoric experiences, presumably during the early phases of child development, supply the prototypes for metaphorical extensions through which cognitive worlds are constructed (see also Lakoff 1987).

These cognitive approaches to language imply, in other words, that language is grounded in and surrounded by nonlinguistic mental processes. This view gains support from neurobiology and cognitive neuroscience. Until recently many cognitive neuroscientists assumed that the mind/brain was basically a "serial symbolic processor." Serial processing was assumed to underlie both the natural language functions of the left hemisphere and the spatial reasoning of the right. According to this idea, symbols encode information in grammatical sequences and these sequences are subjected in the course of decision making to logical permutations and transformations.

Recent research in neuroscience suggests, however, that parallel distributed processing or connectionist models may better reflect what is happening in neural circuits during thinking and perception than serial symbolic processing models (Kosslyn and Koenig 1992). In connectionist models, connections between inputs and outputs are gradually established through a multiplicity of parallel connections across two or more intervening layers or systems. According to this view of the mind/brain, a great deal of mental process is unconscious, and learning and representation do not depend on symbolic encoding and grammatical construction. Rather, they require trial and error. Roy D'Andrade (1991) notes that the mind probably uses a combination of connectionist networks and serial processing.

Neuroanatomy also implies that serial-symbolic processing and language are only part of what is happening in the mind, even at high levels. The right hemisphere shows dominance for configurational thinking, pattern recognition, and motor manipulation. It supports prosody – modulation of volume, tone, and pitch – and recognizes isolated words, as

in swearing and prayer, but otherwise may be minimally involved in the production and understanding of speech. The right hemisphere also is more
concerned with emotionality, perhaps because it mediates recognition of
emotional expression in the self and others (Joseph 1982).

Work on the neural basis of language, moreover, suggests that three distinct neural fields subserve the production and understanding of speech.
Various neural systems in both hemispheres mediate nonlinguistic understandings of the body-self and the external world. A second system, located
primarily in the dominant or left hemisphere, mediates the representation
of phonemes and syntax. And a third system mediates the two-way relations between these first two systems (Damasio and Damasio 1992).
Presumably all three systems are realized biologically in massively parallel,
distributed neural networks. Merlin Donald (1991) theorizes that the evolving hominids could mime events and forms long before they were capable
of complicated spoken language, and he infers from studies of aphasias
that mimetic intelligence is still part of human mental processes.

Edelman (1992) proposes a grand theory of brain function which also
places a generalized capacity for categorization before language. Edelman's
theory, "neural Darwinism," resembles parallel distributing processing
models, but purports to be more biologically accurate. In his theory, neural
networks or groups are fashioned through a winnowing and reinforcement
process in which some neural connections flourish and others perish, and
the surviving networks in turn are connected by "massively parallel" interconnections or "reentrant" pathways. The brain is not a computer that
reads the environment as a symbolic code and subjects it to logical algo-
rithms but rather a living colony of cells and pathways that responds
actively to external and internal stimulation.

A virtue of parallel distributed processing theories and neural
Darwinism for anthropology is that they better enable us to envision a
neurobiological foundation for schema theory and Piere Bourdieu's notion
of habitus (D'Andrade 1992; Strauss 1992a). Schema and habitus imply
that many forms of learning and disposition with cultural relevance
operate at an embodied, prelinguistic level. They involve habits, dispositions, bodily skills and routines, and ways of thinking and feeling that are
hard if not impossible to put into words (D'Andrade 1990, 1992; Holland
1992; Mathews 1992; Strauss 1992b).

Clearly, the evolution of the human mind and the development of culture
involved more than the emergence of a capacity for symbolic communication. Yet it also involved more than an ability to learn schemas. In a paper
that still deserves reading, A. Irving Hallowell noted that culturally mediated social behavior involves a "higher level of psychological integration"
as well as symbolic communication and habitual social behavior. That is, it

involves capacities for "self-consciousness, self-identification and reference, self-evaluation, self-stimulation, self-control, the possibility of relating one's contemplated or actual conduct to traditional ideals and values, etc." (1950: 169–170). Self-awareness permits social actors to become understandable to themselves in relation to a social whole and to hold each other morally accountable. Hallowell then added that human cultures also involve unconscious evaluation and regulation of unconscious wishes and impulses. The "emotional nature" of human beings "becomes structuralized in such a way that anxiety, guilt and depression become indices to the integrative level reached by the personal adjustment of the individual in relation to the symbolically expressed and mediated norms of . . . society" (ibid.: 169). Hallowell was suggesting, in effect, that culture depends on ego and superego functions as well as on symbolic communication.[15]

In biological terms, culture requires the prefrontal cortex, an area that expanded to include more of the cortex during primate evolution. The prefrontal cortex takes up 8.5 percent of the total cortex in lemurs, 11.5 percent in macaques, 17 percent in chimpanzees, and 29 percent in human beings (Fuster 1988: 3). Evidence for the increase of the prefrontal cortex relative to the rest of the cortex includes the large size of the mediodorsal nucleus of the human thalamus, an organ that has close connections with the prefrontal cortex (Armstrong 1990a, 1990b).

The frontal lobes underlie intention and awareness of intentions (Frith 1987). The prefrontal cortex in particular seems to play an important part in relating drives and personal wishes and desires to social ends and to moral ideals. Delusions may result when a person cannot recognize his or her intentions or desires and so falsely attributes them to another person, force, or object. The functions of the prefrontal cortices include self-awareness, self-criticism, and intention. Delusions, then, may reflect impairment of these functions (Benson and Stuss 1990).

The frontal lobes seem to play a role in anxiety, conscience, and repression. Frontal lobotomies reduce anxiety, especially among individuals with obsessive-compulsive personality disorder (Bernstein et al. 1975). The prefrontal cortex also supports empathy. Postlobotomy and frontal trauma patients often ignore feelings and needs in other persons and commonly show little guilt or contrition. In addition, such persons may have weak defenses against impulses and wishes. Dreams and daydreams often express the needs and wishes of frontal patients more directly and concretely than they do for normal people (Frank 1950). Oliver Sacks (1970: 161–165) described a man who murdered a female companion while he was under the influence of phencyclidine (PCP) and then repressed the deed from conscious memory. Later, following a severe injury to his frontal lobes, he remembered the crime with disturbing clarity.

Broca's area of the frontal lobe seems to support the grammatical organization of speech and the ability to produce and comprehend metonymical relations. Anterior portions of the frontal lobe seem to figure in the production of complex sentences and narratives. This may explain why frontal-lobe injuries alter or destroy organized self-representation and even a person's personality. Self-representation includes stories one tells about oneself (see Chapter 4). Narratives are related to superego functions also. There is, Jerome Bruner (1990: 50–51) noted, a moral dimension to stories. They tend to account for departures from usual or conventional behavior; "Stories . . . relate to what is morally valued, morally appropriate, or morally uncertain" (ibid.: 50). Narratives frame moral issues but, also, understandings of motivation and interpersonal relationships. They go beyond logical and literal understanding of what "is" to what "may be" in the future, to alternative possibilities, to perception of multiple motives. They express moral and social complexity with metaphor, metonymy, and other figurative devices. These tropes allow exploration of the connections between the ordinary and the unexpected (ibid.: 59–60). Anticipating the future, planning, posing imaginary scenarios, make-believe, simulating, and acting "as-if" one were experiencing certain emotions (see below, p. 41) may all depend importantly on the frontal lobes, particularly the prefrontal cortices (Damasio 1994).

The prefrontal cortex probably underlies what animal researchers are calling "social" or "Machiavellian intelligence." Social intelligence comprises a variety of skills that allow animals to turn social relations to their advantage (Byrne and Whiten 1988). These include self-awareness and empathy. Self-awareness allows animals to monitor and manage social impressions, and empathy allows them to guess the purposes of social others. Both skills aid in forming and sustaining relationships that may be helpful to the self (e.g., getting food, maintaining social position, or improving reproductive success). To form mutually supportive social ties, animals must seem trustworthy to social others. They may do this either by making sincere emotional attachments to others or by feigning sociability. In the latter case, deception is likely to be more effective if it involves self-deception, since the animal that is unaware of its own motives is less likely to reveal them to social others (Badcock 1991: 101–108). An ability to anticipate what others will do, or what the self will do in certain situations, is part of social intelligence also.

The various functions of the prefrontal cortex – self-control, conscience, planning, self-awareness, narrative, imagination – subserve sublimation, the transformation of drive and emotion into symbolically mediated purpose and social sentiments (see Chapter 7). Frontal injury or lobotomy in human beings may produce "emotional asymbolia," a marked deficit in the capacity for sublimation. Injured or lobotomized persons are less creative and less able to redirect drive or emotion, and they are often less likely to make art and religion part of their lives (Frank 1950).

The semiotic *chora*: drive, affect, trope

At the boundary of drive and thought, at the place where drive becomes emotion and begins to turn into desire, we must imagine another modality, one Julia Kristeva (1986) calls the "semiotic *chora*." Kristeva divides the symbolic in Lacan's work into the "semiotic" and the "thetic," or symbolic proper. The semiotic transgresses and merges with the symbolic, as in poetic expression and other forms of creativity, but it has its own characteristics. An unstructured, unstable organization of drives, it works with opposition and resemblance rather than with judgment, proposition, or symbolic signification. The semiotic traffics in drives, pulsations, energies, and emotions. It corresponds to the unconscious, the primary process, and preoedipal object relations in psychoanalytic theory and to the sensorimotor stage of thought and development in Piagetian cognitive psychology. Going beyond Kristeva's formulation, we might say that it is the place of embodied, subjective experience, the place of images that serve as prototypes for syntactical structures and semantic functions.

We should probably situate emotion or affect in this place between drive energy and fully formed linguistic thought. "Affect" refers to the basic biology of emotion, whereas "feeling" refers to awareness of emotion. Feelings are transient. Moods are feeling states that suffuse experience for long periods of time.

Affect is grounded in human biology. Evidence suggests that emotions and moods are mediated by monoamine neurons projecting from the reptilian brain and by limbic structures which link drives with imagistic representations of social others and, through connections with the cerebral cortex, with symbols and meanings. Thus, there is a sense in which all human beings share the same emotional psychobiology. Paul Ekman (1980) showed that the facial expression of basic emotions (i.e., surprise, sadness, anger, fear, disgust, and happiness) is the same in different cultures. Emotional expression among the Fore, a people in a remote area of Eastern New Guinea, closely resembles emotional expression among the peoples of European countries. Donald L. Nathanson (1992) adds shame, pride, and "dissmell" to this list of basic emotions. The two moods seen most often are euphoria and depression. In mania, enduring excitement and joy become mixed with irritability and anger. In depression persistent sadness dampens pleasure in life.

Antonio R. Damasio (1994) distinguishes between *primary* and *sec-*

ondary emotions. Primary emotions convey information to the thinking mind about instincts, drives, and the condition of the body. They are grounded in the limbic system and instinctual in character. Secondary emotions are associated with situations and objects; they depend on the limbic system and on the cerebral cortex, especially the prefrontal cortex. They are critically important for socially intelligent behavior. Damasio's discussion of secondary emotions implies that object relations and what Kristeva calls the semiotic involve these same neural circuits.

Emotions and moods, like the poetic functions of the semiotic, merge with cognitive processes and cultural schemas. The mental representations of experience are often recorded in memory with emotional associations. Remembering, then, may depend on a specific feeling state (Kiefer and Cowan 1979). On the other hand, mental structures raise or lower the thresholds of emotional experience. Defense mechanisms inhibit emotions or suppress conscious experience of them, whereas cognitive expectations determine the way people feel about themselves and others.

Ordinarily, according to Damasio (1994), emotions are triggered by experience. Physiological changes in the body ensue, and awareness of them then becomes juxtaposed in the mind/brain with the ideas or events that triggered the emotion in the first place. There are, though, "as-if" emotions in which neural devices simulate bodily experience, thus deleting the body from the circuit. It is also possible to fabricate an emotion by thinking about an emotional event or idea, even though it is not congruent with the current situation and its corresponding bodily state. People, like actors, can feign emotion and they can actually induce a false emotion or a good likeness of the real thing by thinking emotional thoughts or remembering emotional events. Both possibilities can, and often are, put into play in the course of trying to influence social others. Language, which allows human beings to represent bodily states symbolically, probably greatly expands the scope of "as-if" emotionality in human beings.

Culture and language also expand the range and subtlety of authentic feelings. Within cultures, many categories, events, and situations take on specific emotional significance. Religious and political symbols and rituals are often especially evocative. Words for emotion capture many subtleties and nuances in these associations between emotion and circumstance. Cultural idioms, practices, and gestures also enrich emotional expression in human beings (Lutz and White 1986).

Condensation and displacement are characteristic of primary process thinking or the semiotic, but they are not peculiar to the unconscious. Spiro (1993b) has shown that tropes based on similarity and contiguity are formally indistinguishable from the mechanisms of displacement and condensation which, according to Freud, inform unconscious or primary process thinking. The difference between primary and secondary process thinking, Spiro shows, lies not in the presence or absence of tropes or trope-like thought processes but, rather, in motivation and defense. Where primary process thinking is in play, the trope may serve a defensive function and the metaphorical meaning, as opposed to the explicit, iconic meaning, may remain unconscious. The use of tropes in everyday speech, in contrast, may be quite conscious.

Consciousness, the self, coherence

Consciousness and self-consciousness are noteworthy features of human nature. Other animals have sensations and chimpanzees seem to have a measure of self-awareness, but there is no doubt about human reflexivity: everyone experiences it.

This experience of reflexivity may be common but it is also profoundly mysterious; indeed, one would have thought it beyond the pale of scientific understanding. Recently, however, various writers, emboldened by rapid and remarkable advances in neuroscience, have theorized what a solution to the problem of consciousness might look like. In a manner that recalls Hallowell's prescient work, they often place the problem in evolutionary perspective and connect it with related questions of self-representation and self-organization (Dennett 1991; Donald 1991; Humphrey 1992).

Edelman (1992) proposes that consciousness is an evolutionary result of Darwinian selection; it exists because it is adaptive. Edelman distinguishes two levels of consciousness: "primary" and "higher-order consciousness." Both are intentional in that they involve will or desire and awareness of objects, but primary consciousness is merely awareness of objects in the world while higher-order consciousness includes a sense of the self in a temporal order as well.

Primary consciousness results, according to Edelman, when there is "global mapping" of entire "scenes" such that familiar and unfamiliar objects are constructed *in toto*. This feat requires massive reentrant relations between separate cortical maps and simultaneous two-way connections between the thalamocortical system, which supplies spaciotemporal configuration, and the limbic–brain-stem system, which supplies values for familiar and unfamiliar objects. Primary consciousness, then, is a sort of "remembered present." It probably depends on the hippocampus, which is important in short-term memory, and the thalamus, which seems to be a critical nucleus for integrating various neural structures.

In higher-order consciousness one is aware of being conscious. Chimpanzees may have some degree of such consciousness. They can clearly recognize themselves as distinct individuals. But the full flowering of higher-order consciousness appears to depend on language. Language allows the subject to symbolically transcend the moment and to situate the self in time and space. With higher-order consciousness, the ability to plan, compare scenarios, and assay the risks and benefits of ambiguous sitations is greatly enhanced. The neural circuity of this advanced consciousness appears to involve all that of primary consciousness plus reentrant loops linking the prefrontal cortex and the language and association areas of the frontal, temporal, and parietal lobes. According to Edelman, primary and higher consciousness are adaptive because they sustain more effective assessment of reward and danger in heterogeneous scenes.

Edelman links higher consciousness or self-consciousness with language, yet there are indications that this is not quite right or, at least, that there is actually not a great deal of difference between primary and higher consciousness at the subjective level. Donald's (1991: 82–86) discussion of the case of Brother John shows that a type of self-awareness and considerable effectiveness in a human environment are possible with little or no production or comprehension of speech and writing. Brother John suffered from epileptic seizures of the frontotemporal lobe. His seizures rendered him completely incapable of understanding language or expressing himself in speech for periods of minutes or hours. Yet, during these periods he remained conscious and self-aware: "Gnosis and praxis were intact, as were episodic storage, self-representation, working memory, social intelligence, and scripts and schemas for action" (ibid.: 86). According to Donald, Brother John's case suggests that language is a semi-autonomous module that feeds into – but is not essential to – the main currents of thought and consciousness.

Damasio (1994) regards the self as an inherent feature of the mind/brain. It is not a localized homunculus. Rather, it is distributed in neural networks that monitor the body and its internal states and hold updated images of the body in short-term memory. Subjectivity involves images of objects that affect the self or body and images of responses to objects as well as images of the organism responding to objects. All this can happen, according to Damasio, in neural networks that have little or nothing to do with language. However, he also notes that language is critical for the "I," that part of the self that formulates linguistic images of its own behavior. The stability of subjectivity, according to Damasio, depends on recurrent bodily experiences and memorable autobiographical events. The self is being constantly constructed and reconstructed on the basis of bodily experience and life events. It persists because many bodily experiences recur and because key autobiographical events can have enduring emotional significance. What endures, he notes, includes not only memories of what was, but also memories of plans for the future.

Saying that the self is self-organizing and that consciousness is grounded in drive, emotion, and bodily experience is not to say that western cultural presuppositions about the inherently acquisitive and individualistic nature of the self are natural or universal. Edelman emphasizes that dialogical interaction and a cultural milieu are crucial for self-formation and second-order consciousness. If this is so, then the self might be expected to vary cross-culturally in important respects (see Chapter 4).

Edelman's theory implies that many mind/brain functions are unconscious. Some are always unconscious and others may become so. This latter type of unconsciousness may occur when the reentrant loops between neural maps are impaired or cut, either functionally or because of trauma or disease. This, he suggests, may be the common ingredient in a whole series of dissociative disorders, including amnesia, dyslexia, aphasia, prosopagnosia (inability to recognize familiar faces), and anosognosia (denial or ignorance of gross neurological deficit). Repression may result from functional processes where cognitive processes stimulated by activity in the limbic–brain-stem system contradict a valued conception of the self. Damasio (1994) does not address the question of repression and the self directly but he makes what may be a pertinent observation. He notes that the mind is capable of simulating or imagining bodily experience. Such "as-if" experiences of the body may inform self-awareness and decision making. Later, I note that an embodied as-if state, or role playing, may be part of the process of repression or dissociation.

A corollary of this perspective is that coherent self-organization and consciousness are interrelated. The mind/brain is a thing of parts but it also tends toward provisional or working integration through activity in reentrant pathways. In a manner that recalls classic psychoanalytic thinking about psychotic delusion (see Chapter 6), Edelman suggests that the bizarre mentation of persons with severe mental illnesses may be understood in part as attempts to reintegrate the self in compensation for impaired reentrant linkages between neural maps in different parts of the brain. Arnold H. Modell (1993) suggests that Edelman's neuronal group selection theory may account for the paradox of the self, that is, the way in which it combines stable structures with fluctuating consciousness of different scenes and objects. Edelman may have described the neurophysiological processes – recategorization of memory and reentrant connections between neural fields – through which value-laden memories (the stable structures of the self) are reworked according to changing conscious experience.

Drive/emotional states and mechanisms underlying smooth motor behavior and physical balance may play crucial roles in integration. Affectively charged representations of the self and other in the emotional brain may underlie the self's sense of wholeness.[16] Ego integration may also involve the cerebellum. Paul Schilder (1950) theorized that body image is the nucleus of the ego, and gave special emphasis to the "postural body," sensations of body positions and movements which together compose the body image. He observed that the vestibular apparatus underlies body awareness. Expanding on Schilder's views, Robert B. Frick (1982) speculated that the "vestibulocerebellar system" may play a role in ego integration in tandem with its role in effecting physical balance and muscular coordination. Areas of the system having connections with prefrontal and temporal cortices expanded greatly during human evolution, implying, perhaps, that psychological cohesion was important for successful adaptation. Following Piaget, Frick noted that abstract, ideational thought develops from sensorimotor intelligence and that the stages of cognitive development represent balanced equilibria in response to external disturbances. He thus suggested that the integration of body movement and body image in the expanded human vestibulocerebellar system may serve as a substrate and a prototype for emotional and mental integration of the ego.

In summary, drive, emotion, thought, and language depend on nuclei and neural networks in different parts of the brain. Drive and primary emotions depend on the reptilian brain and paleomammalian brain. Drive and emotion, on the one hand, and thought and language, on the other, are interconnected in complex ways. The thalamocortical system – ego–superego system in psychoanalytic theory – transforms drives and impulses into desire and will. In combination with the limbic system, it individualizes drives, colors them with emotion, and suffuses them with anticipation (Vincent 1990: 122–123). At the same time, drives and emotions shape thought and energize self-organization and self-awareness.

This division of the mind/brain into a limbic–brain-stem system and a thalamocortical system implies that emotional and mental conflicts are an inherent feature of human psychology. Emotionally colored purposes can conflict with each other or with the results of rational decision making. Some conflicts may be the persistent consequences of formative events in the history of the self. Others may reflect a person's changing tastes and values, current estimates of risks and dangers, and revisions of self-identity. Negotiating dilemmas and approach–avoidance conflicts and seeking substitutive objects are the stuff of myth, drama, and personal narratives. They are also the stuff of dreams, imagination, and play.

Dreaming and play

Freud ([1900]1953) theorized in *The interpretation of dreams* that dreaming integrates recent experience (day residue) and deep-seated erotic memories and wishes. Assuming that undisguised libidinal wishes and impulses can disturb sleep, he suggested that the dreamwork censors them through condensation, displacement, identification, and symbolism. These mechanisms operate on the basis of relations of contiguity and similarity. Displacement uses "allusion" or a change in "accent," that is, metaphor in the first instance and metonymy in the second. Condensation compresses two or more thoughts into the same image. In some cases it may effect a synecdochic concentration of the whole into a part. Identification and symbolism, in contrast, are metaphorical. In identification, one element is replaced by or assimilated into a similar element. "Symbols" in dreams are conventional but unconscious signs for the erotogenic body, sexual activities, and preoedipal and oedipal relations. They are found in folklore and myth as well as dreams. While having these distinguishing characteristics, symbols also make connections on the basis of similarity and contiguity.[17]

That dreams seem to reconfigure experience and personal issues in a language of images and tropes is well accepted, but many students of dreams now question other aspects of Freud's dream theory. Dreams may have more to do with working through problems and integrating and correlating mental processes than with wish-fulfillment *per se*, and there is reason to think that dreams may have a more important function in this respect than simply protecting sleep.

Dreams are generated by biological processes, not by momentary, psychological needs to protect sleep. During sleep brain activity alternates between deep, mostly dreamless sleep, and paradoxical sleep or sleep with rapid eye movement (REM), intense brain activity, motor inhibition, and vivid dreaming. Four or five sleep-dreaming cycles occur each night, with the dreaming periods becoming longer toward morning. J. Allan Hobson (1988) argues that dreaming is turned on by neurological mechanisms, perhaps by cholinergic neurons. In his theory the brain creatively synthesizes the resulting neural stimulation, which is inherently random.

There is, nonetheless, evidence that the libido energizes the dreaming process. Penile erections and increase in vaginal blood flow are common in REM sleep. Orgasms in REM sleep are not unusual, and dreams often involve sexual imagery and conflict around self-assertion (Fisher 1965a, 1965b; LaBerge 1985). Depriving rats of REM sleep lowers the thresholds and raises the response rates for pleasurable brain stimulation; the less rats "dream," the more they self-stimulate when given an opportunity. Conversely, self-stimulation of brain pleasure centers during periods of REM deprivation reduces REM rebound following the deprivation. The implication may be that REM sleep satisfies libidinal drive (Ellman 1985; Steiner and Ellman 1972). The activity of monoamine neurotransmitters also implicates the libido in dreaming. Serotonin neurons, which inhibit dopaminergic activity, are depressed during REM sleep and drug-induced altered states of consciousness (Fischman 1983). Small doses of a dopamine agonist enhance dream detail and vividness and increase the chances of nightmares (Hartmann 1982).

Many dreams, to be sure, are nonsexual and unpleasant. Fights and escapes are common in dreams as are loss of love, abandonment, and death. Often the dreamer is the victim. Ethnographic studies suggest that in many cultures unpleasant dreams are as common as or more common than pleasant ones (Merrill 1992).[18] Freud suggested that unpleasant dreams reflect anxieties about forbidden wishes. Following this suggestion, Ernest Jones ([1951]1959) proposed that nightmares are reactions to incestuous wishes and that they are the experiential basis of European beliefs about demons who rape women and men in their sleep. Derek Freeman (1967) reported that the Iban of Borneo believe that incubi – irresistible male figures – seduce women in their sleep. The demons pilfer the souls of their progeny, causing them to die in miscarriages or during childhood. The incubi, consequently, are both terrifying and fascinating. Freeman speculated that the impetus for dreams about incubi may be the adulterous thoughts of women whose husbands are away, and, possibly, unconscious incestuous fantasies.

Jones's hypothesis about the nightmare and Freud's explanation for unpleasant dreams from which it derives are by no means proven. At least one major study of nightmares failed to find incest in the manifest content of nightmares (Hartmann 1984). Still, there are reasons for thinking that Freud and Jones may have been aiming in the right direction. The libido is active during dreams, and evidence suggests that dreams deal with emotional conflict.

Many writers have observed that dreams seem to process mental and emotional conflicts. Alfred Adler saw in dreaming a "rehearsal of plans and attitudes for waking behavior," a seeking of solutions to emotional problems, and an attempt to find the way to social superiority ([1929]1969: 12, 71–72; [1931]1979: 214). Carl G. Jung discerned a forward-looking, problem-solving aspect to dreaming: "an anticipation in the unconscious of future conscious achievements, something like a preliminary exercise or sketch, or a plan roughed out in advance. Its symbolic content sometimes outlines the solution of a conflict" (1948: 255; quoted in Basso 1992: 87). The anthropologist W.H.R. Rivers (1923) proposed that dreams seek solutions to the problems of waking life. Subsequently, Thomas M. French and Erika Fromm (1964) argued that dreams process emotional conflicts involving contemporary relationships. In their view, the latent contents of dreams are more coherent and rational than in Freud's theory.

Devereux (1951a) described reality testing and problem solving in the dreams of a Plains Indian who was in psychotherapy, and he noted that Plains Indians generally view dreams as aids to solving personal problems. Waud Kracke (1992) argued that dreaming among the Kagwahiv of the Amazon effects a productive "mythopoetic" style of working through personal issues. Among the Sambia of New Guinea, dreams are the subject of private, secret, and public discourse. People share dreams about ritual matters and social conflicts that are already in discussion, whereas they keep private dreams about conflicts over illicit desires (Herdt 1992). The Kalapalo of Brazil believe that dreams reveal aspects of the self as agent or object. Dreaming is "performative" in the sense that it is "a kind of mental operation on current situations that changes a person's feelings, psychobiological motives, or goals" (Basso 1992: 98). It is part of a process of adjusting to the changing circumstances of life. And since human beings use language to deceive themselves and others, "dream images" must be interpreted as "metaphorical symbols" (ibid.: 100).

Experimental studies also suggest that dreaming has a problem-solving function. People who have been deprived of REM sleep have difficulty remembering emotionally charged information, and REM deprivation in animals similarly interferes with shuttle box and complex, unprepared learning (e.g., learning that a rewarding object is dangerous or that a formerly dangerous place is safe). One study found that time spent in REM sleep correlates positively with neuroticism and stress (Knowles et al. 1973). In some infrahuman animals the hippocampus produces synchronous theta waves when the animal is engaged in behavior related to self-preservation. These same theta waves are produced while the animal is in REM sleep. The medial area of the septum, which is evidently involved in theta-wave production, plays a role in learning to avoid a punishing but previously rewarding object or situation. In higher primates the passive avoidance system increasingly involves the frontal cortex (Gray 1987). In a review of the experimental data, Greenberg and Pearlman (1974) suggested that an evolving REM-sleep system allows "the increasingly flexible use of information in the mammalian family" (ibid.: 520), and they proposed that human dreaming integrates emotional experiences according to a person's characteristic defense mechanisms (ibid.: 519). Together with the data implicating the libido in dreams, these findings suggest that when life involves less conflict or more pleasure, the need for dream sleep diminishes and, conversely, when it is less pleasurable and more conflicted, the need for dream sleep may increase. Dreams, in other words, may characteristically deal with conflicts involving drive systems (attachment needs and power- and object-seeking libido) and related fears and anxieties.

Sleep and dreaming in mammalian species may be components of an adaptive system involving active metabolisms and high intelligence.

Comparative physiology suggests that sleep began 180 million years ago and dreaming some 50 million years later. Sleep may have evolved to rest and rejuvenate animals with energetic metabolism. Young mammals are especially active and therefore need even more sleep. Sleep, on the other hand, reduces time for learning in the waking state. Since learning is an essential feature of mammalian adaptation, sleep may have solved one problem but created another. Dreaming may have evolved to allow for learning and practicing drive-related behaviors during sleep (LaBerge 1985: 192–197). More precisely, it may have evolved to allow time for working on emotional conflicts associated with attachment needs and the libido. In this respect, the evolution of dreaming was part of the evolution of social intelligence.

Now, playfulness is also an expression of social intelligence and seems to have increased with evolutionary expansion of the brain (Byrne and Whiten 1988). Karl Groos (1911) observed that play permits experimentation with drives before they are required in serious adult behavior. Nicholas Humphrey (1986) theorizes that play allows children to expand their social experience and knowledge; specifically, by allowing them to take the roles of others it promotes psychological insight into self and others, a major ingredient in social intelligence. Together, the two observations suggest that play allows the practicing of drive-motivated behavior in social interaction.

In this respect, play and daydreaming (the mental counterpart of play) resemble dreaming. Both dreaming and play scenarios involve fear, aggression, and erotic impulses. Sexual play among children has been observed in many cultures. But children's play is also libidinal in a broader sense. It includes not only sexuality *per se* but also experimentation with attachment, separation, and self-assertion. In their little theaters of objects and make-believe children become powerful adults or mythical figures; they capture the prize, hunt game, make a home, nurture babies, and defend imaginary worlds against the forces of evil. Through play and shared fantasies children experiment with cooperation and competition while preparing themselves for adult roles and sociality. They may also play at subverting or opposing adult conventionality and authority.

Dreaming, it seems, is a nocturnal counterpart of waking fantasy and playful discourse. Maeder (1912) theorized that some dreams seek solutions to conflicts which are then tried in practice. And he added that dreams in this respect resemble play. Humphrey (1986) observed that taking the role of the other is common to play and dreaming; like play, dreaming permits the practicing of psychological insight in pretending to be another person. Freud ([1900]1953: 579–580) acknowledged Maeder's ideas but contended that "thinking ahead, forming intentions, framing attempted solutions which may perhaps be realized later in waking life" are secondary to the expression of the unconscious wishes in the dream; "they may persist in the state of sleep as `the day's residues' and combine with an unconscious wish . . . in forming a dream." If unconscious wishes influence conscious intentions, however, the views of Maeder and Freud are actually not so far apart. Indeed, Maeder's suggestion makes Freud's argument more interesting, at least for anthropology. Viewed as a form of play, dreams do not simply or merely satisfy wishes in fantasy; rather, they seek ways in which wishes might find satisfaction in social life.

The prefrontal cortex is active in both play and dreaming. Desire, we know, is organized by the prefrontal cortex, and there is reason to think that dreaming augments the prefrontal cortex's daytime work of negotiating social relations and organizing goals. Jonathan Winson (1985) theorizes that dreaming plays a role in the assimilation of new information and the planning of future activity. During early phases of mammalian evolution, organizing and planning apparently were carried out primarily by the prefrontal cortex. Noting that the primitive spiny anteater has a large prefrontal cortex but no REM sleep, Winson reasons that as organizing and planning became more complex and time-consuming during mammalian evolution, the waking state dealt more with immediate tasks while the dreaming brain took over planning and integration of past and present experience. Winson suggests that this "off-line processing" preadapted primates for the dramatic expansion of the human brain. It did not ensure the evolution of the large hominid brain, of course, but it may have been a precondition for such evolution. Without it the prefrontal cortex in humans would have had to expand to unwieldy proportions.[19]

Along with giving dreams a more adaptive role, current dream theory is blurring the distinction between latent and manifest content. We have already seen that tropes are not peculiar to unconscious, primary process thinking but that they also inform conscious thought, including the conscious portions of dreaming (Spiro 1993b). The mechanisms Freud discerned in the dreamwork are distinguished not by their form but rather by their function of concealing certain wishes from consciousness. But even this feature may be less central to the dream than Freud supposed. The apparent censorship in western dreams may reflect cultural attitudes.

Aram Yengoyan (1990) theorizes that dreams may be more or less congruous with culture and social life depending on whether cultures emphasize proscriptive or prescriptive rules. He notes that according to Freud there is no negation in the unconscious; in the latent content of dreams contrary attitudes or ideas are often juxtaposed. In western culture, however, negative injunctions or proscriptions suffuse discourse. Thus, there is discontinuity between the suppressed wishes in dreams and social life. Among the Pitjantjatjara, in contrast, discourse stresses prescriptive rules. Thus, Yengoyan finds continuity between dreams and social order and cultural norms. Forty-six of sixty-six dreams reported by male informants were explicitly sexual. And 25 percent of these sexual dreams included prohibited relations. Most of these were not with close kin, however. In three dreams featuring sex with close female relatives, the act was not pleasurable and the penis was damaged. Twenty-nine of the dreams dealt with aggression related to structural conflicts in the society or individual conflicts. In other words, images of desire and temptation in the dreams were generally consistent with sexual norms, and representations of aggression were consistent with the sorts of conflict that actually occur in kinship relations.

If censorship is not essential to the dream work, then the tropes (condensation, displacement, identification, imagery, symbolism) in dreams may have another explanation than the one of concealment ascribed to them by Freud. Spiro (1993b: 167) notes that the figurative quality of dreams may follow partly from the way in which they favor images rather than language when expressing dream thoughts. Since many thoughts cannot be expressed literally in images, the images of the dream must become figurative. This formulation, however, raises the question of why dreams favor images over words.

The answer may be the one we have already given, namely, that the dream is a biologically ancient mechanism that is concerned with the motivational and emotional aspects of social activity and social relationships. Animals express their emotions with visual signals and so, too, do human beings, their acquisition of language notwithstanding. Another explanation may lie in the possibility that the dreaming process duplicates and supplements the narrative, poetic orientation of social intelligence. Like narrative intelligence in the waking state, it may use symbols and metaphors because these facilitate the exploration of social conflicts and moral conundrums. Yet another possibility is that primary process thinking in dreams may be more efficient than logical, discursive thought for exploring the relevance of past experience to current and anticipated social and emotional conflicts. In using metonymy, metaphor, and iconographic images while dreaming, the brain may be simply doing what it always does when it organizes experience in terms of prototypical experiences and underlying structures. When trying to understand something new, or when constructing comprehensive semantic structures, the mind proceeds by way of proximity, resemblance, and analogy. Repression and other defense mechanisms may be part of the dream not because they are essential to its formation and function but because they have already affected the memories that are reworked in the dream process. Defense mechanisms may structure social experience from the beginning, and they may again exert effects in the process of remembering. Thus, dreams may work with materials which have already been subjected to rewriting and expurgation.

Many memories of social interaction may enter the dream process, yet, as Freud surmised, the earliest experience and fantasies may be particularly influential. As Winson (1985) suggests, by the middle years of childhood, nonverbal, unconscious memories of social experiences may become, as it were, hardwired. They may thus become stable prototypes for the way the waking and dreaming brain organizes later experience. Psychoanalytic theories of child development suggest that the most important prototypical experiences in this respect involve early object relations.

Freud ([1900]1953) thought that dreams often reflect the Oedipus complex. Since Freud, however, there has been a growing awareness that dreams commonly reflect preoedipal issues of attachment, separation, and individuation. Róheim (1952) discerned the traces of a "basic dream" in dream narratives of many cultures. Male and female dreamers alike enter a cave/the earth/water/a house and then return. Sleep represents death and return to the womb. The id desires uterine regression whereas the ego fears the dissolution of the self and counters with object-oriented eroticism. Oedipal imagery, when it is present, may overlie this conflict between object-relatedness and regressive return.[20] These themes, according to Róheim, are everywhere reflected in folklore and myth. Dreams, of course, may be suffused with local cultural symbols and meanings, and they may be subject to local systems of interpretation, but behind and beneath these local contingencies may lie universal or nearly universal experiences in child development and, beyond that, the common phylogeny of human beings (see also Paul 1987).

Societies are systems of social relations in which persons seek the satisfaction of their needs and wants. Inevitably, the needs and wants of different individuals and groups conflict. It may be that human beings have been finding realizations of their desires and solutions to social conflicts in dreams, daydreams, and play for a very long time. Various scholars have noted that dreaming may influence culture, especially myth and ritual (Devereux 1966; Gregor 1985; Kracke 1978, 1992; La Barre 1966; O'Flaherty 1984; Róheim 1952). Donald (1991) argues that the culture of *Homo erectus* was largely "mimetic." Mimesis, according to Donald, incorporates mimicry and imitation, but goes beyond them to construct intentional representations or models. Still present in ritual, play, theater, and opera, mimesis may have been the dominant mode of representation in the paleolithic. In this case, the modeling of social action and social relations in ritual may have grown out of play. Similarly, P. Reynolds (1976) held that the secret of hominid success was a further evolution of what he called the "flexibility complex": developmental plasticity in behavior, prolonged childhood dependency, learning by observation, and improved parenting. The evolution of this complex involved greater playfulness, the transformations of imitated behavior into behavioral conventions, and the development of survival functions within the simulative mode of play. With the increase in the capacity for more intelligent thinking, imitation could have transposed play to the world of serious activity. Language, Reynolds suggested, may have developed through playing with the vocal–auditory channel and then adapting the results to more serious activities. Play elements may have been pieced into complex patterns of mutual, cooperative play and then transferred to the adult world. In any event, once these complex patterns of mutual play were established and had survival functions, the culture of the play group supplanted the existing culture of adults. "In other words, the behavioural Rubicon of human evolution was crossed by the non-simulative execution of behaviour derived from the simulative mode" (Reynolds 1976: 628).

Summary

Human beings are symbol-making, symbol-using creatures. *Homo symbolicus*, however, offers too narrow a definition of human beings. Work in cognitive linguistics, neurobiology, and cognitive neuroscience shows that drive and emotion are no less a part of human nature than capacities for language and thought. Even the human capacity for language may depend on embodied, precultural experience and nonlinguistic neural maps and pathways in the brain.

Human beings are intelligent, curious, and playful. They form strong attachments to their primary caregivers, usually their mothers, and they are, as a result, subject to separation trauma and anxiety. Like their primate cousins, they are political and territorial. They feel pride when empowered, and shame when their social value is called into question. They are willful, desiring, embodied creatures. They are unusually libidinal. This core of phylogenetic "values" seems central to the self, meaning, and memory. Even language and advanced cognitive processes seem to have a foundation in embodied, subjective, emotional experience and a generalized capacity for categorization.

Human beings, moreover, have capacities for self-awareness, planning, impulse control, and moral reasoning. Given the complexities of social life and mammalian emotional organization, emotional conflicts are an inherent feature of human psychology. The dream mechanism may be an important part of the mind/brain's capacity to deal with such conflicts.

If the parallel distributed processing models or neural Darwinism are even partly right, then the implications for general anthropology are very important. Neither objectivism nor a radical epistemological relativism is correct. Human beings do not read the environment the way a computer reads a diskette, nor do they simply see it through a veil of prearranged words and symbols.[21] Rather, in understanding and constructing their environments, they use prelinguistic capacities for perception, categorization, memory, and evaluation, and when they do formulate their understandings in terms of words and symbols, they may use them in ways that are creative and idiosyncratic. Human beings may subscribe to conventions or they may work against them, and in either event they may do so for reasons that are more or less logical, more or less congruent with common sense, and more or less consistent with empirical observation. It follows that individuals are social creatures but also independent agents.

Human nature, thus defined, is an annotated outline, a plot structure. The complete story includes events, character, action, and dialogue. These details are supplied by child development, culture, and history. They get filled in, too, as individuals talk with each other. Having anticipated the plot, perhaps it is time for us to begin filling in the details.

3   Childhood

Experience gives shape and direction to human nature. Every individual has a share in our common phylogenetic heritage, but what this means for the adult personality depends importantly on experience, especially social experience. Mental abilities and emotional disposition may be inherited to some degree, but even so they take specific form only through interaction with the environment, particularly the human, sociocultural environment.

This process of social learning begins in childhood. In this chapter I focus on experiences and issues during the early and middle years of childhood. The first six to seven years of childhood may be especially consequential for the emotional and mental organization of personality in adult life. By the same token, they may lay the basis for the emotional significance of adult social relations and culture.

I begin by offering reasons for thinking that childhood experiences are significant for later personality. Then I review research and theorizing about the early and middle years of childhood. It should become apparent that there is agreement between what was said about the emotional and mental components of human nature and the broad outline of child development. The drive for attachment, separation anxiety, and the libido play major organizing roles in child development. The mental development of the child includes not only language acquisition and the learning of cognitive skills but, also, the development of a self, self-awareness, a conscience, and moral reasoning, features of personality that reflect the human capacity for social intelligence.

I am interested in two basic issues in this chapter. One is the question of what sorts of childhood experiences are responsible for generic as well as individual features of human personality. Another question concerns continuity. How much psychological continuity is there between childhood and adulthood? Does saying that childhood is important for adult personality mean that childhood experience has predictable consequences for personality differences? Are the consequences of childhood for adult personality sufficiently robust to permit us to try to explain cultural differences on the model of personality differences?

Formative experiences

There is reason to think that the early and middle years of childhood are important for personality formation. Basic emotional and mental structures probably take shape during the first six to seven years of life. Once established, they may condition the way a child continues to develop in later childhood and adolescence. Childhood, then, may lay the foundations for long-lasting features of personality. To paraphrase Freud, the child is parent to the adult ([1940]1964: 187).

Emotional social experiences may be particularly important for personality development. The neonate's behavior is organized largely by subcortical structures. Months and years go by before higher-level cognitive processes and language play a major role in structuring and directing behavior. Even then, the child's first extensive speech productions are "egocentric"; they are mostly self-talk in which the child tries to interpret nonlinguistic sensations, impulses, and desires, some of which arise in the right hemisphere and subcortical areas of the brain (Joseph 1982). The most important of these right-hemisphere and subcortical processes involve affectively loaded object relations and self-representation. These nonlinguistic, emotive schemas begin to develop before language and secondary process thinking. They may also be especially durable. Studies have shown that the visual cortex, while plastic to begin with, may become, as it were, hardwired at an early age. Prefrontal and limbic networks may become similarly fixed during the early years, with lasting consequences for self-organization and interpersonal relations (Winson 1985).

Following psychoanalytic usage, I separate the discussion of childhood into two phases, the preoedipal and the oedipal. The *preoedipal* period covers the first two to three years and involves, primarily, the child's relation with the caregiver. It centers on the attachment–affiliation system and includes the beginnings of self and object representation and mental schemas for managing and experiencing affect. During the *oedipal* phase, the child's behavior and fantasy life express the primate proclivity for triangular play and reproductive politics. The child emerges from the "dual-unity" relation with the mother and begins to deal with erotic feelings, envy, and needs for empowerment within the family and beyond.

There are differences of opinion about particulars. There are various theories about what is happening during the preoedipal and oedipal periods and conflicting opinions about their long-run significance for personality. Many psychoanalysts now think that the preoedipal period is more consequential for personality development than the oedipal period, and most have little to say about oedipality.[1] Feminist writers and some psychoanalysts have critiqued oedipal theory as it applies to women. Many child development researchers doubt that oedipal theory has any value for child psychology.

Oedipality remains a matter of interest for anthropology, however. Oedipal themes and images are common in shared narratives and ritual practices. In later chapters I explore pragmatic explanations for these themes and images. Here, I offer a view of oedipality that takes account of current thinking about it but which also makes sense in terms of both a phylogenetic perspective of human sexuality and the symbolic imagery in social relations and cultural practices.

The preoedipal period

Early psychoanalytic theorizing about child development focused on drive and the erotogenic body. According to the so-called psychosexual theory, the child progresses through a series of phases: oral, anal, and, coincident with the oedipal period, phallic. The phases were deemed to be "psychosexual" because phase-specific erotogenic experience influences thought.

In the oral stage, the child's attention focuses on hunger and feeding, and on pleasure and frustration associated with the mouth and breast. In the second year of life, toilet training ushers in the anal stage, during which power and autonomy become increasingly important issues. In the phallic period, the child becomes more aware of his or her genitalia, and budding erotic urges motivate the Oedipus complex – erotic fantasies about his or her relationships with the parents. Neurotic symptoms and character traits reflect fixations at one or another of these stages. Fixations result from either excessive frustration or indulgence of libidinal drive (Fenichel 1945: 65–66).

Some findings seem to support this view. "Oral" character traits (e.g., dependency, passiveness, oral eroticism) and "anal" traits (e.g., obstinacy, stubbornness, frugality, cleanliness) tend to occur together as the theory predicts (Fisher and Greenberg 1985). Oral or anal preoccupations are described in the clinical literature on schizophrenia and personality disorders. Some cultures also seem to emphasize certain elements of body imagery rather than others. Alan Dundes (1984), for example, speculated that anal themes in German culture may derive from traditional practices of severe toilet training and swaddling. Contrary to what the fixation theory predicts, however, experimental and longitudinal studies have not revealed robust or reliable connections between nursing, toilet training, or swaddling practices and "oral" or "anal" personality traits (Fisher and Greenberg 1985). Cross-cultural studies have also yielded little support for fixation (Whiting and Child 1953).

More recent observations suggest that the bodily preoccupations of children may be more related to social experience than to gratification or frustration of needs for physical pleasure. Attention to body parts and functions may express children's anxieties about autonomy, control, and separation (Roiphe and Galenson 1981).[2] Reactions to dirt and disorder may reflect parental attitudes and general features of family life, not just toilet training (Anthony 1957).

Attachment

Thinking about early child development now focuses on attachment, separation, and object relations. As we have seen, a close mother–newborn relationship is the quintessential feature of mammalian adaptation. Mammals are born immature and dependent. Their development and very survival depend on receiving adequate parental nurture and protection. The pattern is even more marked in human beings, who have even bigger brains and longer periods of childhood helplessness and dependency.

Attachment, in effect, is a primordial motive in mammals, including human beings. Nature reinforces the attachment with powerful emotions. The feeling of being securely attached is highly pleasurable, whereas unwanted separation from a love object can evoke painful negative emotion. Freud ([1926]1959) theorized that separation anxiety may be the prototype for all anxiety. John Bowlby (1969, 1973), taking this observation as his point of departure, organized an entire approach to child development around the phenomena of attachment, separation, and loss. He noted that separation evokes protest, despair, and detachment, and he suggested that these reactions are part of the psychobiology of attachment. Because separation from the mother is life-threatening, infant animals must be motivated to avoid premature separation and to get their mothers' attention when separated. They experience anxiety and anger, and these emotions motivate attention-getting behavior. Bowlby argued that maternal deprivation may lead to emotional disorders.

Mary Ainsworth (Ainsworth and Salter 1982) and her colleagues explored attachment in one-year-olds with a "Strange Situation" technique: the mother and a stranger take turns leaving the child for short periods, and the experimenters observe the child's reaction on their return. They observed three patterns; one seemed to reflect secure attachment (type B) whereas two others reflected insecure, anxious attachment (types A and C). Type A babies avoided the mother on her return and showed little emotion. With other children they were angry and aggressive. The C babies combined clinging with resistance to the mother on her return; they showed anger toward the mother, but less anger in other contexts than the avoidant babies. Later research found that the mothers of avoidant and resistant babies were often insensitive. In addition to being insensitive, mothers of avoidant babies were often angry and rejecting when the child sought contact (Sroufe 1983). In the American population the distribution is about 70 percent secure attachment, 20 percent avoidant, and 10 percent resistant. An analysis of thirty-two studies across eight countries using the "Strange Situation" found similar distributions. Intersample variations were greater within than between countries (van IJzendoorn and Kroonenberg 1988). Variation among the American samples correlates with socioeconomic status. There are more securely attached babies in middle-class families and many more anxiously attached babies (especially type C babies) in lower socioeconomic status families. Anxious attachment correlates in particular with economic insecurity, unstable families, and child abuse (ibid.: 153–154).

The quality of attachment affects emotional and mental development in infrahuman primates and human beings. Harry F. Harlow (1971) found that maternal care in infancy was necessary for the normal development of reproductive behavior and other social skills in rhesus monkeys. There is a rapidly growing literature that is demonstrating continuity from psychological organization in the "Strange Situation" to later personality among western children. Securely attached children at one year of age are more autonomous and empathic in preschool situations (Sroufe et al. 1993). Positive adaptation in infancy correlates with adjustment in early school years, despite difficulties during the preschool period. These findings imply that personality may influence a child's ability to rebound from the effects of adverse situations (Sroufe et al. 1990). Secure attachment at age one is significantly correlated with confidence, purposefulness, industriousness, and sociability at age ten. There is also evidence that insecurely attached children are more apt to ignore gender boundaries in play (Sroufe et al. 1993).[3] Some of the strongest effects of parental insensitivity, rejection, and abuse are seen in people with personality disorders. Emotional deprivation and physical and sexual abuse in childhood increase the risk for personality disorder and mental illness in adulthood (see Shengold 1989; also Chapters 5 and 6 below).

Cross-cultural studies and developmental studies in other cultures also suggest that lack of secure attachment may lead to neurosis and personality disorder in adults. Ronald P. Rohner (1975, 1986) found that parental rejection of children promotes low self-esteem, dependency, anxiety, aggressiveness, and negative outlook. Other studies lend support to the proposition that close, warm, nurturing relationships with primary caregivers encourage self-esteem and security in social relations in later childhood and adulthood. A longitudinal study of eleven children among the Logoli in western Kenya found a significant correlation between frequency of being held by mothers in infancy and optimism, trust, and sense of security in later childhood (Munroe and Munroe 1980). Some research suggests that negative psychological consequences of early experiences may reflect poor attachment and discord within the family more than the negative effects of separation *per se*. Some children thrive emotionally despite poor parenting, particularly when there is someone else who gives them emotional support and encouragement.[4]

Sleeping arrangements and bedtime rituals may be consequential for attachment and, ultimately, for adult personality. A study of 219 Basque women found correlations between sharing the same bedroom with parents during childhood and ego strength and physical and mental health (Crawford 1994). Studies of children's attachments to objects also suggest that parental presence at bedtime fosters a sense of safety and well-being in children (see below).

Object relations

Object-relations theory considers the child's psychic representations of self and maternal object as well as emotion and drive in the child's early relationships. Object-relations theory is largely the result of work by three British psychoanalysts – Melanie Klein, W.R.D. Fairbairn, and D.W. Winnicott. In classical psychoanalysis, the satisfaction of oral needs at the breast was thought to promote attachment to the breast and then to the mother. In the object-relations approach, drive is social from the beginning. In the words of Fairbairn (1952), the libido is inherently "object seeking." Similarly, for Klein, drive is inextricably embedded in social relations.

According to Klein (1975a, 1975b), the young child experiences love and rage in relation to caregivers; the inner world of the child is a battleground for the "life" and "death" instincts. These "instincts," however, are social from birth in the sense that they are directed at the primary caregiver, usually the mother. The young child, having a simple, as yet poorly developed ego, tries to manage feelings of rage and anxiety with rudimentary defenses. Typically, the child begins by adopting a "paranoid-schizoid" position, that is, by splitting the object into good mother and bad mother and by projecting the bad part-objects back onto the world. Since children identify with these projected, persecutory representations, they have pleasant and unpleasant feelings about the self as well. As children experience consistently good caregiving, their rage in moments of frustration becomes less threatening and they learn to integrate the good and bad aspects of the object into a single representation. Similarly, the experience of the self becomes less divided and more coherent. Rage now leads to a "depressive" position as the child realizes that rage and anger might hurt the caregiver.

The child feels guilty and remorseful, and learns to accept disappointments and loss. As children work through the depressive position, they experience gratitude toward the object and try to make reparation.

The child's personality is seen as ordinarily progressing toward integrated and constant representations of self and other. Good and bad parts of a representation, whether of self or other, become facets of integrated representations of the self and the object. This normal progression, however, may get sidetracked by emotional trauma and neglect (Kernberg 1972). Incomplete self–other differentiation and splitting of both self and other are common in persons with severe personality disorders. These characteristics may result from emotional trauma in early childhood. Broken families, parental neglect, and physical and sexual abuse are common in the backgrounds of persons with borderline personalities and other severe personality disorders (Ludolph et al. 1990).

Various studies in fact show that infants' orientations toward their caregivers reflect attachment to particular caregivers and not just the satisfaction of physiological needs. Infants quickly learn the distinguishing characteristics of their caregivers; they recognize, for example, the smell of their mother's milk and prefer it to milk from another mother. Infants cared for by a succession of caregivers are fussy compared with infants under the exclusive care of their own mothers. The infant's attention, moreover, focuses on the mother as a whole, not simply on her breast (Silverman 1987).

Culturally specific patterns of child-rearing may affect the structuring of object relations and their ramifications for personality and social sentiments later in life. The work of Kathleen Barlow among the Murik Lakes people at the mouth of the Sepik River in Papua New Guinea offers an example. Mothering is an important part of the female role among the Murik, but it is also a model and metaphor for valued attitudes and behavior in sociality; giving food and nurturing increases power and prestige, whereas being the receiver of food is associated with dependency and inferiority. Fathership and siblingship are also modeled on the mother–infant relationship; fathers and older siblings should be caring and nurturing like mothers (Barlow 1985, 1990).

This maternal schema begins in experiences of touch, gesture, and facial expression and then is elaborated over time through various symbolic media. Barlow shows, however, that the actual sentiments and behavior are more complicated and ambivalent than the maternal ideal suggests. The mother is a nurturing figure, but she also disciplines her children and has sexual relations with her husband. Older siblings may resent the constantly reinforced obligation to care for younger siblings. Youngest children, free from such obligations, may not develop the proper sense of generosity.

Mothers often attribute threats to others in order to get children to behave (Barlow 1985:214). This same pattern is realized in more dramatic form as the bogey Gaingeen, a leafy, masked figure who appears periodically in Murik villages to chase, terrorize, and delight children aged six months through fourteen years. Gaingeen figures are the most junior in a series of masked representations that at the most senior levels impose sanctions on entire communities. Mothers call for Gaingeen to appear when they want to restrain a toddler from moving too far away or to punish mischievous behavior, or when they want to wean a child (some Murik children nurse until they are six or seven years of age). Children are fascinated with Gaingeen, and they imitate him in their play. Actual Gaingeens are adolescent boys, and they only chase younger children, thereby reversing the rule that older siblings should be nurturing and nonaggressive with younger siblings. Gaingeen thus absorbs the bad aspects of the mother and the older sibling.

Separation–individuation

Margaret Mahler and her colleagues understood early development as a process of separation and individuation. "From the second month on . . . the infant behaves and functions as though he and his mother were an omnipotent system – a dual unity within one common boundary" (Mahler et al. 1975:44). At four to five months of age, the child begins to differentiate from the mother. Instead of molding to the mother's body, the infant strains away from her. With crawling, the pace of separation–individuation accelerates. At first the baby travels only short distances and then quickly returns for "refueling," yet she increasingly asserts herself. She may want to feed herself, and may react with anger if restrained or force-fed. No-saying asserts individuality as the child oscillates between merging with the mother and acting the conquering hero. Increasing awareness of separation may lead to anxiety and fear of strangers, particularly between nine and twelve months. Between ten to fifteen months the child is in the "practicing" subphase. This period begins with the baby's crawling and climbing away from the mother and continues with walking. Elation prevails, although mood may drop when the mother leaves. In the third subphase, walking and advances in representational intelligence further the hatching process, although conflict between being with and separating from the mother recurs. Alternately shadowing and darting away from the mother expresses the contradictory wish for reunion, on the one hand, and the joy of autonomous action, on the other. The press of reality now forces the toddler to recognize the mother's independence and undermines delusions of grandeur, producing what Mahler calls the "rapprochement crisis."

Resolution of the crisis is shaped by the mother's warmth and reassurance, on the one hand, and her encouragement of independence, on the other. Wooing the mother alternates with pushing her away; departures may involve indecision and clinging. The child may split the image of the caregiver into "good" and "bad" part-objects. In the fourth subphase toddlers show increasing tolerance of separation from their mothers, perhaps because they can hold images of them in mind even when they are absent.

The work of the psychoanalyst Daniel N. Stern (1985) qualifies Mahler's view of the first year of life somewhat and, at the same time, offers a previously unexpected insight into the richness of mother–infant interaction. Stern examined films of mother–infant interaction frame by frame. He found that mothers typically and repeatedly engage their infants in interaction games ("Here-I-Come," "Peekaboo," etc.), and that during these games the mother and infant become emotionally and physically attuned to each other. Stern also noticed, however, that some mothers are not so well attuned to their infants, and he wondered if such misattunements might have long-run consequences for emotional disposition and object relations. Attunement may lay the basis for agency and productive inner dialogues later on. In fact, child-development researchers are finding that attunement and misattunement during the first year of life may be precursors, respectively, of secure and anxious attachment in the Strange Situation Test at age one (Isabella and Belsky 1991).

Stern finds that an ability to make perceptual distinctions and to transfer perceptual learning across sensory modalities in infants suggests incipient abstract thinking and, therefore, the possibility that rudimentary representations of self and object begin to form very early. Stern theorizes that infants begin to develop a core sense of self and relatedness to others by the end of the second month or even earlier. Stern's work suggests, in effect, that the agentic subject and the dialogical self begin to take shape very early. The infant's early relation with the mother is not as passive and symbiotic as Mahler suggested.

Stern's work does not undermine the general idea of separation–individuation, however. Infants progress from dependency to less dependency, and from close and frequent contact with the mother to physical and emotional separation. Rather, Stern's work shows that separation–individuation begins early, and that the process of becoming a person and forming a self is dialogical from the start.

The self

Until recently, the earliest organization and development of personality was more the subject of speculation than empirical research. A common strategy has been to assume that severe adult pathology (e.g., grandiose narcissism, loss of ego boundaries, splitting) represents regression to the earliest phases of childhood and, thus, that it illuminates early psychology.

According to classical psychoanalysis, the infant is narcissistic. Only later, as the mother provides libidinal gratification, does the child redirect libido from self to others. Hunger/oral appetite energizes this interest in the mother. The early personality is also unstructured. An internal structure develops gradually as experiences of loss and frustration prompt identification with the object. Even in Mahler's reworking of the classical psychoanalytic view, self-representation grows out of the blurred self-object representations of the symbiotic period. It does not begin to form until the seventh month or so.

As we have seen, these formulations are questionable. Needs for attachment and stimulation may be more important in prompting the child to relate to others than the hunger drive. It follows from this that the behavior and characteristics of non-nursing mothers, fathers, and other caregivers can be crucial for early attachment experience. Stern's work suggests that the early caregiver–infant relationship is less symbiotic for the infant than Mahler supposes. From birth, the infant is a distinct organism, with separate emotions and perceptual and cognitive processes. Social experiences in various modalities lead to a core sense of self and the beginnings of self–object differentiation by two months of age.

It does not follow, however, that the formation of the self results simply or primarily from social experience. Nor does it follow that core structures of personality derive primarily from symbolic experience. Stern's work suggests that the infant is *inherently* social, and that a rudimentary sense of self forms well before the child has much inkling, if any at all, about what words mean.

Michael L. Schwalbe (1991) contends that formation of the core sense of self in the first couple of years of life is autogenetic. Following G.H. Mead, he suggests that "consciousness and the self emerge naturally out of the interaction between human biology and communal life" (ibid.: 270). He goes beyond Mead, however, to draw on recent theorizing about nonlinear (or chaotic) systems to reconceptualize the material grounding of the self. In his view, consciousness and the self emerge as the child constructs images of objects or situations that meet internal impulses. Imagery organizes impulses. Language, once acquired, organizes imagery. "This engenders a more ordered and complex self as the rules that are inherent in language compel further self-organization" (ibid.: 285).

Experiments with mirrors suggest that a fully reflexive sense of self begins to develop in the second year of life. After eighteen months, many children can identify their own marked nose with the marked nose of their mirror image. Not long after this achievement, children refer to themselves with pronouns and by name. Once they have pronouns and names, they begin to construct simple narratives about themselves. Practice in constructing narratives occurs in dialogic interaction with parents and others. The child's reflexive imagination is no doubt further stimulated by stories and fairy tales (Hermans and Kempen 1993: 67–70).

Psychoanalytic theorizing about the early self has been shaped by dealing with issues of self-esteem and ego boundaries in clinical practice. According to Heinz Kohut (1966, 1971, 1977), the "healthy" personality has positive self-esteem, cohesion, and autonomy. Children who get too little recognition and affirmation from their parents may in adulthood be prone to narcissism, emotional emptiness and deflation, and merging or loss of autonomy in relations with others.

One question about the theories of Mahler and Kohut is whether they are too parochial. Some writers worry that their theories may say more about common western values than about universal developmental processes. The notion that children normally progress toward separation and individuality may reflect individualistic values and an inclination to pathologize interdependency.[5]

Recognition and encouragement may prepare children for the rewards and frustrations of a society that emphasizes autonomy, achievement, and individual rights and responsibilities, but they may be less useful for preparing children for social life in some premodern societies that have different norms and expectations for public behavior among adults. In many cultures, sociability and interdependency represent emotional maturity. Robert A. LeVine (1982, 1990) notes that among the Gusii of western Kenya, social norms are oriented toward discouraging inappropriate sexual and aggressive behaviors and, generally, toward inhibiting expressions of assertiveness and boasting. Accordingly, Gusii parenting places less emphasis on encouraging autonomy, self-assertion, achievement, and self-esteem than in middle-class American families. The result is a childhood personality that is less energetic, physically and verbally, and less insisting on attention than its American counterpart (LeVine 1990: 465–466). While this pattern of Gusii child-rearing is suited to premodern society in which obligations to the group and cooperative activities outweigh individual achievement, it may be preparing children less well for the growing emphasis on competition and individual responsibility in modern Kenya.

There may, however, be less western bias in psychoanalytic studies of early development than at first appears. Somewhat paradoxically, the studies actually suggest that secure attachment in early childhood fosters not only sociability but also a capacity for autonomy and agentic action. As the contributions of Bowlby, Stern, Kohut, and others show, an ability to act independently may depend on supportive mirroring by caregivers and a subjective feeling of secure attachment. And by the same token, a measure of autonomy may be a precondition for culturally expected sociability. Ewing (1991) finds that early childhood experiences that promote intrapsychic autonomy may favor rather than hinder the Pakistani woman's capacity to cope with the demands of extended family life in adulthood.

Core gender identity and gender

Core gender identity and gender are probably everywhere central elements of self-representation. Core gender identity is a basic sense of being male or female. Gender or gender role refers to the social and cultural meanings of masculinity or femininity, or any other gender a culture may recognize. Gender is subjective and social. It comprises not only a personal sense of one's bodily self and sexual orientation but, also, a social identity and social role. Anatomical differences inform gender identity and gender constructions, but they are not in and of themselves decisive. Core gender identity need not coincide with anatomy, and some cultures may recognize more than two genders.

Core gender identity begins to form in the first year or two, and it usually becomes permanent by the end of the third year. Children can verbalize a core gender identity as part of their self-concept by eighteen to twenty-four months. Core gender identity rarely changes once established, whereas the content and presentation of gender may well change during development and, for that matter, throughout life (Money and Ehrhardt 1972).

Work on gender identity and gender relations in psychological anthropology has implications for social anthropology. Gender and gender relations are significant features of all social organizations. Thus, gender-identity formation and the teaching of gender roles are part of the psychological and social reproduction of social orders. Some writers, moreover, think that confusion about gender identity – and envy of the female – in the male may be germane to understanding phenomena ranging from customary male fear of women and male aggressiveness to deviant sexual practices (Greenson 1968; Stoller 1975).

Gender-identity formation and gender have long been one of the most controversial topics in psychoanalytic thought. Freud's ideas about gender-identity formation evoked criticism from other psychoanalysts almost from the time they were first enunciated, and nowadays they are either criticized or simply ignored by most psychoanalytic writers.[6] Freud assumed that both the little boy and little girl are essentially masculine and that their first object choice is the mother. Thus, appropriate gender identity formation and object choice are relatively easy for the boy, but for the girl, according to Freud, they are more difficult and conflicted; the girl must shift to a feminine identity and cross-sex object choice and, having made these shifts, she may still envy the male's physical characteristics.

There are various difficulties with this formulation, however, quite apart from its evident sexism. For one thing, there is no evidence for a primary masculinity in normal girls. Girls show feminine characteristics and play at mothering well before the oedipal period. Contrary to what Freud would predict, young girls do not focus exclusively on the clitoris when playing with their sexual parts; to the contrary, it is common for them to explore the interior of their vaginas. Moreover, there is little indication that most young girls feel a significant lack when they first learn about anatomical differences between the sexes. If girls envy boys, it is probably because boys are often given favored treatment (Fliegel 1986). Ironically, envy of cross-sex physical characteristics may be more characteristic of boys than little girls.

Ralph R. Greenson (1968) and others theorized that mother–infant symbiosis in the first year of life encourages identification with the mother and, therefore, femininity in young girls and boys. This theory implies that masculine gender identity requires "dis-identification" with the mother and a counter-identification with the father. Although girls also begin life in a symbiotic relationship with the mother, in their case the early identification with the mother is congruent with their anatomy. In boys it may jeopardize gender identity and individuation.

According to Robert J. Stoller (1968, 1975), primary feminine identification in males and a resulting "protofemininity" may explain why male transsexuals outnumber female transsexuals three or four to one. Transsexuals are persons who identify completely with the opposite gender. Stoller discerned intense mother–son symbioses and ineffective fathers in the early histories of transsexual males, and he suggested that hyper-masculinity, sadism, and perversion in males may be ways of coping with symbiosis anxiety and gender insecurity. Stoller attributed the vulnerability to castration anxiety to insecure gender identity and symbiosis anxiety. So-called "perversions" (e.g., sadomasochism, transvestism, bestiality, necrophilia, pedophilia, Frotteurism)[7] may grow out of a matrix of unresolved protofemininity and symbiosis anxiety. In some instances at least they may represent attempts to reverse childhood insults to a precarious masculine identity with an aggressive stance toward the maternal object and objects that take her place.

Some anthropologists have also theorized that insecure gender identity in males has behavioral consequences. It has been suggested that father-absence encourages insecure gender identity in males and, consequently, expressions of hypermasculinity. Bacon, Child, and Barry (1963) found that polygyny and exclusive mother–child sleeping arrangements, presumably measures of father absence, correlate cross-culturally with male theft and personal crime. Beatrice Whiting (1965) found in a study of six cultures that the Rajput men of Kalapur and the Gusii[8] men of Nyansongo, the two cultures of the six with the least paternal presence, commit assaults and murders and distance themselves from their wives and children more than do the men in the four other cultures. Gregor (1985) used the idea of proto-femininity in a study of child development and expressive culture among the Mehinaku. Among the Mehinaku, the child has a very close relationship with the mother. The father, meanwhile, is hardly present. According to Gregor, this arrangement delays separation–individuation and, in boys, intensifies oedipal fantasies and castration anxiety. These psychological effects of the close mother–child relationship later show up in cultural expressions of ambivalence toward women and sexual pleasure. Ritual, myth, and folklore reveal castration anxiety, identification with women, and hostility toward women. Hypermasculinity and male solidarity may be defenses against symbiosis anxiety and feminine identification.

In a survey of ideas about manhood in various societies, David D. Gilmore (1990) notes that many societies emphasize masculinity for men, and a good many take such emphasis to extremes. Such instances of exaggerated masculinity, according to Gilmore, may represent a defense against traces of early symbiotic union with the mother. Men, because they are raised by women, may be prone to regress to maternal attachment and boyishness. Thus many societies pressure boys to become real men. Gilmore (1990: 224), however, notes that psychology alone cannot account for these pressures. Material conditions also are important: "The harsher the environment and the scarcer the resources, the more manhood is stressed as inspiration and goal."

Chodorow (1978) proposed a corresponding view of female gender identity. Mothers tend to intensify relations with their daughters more than with their sons. This tendency, combined with the father's uninvolvement in child-rearing, encourages daughters to identify strongly with their mothers while reinforcing concern with preoedipal issues of relatedness and nurture. Thus, mothering is reproduced psychologically and socially in daughters whereas sons are apt to distance themselves from nurturing as part of their effort to establish masculine identities.

Ethel S. Person and Lionel Ovesey (1983), however, observed that there is no evidence that either boys or girls are especially feminine in the first year of life. They argued instead that male transsexualism develops out of separation anxiety as a defensive orientation some time after the first year. By merging with the mother in fantasy, the child who will later become a transsexual protects himself against object loss (ibid.: 218). Person and Ovesey concluded that "normal core gender identity" reflects gender assignment and gendered socialization (ibid.: 222). Ethnographic data also raise doubts about the protofemininity hypothesis. Gwen Broude (1990) infers from cross-cultural evidence that male aggressiveness is better understood as resulting from socialization pressures for aggression than as a defense against cross-sex identity. The often-documented connection between father absence and hypermasculinity, she reasons, may reflect the fact that single mothers have difficulty curbing aggression in sons.[9]

Irene Fast (1984) argued that gender identity in boys and girls is initially undifferentiated. Female anatomy supports the gradual emergence of a feminine identity in girls. In this view, both boys and girls may envy the opposite gender when they realize they are being asked to give up something in becoming either male or female. Girls may feel loss on recognizing their lack of a penis, but this is apt to be a fleeting issue. Where it becomes a more serious concern, the underlying issue may be separation anxiety (see also Roiphe and Galenson 1981). Many parents have witnessed the counterpart of penis envy in little boys. At one point, for example, a friend's toddler claimed that he had a baby in his tummy.

The role of bodily awareness and, specifically, genital awareness in gender-identity formation and the sex-typing of other persons is unclear. Roiphe and Galenson (1981) found that the children they studied were aware of their genitals and took pleasure in them by the second year of life. This may not mean that bodily awareness is central to gender identity, however. Sandra Lipsitz Bem (1989) found in an experimental study that only 40 percent of the three to five-year-old children she studied took account of genitals when sex-typing pictures of boys and girls. If they could use knowledge about genital differences, however, they could also correctly sex-type the same children when they appeared cross-dressed. According to Bem, her research refutes the Kohlbergian idea that children who are supposedly at a preoperational cognitive level take gender differences as natural and actively develop them in a rigidly moralistic fashion. Another possibility in Bem's results – not discussed by her – is that anxiety about genital difference blocks use of genital difference in sex-typing. Many of the misrecognitions of gender in her study occurred among boys, and boys were less likely than girls to use terms for the genitalia of the opposite gender.

Gender or gender roles are emphasized in all cultures. Boys and girls are treated differently, and parents and other childcare providers have different expectations for boys and girls. What these expectations are, and how much they differ for boys and girls, vary by social class, ethnicity, and stage in the life cycle. They also vary from one society to another (Whiting and Edwards 1988). This socialization for gender can profoundly influence attitudes, understandings, and behavior.

Transitional object, illusion, and culture

Psychoanalytic thinking about the preoedipal period suggests that cultural representations may reflect parts of the self and the maternal object. It also suggests that cultural objects and social relations – and, ultimately, the whole illusory world of cultural representation – resonate symbolically and emotionally with the maternal object. That is, cultural objects may be in some sense substitutive objects.

Relations with inanimate objects may reflect the child's relation with caregivers and sense of security. Attachments to security blankets, dolls, and stuffed animals are commonplace in young children. Winnicott (1953) noted that young children progress from stimulation of the mouth with fist, fingers, and thumbs to attachments to other objects (e.g., cuddly animals, dolls, hard objects, and make-believe persons). "Transitional objects" and "transitional phenomena" lie between the use of the hand and these attachments. Thumb sucking becomes conflated with mouthing a blanket or a bit of cloth or caressing a ball of plucked wool. This transitional sphere is the area of "illusion." It is both externally present and internally invested with memory and emotional significance. In the child it may serve as a soporific or as a defense against anxiety. It represents the breast or the maternal object. The child asserts ownership of the transitional or substitutive object and cuddles it affectionately. Such objects, according to Winnicott, temper the disparity between the nursing infant's illusion of omnipotence and the inevitable frustrations of growth, especially weaning. The substitutive object sustains the imaginary presence of the actual or ideal mother; it may retain the mother's odor and may represent the mother's breast. The mother's breast, which corresponds to the infant's need, creates the illusion for the infant that it exercises some creative control of its situation; the transitional object recreates this illusion. The infant's ability to accept disillusionment, and to fashion illusion depends on having what Winnicott called a "good-enough mother." Winnicott regarded transitional objects as normal. "Good-enough mothers" frustrate their infants sufficiently to force them to give up their delusional omnipotence for adaptation to reality. The transitional objects ease the process, but they may also express emotional disturbance.

Large-sample studies and clinical cases imply that children's attachments to blankets, dolls, teddy bears, and the like may reflect separation anxiety. One study compared 682 rural Italian children with 450 Italian and 52 foreign children (mostly Anglo-Saxon in origin) living in Rome. Only 4.9 percent of the rural Italian children were attached to inanimate objects as opposed to 31.1 percent of the urban Italian children and 61.5 percent of the foreign urban children. Maternal closeness correlated negatively with substitutive objects and phenomena. Compared with the foreign children, more of the rural children were breast-fed, and they were breast-fed for more months than the foreign children who were breast-fed. More rural children slept in their parents' bed or room and more were rocked to sleep. Fewer urban Italian babies were breast-fed and the ones who were breast-fed were nursed for fewer months than children in the rural group. About the same percentage of urban as rural Italian children slept with their parents but fewer were rocked to sleep (Gaddini 1970).

A similar study compared children in Korea, Korean children in the United States, and non-Korean American children. About 54 percent of the American children, 34 percent of the US Koreans, and 18 percent of the Korean children had attachments to security blankets and dolls. Among children with security blankets, 50 percent of the Americans sucked their thumbs in contrast to 28.5 percent of the US Koreans and none of the Koreans. The Korean and US Korean children were more apt to sleep in the same room with their parents during the first year. Korean children were weaned later than the American children. Although more Korean mothers worked, many left the children with grandmothers who were living in their households. American mothers, in contrast, tended to leave their children with baby sitters. The Korean mothers spent more time with their children (Hong and Townes 1976).[10]

The clinical literature also shows that separation anxiety can motivate children's attachments to substitutive objects. Gregory Rochlin (1953) described the case of little Sam. Aggressive, destructive, and detached, Sam threw toys about and demolished his room. He spurned his mother's efforts to console him, and would sit for hours in a closet rubbing himself with his mother's fur coat. He did not speak until age three and rarely talked after that.

Little Sam was reacting to loss. When Sam was four months old, his mother learned that her husband was unfaithful during his business trips. She quickly weaned Sam, turned him over to her mother, and began to travel with her husband, often leaving Sam for three to four days at a time. She became depressed and angry with her husband and with Sam, whom she saw as an obstacle to a better marriage. Sam, left in the care of his grandmother and house workers, at six months began to suck his fingers. When he was eighteen months old, Sam's mother took him to another country so she could be with her husband. Again, she accompanied him on business trips, now leaving Sam with house workers who spoke no English.

When Sam was three she became pregnant, upon which she returned to the United States and divorced her husband.

In therapy, Sam moved from detachment to interest in candy, to concerns with the placement of things, to emptying drawers, to insisting on staying with Rochlin. His obsessions with order and acceptance expressed a longing for control over his mother. "By the drive first to disown everything and then to possess it, he displayed the fear of losing it and, thus, the need of having and holding on to it" (ibid.: 301). The relationship with the fur coat was an attempt to avoid loss. The fur coat was an inanimate substitute for the mother, one that could not leave or reject Sam. By attaching to the fur coat, Sam turned away from his mother but regained a facsimile of her in fantasy (Rochlin 1953: 306).

The use of transitional objects and activities for emotional support, according to Winnicott, persists into adulthood in the form of art and religion. Art and religion may help people to sustain illusions of being able to create secure and meaningful environments. Through symbols and values they may also encourage empathy, self-awareness, and purpose and, thus, a framework for meaningful social relationships. Alternatively, as in little Sam's attachment to his mother's coat, substitutive objects may become ends in themselves, fetishes that replace or obviate social relationships and interests in the real world.

The origins of paraphilias or perversions are interesting in this respect. There is a hint of perversion in little Sam's attachment to his mother's fur coat, and there are a number of other case studies in the clinical literature which similarly suggest that sexual perversions begin in experiences of rejection and humiliation (Bak 1974; Wulff 1946). Some clinical studies of adults with perverse inclinations point in this same direction. M. Masud Khan (1979) regarded gadgets and fantasies in perversion as symptoms of depersonalization of self and other. In the ten cases on which he reported, the preoedipal mothers related in a sensual way to their children's bodies while ignoring them as autonomous persons. As the children themselves began to show more erotic inclination, the mothers, disturbed by delayed realizations of their excessive closeness to their children, withdrew from them, provoking separation trauma.[11] Louise J. Kaplan (1991) concludes that kleptomania and other perverse strategies in women similarly compensate for deprivations in relations with parents.

The erotic and hateful objectification of the object of desire in perversion, in other words, may be a variant of a more general class of substitutive objectification in which erotic and narcissistic needs fixate on cultural artifacts or on merely the objective and sexual qualities of social others. Later, I suggest that childhood substitutive objects may prefigure displacement and objectification in adults (see Chapter 7). Substitutive objects in this sense may be normal for a particular sociocultural milieu or they may be deviant, or both, depending on social perspective.

The oedipal period

By two to three years the child has the beginnings of symbolic representation, object constancy (an ability to hold caregivers in mind even when they are not present), and a core gender identity. These accomplishments mark the transition to the oedipal phase. During the middle years children begin to deal with the complexities of family relationships as they become increasingly aware of having to compete for parental attention.

The Oedipus complex refers to triangular fantasies about this predicament. The fantasies are thought to emerge, roughly, between four to six years of age. Boys and girls may have feelings of love and attraction to one parent and feelings of envy, fear, and rivalry toward the other. Freud thought that the child could have romantic feelings about either the opposite-sex parent (the "positive" complex) or the same-sex parent (the "negative" complex) or both. The "complete" Oedipus complex, then, is both heterosexual and homoerotic. The complex is superseded when the child represses incestuous desires, identifies with the parental rival, and internalizes the moral order.

Freud found traces of the Oedipus complex in dreams, sibling rivalry, and children's play and phobias. Other evidence included transference – the analysand's passionate attachment to, and hostility toward, the analyst. Freud also noticed traces of oedipality in myth and folklore. In fact, incest and parricide are common in myths, tales, and rituals (Edmunds 1985; Edmunds and Dundes 1983). In a survey of myths and folktales, Allen Johnson and Douglass Price-Williams (1996) find tales about mother–son incest and father–daughter incest in societies of every degree of social complexity. References to parricide and incest, though sometimes more muted or symbolic in complex societies, are discernible nonetheless. In the tales, the son usually initiates mother–son incest, whereas the father usually initiates father–daughter incest.

Quite apart from the clinical and ethnographic evidence and related questions of interpretation, there are a couple of lines of thought suggesting that oedipal fantasies may be fairly common in children. One line focuses on drive and imagination. This, of course, was Freud's approach. In his view the three- to four-year-old child is already attached to the parents. As the child begins to have erotic impulses as well as attachment needs, he or she naturally implicates images of the parents in his or her romantic fantasies. Envy and rivalry are by-products of desire. Alfred Adler ([1931]1979: 207) thought that striving for superiority was a more important motive in human behavior than sexuality. In his view, oedipal fantasies express children's wishes to have the power and stature of mothers and fathers. Freud and Adler thought that they were making very different arguments about oedipality, but given the evidence that dopamine and androgens may underlie both desire and the will-to-power (see Chapter 2), their arguments would seem to be more complementary than contradictory. Both Freud and Adler were, in effect, attributing oedipality to the libido, to the object-seeking libido in the one case and to the power-seeking libido in the other. Oedipality, in other words, may be a developmental expression of the primate propensity for reproductive politics.[12]

The evidence that boys tend to be more assertive and girls more oriented toward attachment implies that oedipality is likely to vary by gender. Chodorow (1978, 1989) contends that the girl more than the boy preserves the nonsexual attachment to the mother during the oedipal period. Thus, the Oedipus complex in the girl combines erotic attachment to the father and a persisting attachment to the mother. It may be, then, that the girl's attachment to the father is less erotic than the boy's attachment to the mother. A daughter looks to her father for recognition of her separateness from her mother and "cares especially about being loved" (Chodorow 1989: 72). Since assertive, masculine sexuality implies dominance, and even abuse in an asymmetrical relationship, the girl may find incestuous fantasies even more disturbing than does the boy. Recall that it is usually the father, not the daughter, who initiates a sexual relationship in folktales about father–daughter incest. That is, tales may reflect the fact that some fathers and stepfathers may use their physical strength and authority to abuse their daughters.

Another way of theorizing about the oedipal period focuses on cognition. In this view, oedipal fantasies in children reflect a stage in the cognitive organization of drive and emotion. The child's achievement of a differentiated gender identity sets the stage for oedipality. Once children think of themselves as boys who differ from girls, or as girls who differ from boys, they also begin to understand the family as a system of gendered identities and social relationships. Father is now clearly a man and mother is a woman. Thus, the child understands his or her relationship to the parent as a gendered relationship also (Fast 1984).

Children's intellectual limitations at this stage may lend oedipal coloring to these first attempts to comprehend gender relations within the family (Fischer and Watson 1981; Watson and Getz 1990). Two-year-old children can only deal with one representation at a time; still egocentric, they are unable to relate one representation to another or to surmise the thoughts of another person. They cannot understand the family as a system of roles, nor can they imagine transformations in the casting of the family drama.

They cannot imagine that they will be men or women when they grow up, because they cannot relate boy to man or girl to woman. In contrast, by ages four and five children do relate one representation to another (e.g., the self replacing mother or father), and they understand that they will grow up to be adults like mother and father. Yet they make these substitutions and transformations only on one dimension at a time (e.g., sex but not age), so they are prone to misrepresenting social role structures. They can imagine cause–effect relations (e.g., if I eliminate my father, I will have mother for myself), but they cannot imagine the full range of effects (e.g., if my father is gone, I will lose him and his affection, and displease mother as well). An exchange between a woman and her five-year-old son illustrates these weaknesses in children's social analysis.

BILLY: Mommy, I'm gonna marry you.
MOTHER: But, Billy, you can't marry me. You're not old enough.
BILLY: Then I'll wait till I grow up, like Daddy.
MOTHER: But when you're grown up, I'll be as old as Grandma.
BILLY: Really?
MOTHER: Yes, you'll be a young man, and I'll be an old woman.
BILLY: Well, I'll just wait till I'm as old as Grandpa. Then I'll marry you.
(Fischer and Watson 1981: 84)

Children at this stage of development, moreover, cannot yet understand that parents can surmise their thoughts. Thus, they are not very skilled at concealing their fantasies. Like Billy, they can say things that would seem to confound the severest critic of psychoanalysis.

"Normal" and "abnormal" oedipality

These considerations suggest that the Oedipus complex is normal. Broadly defined, it is a mixture of affection and desire for parents and related feelings of rivalry and envy. One might say that it is little more than a quality of the relationships with the parents, a triangulation of object relations that reflects a child's growing social skills and intelligence. That is, it merely refers to the child's first attempts to cope with desire and will-to-power in relationships involving three or more persons.

Some conditions may intensify this drama, however. Karen Horney (1937: 161) suggested that children may eroticize their relationships with their parents in fantasy as a way of coping with unfulfilled needs for affection. She also noted that incestuous fantasies may result when parents eroticize relationships with children. Her argument, it will be noted, closely parallels current thinking about the origins of perversion and implies that exaggerated Oedipus complexes may have perverse dynamics.

Devereux (1953) suggested that actual sexual abuse motivates the action of Oedipus in Greek lore. Laius, the King of Thebes and father of Oedipus, raped Chrysippus, the son of the King Pelops. Outraged at the offense, Pelops cursed Laius and thus instigated the chain of events that led to Oedipus killing Laius and marrying Jocasta, his mother. Hera sent the Sphinx to ravage Thebes for this crime, and Oedipus' subsequent exposure may have been a propitiatory offering to Hera in which the sacrifice of Oedipus was to be equivalent to the offense against Chrysippus. If Chrysippus represents Oedipus' double, then patricide and incest in the Oedipus myth are motivated by the initial rape of a son by his father. The Oedipus story itself, in other words, hints that parenting and family patterns may intensify oedipal formations.

Clinical studies suggest that parents who abuse children are expressing issues left over from their own childhoods. They may, for example, have unresolved oedipal fixations and related resentments about feeling rejected or unloved in childhood. The sexually abusive father (more often, a stepfather) is often immature and fixated on his mother. His wife may have been rejected by her mother and her husband. Emotionally withdrawn, she relinquishes the wifely role to her daughter, who also may feel rejected. The wife may represent the negative mother for the husband, whereas the daughter represents the young woman he courted in his youth and the ideal mother (Willner 1983: 145–146).

Family structure may influence eroticization of parent–child relationships. Freud ([1908a]1959) observed what he thought was a common pattern in turn-of-the-century Vienna: while a father devotes himself to work, his wife turns to her children for intimacy, perhaps eroticizing the relationship. According to this scenario, it may be the mother–son relationship in the traditional patriarchal family in particular that gets eroticized, but patriarchal values, by enhancing the power of fathers and stepfathers, may permit eroticization of the father–daughter relationship also. Stepfathers, who may have less affection and regard for daughters than biological fathers, may be especially prone to take advantage of their power within the family. The paternal seduction of daughters is more common than seductive maternal behavior with sons, although the latter is more common than most people realize (Hunter 1990). The US data show that stepfathers are more often sexually abusive than biological fathers and that sexual abuse of children is more common in lower socioeconomic groups in which traditional values of paternal authority and male toughness tend to be more prevalent.

Some researchers have found reason to think that such family dynamics may occur in other societies also. William N. Stephens (1962) contended that customary postpartum sexual avoidance may intensify the male Oedipus complex. Long periods of postpartum sexual avoidance are associated with polygyny, separate mother–child sleeping arrangements, and long nursing periods, all of which may dilute the marriage bond and extend the early "oral" relationship to the mother into the period when the child is becoming more aware of genital pleasure. Stephens further suggested that menstrual taboos, totemism, and initiation rites for boys reflect intensified Oedipus complexes resulting from weak marital bonds. Fitz John Porter Poole (1987) described a five-year-old boy among the Bimin-Kuskusmin. In keeping with his culture – mothers and young sons are especially close and fathers are socially distant – the boy had a very intimate relation with his mother. She rubbed his penis until he was two years old to make it grow, and she nursed him until he was three and a half. Even at age five she and the boy slept naked together. He enjoyed her smell and softness, and sometimes he had erections. The boy's father was emotionally detached from his family and often physically absent. The boy understood that his father was an intrepid "killer and cannibal." He feared his father's anger and expressed the apprehension that his father would castrate him. He also thought that his father was stealing and destroying his treasured objects and playthings. The mother weaned the boy at the father's insistence. The boy resented the weaning, and he worried about his forthcoming initiation during which he would be subjected to penile mutilation and to further separation from his mother. He said, "My mother won't ever cut my penis."

Cultural variations

Psychoanalysts have observed that the Oedipus complex takes various forms. According to Fenichel (1945: 91–98), family organization, parental behavior and personality, sibling relationships, and deaths and losses in the family may all affect oedipal fantasies. Similarly, anthropologists have suggested that the Oedipus complex varies from one culture to another.

Bronislaw Malinowski (1927) discerned a matrilineal form of the complex in the Trobriand Islands. The Trobrianders are avunculocal and matrilineal. Thus, the maternal uncle, not the father, is the actual authority figure, and at age eight or nine a boy may leave his nuclear family and natal hamlet to take up residence with his maternal uncle. Meanwhile, cultural taboos focus on the sister, not the mother. Malinowski found indications of incestuous brother–sister attachment in myths and dreams. He assumed that this familial form implies an absence or modification of the European version of the Oedipus complex.

Following Malinowski's example, anthropologists have linked other variants of oedipality to local family patterns and social organization. In Morocco, the elder brother assumes the hostility felt toward the father (Crapanzano 1980: 59). Among the matrilineal Navaho, incestuous fantasies center on the brother–sister relationship and the maternal grand-father is the authority figure (Proskauer 1980). In southern Italy, the mother is the dominant figure in the family, which may explain the splitting of the maternal image into good, nurturing objects and bad, sexual objects. Food is emphasized in family interaction and the mother's idealized, asexual persona is represented by the Madonna. Men associate their wives and mothers with the asexual Madonna, sexual women with the profane world outside the home. Along with the de-emphasis on passion in mar-riage, there is an erotic undertone to father–daughter relationships (Parsons 1964). In South Asia, mythic expressions of father–son conflict take different forms. In Hindu mythic traditions, fathers may kill sons, whereas in Buddhist myths sons are more apt to express hostility toward fathers. Obeyesekere (1990) surmised that this difference may reflect the greater subordination of the son to the family in Hindu culture than in Buddhist. In Japan, an intense dyadic relationship between mother and son, involving undertones of anger toward the mother and a special form of guilt, may have more cultural implications than the classical form of the Oedipus complex (Spain 1992).

Some of these apparent variations may overlie the classical Oedipus complex, however. Spiro (1982) argued that the brother–sister and nephew–maternal uncle relationships in Trobriand culture reflect oedipal fantasies involving the mother and father, and he adduced various ethno-graphic facts and considerations in support of this reinterpretation. Despite the descent system, the biological father is a social father until the boy leaves to live with his uncle. Traditional Trobriand culture, moreover, approves of a long nursing period, postpartum sexual abstinence in mar-riage, and exclusive mother–child sleeping arrangements, customs that intensify – and may eroticize – the mother–child relationship. Moreover, there are indications of hostility toward the father and incestuous attach-ment to the mother in myth and folklore: the sons of chiefs have adulter-ous affairs with their co-mothers, and there are allusions to patricide in myth and *kula* legend. When a man dies, Trobrianders suspect his wife and children of sorcery.

James M. Taggart (1992) reaches a conclusion similar to Spiro's in a comparative study of myths in a Sierra Nahuat community in Mexico and Cáceres, Spain. Noting that oedipal themes in folklore and concerns with preventing brother–sister incest are more pronounced in the Nahuat com-munity, Taggart suggests that a more intense preoedipal relationship with the mother in the Sierra Nahuat community may contribute to these differ-ences by promoting a stronger Oedipus complex. But he also notes that the myths may reflect the fact that the greater authority of males in the Nahuat community puts women at greater risk of sexual abuse.

Superego and the passing of the Oedipus complex

The dissolution of the Oedipus complex and the formation of the superego or conscience are closely linked in classical oedipal theory. Freud thought that the Oedipus complex contained the seeds of its own resolution. Fear of punishment and rejection may cause the child to suppress oedipal fantasy. Charles Brenner (1982) also traced superego formation to oedipal conflict. In his view the superego reflects compromise formations dating from the oedipal period. Children, he argues, may develop different strategies for avoiding punishment and loss of love during the oedipal period. Some children may derive masochistic pleasure from their submission to parents, but they all have superegos in the sense of having arrived at some sort of strategy.

Yet, as Freud himself realized, superego development is not confined to the oedipal period. It begins during the preoedipal period and continues long after the oedipal phase. In keeping with this protracted development, the superego is heterogeneous.

Classical oedipal theory may also exaggerate the role of fear in superego formation. Children are more likely to identify with parents who are warm and respectful than with those who are threatening and punitive (Fisher and Greenberg 1985: 207–212). In other words, secure attachment is more effective in promoting moral development than fear of punishment. The ego-ideal may even begin in the self-object illusion, that is, in an underlying sense of secure attachment to a nurturing object, whereas superego defects may begin with emotional trauma or deprivation during the preoedipal period. Brenner's point about compromise formation in superego formation is interesting. All older children have superegos in the sense that they can exercise social intelligence in their own self-interest. But by implying that superego functioning is always egocentric, Brenner ignores emotional and cognitive differences.

Superego development is continuous and occurs in various ways. Identification with the parents during the oedipal period is probably only a continuation of processes of identification and imitation that begin at an earlier age. Intentional instruction is also part of the process. Considerable parental effort in child-rearing is directed toward inculcating specific rules and ethical principles. Recent studies in western culture and others have shown that parents and teachers subject children almost continuously to moralizing discourses and narratives (Dunn 1988; Miller and Moore 1989; Schieffelin 1990; Shweder 1991). Children also develop important components of superego function while interacting with each other. Moral reasoning develops in play as children learn to take the perspective of the other. The role of empathy in moral behavior, however, suggests that the quality

of the child's attachment to the caregivers ultimately may be more significant than any of these factors. Particularly suggestive in this regard is the
well-documented connection between abuse and psychopathic personality,
the prime example of defective superego and inability to love.

The passing of the oedipal phase is a separate problem. Psychoanalysts
have noted that oedipal fantasies may evoke fears of punishment (castration) or anxieties about loss of love. Children's mere appreciation of their
physical immaturity and their uncertainty about the whole mysterious business of bodies and babies may be sufficiently aversive to discourage conscious oedipal desires (Chasseguet-Smirgel 1984: 52). Robin Fox (1983)
suggested that frequent physical interaction between siblings is sexually
arousing but also sexually frustrating, perhaps in part because children do
not know how to have intercourse and are apt not to succeed even if they
try. Repeated frustration, according to Fox, leads to aversion. The same fate
may befall the oedipal wishes of boys and girls toward their parents, for
such wishes too are bound to prove frustrating.

Continuing cognitive development may further undermine an oedipal
project. Oedipality begins to wane when children can appreciate its
impracticality and when, aware of their parents' ability to guess their
thoughts, they begin to conceal their fantasies from their parents and themselves (Fischer and Watson 1981). At some point the child learns about the
incest taboo. There is, moreover, the simple fact that in the end the world
outside the family provides a rewarding field for will and desire.
Competition among peers offers more chance of success than competition
with parents, and love objects outside the family are apt to seem more exotic
and attractive than siblings or parents. With close relatives there is always
ambivalence, but with others there is, initially at least, the possibility of
infatuation, the fantasy of the perfect object.[13]

Variations in family organization, socialization practices, and childhood
play may affect the process of separating from the mother and the kinds of
substitutive formations that replace the Oedipus complex. Stanley N. Kurtz
(1991) finds evidence for his relativistic version of childhood determinism
of personality in Trobriand and Hindu socialization practices. He argues
that any oedipal desires within the Trobriand nuclear family are quickly
and thoroughly diffused through erotic activity in children's play groups. In
some Trobriand folktales and in beliefs about the spirit world, women
incorporate men into group sex life in an aggressive manner which, according to Kurtz, mirrors the situation in the children's play group and reflects
a process of "polysexualization" in which the child is weaned from incestuous fixation on the mother.

In a study of Hindu culture, he contends that the Hindu mother encourages emotional separation by interspersing emotional rejection with phys-

ical nurturing (Kurtz 1992). The emotional availability of "in-law mothers" and the solidarity of the extended family, meanwhile, encourage a distinctly Hindu resolution of the boy's ties to his mother: he learns to renounce selfish desires and to focus on the in-law mothers as substitutes for the mother. Because development depends on renunciation rather than repression, the unconscious meanings of collective representations are more explicit. In Hindu myth, the hero is castrated (a symbol of renunciation) but then the phallus is restored as he puts self-interest aside and identifies with the group (the mothers) on a spiritual and moral plane.

Spiro (1992) questions Kurtz's treatment of the Trobriand material. He doubts that girls play an aggressive role in initiating young boys into the play group, and finds other problems in Kurtz's argument as well. Kurtz's treatment of the Hindu material raises similar concerns. Kurtz may underestimate the emotional nurturing that mothers give their children in more private moments, and he may exaggerate the attention children get from their in-law mothers. But a more serious problem may be Kurtz's assumption that children must be weaned from incestuous attachments through seduction, an assumption that ignores the child's internal emotions and cognitive resources in resolving oedipality and seems to misconstrue the origins of emotional and mental disorder. Kurtz ignores the evidence that abuse and emotional deprivation in the preoedipal period may be a more significant source of oedipal fixations and emotional disorder than the absence of social mechanisms for resolving oedipality. In emotionally healthy, thriving children, oedipality may be little more than a constructive process of learning about internal feelings and family role structure, and it may be largely self-extinguishing in any case. Theory and evidence alike suggest that psychosexual fixations in neurosis and perversion are more likely to result from a combination of sexual stimulation and emotional deprivation than from an absence of sexual play partners or other substitutive objects. Substitutive objects exist, but everything suggests that children and adults find or invent them on their own (see Ingham, in press).

The speaking child

Another way of thinking about the early development of the child considers the acquisition of language and what it means for the structuring of thought and emotion.

The linguistic unconscious, according to Lacan, emerges as the child disengages from a prelinguistic relation with the mother. The child begins in unruptured wholeness with the mother. Then, at the "mirror stage" (six to eighteen months), the child sees the self in the mirror; the specular image of the self becomes an ideal self that opposes, or contrasts with, the child's fragmented bodily experience. The mother duplicates the self-alienation set in motion by the mirror. Her smile, like the specular image, establishes an ideal self in the child separate from the real self. The rupture or division within the self, and between the mother and the self, is completed by the Other – the "Name-of-the Father," "Logos," or "Phallus" – which intervenes between mother and child but offers another possibility of wholeness, that of completing the self through cultural symbols. This wholeness, however, is illusory because cultural desiderata are forever changing and often unreachable and because culture is more durable and inclusive than the self.

Lacan situated the paternal metaphor in the Other where it governs the substitution of symbol for the thing itself and infuses language, family, and social organization with discipline and order. The boy yields to the moral and symbolic order of culture by accepting "castration," that is, by letting go of *being* the phallus for the mother – the object of her desire – and by identifying with the father, the person who *possesses* or *represents* the phallus. The boy passes from the domain of images to the domain of symbols. The transition, once accomplished, opens the way to self-awareness, to organizing the self, to the future, to meaningful social relations. "The-Name-of-the-Father" refers not to the actual father but to culture. It intervenes in the daughter's primordial, prelinguistic relation with the mother no less than it does in the son's.[14]

Lacan's appeal to some scholars lies in the emphasis he gives to language and culture in structuring unconscious mental process, a revision of psychoanalytic thinking that seems to open the way for cultural studies and for more attention to culture in personality theory. These virtues, however, entail a peculiar view of child development and an inability to say very much about individuality, motivation, and agency, not to mention a questionable use of masculine metaphors for culture. Lacan's idea that early development involves self-alienation is doubtful, and the destructive role Lacan assigns to the mother is inconsistent with the evidence that emotionally supportive parents nurture a coherent, authentic sense of self (Dervin 1987). Nor is paternal presence essential for separation–individuation or learning language and culture. Children have an inherent drive to individuate, and children raised in absent-father families learn to speak.

Still, the use of the father as metaphor for language and moral order has some cogency. Many studies have shown that father absence correlates with teenage pregnancies, drug abuse, delinquency, and lower scores on tests of moral development. Boys who grow up in absent-father households are more rebellious and aggressive, and they show more hypermasculine behavior and more hostility toward women and more depreciation of femininity. Girls who grow up without fathers are more hostile toward men, more sexually active from an early age, and less likely to bond with a single male (Draper and Harpending 1982).

These correlations, to be sure, may reflect the effects of poverty in single-parent families and the understandable difficulties of some single mothers in exerting strong supervision over their children, but they also imply that fathers can and often do play a special role in encouraging moral development in their children. Where there is no third person, the developing child may have trouble separating from the mother and entering the social world outside the family. Thirdness appears in a relationship between mother and father which is both linguistic and independent of the mother–child relationship; alternatively, it may become apparent to the child when he or she realizes that the mother has a life apart from the child, a life that includes others, although not necessarily the father.

Politics begins with the presence of a triangle: with two plus a third. In the realm of the triangle, there is not only gratification and frustration but also competition, duplicity, and unfairness. There is also language. Children use narratives to explain departures from social expectations and to assert their positions (Dunn 1988; Miller and Moore 1989). In this sense, at least, Lacan is right in suggesting that language and culture lie beyond and stand opposed to the earliest relationship between child and caregiver.

Continuity

The question of continuity between childhood experience and adult personality is a major issue in psychological anthropology. Psychoanalytic anthropologists assume that childhood is consequential for adult personality. In particular, they are likely to emphasize the ramifications of emotional experiences in childhood. Culturalists and social constructionists, on the other hand, are more apt to emphasize socialization, especially the intentional inculcation of moral norms. In keeping with their emphasis on the instability and fragmentary nature of the self, some postmodernists even question whether personality as a whole has important roots in childhood or, for that matter, whether the very notion of personality is still useful.

Evidence for childhood origins of personality takes various forms. Qualitative evidence includes clinical observations of neglect and abuse in the backgrounds of persons with severe personality disorders (Shengold 1989). For psychoanalysts, at least, it also includes transference, the way in which analysands often seem to reenact earlier parent–child relations in relationships with their analysts. Such impressionistic evidence can be persuasive in particular cases, at least for scholars who are already predisposed to assume that childhood has important consequences for personality formation, and it can certainly disclose the complexities and idiosyncrasies of individual psychological development. Perhaps more persuasive for the continuity question are longitudinal studies involving sizeable samples.

Some research suggests continuities between emotional adjustment in childhood and adjustment in early adulthood (Thomas and Chess 1984). An examination of data from the Berkeley longitudinal study has shown that dependency, shyness, and irritability in childhood persist in styles of social interaction and coping throughout the lifespan (Caspi et al. 1990). Aggressiveness and antisocial behavior show substantial continuity from childhood to adulthood (Farrington et al. 1990). Ability to delay gratification at age four in an experimental setting correlates significantly with social and academic competence and the ability to tolerate frustration and plan ahead in adolescence (Mischel et al. 1989).

Whether similar continuities between childhood personality and adult personality hold in nonwestern cultures remains to be seen. In anthropology, attempts to show continuity often have taken the form of cross-cultural correlations between child-rearing practices and putative cultural measures of psychological variables. Some significant and theoretically interesting correlations have been found, but many have been moderate at best, and often they permit alternative, nonpsychological interpretations. Comparative and cross-cultural studies have even been used to argue against continuity.

Cynthia A. Cone (1979) concluded that child-rearing practices do not account for the often-noted character differences between settled farmers and more mobile pastoralists. Pastoralists tend to be more independent, aggressive, and extraverted than farmers, but these traits may reflect the social conditions and religious beliefs of pastoralists more than the effects of intentional socialization practices. Paul Riesman (1983) compared the Fulbe and Riimaaybe of the Upper Volta. The Fulbe are restrained and dignified, whereas the Riimaaybe, their former slaves, are more aggressive and extraverted and have less sense of pride. Riesman found similar child-rearing practices in the two groups and concluded that child-rearing may have little influence on adult personality and that personality is a sense of self that derives from social situations. The Fulbe have strong lineage organization and social controls, ancestors to worry about, and a proud tradition, whereas the Riimaaybe have no corporate groups or ancestors and little cultural pride. Riesman, however, did not consider the possibility that the social characters of the Fulbe and Riimaaybe parents may themselves be important influences on their children.

Overall, the research offers some support for the childhood origins of personality. This, however, does not mean that all childhood experiences are formative to the same degree, or that their consequences for adult personality are highly predictable. Some child-rearing practices (e.g., age of weaning or toilet training) may have little or no effect on personality. The acceptance or rejection of children, the availability of role models during gender identity formation, and socialization for moral and ethical behavior, meanwhile, may well be consequential for particular components of personality. In these areas, however, the personalities and idiosyncrasies of parents, traumatic losses, and the social condition of individual families may prove more decisive than customary child-rearing practices. Rohner's research implies that some peoples may be more accepting of children than others as a matter of practice, but it seems that we should be especially cautious here. Before concluding that the mothers of a culture lack love or empathy for their children, we ought to be sure that we are not superimposing our own expectations about maternal behavior; it may be that parents show pride and acceptance in different ways in different cultures. What may matter, then, is not appearances but the children's subjective experience of being accepted or rejected. Altogether, the data suggest that emotional disposition, object relations, and core features of self-representation and moral reasoning may have stronger roots in childhood experience, whereas social values and attitudes, social identities, and styles of presenting the self are more apt to reflect social expectations.

Constitutional factors and the child's active, self-forming imagination further complicate the picture. Neuroticism, extraversion, and sensation-seeking reflect inherited disposition to some degree (Dunn and Plomin 1990; Zuckerman 1991). Such temperamental dispositions structure normal personality and, in combination with other factors, they may steer a person toward one or another form of mental disorder (Claridge 1985). Recent research suggests that a large portion of the personality traits shared by siblings reflects common genetic inheritance, not shared environment. Meanwhile, the differences between siblings may reflect the effects of nonshared environment within and outside the family (Dunn and Plomin 1990). Children, moreover, interpret the events in their lives. How they interpret their experiences and work them over in imagination and play affect the ways in which experiences influence personality. Subjectively, then, the same family may be a different environment for different children.

Conclusions

In the discussion of human nature I present reasons for thinking that attachment, desire, empowerment, and safety are key motives in human behavior. I also note that social intelligence and a capacity for moral reasoning are human characteristics. In this chapter I notice how the preoedipal and oedipal periods are organized around just these motives and mental characteristics.

Current work in child development and psychoanalysis suggests that the most consequential developmental experiences affect attachment, core gender identity, preoedipal and oedipal object relations, and moral development. Contrary to what psychoanalysts – and a fair number of anthropologists – once thought, bodily experiences (e.g., nursing, toilet-training, sexual play) have relatively little impact on personality except insofar as they are part of social experiences involving attachment, separation, loss, rejection, or learning to deal with assertiveness and sexual impulses in dyadic and triangular relationships. Overall, the cultural content of what children learn about moral and other matters through direct socialization may be less significant than the quality of the social relationships in which the learning takes place. Parental acceptance and rejection, paternal presence, and the way in which parents model moral and ethical behavior may have significant long-run consequences for personality.

The effects of even the most influential childhood experiences, moreover, are hard to predict. Inherited differences in mental ability and emotional disposition and the child's creative imagination affect how a child interprets objective events. In important respects the child authors the significance and consequences of his or her emotional/social experience. The strongest continuities between "objective" childhood experiences and later personality traits appear in the literature on developmental psychopathology. Even here the evidence simply suggests that certain experiences increase the risk for certain types of personality disorder or emotional problems, not that they shape the final form of personality with great precision.

The idea that cultural differences can be explained on the model of psychological differences and, specifically, psychological differences resulting from specific childhood experiences, seems to be a logical consequence of the psychoanalytic idea that personality begins in childhood. This idea, however, is less psychoanalytic than it may at first seem. Freud realized that the effects of childhood experience for later personality are multiform and unpredictable. He pointed out that child development is shaped by inherited mental and emotional characteristics and by the child's creative imagination as well as by objective events. Furthermore, he noticed that memories of early experiences undergo revision with subsequent experience and changes in mental habits and outlook. Mental traces of the past, he concluded, are subject to "retranscription" or restructuring (*Nachträglichkeit*) under the influence of subsequent fantasy, thought, or experience. It is not simply that the past shapes the present; the present also shapes the past (Modell 1990).

These considerations suggest that it is time to reformulate the way in which we think about the anthropological implications of childhood. Childhood can help us to understand individual agency and mental disorder. And it may help to account for specific institutions and behavioral proclivities in a society. Child-rearing practices are not likely to take us very far in the effort to explain the overall differences between societies, however. Even in traditional, relatively homogeneous societies in which child-rearing is highly standardized, children do not have exactly the same developmental experiences.

Still, there is good reason to assume that cultural beliefs and practices are emotionally meaningful for individuals. There is also reason to think that they are meaningful because they tap unconscious memories of childhood experience and fantasy. It need not follow that people must have exactly the same unconscious memories in order to share the same cultural beliefs and practices, however. In some respects their memories may be idiosyncratic and in others they may reflect universal or nearly universal issues in human child development. In later chapters I suggest that pragmatic uses of cultural beliefs and practices and related processes of retranscription tap both these idiosyncratic and generic childhood experiences.

4   Personality

The chapters on human nature and childhood present reasons for thinking that personality comprises basic drives and emotions, preoedipal and oedipal motivational structures, an embodied subject and dialogical self, and moral reasoning, among other things. Such a view of the personality lays a basis for interpreting the motives and intentions of subjects and the ways in which sociocultural milieus affect subjectivity. Although it has fallen from favor in psychological anthropology, I revive the notion of *personality* because it embraces the whole range of emotional and mental elements that make up the intrapsychic organization of a person.

In this chapter I add more detail to this picture of personality. I begin with emotional drive and then go on to discuss various mental aspects of personality. My treatment of personality in this chapter implies that the basic components of personality are rooted in human nature and the human condition but I also show how these components are instantiated in different ways depending on personal histories and sociocultural contexts.

Emotional disposition, desire, and agency

William James ([1892]1985: 271–272) noted that human personality includes sexual passions, parental impulses, love, ambition, acquisitiveness, fear, and "the selfish zest of the battle of life." Freud ([1931]1961) theorized that personalities are energized in differing degrees by the libido, aggressiveness, and anxiety. The "erotic" personality focuses on loving and being loved; the narcissistic person is aggressive and active; and the "obsessional" individual is ruled by "anxiety of conscience."

Empirical studies have suggested similar schemes. H.J. Eysenck (1967, 1982) found that introversion versus extraversion and neuroticism versus non-neuroticism account for much of the variance in personality. The neurotic person is emotional and restless; the normal person is calm and carefree. The introverted person is cerebral and asocial, while the extraverted person is sociable, impulsive, and action-oriented. Since extraversion and neuroticism are independent, they in effect delineate four psychological orientations: the neurotic introvert, the neurotic extravert, the normal introvert, and the normal extravert. Jeffrey Gray (1987; Gray et al. 1983) accepts this distribution of traits but argues that anxiety and impulsiveness are the underlying axes of personality. Neurotic introversion expresses anxiety while neurotic extraversion expresses impulsiveness. A number of other studies find five components or variables in personality: surgency/extraversion versus passivity; agreeableness versus hostility; conscientiousness versus carelessness; neuroticism; and openness or intellect (Goldberg 1993). An alternative theory distinguishes sensation-seeking, sociability, aggression/hostility, neuroticism/anxiety, and activity as the basic components of emotional disposition (Zuckerman 1991, 1992).

These models are consistent with the discussion of emotion and drive in Chapter 2. Activity or conscientiousness corresponds to what I am calling "social intelligence" and "moral reasoning." The other four factors correspond to flight, fight, attachment, and the libido in the scheme I presented in Chapter 2 or, to put it another way, they fit the distinction between self-preservative drives or emotions, on the one hand, and reproductive drives, on the other.

Anxiety is part of the self-preservation system. I suspect that impulsiveness is another expression of this system. Gray et al. (1983) offer several hypotheses about impulsiveness. Perhaps the most plausible of these hypotheses views it as a by-product of aggressiveness. The connection between aggressiveness and impulsiveness is well documented (Goldstein 1986: 48–51). Rage and impulsiveness are common in narcissistic personalities, and narcissistic insult is a prime source of human aggression (Kohut 1972; Rochlin 1973).

Sociability and sensation-seeking are expressions of the reproduction system. Sociability represents a further development of the attachment–affiliation system in children (Weiss 1982).[1] Extraversion and, to some extent, impulsivity, may be measures of sexual and power-seeking libido. Extraversion correlates with sensation-seeking and risk-taking, inclinations that seem to be associated with the libido. Preferences for risky sports, travel, exploration, and drug and alcohol use correlate with sexual activity and assertiveness in social relations. They also correlate positively with gonadal hormone levels and negatively with dopamine beta hydroxylase and monoamine oxidase levels in the blood, possible measures of dopaminergic activity in the brain. Libidinal hormones may increase brain dopaminergic activity by suppressing monoamine oxidase, which metabolizes dopamine (Zuckerman 1991).[2]

There is an energetic quality in human motivation and, as was noted in Chapter 2, this quality reflects neural activity in the reptilian brain. At the same time, the drive and arousal mechanisms in the core structures of the brain are stimulated and modulated by processes in the emotional brain and cerebral cortex.

In psychological terms, drives are stimulated and organized by emotion-charged representations of self and others. The expression of drives and emotions is also mediated by cultural understandings, rules, schemas, models, and moral reasoning. Some anthropologists argue that the very presence of goal-oriented cultural schemas in the mind may help to account for motivational disposition.[3] In fact, drives/emotions probably involve both self-object and cultural schemas. Robert A. Paul (1990: 440) says that drives are "affective colorations of accretions of intense positive and negative early object-related experiences organized into images and fantasies; and one may speak of their derivatives by and large in the ordinary human language of wants, desires, fears, strategies, intentions, and reasons." Cultural symbols, schemas, and narratives assume personal meaning for individuals, according to Paul, as they arouse and direct these underlying emotion-colored self-representations and object-relations schemas. Thus, unconscious traces of preoedipal and oedipal schemas may continue to influence desire and will in adulthood.

Memories of early object relations may influence social interaction and styles of coping with loss, frustration, and disappointment; when representations of the object are fragmented, a person may react to disappointment with splitting and projection. Triangular or oedipal structures may influence gender relations and competitive social relations in various ways. Clinical observations point particularly to the ways in which unconscious traces of childhood oedipal experience may influence romantic relationships (Kernberg 1988; Person 1988) but they also suggest that oedipality may inform agency, fantasy, and conflict (Greenberg 1991).

Agency concerns the possibility of taking action and exerting power in social situations. Agency does not depend solely on social circumstances and objective possibilities, however. It is also a disposition, an expression of desire or will, even a style of being in the world. David Bakan (1966) saw agency as a principal modality in human experience and activity. It manifests itself in self-protection, self-expansion, self-assertion, and in asceticism, repression, and aloofness. In psychoanalytic terms, it reflects the libido in its power-seeking aspect; agency, Bakan observed, correlates with hormonal androgens.

Agency is a major feature of social life, but it is not the only social motive. Bakan distinguished agency from communion, which he said is evident in union, contact, and oneness. In effect, Bakan suggested that power-seeking libido and self-preservative impulses inform one major modality of social existence, whereas the attachment–affiliation system informs the other. Whether the underlying structure of social motivation is quite this dualistic is debatable, but Bakan's scheme is a useful corrective to the emphasis on the will-to-power in current social and cultural studies.

Perhaps the notion of agency should be expanded to include motives other than power. According to Modell (1993: 167–177), the subjective sense of agency depends on being able to recategorize value-laden memories with ongoing experience in a way that enhances a sense of competence. While this process may involve memories built around the need for power it may also involve other drives or affects.

Representations of the self also inform and organize desire and agency. What persons consider desirable or empowering reflects the stories they tell about themselves as well as, and perhaps more particularly, their imaginary future selves and ego-ideals.

The self: embodied and social

Many writers agree that a central feature of personality is self-organization or, simply, the self. Various students of personality have noticed that the complete self has both active and passive qualities, although they may give different names to them. James ([1892]1985) distinguished the "*I*" and the "*Me*" as two aspects of the complete self. The *I* is the volitional self, the active, speaking subject. The *Me* is the object of reflection, the representation of the self. The *I* "knows" and acts, the *Me* is the passive "known." Similarly, Freud used "ego" in the sense of both *I* and *Me*. Eventually, he broadened the meaning of the term "ego" to include perception and the mechanisms of defense (A. Freud 1946; Hartmann 1964).

The *I* is the part of the self that exerts agency. According to George Herbert Mead (1934), the *I* is associated with instincts, creativity, and innovation. Winnicott (1965) similarly suggested that the true self is energized by instincts in contrast to the false self, which is oriented toward the social world.[4]

Ego psychoanalysts and object-relations theorists have used "self" to refer to self-representations (Jacobson 1965; Sandler and Rosenblatt [1962]1987). Roy Schafer (1978) subsequently distinguished between the "person" or agent of action and the "self" as representation and reflexive experience. Helena Harris (1987) observes that representations of the self are themselves social. The way we see ourselves is affected by how we think others see us. Our "identities" are combinations of our private selves and our images of how others see us as social persons: "the world knows a person, but only a person knows the self. And only the person knows his or her identity because identity includes elements of both self and person representational actions" (ibid.: 10). The self and person are parts of a single personality. Accordingly, some writers use "self" and "person"

interchangeably to refer to the complete self. Heinz Kohut and his followers combine the self as agent or actor and the self as self-image or self-con-
ception into a single, cohesive unit (Wolf 1988).

Grace Harris (1989) suggests that "individual" refers to the separate existence and species-nature of the person, including human capacity for language. The "self" refers to the locus of experience and includes both the
"existential" *I* and the *Me*. The "person" is the individual as social actor,
the one who exercises purpose and agency in social relations (ibid.: 602).
The notion of person emphasizes the public or social nature of the individual, the way in which the individual exercises agency, gains a reputation,
and assumes moral responsibility in social relations.

Personhood depends on the possibility of realizing agency. Personhood
can be "bestowed or removed, confirmed or disconfirmed, declared or
denied" (Harris 1989: 604). It is determined by social position, material
conditions of life, and position in the life cycle. Thus, personhood is
achieved more by some individuals than by others. Personhood among the
Tallensi, for instance, is a social status bound up with social offices, power,
and achievement (Fortes 1987; La Fontaine 1985). The notions of person
and agency focus attention on the public self and the will-to-power in
human motivation.

Various writers, then, recognize an active part of the complete self or
personality. The *I*, the person, the true self, the speaking subject, the agent
variously evoke this active element. Writers also recognize an objective self.
The *Me*, the self, the false self, self-representation, self-image refer to a subjective representation of the self, often with the implication that it is socially
constituted and shapes the way in which the person presents himself or
herself to social others.

The "subject" is not synonymous with the philosophical notion of a fully
self-conscious, self-determining individual. The subject is not altogether
conscious nor altogether self-determining. It has been subjected to social
influence, and it reflects or encompasses unconscious wishes, desires, fantasies, and semiotic processes.

The self or *Me* can be seen as comprising various components or part-
selves. According to James, the *Me* has "material," "social," and "spiritual"
components. The complete personality for Freud is a tripartite structure
similar to the material, social, and spiritual selves in James's scheme: it
includes the id, or source of psychic energy; the ego, in its expanded sense;
and the superego, or moral agency of personality.[5]

In James's formulation, "The *body* is the innermost part of the material
me in each of us; and certain parts of the body seem more intimately ours
than the rest. The clothes come next" ([1892]1985: 44). Similarly, Freud suggested that self-reflection begins with awareness of the body, especially its

surface, the organ of sensation; "[t]he ego is first and foremost a bodily ego" ([1923a]1961: 26).

The sense of having a male or female body (or, in rare instances, the body of a culturally recognized third gender) may be a core feature of self-representation for all persons in every culture. Other qualities of the body also may inform self-image and self-representation. Size, strength, beauty, agility, dexterity, quickness, and physical health may enhance positive self-image whereas deformities, impairments, and physical illness may have the opposite effect (Schilder 1950). Various social activities – e.g., work, recreation, ritual – entail familiar and repetitive patterns of movement and postural balance which inform a person's social identity. In this way the body becomes a ground not only for the self but also for culture. What Bourdieu (1977) calls habitus – largely unconscious, taken-for-granted, embodied patterns of perception, thought, and action – are part of the bodily self.

Cultural meanings may be experienced and expressed in the body and bodily movement. Demonic possession, spiritual inspiration, and speaking in tongues, for example, embody religious experience for charismatic Christians (Csordas 1990). The body also blends with the social self or persona. Social status is inscribed in the image and appearance of the body. Dress, cosmetics, hair-style, jewelry, perfume, tattooing, scarification, depilation, or foot-binding signal social identities.

The social subject expresses itself through the body but its principal mode of expression is speech. Peirce described the tongue as "the very organ of personality" (quoted in Singer 1984: 90). According to Cooley (ibid.: 88), the essence of the *I* is the "assertion of self-will in a social medium of which the speaker is conscious." Speech is also the means of self-definition. The person authors the self through "I-statements" (Auerbach 1985) or by telling stories about the self (Bruner 1990; Sarbin 1986; Schafer 1978). The many facets of the self unfold in a series of statements. Persons identify themselves with the pronoun "I" in speech acts that refer forward and backward to other pronouncements (Crapanzano 1982).

Self-narratives may be explicit, allegorical, or implied. They may occur in soliloquies and in monologues. In every culture self-assertion occurs in such standard genres as boasting, repartee, joking, speechifying, and singing. Among the Guayaki of Amazonia, a man glorifies his virility and hunting skills in song. "I am a great hunter, I am in the habit of killing with my arrows, I am a powerful nature, a nature incensed and aggressive!" The singer then emphasizes his points by exclaiming "me, me, me" (Clastres 1987: 113).

According to Mead (1934), the formation of the *Me* is a social process. The person learns to speak about the self as social others speak about it. The self or *Me* is not an objective third person but rather the second person in a conversation with the first person or *I* (see Habermas 1992). These internal conversations of self-definition may reflect dialectical and dialogical processes with social others. The person learns to define the self by objectifying others and by defending the self against unwanted characterization and objectification (Crapanzano 1992). Similar processes occur in discourse between rival groups and factions. And since individual identities reflect group memberships, these group-level discourses also affect self-representation (Dominguez 1989). Even soliloquies are dialogical inasmuch as they involve speaking to and listening to the self. Dorinne K. Kondo (1990) describes how the Japanese fashion the multiple facets of their selves in relations involving power. Vincent Crapanzano (1992) notices that individuals express their desires in and through their typifications of self and social others and within the constraints offered by language and the resistance of their interlocutors. Characterizations of others may seem to describe essential traits or attributes of the Other but, in fact, they are often pragmatic; they typify the self or Other in order to construe something about the quality of the relationship (e.g., difference in power or right to some possession or object).

Self-narratives are often stories about spatial practices. Thus, they connect the experiences of the material and social selves. M. Brewster Smith (1985) holds that the self is an "as-if" system of metaphors about the embodied self moving in space. Hermans et al. (1992) suggest that the *I* or subject moves in actual or imaginary space, whereas the *Me* is the self observed moving in space. The *I* moves within the mental theater as though it were travelling through a landscape or the rooms of a house or across a stage, taking up one stance and then another. The *I* can invest one position or its opposite, giving them voice and creating, as in a novel or drama, a dialogue. Following Bakhtin, Hermans et al. (1992: 28) theorize a polyphonic, dialogical self in which the subject assumes various positions in an "imaginal landscape."

The significance of any one dialogue or monologue for constructing or reconstructing the self depends on the identity of the interlocutors. Social actors notice how others respond and adjust their self-representations accordingly. The others who matter most, as James ([1892]1985: 46) noted, are loved ones and those who decide the person's fame and reputation.

The complete self includes one or more identities based on social statuses and roles. Age, names, family membership, kinship affiliations, home and neighborhood, ethnicity, and occupation all define the social self. Cultural understandings about the body, emotions, psyche, soul, and purpose and meaning of life may also inform self-representations (see Fogelson 1982).

Public selves may differ from private selves. Wearing social masks – personas – is an inherent feature of social life. Sometimes these public selves or personas take on lives of their own. They may become false fronts that differ from the true or inner self. To put it another way, persons may become so caught up in the wearing of social masks that they become estranged from their inner selves. Winnicott (1965) captured aspects of this internal differentiation with his notions of true self and false self. The true self, as noted earlier, acts on impulse and feeling; it is rooted in bodily awareness, feels alive, and experiences itself and its vital relationships as genuine. The false self may develop to normal or abnormal degrees. Ordinarily, it is polite, mannerly, and accommodating to social expectation. In a more defensive posture, it becomes an apparatus for protecting the true self from harm or annihilation. This social orientation of the false self, Winnicott observed, is not necessarily synonymous with social effectiveness. Creative engagement in cultural life depends on some measure of integration between true and false selves, and on an ability to live in the transitional space between dream and reality. People in whom there is a marked split between the two selves are often restless and unable to commit fully to cultural activity.

The conscious, intentional *I* – the *I* of enunciation – moves around amid these various selves or subjects within the personality. It successively becomes the subject of the self's various selves and part-selves. It may for the moment experience the world from the point of view of the inner self, a true self, a false self, or one of the various social selves. It may also take the position of the nurturing, protective parent or punitive conscience (Bollas 1987). The *I* may be present in dreams, private fantasy, and social behavior, and aspects of the self may be either very private or altogether social. Often the *I* invests the social self in public spaces, but this is not necessarily the case; persons may rehearse public presentations of themselves in private or entertain private fantasies amid public places.

Impression management and mechanisms of defense

There is a theatrical quality to social life. Persons play social roles, act their parts, and "manage" the impressions they make (Goffman 1959). In relating to others, particularly in public arenas but, also, in courtship, the subject may be something of an actor or actress. Desired impressions are conveyed by displaying or disclosing some features of the self while concealing others. Such pragmatic tactics presume self-control, an intentional use of the human ability to conceal or embellish facts about the self. They also may depend on an internal impression management, on self-deception, since persons who can fool themselves are apt to be more convincing when deceiving others.

Social impressions are staged through dress, manners, tastes, speech habits, and expertise. People may affirm social status by dropping names or alluding to their occupations, pastimes, and other activities. The notion of "defense mechanism" ordinarily refers to the way in which individuals manage impulses and self-representation. But the functions of defense mechanisms are not merely subjective or intrapsychic. The control of disturbing impulses, thoughts, and feelings figure in discursive practices oriented toward influencing social others. The use of defense mechanisms informs discourse about self and other. Thus it can play a role in persuasive characterizations of self and other (Ewing 1987: 28; Swanson 1988).

The psychoanalytic literature includes descriptions of various defense maneuvers. The descriptions focus on intrapsychic processes, but it is not difficult to see that they may affect a person's relations with social others.

Repression is the basic mechanism of defense. It banishes an impulse, desire, or thought from consciousness. The very fact of repression disappears from consciousness along with the content of what is being repressed.[6]

In *suppression* there is some awareness of excluding an impulse or idea from consciousness.

In *reaction formation*, one attitude, thought, or feeling replaces its opposite, for example, when a person acts affectionately to cover up hostile feelings.

Undoing attempts to reverse a state of affairs, often through magical thought or action.

In *isolation*, emotions and thoughts or parts of a train of thought may get disconnected from one another.

Projection attributes one's impulse, emotion, or thought to another person or object.

Still another defensive maneuver is to identify with the source of danger. *Identification* can be a way of coping with subordination and loss; identification with the aggressor may provide a sense of control while identification with the love object may be a way of coping with loss or separation anxiety (Brenner 1955: 88–107; Fenichel 1945: 141–167, 220–223; A. Freud 1946).

Psychoanalysts have also observed several so-called "primitive" defenses, especially in persons with severe personality disorders. *Introjection* and *incorporation* refer to elementary forms of identification modeled on ingestion. *Splitting* divides love objects into separate good and bad persons. In splitting, an object may be idealized at one moment and seen in completely negative terms at another. In *projective identification* the person attributes an aspect of the self (e.g., anger) to the object and acts to provoke that quality in the other while continuing to experience it as part of the self.

Differing forms of *merging* with the other can have this implication. In *denial*, the person stubbornly denies some feature of the real world.

The spiritual self

James ([1892]1985: 62) recognized a spiritual component of the self. In its "self-seeking" aspect it is concerned with "religious aspirations" and "conscientiousness" and in its "self-estimation" aspect, with senses of moral superiority and inferiority or guilt. He suggested that "the very core and nucleus of our self" is associated with "*active–feeling* states" of the spiritual self (ibid.: 48). James noted that people have actual selves and future selves, and he suggested that the focus of the whole self may progress in time from the bodily and social selves toward a fuller realization of the spiritual self.

Hazel Markus and Paula Nurius (1986) have discussed "possible selves," selves which, in contrast to the now self or working self, represent what a person might become in the future. The possible selves may express individual creativity and purpose but they also draw on cultural values and images of social roles. Possible selves orient the person toward the future and, simultaneously, provide a cognitive framework for evaluating the actual self. Positive and negative possible selves affect motivation. In modern societies many individuals spend considerable time daydreaming about who they would like to be or what they would like to have. Such daydreaming becomes part of the organization of will and desire. Thinking about possible selves may be less developed among victims of racism and discrimination for whom there are fewer objective opportunities for self-transformation. Disadvantaged persons also may focus on negative possible selves that reinforce pessimism and anxiety. It occurs to me that fantasies about possible selves may be less elaborate in traditional societies in which there are fewer roles and occupations and less orientation toward the future.

The spiritual self in James's psychology corresponds to the superego in psychoanalysis, the part of the psychic apparatus that suppresses antisocial impulses and orients behavior toward social goals and moral ideals. Like the spiritual self, the superego is especially concerned with the future. According to Freud ([1914]1957, [1923a]1961, [1940]1964), the superego includes the conscience and the ego-ideal, that is, both a capacity for punishing the self and the values, tastes, and norms of the group, social class, or society.

The conscience represents the punitive parents or at least the parents who say "no," whereas the ego-ideal is based on identification with loved and admired objects, identification with the "good" child as portrayed by parents, and identification with admired qualities of the self. One aspect of Freud's notion of the ego-ideal is the ideal self, the most ideal form of the self (Sandler et al. [1963]1987). The ideal parent and the ideal self are possible selves that are part of a higher-order executive function that organizes the whole ensemble of possible selves in terms of moral and cultural values. They guide and direct striving for social superiority and moral perfection (see Piers and Singer 1953: 14–15).

Real and ideal-self representations influence emotions and moods. Mismatches between real and ideal selves produce shame and guilt, whereas elation results when the person approximates the ideal in reality, fantasy, or delusion. "There is always a feeling of triumph when something in the ego coincides with the ego ideal. And the sense of guilt (as well as the sense of inferiority) can also be understood as an expression of tension between the ego and the ego ideal" (Freud [1921]1955: 131). Guilt results when a limit set by the superego is touched or transgressed, whereas shame is a feeling of inferiority in response to failure (Piers and Singer 1953).[7]

Cultures vary in the emphases they give to shame and guilt (ibid.). There once was speculation that many traditional cultures may be more shame-based than guilt-based. Japan was portrayed as a prime example of a culture that emphasizes shame. In fact, most cultures probably involve mixtures of shame and guilt.

Japanese culture encourages guilt in certain situations (De Vos 1973a). Takie Sugiyama Lebra (1971, 1983) found that guilt in the Japanese is a reaction to unjustifiable injury to another or to being in debt, whereas shame accompanies the thought that one does not deserve a status position. The Japanese, she says, often feel guilt when their failures bring shame on their families or reference groups. Guilt is a common feeling in western societies, but so too is shame (Nathanson 1992). In Tahiti, shame is associated with physical and social inadequacy, some sexual behaviors, and incest. The connection with incest also links it with disorder, dirt, and disgust. Shame and embarrassment are culturally elaborated; there are words for them and standard ways of coping with them. Guilt, meanwhile, is de-emphasized, at least conceptually. Tahitians have no word for guilt as such. Nonetheless, they have a notion of transgression or sin, and they believe that self-control in social behavior depends on having empathy or compassion for others (Levy 1973).

Comparing and contrasting individuals and cultures in terms of shame and guilt poses the question of whether individuals vary with regard to strength and style of superego function. The psychoanalytic literature suggests that the superego may be well or poorly developed, reasonable or harsh, well organized in some areas and weak in others. Cognitive theorists find differences in the quality of moral reasoning. Lawrence Kohlberg discerned three distinct levels or styles of reasoning about moral dilemmas: preconventional, conventional, and postconventional. He further discerned two phases in each level, thereby distinguishing six stages altogether. Preconventional reasoning (obedience and punishment orientation, and instrumental purpose and exchange) is selfish and emotional; conventional reasoning is still emotional but takes the perspective of others (interpersonal accord and conformity, and social accord and system maintenance); postconventional reasoning defines right and wrong in terms of abstract, universal principles that take account of the rights of all individuals (social contract, utility, and individual rights, and universal ethical principles). The stages are said to be sequential. Most individuals attain conventional moral reasoning, but few individuals show signs of postconventional or abstract, universalistic approaches to moral issues (Colby and Kohlberg 1987). Various studies suggest that stages five and six are uncommon in most societies and absent altogether in some (Snarey 1985).

Anthropologists are interested in the influence of sociocultural milieus on superego and moral reasoning and with the effects of moral agency on actual social behavior. These concerns have raised various questions. One relates to cultural bias. Shweder, Mahapatra, and Miller (1990) aptly note that Kohlberg's notion of postconventional reasoning reflects the importance of individual rights and fairness in modern, contract-based societies. Moral principles involving the core assumptions of a contractual society seem "natural." Others may seem conventional or arbitrary, the implication being that individuals can choose to ignore them without violating deep moral principles. Shweder, Mahapatra, and Miller wonder whether forms of postconventional moral reasoning vary from culture to culture. They suggest that Hindu moral reasoning begins with a principle of duty, not rights; and they find less inclination to recognize a sphere of conventional morality. Since most norms and rules are tied up with social responsibility or duty, most of them are considered natural. Shweder and Much (1991) note that Kohlberg's scheme may overlook implicit universalistic reasoning based on local moral and philosophical understandings. The moral reasoning of their Hindu informants seems conventional because it is more obligations- than rights-oriented, yet it is postconventional in following abstract notions of dharma. Steve Derné (1992) suggests that Hindu men are more responsive to social circumstances in making moral decisions, whereas westerners may be more governed by a combination of selfish desires and abstract principles. Barbara V. Reid (1990) concludes from a comparison of moral reasoning in Samoans and Europeans in New Zealand that world views affect moral reasoning. New Zealanders are egocentric whereas Samoans are more sociocentric. Kohlberg's scheme, she avers, reflects European individualism, and she suggests that the inclusion of "abstract principles of care, responsibility, and religious belief" in the definition of postconventional moral reasoning will uncover more post-conventional reasoning in other societies (ibid.: 67). Postconventional levels of moral reasoning correlate positively with years of formal school-ing and intellectual ability. It may be, then, that Kohlberg's measures of moral reasoning are biased by both western values and academic thinking.

Shweder focuses on the moral assumptions of a culture and the ways in which adults intentionally inculcate moral rules and principles in speech. His approach emphasizes cultural differences in moral reasoning. However, it has less to say in respect to common moral attitudes (i.e., the nearly uni-versal condemnation of murder, incest, genocide, theft, and gratuitous vio-lence against helpless victims).

Another issue concerns the relation between the moral faculties of per-sonality and actual behavior. Shweder's approach suggests that moral behavior reflects cultural knowledge, especially knowledge about moral principles, rules, and norms. In this respect, it resembles Freud's idea that the strength of the superego depends on identification with moral authority.

Knowledge of rules and norms alone, however, does not ensure moral or ethical behavior. Psychopathic personalities are often well aware of social norms but may disregard them nonetheless. It is also unclear to what degree so-called higher stages of moral reasoning actually predict moral behavior. Some studies suggest they may (Colby and Kohlberg 1987: 373–375), but the many examples of immoral and unethical acts by educated, intelligent persons suggest that there is more to virtuous and ethical behavior than cultural learning or intellectual sophistication. Indications of what these additional ingredients may be have emerged in studies of gender differences in moral reasoning. They are also apparent in studies of antisocial personalities.

In a comparison of moral reasoning in males and females in the United States, Carol Gilligan (1982) found that women are influenced by caring, concern, and empathy more than men.[8] These elements may insure moral and ethical decision making in real situations more effectively than either intellectual sophistication or knowledge of rules and norms. Psychopathic persons are again instructive in this regard. Their deficiency may lie not so much in knowledge as in self-control and in lack of compassion and ability or willingness to see others as real persons. What is true of psychopaths can be true of groups. Objectification and dehumanization of the other are often present wherever groups engage in collective violence (see Chapter 8).

A certain type of psychological integration – in a word, "integrity" – may be another ingredient in moral behavior. Psychoanalysts have noted that some people seem to have lacunae or gaps in their superegos. Similarly, students of moral reasoning have found that level of moral reasoning can vary with the nature of the moral dilemma; a person may reason at one stage about theft and at another about tax evasion or extramarital relations (Shweder et al. 1990: 141). An inclination toward splitting or dissociation may favor superego lacunae and inconsistency in moral reasoning and, thus, an inability or unwillingness to apply moral or ethical principles to behavior in specific situations.

Boundaries, multiple selves, autonomy

Emotional disposition, a desiring, willful, and anxious *I*, and the Jamesian and psychoanalytic ideas about the structure of personality allude to what may be some of the important components of personality. Psychoanalytic and anthropological literatures suggest that autonomy and cohesiveness are also significant variables in personality. Clinical observation has revealed wide variations in dependence/independence, firmness of ego boundaries, and integration/fragmentation of the self. Variations along these dimensions have figured in cross-cultural comparisons, especially in comparisons between western and nonwestern societies. They are also playing a role in psychoanalytic and postmodernist assumptions about the very nature of personality; psychoanalytic writers often find variations in dialectical tensions between integration and fragmentation, autonomy and dependence, and egocentricity and sociability, whereas postmodernists regard fragmentation, dependence, and sociability (or, in some versions, narcissism) as the usual state of human beings.

Comparisons involving these qualities of personality have been made between nonwestern and western societies, or between simple, traditional societies and complex, modern/postmodern societies. The self in traditional society is said to be less autonomous and more "sociocentric." Marcel Mauss ([1938]1985) called attention to the social nature of cultural notions about the person. He noted that in traditional tribal societies the person inherits a spirit, name, and corresponding rights and obligations as a member of a kinship group. The person is a personage, a social actor who wears a mask and plays a role. In Roman culture this notion of the persona took on the nuance of legal person or citizen. According to Mauss, this incipient notion of the person was then reworked by Christian thinkers and philosophers until it became the modern idea of the person as conscious, moral individual.

Shweder and Bourne (1991) contrast what they take to be two divergent ways of understanding the person and social relations. In western cultures, an "egocentric-contractual" model portrays an independent individual in abstract terms, whereas in societies with a "socio-centric organic" perspective the person is placed in a context and seen as having distinctive characteristics. A comparison of language used in describing others in the United States and India seems to illustrate the difference. According to Shweder and Bourne, the Oriya of India can think abstractly, yet in contrast to the Americans in their study, their thought about persons and social relations is concrete and contextual as a matter of cultural style.[9]

Similarly, Michelle Z. Rosaldo (1984) found little fit between the western notion of the independent, inner-directed individual and personality among the Ilongot, a tribal people in the Philippines. Private and public parts of the self are not well differentiated and the sense of self shifts from one social context to another. The Ilongot seem to lack a well-developed sense of personal responsibility or an ongoing self; they blame the spirits for misfortune, and they ignore continuities in personal history. Emotions are more a function of social context than enduring disposition. Some researchers working in South Asia have inferred from interdependency in interpersonal relations that psychological autonomy in the western sense is neither present nor necessary for effective participation in social life (e.g., Roland 1988).

Many studies imply that the self and emotional expression in any one traditional society are apt to fit a single pattern. They also suggest that the self is more coherent in traditional societies and more fragmented and more isolated or autonomous in modern, complex societies. In modern/postmodern societies, individuals play various roles and encounter diverse and often unexpected situations. Thus, they may have various personas, and they may actively experiment with wearing different "masks" as they try to cope with social exigencies. Gergen (1972) argued that the wearing of many masks is typical in modern culture and that the attempt to "remain true to oneself" may be an unworkable, even dysfunctional ideal. The contemporary self, according to Gergen (1991), is "saturated" with communication from different directions, and confronted with a multiplicity of expectations and points of view. It thus learns to adjust to changing circumstances. Similarly, Robert Jay Lifton (1993) describes the modern self as resilient, fluid, and multifaceted.

Some work implies that the self in complex traditional societies lies somewhere in the middle of the unified–fragmented continuum. According to Geertz (1983), traditional Javanese and Balinese personalities are sociocentric but also marked by internal differentiation between private and public selves. The Javanese conceal their feelings while interacting with others in the public sphere; they separate the inner world of modulated emotion from the outer world of socially patterned behavior. In Bali, where the society is characterized by formalized status distinctions, the idiosyncratic self, according to Geertz, is further removed from social interaction.

Society is a hierarchical drama in which the dramatis personae conceal their inner selves. The Balinese live with the fear that they will blunder in public performances and shamefully expose their inner selves.

Characterizations of culturally constituted selves, however, probably minimize individual variations, psychological complexities, and the non-cultural dimensions of personality. Typifications of societies as sociocentric or egocentric overlook the complexities and subtleties in the content and organization of persons and their cultures. The Japanese self, for example, may be other-oriented in some sense yet it clearly has inner-oriented qualities as well. Nancy R. Rosenberger (1989) describes private and public aspects of selfhood in Japan. The Japanese regard energy as radiating from the heart and expressing itself in either disciplined or spontaneous behavior. Both forms of behavior may assume public or private expression.

Marina Roseman (1990) describes selfhood among the Temiar, a Senoi people in Malaysia, as multiple and sociocentric. In the local folk psychology, the sense of the self's complexity is reflected in Temiar recognition of head, heart, shadow, and odor selves. "The various selves can detach, interact, and even intermingle as bound 'soul' becomes unbound 'spirit'" (ibid.: 230). The detachability of these soul components expresses Temiar sociability but ideas about soul-loss and illness also reflect the desire to maintain the autonomy and integrity of the self. Roseman (ibid.: 237) writes that "[b]oth egocentric and sociocentric societies . . . contain cultural subscripts that implicate their opposites." Poole (1991) shows that Bimin-Kuskusmin men express their individuality in narratives although they are sociocentric in some respects.

Katherine P. Ewing (1990) suggests that persons in many cultures may have multiple self-representations that shift in and out of focus depending on the requirements of situations. The self-description of a Pakistani woman seems to entail several self-representations. Thus, Ewing suggests that the unitary self may be a subjective illusion, even in traditional societies. Anthony Giddens (1991) notes that the contemporary subject engages in a project of constructing a self amid social and cultural diversity but he also observes that this process may result in either fragmentation or integration. Unni Wikan (1987) shows, contra Geertz, that the Balinese social self is not merely an expression of culturally valued aestheticism or a fear of social clumsiness. The whole Balinese world, she notes, is suffused with an undercurrent of violence and fear of violence. The social self, then, has the qualities of what Winnicott calls the false self: it is a defensive structure oriented toward suppressing dangerous impulses and protecting the self from dangerous others (see also Spiro 1993a).

Ewing (1991) points out that typifications of the self in nonwestern societies may confuse actual social relations or discourse about social relations with self-representations and unconscious object relations. Social relations and cultural expectations, on the one hand, and intrapsychic organization, on the other, are different things. Social interdependency, in other words, is not equivalent to psychological disposition toward dependency or diffuse ego boundaries in the psychological sense. To the contrary, an ability to participate effectively in interdependent social relations may require psychological autonomy in the psychoanalytic sense. Ewing shows how the psychological consequences of childhood difficulties with separation–individuation may have led several of her Pakistani subjects to have difficulties adjusting to their husbands' extended families.

Personality and cultural ideas about the person are not the same thing. Nor are the number of roles a person plays necessarily an indication of fragmented personality or of willingness to experiment with different presentations of the self. We should also observe that individuals may be more or less aware of their own characteristics. Lakshmi Bandlamudi (1994) writes about how immigrants in New York develop dialogical and dialectical understandings of self and culture. These sophisticated understandings are associated with recent immigration and frequency of visits to home countries. The immigrant experience seems to promote a split identity in some sense but also an awareness of the dialogical nature of the self and culture.

In contemporary America at least some persons are more inclined to adjust their presentations of the self to fit changing situations than are others, even though they may have no more social roles to play (Snyder 1987). These "self-monitoring" persons are social actors who think of themselves as flexible and pragmatic. Persons low in self-monitoring, in contrast, tend to remain the same in different situations and to regard themselves as principled and consistent. Persons high in self-monitoring form diverse and diffuse relations, and they are more apt to relate to others by activity preference. Persons low in self-monitoring form strong emotional attachments to friends and loved ones, and they are more likely to associate with people by social feelings. Low and high self-monitors also differ in romantic and sexual orientations. High self-monitors are more likely to notice physical appearance than inner qualities. They seek out a variety of sexual partners, and they are slower to commit themselves to romantic relationships and more apt to be unfaithful to partners. They also report more sexual thoughts and fantasies. High self-monitors become depressed when they fail in social performance, whereas low self-monitors become depressed following separations from loved ones or failures to realize their ideals. High self-monitors are more exhibitionistic, playful, and dominance-seeking.

The subjective or mental boundaries between self and other are everywhere somewhat murky, even in more individualistic societies. James ([1892]1985: 44), writing in late nineteenth-century United States (and with the characteristic sexism of the period), said that a man's self includes "not only his body and his psychic powers, but his clothes and his house, his wife and children, his ancestors and his friends, his reputation and works, his lands and horses, and yacht and bank-account." While boundaries may be somewhat fuzzy in all individuals, they may be more so in some individuals than others. Contemporary psychotherapists observe various kinds and degrees of merging between self and other. Kohut (1971) wrote about "self-objects," that is, images of social others that support the individual's narcissistic aims and self-esteem. Self-object relations, according to Kohut, range from "twinship" to "merging." At one extreme they include such mundane identifications as teenagers dressing like their rock-star idols while at a concert and, at the other, psychotic confusion between the self and the other.

Some personality types and mental conditions take uncertain boundaries, inconsistency, and dissimulation to extremes. Histrionic personalities are prone to role-playing. Persons with multiple personality disorder diagnoses supposedly have two or more personalities, while persons with borderline personality disorder may show identity confusion and merging. Persons with borderline personality organization in the broad sense tend to entertain a multiplicity of possible identities or selves in fantasy and dreams (Fast 1974). Although everyone tries to manage impressions to some extent, and although social grace and tact require discretion if not deception, histrionic, narcissistic, imposturous, and psychopathic personalities are often downright dishonest as well as artful and deceptive (Greenacre [1958]1971). The "as-if" personality described by Deutsch (1942) may seem normal enough, but the presentation of self may mask an inner emptiness and a lack of vitality, originality, and moral center. Persons with schizophrenia evince inclinations toward weak boundaries and various tendencies toward psychological fragmentation (see Chapter 6).

Certain social conditions and developmental experiences may promote a fragmented or poorly bounded self. These may be counterbalanced by various psychological and cultural processes. Ewing (1990: 273) wrote that people maintain the illusion of internal cohesion by connecting their disparate roles, selves, and social experiences through metaphor, metonymy, transference, and identification. She also notes that emotion unifies experience and that the very ability to adjust orientations to different situations can sustain a sense of wholeness.

Body image and embodied experience may also unify experience. Body image and kinesthetic experience are important, perhaps central, elements in self-awareness. As we have seen, some writers have theorized that coordinated body movement underlies or informs ego integration. Unchanging features of the body, and the subjective experience of coordinated movement and postural balance may underpin a sense of coherence or wholeness. A stable sense of having a male or female body may be an important element in the subjective sensation of unity. Schizophrenia, perhaps the outer limit of psychological disunity, is instructive here. Gender-identity confusion, depersonalization (mind–body separation), loss of boundaries, stilted and awkward movement, and body dismemberment fantasies are common features of schizophrenia.

The self is also unified by the ego-ideal. The person may play different roles in different situations, but commitment to a set of values and ideals may underpin a stable identity. Significantly, wanting to be a good person is a theme in the diverse self-representations of Ewing's (1990) informant. Crapanzano (1990: 420) seems to allude to this phenomenon when he suggests that conscience reinforces "the referential conventions of language that mask the pragmatically induced instability of dialogical exchanges."

Vincent Crapanzano, like other postmodernists, seems to think that the sense of wholeness is an illusion. Characterizations of the self and other are unstable and somehow less real than stable structures of personality. The implication is that dialogue is constantly working against stability or creating, at best, illusory structures. The relation between stability and dialogue may be more complex than this, however. What people say to each other may reinforce self-conceptions and coherent views of the world or, when social tension or conflict is present, it may encourage psychological conflict. Similarly, internal dialogues may move toward either subjective wholeness and integration or splitting and fragmentation. Whether dialogues move one way or the other may depend on how much empathy or respect one voice has for the other or on how much one is willing at least to listen to the other. Neurotic personalities are generally divided in one way or another. Perhaps they have difficulty listening to themselves or, alternatively, they are too wrapped up in recurring self-talk to find solutions to their problems. Clearly, they are often too absorbed in themselves to listen carefully to what others are saying.

Every personality, it seems, consists of various *I* positions that converse with each other. These positions include the inner or "true" self, social selves, or parts of these selves, self-objects, and others or aspects of others. The existential *I*, through imagination, invests each by turn as it remembers and anticipates social situations and dialogical interactions. Individuals, however, may vary with respect to where the *I* usually resides and to how freely and consciously it moves among the various positions. So-called self-monitoring personalities (the term is something of a misnomer) are aware of themselves in relation to situations but may have a dissociated lack of insight about their inconsistency and insincerity. They are more adept at taking the role of others cognitively, but they have less emotional empathy (Snyder 1987: 124). Different sorts of "pathological" fragmentation may represent even more extreme versions of this tendency. In multiple personality disorder, histrionic personalities, borderline personalities, and as-if personalities, and in persons with schizophrenia the central *I* position of the subject becomes very unstable and the capacity for genuine empathy is even less well developed.

These reflections suggest that cultures may nurture either subjective wholeness or fragmentation. Whether the self is homogeneous or fragmented may depend in part on the pace and complexity of social life. Yet even where some conditions promote fragmentation, others may restore the sense of wholeness. Many complex societies, both traditional and modern, seem to have devised strategies for unifying the self or, at least, for promoting feelings of inner harmony. Recreation, sport, song, poetry, art, intimate conversations, moral instruction, psychotherapy, and religious disciplines like prayer and meditation may all, in different ways, serve the aim of buttressing and restoring feelings of physical, social, and spiritual integrity. A Japanese person, for example, may integrate different selves by balancing activities and by practicing Zen and traditional arts (Rosenberger 1989). Benjamin N. Colby (1987) has argued that human beings have a deep-seated need for order and coherence in their experience, and he thinks that cultures address this need in systematic ways. He also suggests that whether people satisfy their needs for coherent experience and meaning may have significant consequences for their physical and emotional well-being. Colby (1991) shows how the Japanese tea ceremony restores a sense of social and internal harmony by de-emphasizing social differences and refocusing attention on nature and on widely shared and highly valued cultural achievements.

"Neurotic styles"

So-called personality disorders, at least insofar as they have been described for western societies, form a continuum with so-called normal personality; there is no sharp break between normal and abnormal, and often the characteristics that distinguish persons with personality disorders exist in less developed forms in normal persons. Personality disorders, then, are interesting for personality theory because of the way they underscore the emotional and cognitive components of personality.

David Shapiro (1965) referred to "neurotic styles" to emphasize that so-called personality disorders are, among other things, habitual patterns of perception and thinking as well as organizations of drive and conflict. Patterns of perception and thinking, of course, are influenced by culture. It follows that there may be a cultural component to personality disorder. Many personality disorders recognized in western psychiatry fall along a continuum running from obsessional to impulsive. How much of this continuum reflects human nature? And how much reflects western culture? Inasmuch as personality disorder elucidates personality in general, the question becomes still another way of wondering whether we may theorize about personality in general terms or whether we need a special theory of personality for each culture.

Obsessional styles

The obsessive-compulsive personality in the literature of western mental health professionals is said to be unusually thoughtful and conscientious. David Shapiro (1965) observed the self-preoccupations and intense concentration of obsessive persons. They are cool and inattentive with others. Their lives often center on work (ibid.: 31). Work and other activity is driven by conscience. "When the obsessive-compulsive person acts as his own overseer, he also feels that he acts in response to the requirements of some objective necessity, particularly some moral necessity" (ibid.: 39).

Asceticism, moral dogmatism, and perfectionism are ways of gaining control. Many obsessive persons are anxious unless they are making money or otherwise climbing the ladder of social success. The passage of time is disturbing for obsessive persons because it is uncontrollable and because it leads to death. Obsessive persons may counter this threat by ignoring time, by taking risks, or by formulating grandiose projects for lasting social recognition. Yet, the obsessive person is plagued with doubts, indecision, apprehensions. He has trouble enacting his plans (Salzman 1968).

Aversion to dirt and contamination may express this apprehension about death. For the obsessive, death is "ubiquitous, amorphous, ungraspable. It exists as an infinite potentiality, as a demonic power, which scoffs at all counteraction" (Straus 1948: 9). Germs, pollution, and disease suffuse, leaving little space for spontaneous movement. The obsessive person lives in a world permeated with malevolence. Obsessive thoughts, orderliness, and cleanliness represent efforts to control the evil. Yet, neither the mental incantations nor magical rituals succeed in providing anything more than temporary relief from anxiety. While they may want omnipotence, obsessive persons usually experience themselves as subject to thoughts and circumstances that are beyond their control.

Several passive personality types resemble the obsessive pattern. Passive-aggressive personalities combine passivity with veiled aggressiveness and hostility. In work settings they express their hostility toward bosses and supervisors in stubbornness, forgetfulness, and procrastination. The passive-aggressive person resembles the masochistic person in the psychoanalytic literature. Masochism can be sexual, but more often it takes the form of moral masochism. In either case, the goal, among other things, may be a roundabout acquisition of power. Masochistic persons may secretly identify with their more powerful tormentors, perhaps with the expectation of eventual triumph. Theodore Reik ([1941]1962) concluded that hidden superiority feelings and pride are prime features of the masochistic orientation. "The saint who shows off his humility seems to prove his pride in being humble" (ibid.: 262).

The paranoid personality also shares features with the obsessive-compulsive personality (Shapiro 1965). Paranoid persons are ambivalent about power and submission, but they focus on external threats and dangers. They are vigilant, mistrustful, and often hostile and argumentative. They exaggerate their importance, envy more powerful persons, and deprecate persons they see as weak or flawed (American Psychiatric Association 1987: 337–338). "Playfulness disappears, and playful interests are usually absent" (Shapiro 1965: 78). Paranoid persons fear subjugation, and they feel humiliated by personal imperfections, especially when they are criticized by superiors (ibid.: 81–82, 85–86). They may rationalize their fears in terms of political and religious ideas.[10]

Impulsive styles

Several personality types are more impulsive (i.e., narcissistic, histrionic, psychopathic, and borderline personalities). Current research and theory suggest that these impulsive personality types share "borderline personality organization" (Kernberg 1985), a combination of impulsiveness, hostility, the use of primitive defense mechanisms, and poor ego and superego organization (Svrakic et al. 1991).

Narcissistic persons are self-assured, aggressive, and ambitious, at least in fantasy. Imagining themselves quite special, they fantasize about power, brilliance, success, and physical beauty. Many persons with narcissistic personality organization are social actors. This "as-if" mode of presenting the self can become imposturous (Greenacre [1958]1971) and even exceedingly pretentious. Jones ([1913]1964) observed a variant of narcissistic personality which he called "the God complex," a constellation of traits that includes identification with God, fantasies of omnipotence and omniscience, aloofness, mystification of the self, belief in personal immortality, conviction of creative power, interest in psychology, and, among other things, a presumed ability to predict thunderstorms! In a classic contribution to the literature on narcissism, Henry A. Murray (1955) described an undergraduate who reminded him of the mythic Icarus who made wings of wax and feathers to escape the island of the tyrannical Minos. Consumed with the elation of flying, Icarus ignored his father's warning and flew too close to the sun. His wings melted, and he fell into the sea. Murray's subject was an under-achiever who fantasized having great power, prestige, and wealth. Surrounded by talented people, he preferred sloth to competition and the risk of failure. His fantasies included urethral eroticism, wishes for immortality, depreciation of women, and rising up and falling down: "[t]he wish to overcome gravity, to stand erect, to grow tall, to dance on tiptoe, to walk on water, to leap or swing in the air, to climb, to rise, to fly, or to float down gradually from on high and land without injury, not to speak of rising from the dead and ascending to heaven" (Murray 1955: 631). The young man said, "I am just biding my time and waiting for the day when my 'soul' will ignite and this inner fire will send me hurtling (two rungs at a time) up the ladder of success" (ibid.: 633).

The psychopathic or antisocial personality may have a long history of lying, cheating, and otherwise antisocial behavior. He knows the rules but ignores them whenever it suits his convenience or self-interest. Caring little about others, he wants only power and possessions. In contrast to the nar-cissistic person, who has a grandiose self and punitive superego, the anti-social personality idealizes the bad parents and has a destructive self (Svrakic et al. 1991). He is irritable, aggressive, impulsive, restless, and bored. He has little love or empathy for others, and he is often destructive when acting on sexual impulses. Many psychopaths are actors; wearing masks of legitimacy, they make effective swindlers (Millon 1981: 181–215).

The hysterical or histrionic person is self-dramatizing and given to romantic fantasies. A proclivity for role-playing may, in the female, take the form of a coy, seductive exaggeration of femininity. On another level, this romanticism may be expressed in a readiness to join in fads, trends, and religious and political movements. Thought is impressionistic, diffuse, and global, and there is a tendency to deny, dissociate, and repress (Shapiro 1965). Histrionic persons are prone to idealism and nostalgia, but of a superficial sort. Their fantasies are rather thin and susceptible to sugges-tion. Claiming helplessness, they tend to blame problems on conditions beyond their control. Having denied or failed to nurture an authentic self, they may identify with leaders and celebrities and fantasize relationships with them. Chameleonlike, they adapt to whatever cultural trend supports their passivity and dependency. They may play a sick role or get involved in cults or political movements (Krohn 1978).

Descriptions of histrionic personalities often read like caricatures of traditional femininity (Chodoff and Lyons 1958). Men may have histrionic traits also, but they are more apt to fit other personality profiles, particularly if they exaggerate masculine toughness. In western culture, aggressively masculine men with histrionic traits are apt to be seen as narcissistic or antisocial (Nuckolls 1992).

Persons with borderline personalities exhibit instability in self-image, interpersonal relations, and mood.[11] They often lack a coherent and firm sense of self and may depend on others for their sense of realness. They have trouble tolerating solitude and independence yet they have difficulty maintaining relationships. They begin passionate attachments idealizing their partners but inevitably they discover "major" flaws and end up feeling disappointed and disenchanted. Because they manipulate others, they often turn them "off" and set themselves up for rejection. They complain about boredom, inner emptiness, and separation anxiety. They may engage for periods in promiscuous and perverse sex or go on bouts of substance abuse. Many cut their wrists or burn themselves with cigarettes. These moments or periods of impulsive acting out alternate with periods of depression and anger. Persons with borderline personality disorder are also prone to eating disorders. Splitting, projective identification, and denial are common among them, particularly when they are under stress. When stresses become acute, they may become temporarily psychotic (Gunderson 1984; Kernberg 1985; Stone 1980).

Personality theory and psychic unity

Neurotic styles magnify common variations in emotional disposition and mental organization. Obsessional personalities are unusually anxious and conscientious. Impulsive personalities are more aggressive, hostile, and impulsive. Whereas the obsessive personality relies on reaction formation, the impulsive personalities are prone to using denial, splitting, and projective identification.

Individuals and groups may vary along these dimensions in other cultures also. They may show more or less impulsivity or more or less anxiety of conscience. In certain respects, however, descriptions of personality disorders may reflect modern culture. The obsessional personality seems to take asceticism and the work ethic to the extreme. The paranoid person's concern with perfection and the passive-aggressive person's ambivalence in hierarchical relations may reflect the emphasis on achievement and the disparities in wealth and social status in industrialized societies.

The obsessive personality may have been more common in earlier stages of capitalist society. Erich Fromm (1947) described a change in the dominant character structure of society from a "hoarding" orientation (i.e., an obsessive-compulsive style) to a "marketing" orientation, and David

Riesman ([1950]1962) observed a trend from "inner directed" personality to "other directed" personality. Clinical psychologists and psychoanalysts have noticed a shift from classical neuroses to personality disorders (especially, narcissistic and borderline disorders) in their practices. Christopher Lasch (1978) suggested that contemporary society and culture are increasingly narcissistic. The cynicism, boredom, anger, egocentricity, superficiality, lack of social and moral commitment, and uncertainty about identity and values in impulsive personalities are arguably widespread in contemporary American society. Gergen (1991) discerns in postmodern society an increasing "multiphrenia" and a passing of commitment, truth, personal morality, intrinsic values, and sincere emotion. He doubts that these trends are pathological, and even tries to cast them in a positive light, but the similarity between them and borderline personality organization is obvious and intriguing.

Cultural interpretivists and social constructionists argue that western psychology is culturally biased. In an often-quoted passage, Geertz (1983: 58–59) clearly articulates this idea.

The Western conception of the person as a bounded, unique, more or less integrated motivational and cognitive universe, a dynamic center of awareness, emotion, judgment, and action organized into a distinctive whole and set contrastively both against other such wholes and against its social and natural background, is, however incorrigible it may seem to us, a rather peculiar idea within the context of the world's cultures.

Scholars who agree with Geertz cite ethnographic examples to show that local cultures make different assumptions about the person. They argue that the self is socially constructed and, therefore, different from one historical or cultural setting to another. And they assert that the notion of the autonomous self reflects western individualism (Gergen 1990; Sampson 1989; Shweder and Bourne [1982]1991; Kirkpatrick and White 1985).

Western notions about personality may be culture-bound to some extent. Psychiatric typifications of abnormal personality in particular seem to reflect western values and conditions. Westerners may be more individualistic than people in many traditional societies. Emotional expression, self-representation, identity, boundaries, and internal controls may also vary from one society to another.

Generalizations about cross-cultural differences in personality are risky, however. They tend to gloss over individual differences and cultural complexities. North Americans, for example, are individualistic in some contexts but communal in others, and they vary widely with respect to autonomy, psychological integration, moral integrity, and emotional dynamics. Typifications also may exaggerate the differences between peoples.[12] Notwithstanding Geertz's claims about the peculiarity of the western concept of the person, there is no reason to conclude that peoples in other societies lack consciousness, emotion, judgment, or intention or that they are unaware of the difference between themselves and others.

Dialogic interaction, stability, and situation

The self is constructed and reconstructed to some extent in dialogic interaction. For some writers this implies that the self is inherently fragmented and changeable. Indeed, the dialogical nature of the self suggests to Gergen (1990) that we should avoid substantive notions about the mind altogether. Desires, emotions, and beliefs become ephemeral properties of verbal exchanges in social relations (Gergen 1972, 1990). Similarly, Shweder (1991) concludes that personality traits are unstable across time and that correlations between personality traits and behavior in different situations are usually weak. He maintains instead that most behavior makes sense in terms of cultural definitions of, and assumptions about, situations.

These assessments of the personality concept may be too pessimistic, however. Conversations may involve pragmatic characterizations of self and interlocutor, and behavior often does make considerable sense in terms of cultural schemas regarding appropriate behavior for specific situations. Studies also show that individuals adjust their self-representations to the changing circumstances of life, and that they put on different social masks or personas in different situations. It does not follow, however, that personality is unstructured, ephemeral, or inconsequential for behavior. In fact, the research shows that self-representations are remarkably stable over time and that individuals strenuously resist the attempts of others to change or contradict their own self-characterizations (Markus and Nurius 1986). The best longitudinal studies, moreover, find continuity in emotional disposition as well as self-representation.

Jack Block (1981), for example, compared extensive psychological evaluations of eighty-four men and eighty-seven women at adolescence with evaluations made when they were in their thirties. Many traits showed statistically significant continuity. Males and females tended toward well-adjusted, anxious, or impulsive personality styles at adolescence, and many of them displayed variants of their adolescent style years later. The three styles, moreover, correlated significantly with different patterns of behavior in work, family life, and social relations.[13]

Block's research suggests that a stark choice between stability or instability may put the matter too simply. Patterns of emotional disposition, object relations and transference patterns, core features of self-representation, and certain aspects of moral reasoning may tend to remain stable across situations and may indeed influence behavior in significant ways. More superficial aspects of personality may be less influential in this respect. Ironically, the inclination to change in response to situations may itself be a stable feature of personality, one that varies from individual to individual and, perhaps, from one historical or cultural moment to another.

Conclusions

Human beings are products of nature and nurture. They preserve features of their primate and hominid ancestors. They are emotional, desiring creatures. Yet they are also moral, symbol-using creatures. The various ways in which human beings adjust and realize these inclinations and capacities reflect their inherited dispositions and their personal histories.

By recognizing nature and nurture in human subjects in this way we are in a better position to understand agency, innovation, and resistance in social life and, reciprocally, the effects of socialization and social persuasion on the individual. The same drive systems that energize assertive, goal-seeking behavior in social life are also the ones that make people susceptible to social influence. By combining an appreciation of nature and nurture in our view of personality, we can accommodate fragmentation, multiple motives, and conflict in personality as well as unity and cohesion. We are, moreover, in a better position to understand emotional and mental disorders and the psychological foundations of social relations and cultural beliefs and practices.

5   Depression and hysteria

The mental structures of the ego and superego ordinarily organize and direct desire and will according to social norms, effecting a shift, to use Kristeva's terminology, from the "semiotic" to "the symbolic." This shift marks the passage from early to middle childhood but it is also an ingredient in everyday sociality; to interact effectively with social others, individuals must regulate their drives, emotions, and primary process thinking, and they must make sense to others with signs and symbols.

This movement from semiotic to symbolic is susceptible to various forms of exaggeration, arrest, or regression. Excessive intellectualism or moralism may leave little room for feeling or empathy. The person may disregard internal and external voices of common sense or morality. Repression or dissociation may short-circuit imaginary dialogues with the self and social others and, therefore, a person's social skills. In hysteria, depression, and madness, splitting and disruption of the dialogical process may severely compromise a person's capacity for social life. In hysteria, cryptic bodily symbolism may replace explicit communication; in depression the person may sink into stuporous asymbolia; in madness, the semiotic may replace or overwhelm the symbolic.

In this chapter and the next I consider emotional and mental disorders, building on what was said earlier about human nature and personality. I show how vulnerability to emotional and mental disorder is inherent in the psychological characteristics of human beings. I also note that disorder, like personality generally, is a response to life events and social circumstances. Social experience may figure in the origins of disorder, and it always affects the inner experience and outer manifestations of disorder.

Disorder is anthropologically interesting because it can have both disruptive and productive effects in social life and cultural activity. I consider this productive aspect of disorder in later chapters. In this chapter I focus on the phenomenology and origins of depression and hysteria. In the following chapter I examine the phenomenology and origins of eccentricity and schizophrenia.

Understanding depression and hysteria begins with emotion and, more particularly, with the social matrix of emotional experience. It also involves realizing that emotional expression is both a natural and socially constructed part of social interaction. Before turning to depression and hysteria, therefore, I want to make some general observations about the sorts of social situations that engender strong emotions in human beings. I also want to emphasize that emotion is expressed in language as well as in the body.

Trauma, affect, and speech

Emotion occurs within the mind and body, but it is also a social phenomenon. Human beings experience emotion when they remember, imagine, or participate in social interaction. Emotions color attitudes toward social others, and mark the vicissitudes of social relations. Positive affect often accompanies love, attachment, and empowerment. Negative affect is often a response to losses of love, status, or reputation.

Social status and reputation are everywhere emotional matters (Kemper 1978, 1984). People in subordinate positions may feel shame about themselves and envy, resentment, and anger toward those in higher positions (Foster 1972). Young Ilongot men in the mountains near Manila, for instance, feel ashamed in the presence of their fathers and peers until they have proven themselves by taking heads (M.Z. Rosaldo 1983, 1984). Among the Maya Indians of southern Mexico, shame accompanies and perhaps reinforces subordination to Spanish-speaking Ladinos (Aguilar 1982). On the Nissan Atoll in Melanesia, people feel shame when they fail or go into debt. The Nissan defend themselves by shaming assertive, boastful, or self-serving persons, that is, persons who by their aggressive actions make others feel inferior (Nachman 1984). Guilt also correlates with social hierarchy. Indebtedness may encourage guilt, even among the wealthy. Edward Sapir ([1939]1963:589) speculated that a business person may suffer from "that obscure, perverse, guilt feeling which, the psychiatrist tells us, so often festers in one's heart of hearts when one tries to balance one's usefulness to society with the size of one's income."

Aggression and rage are often reactions to real or imagined attacks against the self (Rochlin 1973). Since self-image is tied up with social position and reputation, hierarchical relations are conducive to hostile feelings and aggression. People in subordinate social positions may react with anger or rage when they feel shamed by social superiors, whereas the latter may react with anger and aggression when they perceive social subordinates as threatening their social positions and prerogatives.

Hostility and shame are interconnected. The feeling of being shamed may evoke vengeful anger, and such anger, when sufficiently righteous, may induce shame in social superiors. Assertions of superiority that encourage feelings of inferiority and shame in others may be taken as aggressive. On Nissan Atoll even virtuous behavior is deemed aggressive since it shames the less virtuous (Nachman 1984). Aggression toward others may be expressed indirectly by turning it against the self or self-objects. When shamed by social subordinates or superiors, individuals in Melanesia and elsewhere may destroy their property or commit suicide to shame the person doing the shaming. For the Japanese, suicide may occur when aging or social disappointment damage the self-image; alternatively, it may represent a veiled attack against a person or persons seen as responsible for ego's misfortune (De Vos 1973b).

Unpleasant emotion occurs with loss of love and separation. Almost everyone is familiar with loneliness and the pain of bereavement, separation from loved ones, and rejection. A romantic triangle can promote envy, jealousy, and other negative emotions. Separations may engender guilt; a child may experience guilt when separating from its mother, and this experience, in turn, may lay the basis for guilt feelings later in life when the adult person survives loved ones or rejects or leaves significant others (Modell 1971).

Needs for love, empowerment, and passionate attachment are expressed in discourse. Similarly, people work through disappointments of needs and desires in speech and cultural idioms. Affective speech and practice may be therapeutic, first through emotional catharsis but also through the effects on the beliefs and sentiments of social others, including those others who form the social matrix of the subject's emotional experience. Such speech does not operate freely, however. It is constrained by convention and social relations, particularly by hierarchical relations and related understandings about what is licit communication between social superiors and social inferiors.

In recent years there has been growing attention to the pragmatic expression of affect among women and other socially subordinate individuals (Ong 1987; Raheja and Gold 1994; Trawick 1988). Suggestive for psychological anthropology in this regard is the work of Lila Abu-Lughod (1986, 1993). In her study of a Bedouin community in Egypt, she discerned a dominant speech of honor and modesty and a subversive poetry that expresses suppressed feelings of loss and frustrated needs for agency and passionate attachment. The dominant idioms turn on a morality of noble ancestry and its values of assertiveness, fearlessness, and autonomy. Modesty, especially for women, is part of this ideology of honor because women can undermine the purity of blood in the male line with improper sexuality. These values of honor are realized by older men more than younger men and women, for whom they can represent frustration, failure, and inadequacy.

Two-line poems in this context permit women and subordinate men to express their unfulfilled needs for intimacy, pleasure, and empowerment and resistance to the dominant order.

Abu-Lughod mentions the case of Nāfla, a woman who protested against being married at the early age of fourteen. When her remonstrations failed to deter her father and his relatives, she feigned spirit possession: "I tensed my body, rolled my eyes, and everyone rushed around, brought me incense and prayed for me" (1986: 102). When Nāfla emerged from her seizure, her thankful family decided that perhaps fourteen was indeed too young an age for marriage.

Abu-Lughod notes that possession, like poetry, can express resistance. Some, like Nāfla may "fake" possession, but many others do not, at least not consciously. In this respect, Abu-Lughod's observations are paradigmatic for what I wish to suggest here. Poems, laments, humor, and songs may not always satisfy suppressed needs and desires. When expression fails to bring relief, the result may be emotional disorder. "Depression" and "hysteria," or some combination of the two, are imperfect but serviceable rubrics for the forms such disorders often take. In hysteria the poetry of the resistance is expressed in the body rather than in speech, in lapses of consciousness, or fragmentation of voice, whereas in depression interpersonal and internal dialogue and discourse deteriorate.

Depression

The symptoms of depression include sadness, loss of appetite, disturbed sleep, feelings of hopelessness, and suicidal thoughts. For persons with depression, loss of pleasure in life is also common. Kristeva captures these and other features of depression in the opening pages of *Black sun: Depression and melancholy*:

An infinite number of misfortunes weigh us down every day . . . All this suddenly gives me another life. A life that is unlivable, heavy with daily sorrows, tears held back or shed, a total despair, scorching at times, then wan and empty. In short, a devitalized existence that, although occasionally fired by the effort I make to prolong it, is ready at any moment for a plunge into death. An avenging death or a liberating death, it is henceforth the inner threshold of my despondency, the impossible meaning of a life whose burden constantly seems unbearable, save for those moments when I pull myself together and face up to the disaster. I live a living death, my flesh is wounded, bleeding, cadaverized, my rhythm slowed down or interrupted, time has been erased or bloated, absorbed into sorrow . . . [Kristeva's ellipses]. (Kristeva 1989: 4)

The depressed or melancholic person "ends up in asymbolia, in loss of meaning: if I am no longer capable of translating or metaphorizing, I become silent and I die" (ibid.: 42). A feeling of meaninglessness and absurdity, a sense of emptiness or soul loss, may be the common experiential core of depression in many cultures (Shweder 1985).

Other features of depression vary. Verbalization of dysphoria, guilt, and self-criticism is characteristic of educated westerners, whereas among people in lower social strata and many nonwestern cultures depression may appear as fatigue, loss of appetite and energy, or bodily pain (Marsella et al. 1985). Level of education explains some of these differences, but there are other considerations. In some settings, somatic symptoms are less socially disruptive than verbalizing one's loss, sins, or failings (Kleinman and Kleinman 1985), or the choice of bodily expression may reflect a lack of cultural support for verbalizing feelings (Lesser 1981: 538).

Origins and dynamics

Early psychoanalytic theorizing about depression focused on affect and internal representation, using mourning as a model. Mourning lacks the exaggerated self-denigration often seen in depression, and the grieving person returns to a normal state in a more predictable manner, but otherwise mourning and depression have similar features. In each there is sadness, dejection, and withdrawal from sociality. Depression, like mourning, can begin with loss. The two conditions, moreover, can involve increased irritability and feelings of anxiety, guilt, and rage.

Freud ([1917]1957) reasoned that depression results from identification with, and anger toward, a lost object. The grieving person identifies with the missing object as a way of restoring it to him- or herself. The object becomes, in some sense, part of the self. The mourner feels anger toward the object for his or her departure. When the object becomes part of the self, the anger is directed in effect against the self, and the result is depression.

Freud noted that depression is a heterogeneous category and his hypothesis was only intended to apply to those forms of the disorder having psychological origins. Many experts, including psychoanalysts, would now question the idea that anger directed inward is the main cause of depression. There is no doubt, however, that depression is related to loss and anger.

Loss can predispose a person to depression and trigger the onset of depressions. An infant's separation from the mother provokes fear, distress, and anger. When separation is prolonged, it can lead to detachment and depression (Bowlby 1980). René A. Spitz (1945; Spitz and Wolf 1946) described depressive reactions (i.e., crying, withdrawal, dejection, stupor, retarded development, anorexia, and insomnia) among hospitalized infants separated from their mothers. Temporary separations and losses are painful for older children and adults as well. Childhood losses and separations may be precursors of some adult depression. A study in England found a correlation between early death of the mother and adult depression in women (Brown 1982; Brown and Harris 1978).

This tendency for depressive reactions to follow loss is part of our primate heritage. Orphaned chimpanzee infants and youngsters tend to become lethargic when their mothers die, and if they survive they often show retarded physical and sexual development. Flint, eight and a half when his mother died, spent much of his time near his mother's body and became increasingly lethargic. He passed away himself within a few weeks (Goodall 1986: 101–104). The depression-withdrawal syndrome is a characteristic human response to sudden, massive trauma, and seems to have counterparts in playing possum, cataplexy, and sham death among animals (see Chapter 2).

Fenichel (1945: 390–391) observed that depression often follows a "loss of self-esteem" or of the "supplies" that support self-esteem, that is, a loss of prestige, money, or love. Adverse economic conditions increase the risk for depression. "Unstable times and economic depressions," according to Fenichel, "by depriving people of their satisfactions as well as of their power and prestige and habitual ways of regulating self-esteem, increase their narcissistic needs and their oral dependence" (ibid.: 406). He added that persons who have orally dependent character structures as a result of early experience are especially vulnerable to social and economic adversity (ibid.). The notion of oral fixation is now out of date in psychoanalysis. A contemporary formulation would be that unrealistic narcissistic needs and anxious attachment increase vulnerability to depressive reactions.

In any event, losses may trigger depression or lay the basis for disposition toward depression. Research in the Peoples' Republic of China found that loss of power and socioeconomic status contributed to depression. Some depressed patients were from landlord and intelligentsia families that had suffered financial and social decline during Chairman Mao's Cultural Revolution (Kleinman and Kleinman 1985). Among women in England, early loss in combination with unemployment, having three or more children under fourteen, and low intimacy with husbands, increased the risk for depression (Brown 1982).

Susto (fright), an ailment in rural Mexico and other parts of Latin America, also shows that loss of love and blows to self-esteem can provoke depressive reactions. The term *susto* covers various organic and psychiatric conditions, although dysphoria may be its main referent. The symptoms include sadness, fitful sleep, and loss of appetite. In Tlayacapan (Mexico), some *sustos* follow losses and failures in role performance. One young woman became *asustado* when her aunt was dying of cancer. The young woman's mother became *asustado* when a thief stole her purse and, with it, a large amount of money (Ingham 1986: 74–76, 178–179). O'Nell and Selby (1968) viewed *susto* in two communities in Oaxaca, Mexico, as a reaction to stress resulting from the self's perceived inadequacy in role performance. Women were afflicted more than men, and women had more stressful lives than men. From childhood on, the social expectations for females were more demanding than those for males: since residence was patrilocal, young women were subjected to the demands and criticisms of their mothers-in-law; women had much less freedom of sexual expression than men; women's work was continuous, whereas men had periods of leisure and the freedom to enjoy them; and women had primary responsibility for the care and health of children. Another study in Oaxaca found that *susto* correlated with failures in role performance and organic illness (Rubel et al. 1984). Similarly, loss of loved ones and blows to self-esteem and social status are risk factors for depression in Native American communities, where depression is often four to six times more prevalent than in the US population as a whole. Among the Hopi, circumstances surrounding the onset of depressive symptoms include the deaths of loved ones, unemployment, crop failures, divorces, sexual jealousy, political setbacks, and supernatural sanctions (Manson et al. 1985).

Internalized anger may exacerbate the depressive process. Depression may be more common in cultures that inhibit aggressiveness (Fernando 1969; Kendall 1970). and less common or even rare where aggression and anger are more acceptable, as among the Kaluli, a Papua New Guinean people who freely express grief and anger in public ritual (Schieffelin 1985). The connection between anger and depression, however, may not work quite the way the classical theory envisioned. The link between role failure or status loss and depression suggests that anger may be secondary to more fundamental causes. In moments of failure people often feel shame and humiliation. Helen B. Lewis (1986) argued that depression and shame are strongly associated. Shame provokes anger, even rage. This anger is internalized, she wrote, because to express it publicly would result in more shame. Unlike guilt, which centers on specific transgressions, shame fills the entire self with a sense of failure and helplessness. The humiliated rage that goes with shame may reinforce this felt helplessness. Shame also may involve anxiety about the possible reactions of others to one's failures and feelings.

Sustained fear and anxiety may promote depression by their effects on neurotransmitters in the brain. The rapid firing of noradrenergic neurons in the locus coeruleus during panic and stress eventually decreases the available noradrenaline and, possibly, the activity of the adrenergic receptors at the synapses. According to this theory, the noradrenergic hyperactivity mediates dysphoric arousal whereas noradrenergic depletion, after excessive firing in the locus coeruleus, mediates the vegetative features of depression (Siever and Davis 1985). In other words, just as the use of the word "fright" for dysphoria in Mexican folk culture implies, fear and anxiety may lead to depression. Whether they do so may depend on an individual's coping strategy as well as his or her economic and social resources. The person who succumbs to depression, lacking defenses against anxiety-producing thoughts and experiences, or the reassurance of a supportive environment, may experience one anxious moment after another (Barlow 1988: 276–281).

Emotion reflects unconscious object relations and cognitive schemas. Cognitive processes, then, may determine whether certain emotions occur and whether they lead to depression. Some research on depression suggests that mental habits that distort or exaggerate losses and failings may increase the risk for depression. A learned style of acting and feeling helpless may also have this effect (Beck [1967]1972). Cultural patterns of dealing with emotion, and cultural understandings that foster hope or despair, may also influence the prevalence of depression (see Chapter 9).

Dissociation/hysteria

Some personalities are more prone to fragmentation than others (see Glass 1993). A disposition to fragmentation can take the form of hysteria, a term I use as a catchall for conversion disorder, Briquet's syndrome, and various other dissociative disorders. In conversion disorder a symptom having little or no organic basis represents an unconscious fear or wish. Symptoms may include aches and pains, tics, twitches, paralyses, or other problems with movement, and loss or diminution of hearing, sight, speech, and tactile sensations. In the stable syndrome of hysteria (Briquet's syndrome) a patient has a history of psychogenic pain or conversion symptoms, dysphoric mood, sexual dysfunction, and surgical procedures (Guze 1975). Dissociative reactions include fugue states, some temporary psychoses, and so-called mass hysterias. Hysterical or histrionic personality and multiple personality disorder evidently belong to this family of clinical phenomena. Counterparts of these syndromes in traditional societies may include spirit intrusion and malevolent spirit possession. In spirit intrusion, a spirit enters the body causing physical symptoms. In possession, a spirit enters a person's mind and replaces some or all of a person's voice. In western terms, spirit intrusion resembles conversion disorder, whereas possession is more akin to fugue states, multiple personality disorder, or temporary psychosis.

The word "hysteria" derives from thinking in ancient Greece that linked ailments in women with uterine disorders. It thus carries the erroneous implication that hysteria occurs only among women. The adjective "hysterical" is often misused in everyday language to describe any sort of behavior that seems too emotional. It thus has off-putting connotations that add little if anything to genuine understanding. The notion of hysteria also lumps together a number of clearly distinguishable conditions. The earlier literature on hysteria often implies that hysterical personality, Briquet's syndrome, and conversion disorder are the same phenomenon. While they can occur together, it is now clear that they often occur as distinct syndromes.

To avoid these difficulties, the *Diagnostic and statistical manual of mental disorders (third edition, revised)* (*DSM-III-R*) and its successor, *DSM-IV*, discard "hysteria" and replace it with various somatoform and dissociative disorders. In cross-cultural psychiatry and anthropology, what used to be called hysteria is often discussed under the heading of "culture-bound syndromes," that is, disorders that are presumably unique to local cultural traditions.

These strategies direct attention toward the distinctive features of particular syndromes and avoid the gender bias and critical connotations associated with the word "hysteria." Unfortunately, they also divert attention from the common features of these disorders. Since I prefer to emphasize these common features, I use the word "hysteria" as a rubric for various conditions, with the caveats that hysteria can and does occur among men and that it is not necessarily morally reprehensible.

Hysterical disorders have both emotional and social role-playing components. Disorder may originate in emotional trauma, but it also fulfills cultural expectations, and it can be seen as veiled communication. Later in this chapter, I explore how emotion, role-playing, and communication fit together. First, however, let us consider some examples.

Spirit possession and multiple personality

Borderline personality, multiple personality disorder, and other dissociative disorders may be the counterparts in developed countries of malevolent spirit possession in traditional societies. Larry G. Peters (1988) describes Betsy, a 30-year-old California woman who had been diagnosed as a borderline personality. She had a history of severe anxiety, suicide attempts, and transient states in which she hallucinated spiders and frightening beings who were "tearing at her flesh." Her frequent acts of self-mutilation followed sensations of internal pressure caused by a "witch" who took control of her and filled her with "pus, worms, and maggots." Betsy's father had been verbally and sexually abusive. Her mother had remained aloof. Betsy often felt depressed, empty, and abandoned by her mother. She hated her mother for not protecting her and called her a "witch." Self-mutilation may have distracted Betsy from her pain. Peters notes that the borderline disorder shares several features with other dissociative disorders and suggests that transient psychotic states in the borderline personality and in negative spirit possession are variants of hysterical psychosis.

In India the victims of spirit possession are usually culturally conservative women in lower socioeconomic strata. An example is Daya, a fifteen-year-old bride and a member of the leather-working caste in the village of Shanti Nagar described by Stanley A. Freed and Ruth S. Freed (1964). During states of possession, Daya lost consciousness and her voice was taken over by a ghost. She also complained of pains and feeling hot and tired. Her first possession began a few days after she arrived at her husband's home to stay (village exogamy is the norm in rural India). Like other brides, she had sexual intercourse for the first time during her second visit. The marriage was stressful. Since her husband's family was less well off, it probably represented a loss of status for Daya, and she said she felt lonely in her husband's village and feared sexual intercourse. She recounted the sexual exploits of two dead friends. Chand Kor, one of these friends, had been driven to suicide by her father after she became pregnant. In Shanti Nagar, unmarried adolescents who become pregnant or brides who refuse to have sexual intercourse with their husbands are either forced to commit suicide or are murdered by their fathers. A second friend had sexual relations with a teacher; according to Daya, her father raped the young woman, slit her throat, and dumped her into a well. It was Chand Kor's spirit that possessed Daya.

In *Medusa's hair*, a study of a Hindu–Buddhist cult in Sri Lanka, Gananath Obeyesekere (1981) discussed spirit attacks or spirit possession in several individuals with histories of traumatic loss and emotional deprivation. The case of Pemavati Vitarana (age 45) illustrates themes that appear in other cases Obeyesekere discusses.

Pemavati's father deserted his family when she was a young child. Her stepfather abused her, and her mother was preoccupied with five other children. Her uncle looked after her, and she was closely attached to him. Fainting spells in early adolescence were interpreted as erotic attacks by the god Kalu Kumara. Her parents disowned her when she married, and her marriage was unhappy. She also felt guilty about her uncle's death, perhaps because she left his house in anger at fourteen after fighting with his eldest daughter. Some months after giving birth to her last child, Pemavati was possessed by the uncle's spirit and, as a result, suffered from fainting attacks and developed a "revulsion for food" (Obeyesekere 1981: 60). Her dreams expressed a wish to be closer to the gods. In one dream, the god Huniyan, wearing a garland of fire and carrying a sword, jumped on her. He wore "transparent cloth" and "cobras around his waist." "'He came to scare me. He threw one of the snakes from his waist at me; it fell near me. But I smiled and felt a great pleasure. It was such a beautiful snake'" (ibid.: 57). In these and other cases in *Medusa's hair* guilt is experienced as spirit intrusion or possession. Possession seems to recreate a lost relationship. When the attack is by "the Dark Prince," the erotic connotations of the spiritual relationship may compensate for a bad marriage while alluding to a lost object of childhood.

Grace G. Harris (1957) noticed a role-playing element in spirit possession among the Taita of Kenya. At the time of her study, the Taita were a herding people who were turning increasingly to cash-cropping and wage labor. Many Taita women experienced *saka* (spirit possession) following a period of restlessness and anxiety. The sight of motor cars, cigarettes, bright cloth, bananas, and other objects with masculine connotations triggered the convulsive states. If the objects were not directly connected with men, they were at least associated with the outside world to which men had privileged access. The Taita treated *saka* with a ritual dance in which the patient and other women wore special dresses fashioned from exotic and masculine elements. Harris noted that *saka* had social meanings, and that many affected women were probably simulating possession. Men competed for power and prestige in kinship, economy, politics, and ritual action and knowledge, whereas women participated in the public world mainly as consumers of manufactured goods. *Saka* voiced women's desires for consumer goods and male support, and since it resembled, and perhaps emulated, the shrine complex of the males, it may also have expressed women's wishes for power and freedom commensurate to those of their menfolk.

Erika Bourguignon (1989) compares the case of Ms. G., a black woman in New York, and Joao, a mulatto man in Sao Paulo, Brazil. Ms. G. had an alter personality named Candy. Joao was possessed by a female spirit named Margarida. Ms. G. sought psychotherapy after experiencing the difficulties caused by Candy. Joao participated in an Umbandista cult, which takes an accepting attitude toward possession. Candy was regarded as a pathological instance of dissociation by Ms. G.'s therapist. In contrast, the Umbandistas believed that Joao's possession was a sign that he needed to talk with helpful spirits. Similar personality structures, as Bourguignon illustrates with these examples, may be subject to different cultural construction and interpretation; although syndromes in different cultures may involve similar histories of abuse and a similar use of dissociation or splitting as a defense, the way in which they are culturally constructed and understood may be quite different.

Psychiatric reports in India also suggest that multiple personality disorder is an artifact of modern society. Reports of spirit possession are common, but documented cases of multiple personality, although perhaps on the rise, are still rare. In several such cases a secondary personality emerged following family disapproval of a romantic relationship. In all three cases, the secondary personalities mentioned they lived with or wanted to be with their "mothers." Two of them identified strongly with western values (Adityanjee et al. 1989).

Latah

In *latah* the afflicted person reacts to a loud noise, tickling, a word, or a command with a startle, obscene words, and mimicry. Sometimes the person becomes submissive and compliant, even when told to do something embarrassing or dangerous to the self. The condition is well known in Malaysia and Indonesia, but similar maladies occur in Siberia, North Africa, and among the Ainu of Japan (Winzeler 1984).

In Southeast Asia the obscene words are sexual. The person with *latah* blurts out obscene language or interpolates it into otherwise ordinary sentences. The immediate provocation may be a loud noise, a prod to the ribs, or a sudden movement. Some reports suggest that sexual dreams trigger *latah*. In Sarawak, people attribute *latah* to bereavement, to giving birth, and to disturbing dreams. About one-third of the *latahs* remember having dreams with sexual content before their episodes (Chiu, Tong, and Schmidt 1972).

David Aberle (1952) theorized that *latah* is an ambivalent reaction to a threat of being overwhelmed by a sexual attack. Tickling has erotic connotations. Impulsive swearing, then, may be an attempt to repel the attacker and, perhaps, an expression of repressed desire. Hildred Geertz (1968) found support for this hypothesis in Java where *latah* usually affects older women, often in working-class, urban settings. Geertz observed that the Javanese are sensitive to social slights and minor differences in status, and so they place great emphasis on etiquette and deference. They are also modest and circumspect about sexuality. *Latah*, which inverts these values, may be a reaction to social subordination. *Latah* often occurs in the presence of social superiors. Women, however, are not especially subordinate to males in Javanese culture. Geertz (ibid.: 103) suggested that "their very freedom accentuates an ambivalent desire for and fear of submission."[1]

Arctic hysterias

Frenzied dissociated states occur in both Siberia and the Arctic. Loss of appetite and withdrawal give way after a few days to boasting, violence, disrobing, or erotic language. Among the Polar Inuit, these reactions, called *piblokto*, begin with running and end with seizures and collapse. The disorder occurs in both sexes but is more common in females.

Brill (1913) interpreted *piblokto* as hysteria and traced it to lack of love. Gussow (1960) suggested that economic and environmental stress may trigger *piblokto*. Attacks occur more often in the winter when accidents and hunger are more likely. Death and disappearances of hunters are doubly disturbing for women since they threaten starvation and loss of love. *Piblokto*, then, may dramatize needs for support and love while expressing denial of helplessness and danger. Edward F. Foulks (1972) attributed *piblokto* to Inuit society and culture, especially to the child-rearing practices. Children are indulged and pampered. They are expected to obey adults; shaming and ridicule are common techniques of control in the family and in society. The resulting personality may have trouble dealing with frustration in situations in which others are not exerting a controlling influence. *Piblokto* and shamanic soul trips may be ways of acting out frustration and avoiding social control. In a study of ten individuals with histories of *piblokto*, Foulks found traditional parental control, traumatic losses, and shaming by peers. Freeman, Foulks, and Freeman (1978) suggested that dependency, separation anxiety, and lack of individuation predispose males to *piblokto*. Attacks may follow separations from mothers or wives, the deaths of mothers or wives, or failures to meet women's idealized expectations of men.

The couvade

"Couvade" (from the French *couver*, to hatch) describes bodily symptoms men have during their wives' pregnancies and birthings. It also refers to cultural restrictions on male work activity, eating, or sex during the birth cycle and the customary patterns of men taking to their beds during and after the birth of a child.

Many men have physical symptoms during their wives' pregnancies. Some may be reacting with separation anxiety. They may be feeling rejected by and angry with their wives during the prenatal period, perhaps because they were anxiously attached to their own mothers. Birth may trigger separation anxiety in various ways. The mother or neonate may die or the child may be born defective. Or childbirth may arouse worries about the wife's faithfulness and, in any event, it confronts the father with a rival for the wife's attentions. Some husbands seem to identify with their wives out of sympathy for their suffering (Curtis 1955; Trethowan 1968; Trethowan and Conlon 1965).

Reik (1931), noting that sexual abstinence is common in the later stages of pregnancy, suggested that the couvade may be a defense against hostility toward the wife and that the infant may remind the father of childhood rivalry with his own father. Many societies require sexual abstinence during pregnancy and the postpartum period. In Tlayacapan, Mexico, a community where such rules are traditional, some first-time expectant fathers experience body pains and fatigue during their wives' pregnancies. One treatment is for the wife to make a bracelet, necklace, or belt for the husband with material from the hemline of her dress. The remedy seems to effect a symbolic compensation for the loss of sexual intimacy with the wife: what is around the mother and fetus is put around the husband (Ingham 1986).

Couvade symptoms also have been interpreted as envy of female reproductive capacities. Roger V. Burton and John W.M. Whiting (1961) found a cross-cultural correlation between the couvade and exclusive mother–infant sleeping arrangements and matrilocal residence. They suggested that the mother–infant sleeping arrangements encourage cross-sex identification in boys and that matrilocal residence further diminishes the presence of male role models. In these circumstances the couvade expresses feminine gender identity in men. Among the Garifuna (Black Caribs) of Belize men are often migratory laborers and family and culture are mother-centered. Many men report having pregnancy symptoms, and many of these same men observe couvade restrictions during the birth cycle. Absence of adult males from the home in the first three years of life and several measures of feminine identification are significantly correlated with couvade observances in adult males (Munroe et al. 1973). Mexican-American men in Texas who report having pregnancy symptoms tend to be more effeminate than other men and often prefer being with their wives and families to joining men in the cantinas (Rubel and Spielberg 1966).

Other writers question the cross-sex identification theory of the couvade. Broude (1988) contends that exclusive mother–child sleeping arrangements do not entail actual father absence in couvade-practicing societies. Janet M. Chernela (1991) doubts that the couvade represents male imitation of maternity among the Garifuna. The father may seem to imitate a recovering mother after birth but his real aim may be one of asserting identification with the child. The mother's brother becomes the provider during the ritual period. The mother's group as a whole provides nourishment to the childlike father. Chernela concludes that the "couvade is an elaborate symbolic battleground on which people struggle over contradictory relationships and the rights to reproduction" (1991: 63).

Couvade rituals have social meanings and functions. Bachofen (1861) explained the couvade as an attempt to assert paternity during historical transitions from matriarchy to patriarchy. In support of this hypothesis, Tylor (1889) found that the couvade occurs more often in societies with both patrilocal and matrilocal residence. Karen Ericksen Paige and Jeffery M. Paige (1981) interpreted reproductive rituals (e.g., puberty rites, menstrual avoidances, birth practices) as efforts to maintain or enhance power. They saw the couvade as an assertion of paternal authority and rights in cultures where men lack the support of fraternal interest groups, that is, groups of genealogically related, co-resident males. They found that fraternal interest groups usually occur in societies with patrilocal and avunculocal residence, valued property, patrilineality, and bridewealth. The couvade and fraternal interest group strength are negatively correlated (-0.48). The implication may be that men who have the support of an agnatic group do not need the couvade.

Rancour-Laferriere (1985) theorizes that the birth of a baby may have phallic associations for women and associations with castration for men: the sight of the bloody neonate emerging from the vagina suggests a severed penis; in Indonesia and Malayasia there is "a widespread belief that the spirit of a female who has died in childbirth returns to castrate males" (ibid.: 365). Yet Rancour-Laferriere also theorizes that the couvade implies that identification with the wife plays a role in paternal inclinations. In couvade cultures, he suggests, castration anxiety is a minor theme, envy of or identification with the mother is the major theme. In his view, fraternal interest groups and the couvade tend to have a complementary distribution because fraternal interest groups are alternative expressions of men's identification with the mother, that is, they represent a symbolic appropriation of the reproductive powers of women.

Rancour-Laferriere suggests that castration anxiety and paternal inclination, modeled on biological motherhood, represent negative and positive sides of the same coin. The argument may complement the notion that reproductive ritual is part of political rhetoric. Social concerns about becoming a father and its political implications may reverberate with personal anxieties about the body and separation. The Bimin-Kuskusmin have patrilineal clans and cognatic kindreds. Thus, paternal and maternal relatives may compete for the child's attention. Firstborn sons can start lineages and develop paternal rights by having children of their own. Significantly, the men with more history of couvade symptoms are often firstborn sons without children or firstborn sons who have lost wives in childbirth or newborns through miscarriages. That is, the couvade affects men who are experiencing anxieties about separation, loss, and living up to social expectations (Poole 1982a).

Koro

In *koro*, a condition that occurs in South China and among Chinese in Southeast Asia and, occasionally, other peoples in Southeast Asia, the penis is thought to retract into the body. The retraction, whether real or imagined, is very anxiety-provoking because people believe that it can cause death. To prevent penile shrinkage, a person having a *koro* attack may grab the penis with his hand or attach a penile clamp, a jeweler's clamp, or loop of string; or the wife, mother, grandmother, or a friend may hold the penis. Anxieties about virility, nocturnal emissions, masturbation, and sexual self-indulgence may be predisposing conditions (Edwards 1985; Gwee 1985; Lehmann 1985; Rubin 1982).

Hysterical psychoses

Transient psychotic states with impulsive behavior occur in many cultures. Typically, the person behaves strangely and experiences delusions and hallucinations following a period of acute stress. Later the person may have no memory of the episode. These "brief reactive psychoses," as they are now called, were once termed "hysterical psychoses" (Langness 1967).

A violent form of this condition known as *amok* occurs in Malaysia (see Chapter 8). The *pengamok*, or killer, explodes in a murderous spree using a knife or sword following a period of sulking and withdrawal. If he is not killed himself – the killers are almost always males – he then lapses into a stuporous state in which he cannot remember the destructive behavior. The victims are usually kin, affines, or neighbors (Yap 1951, 1969).

Reactive psychosis with mock aggression also occurs in some cultures. Philip L. Newman (1964) described the agitated, "wild man" behavior of a young man of the Gururumba tribe of the New Guinea Highlands. L.L. Langness (1965) reported a similar hysterical psychosis syndrome for the Bena Bena. Some young men suddenly act aggressively toward clansmen, wives, or their children. During these episodes, which last about twenty-four hours, they cannot hear and later they cannot remember what happened. Young adulthood is a stressful period for Bena Bena males.

Mass hysteria

Conversion hysteria and anxiety can be contagious. Such instances of infectious conversion disorder and panic resemble crazes, passionate political and religious activity, and shared delusions. While these phenomena may involve dissociated thinking also, clarity is served by restricting "mass hysteria" for contagious collective anxiety and conversion disorders. Examples include "biting nuns," fainting school children, gassed factory workers, and attacks by anaesthetizing prowlers (Wessely 1987). In one instance, a class of eight adolescent females experienced falling attacks in association with preoccupations with love, death, and sexuality. The young women sensed a conflict between God and Devil and were struggling with guilt over sexuality (a classmate had died in childbirth and two others were feeling anxious about their sexual experiences) (Benaim et al. 1973).

Contagious anxiety hysterias seem to occur mainly among school children and are often self-propagating. Mass motor hysterias (e.g., shared paralyses), in contrast, occur in many different types of social groups and historical situations, often in association with social and economic stress. Mass hysterias in Malaysia have been attributed to loss of faith in local authorities and to stresses of modernization (Wessely 1987). During a period of public concern about estrogenic hormones in chickens, a mass *koro* episode occurred in Singapore in 1967 when a newspaper reported that a pig had expired from *koro* after being treated for swine-fever (Rubin 1982). Aihwa Ong (1987) interprets shared hysterical reactions among women factory workers in Malaysia as resistance to male power in high-tech urban factories. Subjected to stressful pressures to increase production, the women resist by working more slowly, crying, requesting time for prayers, going to the locker room, and absenteeism. Spirit possession may be a variation on these tactics; the spirits often seize the women in prayer rooms and locker rooms, the very places where the women seek relief from the pressures of the factory floor. The offending spirits are said to include were-tigers and aboriginal earth and grave spirits disturbed by factory construction.

Mass anxiety and motor hysterias presumably involve identification with the first victim. Common fears, anxieties, and fantasies may also play a part (Sirois 1982). Some studies find among participants in shared hysterical reactions more neuroticism or anxiety (McEvedy et al. 1966; Moss and McEvedy 1966; Tam et al. 1982), hysterical personality traits (Colligan and Murphy 1979; Knight et al. 1965), or paranoia (Goldberg 1973). One study of mass hysteria among children found significantly more histories of parental divorce and loss in the most severely affected children (Small and Nicholi 1982).

Other studies, however, reveal little or no psychological disposition (Olczak et al. 1971; Small and Borus 1983). Robert E. Bartholomew (1990) even opines that "mass hysteria" is a pejorative construction of objectivist western psychiatry. In his view, it pathologizes diverse expressions of "collective exaggerated emotions." He prefers to interpret instances of "mass hysteria" in terms of local cultural meanings and contexts.

Theoretical perspectives

Psychiatric and philosophical interest in hysteria and dissociative states was strong throughout the nineteenth century and this is reflected in the many cases of split or multiple personality that were described. In 1859 Paul

Briquet published the results of his investigations of 430 patients with hysterical symptoms. Various investigators commented on the similarities among hysteria or somnabulism, catalepsy, hysteria, and multiple personality, and they observed that hypnosis could be used to induce catalepsy and ecstatic states and to relieve conversion disorders. These investigations produced notions of unconscious mental process and motivation, a recognition of sexual motivation in human psychology, and two- and three-part models of the structure of the human mind (Ellenberger 1970). There was, moreover, speculation that hysteria exemplified a trend toward social dissolution in modern society (MacMillan 1991:44).

At the end of the nineteenth century, theorizing about hysteria ranged from the psychobiological to the psychological. Jean-Martin Charcot tried to account for the underlying structure of hysteria and hypnosis in terms of a common physiology; in his view, hypnosis progressed through stages – from lethargy, to catalepsy, to artificial somnambulism – in ways that seemed to imply biological foundations. Hippolyte Bernheim, in contrast, contended that hysteria was a consequence of suggestion, not physiology. Pierre Janet, Charcot's student, concluded that hysteria reflected a lesion or constitutional weakness in cerebration. Moving away from Charcot's position, however, he recognized that Charcot's stages had been artificially produced by hypnotic suggestion, and he theorized that mental representations of experienced events could break off from the main stream of conscious process and form subconscious structures. He also theorized that emotional trauma could be the impetus for the formation of such subconscious structures. Secondary, subconscious personalities, according to Janet, might form by giving a name to a cluster of thoughts and associations.[2]

Breuer and Freud ([1893–1895]1955) took account of these ideas and observations but focused on two prominent features of the disorder: emotional trauma and psychic defense. In Breuer and Freud's joint publication on hysteria, Breuer theorized that hysterical dissociation results from "hypnoid" states occurring during traumatic experiences. Freud proposed that the splitting of the mind can be a defensive maneuver, and he later rejected the hypnoid state hypothesis. He also rejected Janet's idea that the mind could have two or more separate loci of consciousness. The paradoxical notion of an unconscious consciousness made no sense to Freud. In his view, consciousness was a quality that alternated between two or more personality structures (Freud [1912]1958). Any mental impairment in the hysterical personality, according to Freud, was more likely a result than a cause of the condition.

In recent years there has been a resurgence of dissociationist thinking among mental health professionals and an explosive increase in the number of reported cases of multiple personality disorder (MPD), particularly in the United States. Therapists who are treating MPD patients find histories of physical and sexual abuse in as many as 90 percent, and as many as 20 percent of MPD patients are said to be victims of Satanic abuse.

Many therapists who work with MPD patients are critical of psychoanalysis. They claim that psychoanalysis emphasizes unconscious fantasy at the expense of serious attention to actual events. Richard J. Castillo (1994a, 1994b) views spirit possession in South Asia as a local version of trauma-induced multiple personality disorder. There is no need, according to Castillo, to postulate unconscious desires or guilt.

Developmental and social trauma

A history of emotional trauma is a recurrent theme in the literature on hysteria and dissociative disorders. Some researchers now view these disorders as forms of post-traumatic stress syndrome, and many think that actual physical and sexual abuse often play a role in their etiology. Trauma, however, does not always result in dissociative disorder. It seems likely, therefore, that the child's interpretation of objective events shapes their consequences for later mental functioning.

Breuer and Freud traced hysterical symptoms to traumatic sexual experiences in childhood and adolescence. Freud observed that sex in young women can be anxiety producing. In his study of Katherina he found that anxiety over sexuality might produce a hypnoid state. In another publication he discussed eighteen cases of hysteria involving sexual abuse by other children or adult strangers, caretakers, or teachers (Freud [1896]1962).

Eventually, Freud concluded that the child's imagination and social experiences influence the meaning and memory of traumatic events. One source of anxiety in hysteria, then, was sexual trauma that had taken on oedipal nuances. The actual hysterical symptoms, according to Freud ([1908b]1959), represent the influence of unconscious fantasies or daydreams; the hysterical symptoms and attacks may recreate traumatic experiences, express sexual wishes, and effect compromises between tendencies toward suppression and expression of wishes. "Hysterical attacks" are "pantomimic" representations of underlying phantasies which remain disguised through mechanisms of distortion like those in the dreamwork. The hysterical attack, more precisely, mimes the body in sexual coitus in motoric and physiological detail (Freud [1909]1959).[3]

In keeping with this line of thought, psychoanalysts have noted that sexuality is often inhibited or disturbed in persons with hysteria (Fenichel 1945: 231–232). Similarly, Ernst Kretschmer (1960: 21, 28–29) traced hysteria to "disappointments in love," "erotic conflicts," and "mortal danger" and H.J. Eysenck (1982) interpreted hysteria as expressing approach–avoidance conflicts, particularly about sexuality; hysterics in his study had increased sexual activity and interest but also more guilt and unhappiness about sex and more hostility toward sexual partners.

Some ethnographic examples fit these formulations and observations. *Latah* may be a reaction to unwanted sexual advances or abuse by a socially superior male. The marriage of Daya, the young Indian bride, was a step down in social status, and sex implied threats to her self-preservation and, possibly, unconscious oedipal meanings. The replacement of spirit possession or intrusion with an ecstatic relation with the Dark Prince in the Kataragama cult also implies that symptoms can represent frustrated or dangerous desires. Goodwin, Simms, and Bergman (1979) reported six cases of "hysterical seizures" from the American Southwest in which incest was a factor. In all six cases (four Anglos, one Mexican-American, and one Navaho) psychotherapeutic exploration of the memories of incest relieved the symptoms. The investigators observed the similarity between orgasm and seizures and suggested that the seizures may represent an attempt at gaining mastery over the trauma. They noted, too, that Galen as well as the Navaho attribute epilepsy to incest.[4]

Disturbed preoedipal object relations may lie behind oedipal fantasies or sexual abuse in some cases of hysteria. Melitta Sperling (1973) observed that expressed concerns with attachment to and separation from the analyst are recurrent features of transference in the psychoanalyses of hysterical patients. These concerns may have childhood origins. Caregivers of future hysterical persons may reinforce dependency in their children while denying them opportunities for self-expression and self-assertion. They may also give their children special attention when they are sick, thus encouraging the illness role as a way of maintaining attachment. Some parents of future hysterics may be indulgent and seductive but also controlling (Krohn 1978: 132–138). The exaggeration of male and female gender roles in hysterical personality suggests that insecure gender identity may be another ingredient in some instances of hysteria. Couvade symptoms, for example, may reflect both anxieties about object loss and insecure gender identity.

Stressful experiences in adolescence or adulthood may trigger hysterical symptoms by rekindling preoedipal and oedipal anxieties or memories of traumatic sexual abuse. Loss and separation anxiety are often antecedents to hysteria (Krohn 1978: 138–144). Schiffer (1962) described a woman in whom a succession of symptoms throughout her body represented her attempts to control loved ones; by identifying her husband and children with parts of her body, she seemed to compensate for the early deaths of her mother and other relatives. Losses may play roles in *amok*, couvade, and *piblokto*. Proskauer (1980: 44) noted that dissociative reactions and hysterias among the Navaho often accompany bereavement.

Anger and resentment about social subordination figure in the etiology of some hysterical conditions. I.M. Lewis (1971) argued that anger and resentment about male privilege and power are common motives in female spirit intrusion and possession in many cultures. The *saka* complex lends itself to this interpretation, but so, too, do many other examples. Hysterical psychosis may originate in grieving over real or imagined loss of social status. Mass hysterical conversion may reflect anxieties about powerlessness and vulnerability to abuse and exploitation. Social subordination may be experienced as an injury to self-esteem, but it can also carry the risk, especially for women and children, of sexual abuse. The more powerful person may use a position of power to act out impulses or fantasies.

These considerations suggest that hysteria may be more prevalent in highly stratified societies with strict sexual mores. Where these societies are patriarchal and where sexual repression falls more heavily on women than men, which is often the case, then hysteria may be more common among women than men. Historical data and cross-cultural data seem to confirm these expectations. In European countries values were more patriarchal and more restrictive regarding female sexuality in the nineteenth century, whereas they became more egalitarian and more liberal in the twentieth century; accordingly, the prevalence of hysteria seems to have declined. Meanwhile, the incidence of hysteria remains higher in developing countries (Leff 1981), many of which continue to have patriarchal value systems, prudish sexual mores, and double standards for male and female sexual behavior.

D. Wilfred Abse (1950) compared the ratios of anxiety states to hysteria in a British military hospital and Indian military hospital during World War II. The ratio was 12 percent versus 57 percent in the Indian hospital and 50 percent versus 24 percent in the British hospital. A comparison of British and Indian soldiers in Burma produced similar statistics (Williams 1950).

These same considerations suggest that hysteria is more common in traditional agrarian societies than among simple societies. In a study of 488 societies, Bourguignon (1973, 1976, 1979) found that spirits are thought to affect people in most societies. She divided her sample into societies that recognize spirit possession and spirit intrusion, on the one hand, and those that only recognize spirit intrusion, on the other. Possession and spirit intrusion are strongly associated with social complexity, whereas spirit intrusion alone is more characteristic of simple societies. Bourguignon also suggested that these differences may reflect the effects of child-rearing practices in the more complex societies. Simple societies are more likely to socialize children for independence and achievement motivation whereas the more complex societies usually encourage dependency and obedience (Barry et al. 1959).

Differences between simple and complex societies with respect to possession may also reflect differences in marital relationships and the quality of
sexual experience. Many complex societies have separate sleeping arrangements for husbands and wives (Whiting and Whiting 1975). Also, many are
patriarchal and hold women to stricter standards of sexual conduct than
men. Women in such societies may fear that complaints about lack of intimacy or sexual frustration may elicit censure or abuse. These same conditions may increase the likelihood of child abuse. Although little is known
about the prevalence of physical and sexual abuse in traditional societies,
the evidence that incest is associated with male dominance and patriarchal
values in developed societies suggests that incest occurs with some frequency in traditional societies (deMause 1991).

Suggestion and role-playing

Descriptions of hysterical patients in western societies frequently read like
caricatures of traditional femininity (Chodoff and Lyons 1958), and
women are far more likely than men to receive a diagnosis of Briquet's syndrome or hysteria proper. Szasz (1961) interpreted conversion symptoms as
role-playing in which the hysterical person mimics a physical ailment to
assert or reassert control in relationships. Michael G. Kenny (1983) viewed
latah as a social role. Harris (1957) noted that some Taita women seem to
fake saka convulsions. Reports of multiple personality disorder are on the
increase in the United States, and they may become more common in India
and other developing countries with modernization. Adityanjee, Raju, and
Khandelwal (1989) suggest that traditional religion supports beliefs in
spirit possession in Asian countries, whereas the acceptability of social
role-playing in modern societies is conducive to multiple personality disorder. Possession may have a role-playing aspect also, but the multiplicity
of social roles and the disjointed, pastichelike quality of postmodern
culture in advanced capitalist societies may be conducive in some sense to
a multiple splitting of the self.

It may also be that multiple personality disorder is promoted by suggestion in the course of psychotherapy. The prevalence of the disorder seems
to wax and wane with theoretical fashion in clinical psychiatry. Early
psychoanalysts were critical of dissociationism. They preferred to
conceptualize their patients' problems in terms of repression and defense,
and they suspected that multiple personalities might be an artifact of
hypnosis and suggestion. Accordingly, the apparent prevalence of MPD
declined as psychoanalysis gained influence in medical circles. Recently,
MPD diagnoses have come back into fashion as psychoanalysis has become
less affordable and influential within the mental-health care delivery

system. It has been pointed out that patients with MPD diagnoses are easily hypnotized and may be highly suggestible. It has also been argued that some recovered memories of parental abuse and many memories of Satanic abuse are improbable (Lotto 1994).

Kenny (1986) suggests that MPD patients and their therapists are involved in a process of social construction that amplifies the perception of MPD and, through hypnosis, may transform garden variety psychic fragmentation into virtual realizations of MPD. That is, MPD may be an *iatrogenic* condition. He suggests that a western inclination to split the self into good and bad parts may be a facilitating condition, along with the problematic nature of identity formation in modern society. Kenny discusses several cases of nineteenth-century multiple personality disorder. In these early reports, in his view, a split between two roles or personalities reflected dualism in traditional western religious thinking, whereas an increasing prevalence of persons with ten or more personalities in the late twentieth century may reflect increasing interest among mental health professionals and the lay public in multiple personality. Thus he argues that "the form mental disorder takes is influenced by the acquisition of a culturally specific idiom of distress in collusion with local circumstances" (ibid.: 163).

We know that personality is inherently fragmentary, and that the parts that make up whole selves are less integrated in some personalities than in others. We know, too, that more severe forms of fragmentation are often sequelae of emotional trauma, and that a disposition toward psychic fragmentation is associated with willingness and ability to play roles. There is in fact a great deal of physical and sexual abuse of children in the United States and even more emotional abuse and neglect. Given these observations, it is not difficult to imagine how multiple personality disorders might be created or elaborated in therapy when therapists are expecting to find them.

Given this possibility that MPD is an iatrogenic disorder peculiar to the west, Castillo's criticism of psychoanalysis and his use of the dissociationist perspective of MPD for understanding spirit possession in South Asia seems risky, if not naïve. Trauma can promote dissociation or repression, but it is unlikely that the memories of trauma recovered through hypnosis are always accurate. They may be retranscriptions of trauma or defensive screens (e.g., patients may find it less painful to suppose that their parents abused them sexually because of cult membership than emotionally on their own volition). It is also naïve to think that trauma automatically leads to identity disorders. Suggestion and cultural expectations play a role in shaping psychic responses to trauma. Therapists may create multiple personality disorder by labeling self-fragments. In the person who is prone to dissociation this labeling process may be facilitated also by the spread of reported cases of MPD in the media. Mimesis or identification with the other is part of the *modus operandi* of the person who tends toward self-monitoring and dissociation. Castillo's critique of psychoanalysis also ignores current trends in psychoanalysis. Psychoanalysts have incorporated "dissociation" into their vocabulary, and they are concerned with the psychological effects of traumatic experiences. Psychoanalysts regard dissociation as a defense, however (Marmer 1991; Paley 1988).

Psychology and role-playing: a synthesis

Fright is evidently part of hysteria. Kretschmer (1960) observed that hysteria resembles escape behavior in animals. Agitated hysteria recalls the disorganized flight of frightened animals while dissociated states resemble sham-death or animal hypnosis. Hysterical reflexes, anesthesias, and hypnoid denial, according to Kretschmer, are perpetuated in human beings through semiconscious attention to affective stimuli or intentional muscle tonus. Later, they become "objectified" and, like "bad habits," elude conscious control.

Kretschmer contrasted a "purposive will" with a "hypobulic will," a "double" of the former. "Purposive will" entails future orientation and goal-seeking, whereas "hypobulic will" is impulsive and bound to the present. The second displaces the first in hysterical reactions, whereas the two wills act in concert in ordinary persons. In the hysterical person the hypobulic will is stronger than the purposive will. Kretschmer's formulation recalls Freud's analysis of the woman who could not nurse. Her conscious will to nurse her babies was undermined by an unconscious unwillingness to nurse (see Chapter 1).

Freud's idea was that depressive dispositions weaken the conscious will in hysteria and in neurosis generally ([1892–1893]1966: 121). Ordinarily, the will suppresses antithetical ideas that may be associated with intentions and expectations, but in hysteria antithetical ideas are dissociated from consciousness and take on a life of their own in the unconscious. In fact, there are peculiarities in the cognitive functioning of hysterical personalities, including deficits in attention and memory and tendencies toward global thinking (Shapiro 1965; Abse 1966). Somatization is frequent in depression, and hysterical persons are prone to depression (Klerman 1982). Suggestibility is common in both histrionic and dysphoric personalities (Eysenck 1982). Psychometric studies suggest that dysfunction in the dominant hemisphere of the cerebral cortex may account for imprecise communication, inappropriate emotion, and a tendency for conversion symptoms to appear on the left side of the body in persons with the stable syndrome of hysteria or Briquet's syndrome (Flor-Henry et al. 1981).[5]

I noted earlier that Breuer and Freud differed about the basic mechanism in the production of hysteria. Breuer thought that hysterical formations originate in hypnoid states. Such states, he observed, could occur through hypnosis or self-hypnosis or because of "emotional shock." The vacuous mental state created by hypnosis, according to Breuer, separates irrational associations from critical evaluation and thus allows their subsequent elaboration. Hypnoid states are the starting point for the splitting of consciousness in conversion disorder and dual personalities. Freud, in contrast, concluded that hysterical symptoms reflect the operation of defensive maneuvers, especially repression.

A synthesis of these ideas may be possible. From a phylogenetic perspective, the hypnoid condition is itself defensive; it is a manifestation of mammalian capacity for freezing, catelepsy, and dissociated withdrawal. In other words, autohypnosis and repression may be different words for a common process. Freud ([1916–1917]1963: 103) suggested that post-hypnotic suggestion demonstrates the existence of a dynamic unconscious. In another connection, Freud may have hinted that freezing, and thus a biological capacity for hypnosis, was the phylogenetic precondition for repression in human beings. Marmer (1991) has noted that the patient with multiple personality disorder seems to have a habitual tendency to repeat terrifying experiences and to respond to them with quiescent dissociation. Simultaneously, the subordinate personality may be aggressive, perhaps with the aim of acting as a guardian. This cluster of aggressiveness, repetition, and passivity reminds Marmer of Freud's death instinct, a label Freud gave to a nexus of aggression, a compulsion to repeat, and self-destructive behavior. In multiple personality disorder the primary self seems to prefer the death of the self to remembering the original trauma. Gordon H. Bower (1990) discusses posthypnotic suggestion as a model for repression.

A link between animal hypnosis or sham-death and defensive repression suggests a phylogenetic basis to the link between trauma and role-playing in hysteria. Just as the animal "plays possum," there is a theatrical or role-playing aspect to hypnosis and hysteria.

Earlier I noted that an ability to fantasize, including an ability to simulate emotional experience, is a characteristic of the prefrontal cortex. Hypnosis and dreaming illustrate this capacity. The ability of an animal to freeze, when it is experiencing terror, may depend on this capacity for simulating feeling. Here, an "as-if" pleasant feeling may displace or override the actual, embodied feeling of fear.

As-if simulation may be a way of dealing with both actual trauma and memory of trauma. Autohypnosis allows as-if simulation of a pleasant feeling during trauma; repression facilitates this effect whenever memories of painful events threaten to surface with emotional force. In split or multiple personalities, the alternate self may be more aggressive or libidinous than the frightened self. In *latah* or the *hysteric deleria* of medieval nuns who used licentious language or blurted blasphemies, the subordinate will seems to take a counterphobic attitude toward what is frightening, i.e., eroticism, aggression, and, perhaps, powerful males.

In conversion disorders and Briquet's syndrome the subordinate will seems to imagine a bodily state. The imaginary image then may become a schema for the motoric production of a physical simulation of the bodily condition (e.g., an anesthetized leg). Lack of conscious awareness of the symptom (the famous *la belle indifférence* of hysterics) may then permit the symptom to consolidate (Ludwig 1972). The symptom may be a compromise formation, one that involves conscious pain and inconvenience and an unconscious counterphobic repetition of the traumatic circumstance or idea.

Suggestibility may be a consequence of depression or cortical dysfunction, especially dysfunction in the speech-producing areas of the cerebral cortex. Suggestibility may facilitate switching from one social role to another. Absorption in one's social role, for its part, may have hypnoid, dissociative qualities. It is well known that actors can become totally absorbed in their parts; similarly, the playing of a role in social life may involve dissociating the role from other aspects of oneself and social relationships. Hypnosis, according to Sarbin and Coe (1972), resembles role-playing; like role-playing, it engages a person's capacity for as-if thought and behavior. It is also interesting that hypnosis, like hysteria, may involve right hemisphere dominance and partial inhibition of the neocortex. Predominant left lateral eye movement, an indication of right-hemisphere dominance, is associated with hypnotizability (Bakan 1969). According to Ernest R. Hilgard (1986: 216–241), the psyche comprises many hierarchically arranged semi-autonomous cognitive systems. Ordinarily the executive ego controls subordinate systems. This control is relaxed during hypnosis, perhaps with corresponding diminution of cerebral activity and increase in subcortical emotionality (Gellhorn 1967: 61–65). Defensive repression, splitting, and dissociation, and a resulting disinhibition of an unconscious will can be understood in these terms as an extreme version of the connection between suggestibility and role-playing.

There is a representational, intentional quality about conversion symptoms. If their production involves a hypnoid process, as seems likely, then this is like saying that conversion involves regression from the symbolic to the semiotic. Freud was, with his increasing attention to the symbolism of conversion symptoms, moving closer to concerns with suggestion and culture, although he never really freed himself from an associationist theory of symptoms (e.g., a facial pain is a symptom because the person was experiencing a toothache at the time of the emotional trauma).

Monique David-Ménard pursues the linguistic approach further. For David-Ménard (1989), the physical symptoms of hysteria bespeak not a psychosomatic process but, rather, a registration of intense pleasure and disgust in a code of bodily position and movement. The erotogenic body becomes an hysterogenic body; pleasure is displaced from one area to another and converted into unpleasure. Abandoned sites of pleasure become anesthetic, as if, as David-Ménard (ibid.: 66) puts it, "[t]he hysteric has no body." Meanwhile, the hysteric behaves as if she wants to transform the site of the displacement into the whole body. Whereas the bodily is ordinarily a field of pleasure in symbolic discourse with others, it becomes in the person with hysteria an arena in which representation turns back into presentation; whereas symbolic representation is predicated on the acceptance of the absence of the object – the sign is not the referent – hysteric presentification mimics in bodily movement or sensation an early pleasure or object relation. In the process, the hysteric person foregoes a pleasurable body in actual social relations. "The failure in the symbolization of her desire, the prohibition of jouissance [sexual pleasure] that polarizes the history of her body, simultaneously eradicates the reality, even the perceptual reality, of that body" (David-Ménard 1989: 44–45). Since the signifier is never the thing represented in representation, there is always a lack, an absence which the person with hysterical disorder, unwilling or unable to accept, replaces with a plastic, figurative "presentification" within the body itself. This meaning in hysterical complaint becomes evident when attention turns to movement, and to the body's history of movement in relation to social others.

David-Ménard's formulation is congruent with the evidence for a weakening of activity in the dominant or linguistic hemisphere. The dysfunction may be functional or organic, but in either event the result is retreat to underlying motoric structures, to a replacement of discourse with pantomime. The partiality of conversion symptoms for the left side of the body, noted earlier, fits this picture of left- or language-hemisphere impairment and, possibly, right-hemisphere activation.

This regression from language to motoric communication also recalls the evolutionary architecture of the triune brain and its ontogenetic development: motoric communication comes before symbolic communication in both evolution and individual development. We are reminded here of Donald's thesis that mimetic culture preceded language-based culture in human evolution, of Piaget's contention that the child develops a sensorimotor intelligence before an abstract, symbolic intelligence, and of Johnson's (1987) thesis that abstract thought develops as metaphorical elaborations of bodily experience. The shift in register in hysteria from verbal to bodily communication, it seems, effects a sort of phylogenetic and ontogenetic regression or at least an elision of linguistic communication about certain emotionally loaded issues. By returning to a language of the body or by speaking with multiple voices, hysterics manage to say what they would be afraid to say otherwise. They replace verbal expression of genuine emotion (e.g., fear, fear of pleasure, desire for pleasure) with a motoric expression of fear or a bodily substitute for pleasure or attachment.

This problematic nature of discourse in hysteria places the disorder in a social field and leads David-Ménard (1989: 182) to "wonder what type of man makes a woman hysterical." She suggests as a prototype for the man in question the scholar who effects a radical separation of the work of the mind from the needs of the body and the affairs of domestic life. (Although, in view of the prevalence of hysteria in agricultural and pastoral societies, we might broaden her formulation to observe that there are other activities that privilege men's concerns while excluding and demeaning women – e.g., subsistence, warmaking, business.) In any event, gender relations – including their sexual, emotional, social, and political aspects – seem to have a central place in the social and psychological production of hysteria.

Conclusions

Emotional and mental disorder is widespread in human societies. Many of these disorders seem to correspond to affective and dissociative disorders in western psychiatry (i.e. depression, conversion disorder, Briquet's syndrome, multiple personality disorder, borderline personality disorder, or fugue states). Often they are conceptualized as soul loss, spirit possession, or spirit intrusion in traditional cultures.

In the west, depression and hysteria have fuzzy boundaries. They take different forms, and they can overlap. Persons with dissociative disorders are often depressed. Depression may take the form of somatic symptoms as well as guilt and despair, and violent hysterical psychoses often begin in depressive brooding. Suggestion and role-playing are evident in both conditions, especially in hysteria.

The histories of persons with depression and hysteria, moreover, can resemble one another. Both can originate in traumatic experiences. In hysteria frightening experiences may lead to hypnoid dissociation and flighty thinking, whereas in depression they may lead to withdrawal and helplessness. Such frightening experiences may include threats to self-preservation, loss and separation, loss of social position and other narcissistic injuries, sexual abuse, and oedipal conflicts.

Communication is impaired in hysteria and depression, but this need not mean that communication is absent. It may be there, but in cryptic form, perhaps as a way of circumventing strictures on permissable discourse.

Singly or in combination, hysteria and depression cover a wide range of complaints and symptoms. Both are subject to social and cultural conditioning, hysteria particularly. Both may imitate the roles of the sick or may become culturally patterned behavior in their own right. Hysteria can also blend with cultural fashions and religious and political enthusiasms. This means that distinctive instantiations of depression or hysteria may vary from one cultural or historical setting to another, sometimes in ways that are striking and unexpected. This also means that individual instances of depression and hysteria may or may not be regarded as disorder by particular individuals or groups or in particular cultural and historical circumstances. Such variation is not an argument against universal psychological issues and processes, however. To the contrary, depression and hysteria in their manifold guises illustrate widespread and recurrent themes in human suffering and sociality.

6 Eccentricity and madness

Hysteria illustrates the susceptibility to fragmentation in human personality: unconscious wishes and fears may wrest control of the body from the conscious ego, and the ego itself may develop separate selves. Portions of the feeling, motoric body and parts of the self may seem to break away from the main currents of body image and self-organization. In this fragmentation there may be an artful quality about the person's being in the world; the subject may act "as if" she were another person or "as if" she had a physical illness.

A more severe fragmentation occurs in schizophrenia. "Molecular" rather than "molar," the disintegration is more extensive; splits occur in the very structure of language and thought (Abse 1950). The person with a hysterical or dissociative disorder may be unaware of playing sick, but the person with schizophrenia may lack a capacity for artfulness and may confuse the imaginary with the real. Missing or severely impaired is the essentially human capacity for engaging in a playful, as-if mode of thinking; for the schizophrenic, words may be things, and the play, life itself.

There is a spectrum of schizophreniform disorders, ranging from what may seem like little more than garden variety eccentricity to serious mental illness. These more severe forms of schizophrenia can radically undermine a person's capacity for productive activity and social relationships. James M. Glass (1985) even likens schizophrenia to regression from culture to nature: persons with schizophrenia may find themselves in uncivilized worlds of raw power and humiliating submission. Schizophrenia, therefore, may reveal the psychological or psychobiological preconditions of culture in a more fundamental way than either depression or hysteria.

Paradoxically, schizophrenia can mimic psychological processes in the production and reproduction of culture. As Glass also notes, there are similarities between schizophrenic delusions and political and religious beliefs. Persons with schizophrenia can have philosophical and artistic bents, and they can be witty and creative in their use of language.

Like depression and hysteria, schizophrenia occurs in social and cultural contexts. Understanding how social and cultural factors contribute to the

144

etiology of schizophrenia, then, has been part of anthropological interest in schizophrenia. I shall review some of the research on social and cultural factors in schizophrenia, but more interesting for us is what schizophrenia implies about the psychological foundations of sociality and cultural activity. Social experience may play a smaller role in the origins of schizophrenia than in depression and hysteria, and it may also have less to do with shaping the actual form of the disorder.

Eccentricity

Schizophrenic subjectivity, though strange, is not beyond the pale of ordinary subjectivity. Emanuel Kant suggested that we are all insane in our dreams, and Freud incorporated his knowledge of psychotic mental process into his characterization of normal unconscious thought process (i.e., primary process thinking). Michael Eigen (1986) theorizes that every personality has a "psychotic core." It may be added that psychotic traits (e.g., illogical thinking, ungrammatical language, delusions and illusions, subjective depersonalization and derealization, emotional instability, lack of purpose and direction, poor self-esteem, egocentricity, distrust of others, etc.) are, when taken separately, common in normal populations.

Eccentricity also points to a continuum between normality and schizophrenia. Almost every society includes some eccentrics or otherwise marginal persons. Some may be social recluses. Others may seem odd or disturbed. And still others may be unusally wise and a bit mad all at once. The *DSM-III-R* recognizes several eccentric personality types that share features with schizophrenia. "Avoidant personalities" are shy, timid, and unusually sensitive to the opinions of others although inwardly they may want social ties and recognition; fearing criticism and rejection, they remain aloof. "Schizoid personalities" avoid others because they have little or no conscious social desire or feeling; often they have solitary hobbies. "Schizotypal personalities" are eccentric in thought, behavior, and speech and aloof and awkward in interpersonal relations. They report strange experiences, have odd beliefs, display inappropriate emotion, and may engage in magical thinking (Millon 1981).

The anthropological literature includes two exemplary studies of persons with schizophreniform personalities: *Oscar: An inquiry into the nature of sanity* (Wilson [1974]1992) and *Tuhami: Portrait of a Moroccan* (Crapanzano 1980). Oscar and Tuhami were aloof and eccentric. Both were storytellers and comics with traumatic histories.

Oscar lived on Providencia, a small island near Colombia inhabited by English-speaking, Protestant people of mixed African and European descent. He was a fisher, farmer, tramp, thief, gossip, confidant, and prophet who went "in" and "out" of madness, delivered impressive sermons, recited his own poems, expounded on matters of philosophical moment, publicly condemned other islanders for their transgressions, invaded their privacy, pilfered small items and left worthless objects in return, and begged for food. One notices in Oscar's speech concerns with power and romantic relationships. "I determined at a very early age," Oscar said, "that I would improve beyond my father's capacity and be apt to associate my ideas with other men. . . . In my youth I followed the gardening or farming profession and became an eminent fisherman" (Wilson [1974]1992: 16). "I became a devoted lover at the early age of eighteen. My admirers were many and my girls not a few" (ibid.: 27–28). He asserted the value of education, of being ambitious, of rising above others.

Traumatic losses and blows to self-esteem may have figured in Oscar's condition. A woman friend became pregnant and, though she was not right for him, they married and had five children. He then went to the Adventist Training College in Panama with the aim of becoming a minister but, once there, he may have worked only as a gardener or servant. Meanwhile, his wife left him and became a prostitute, and his children forgot him and either died or disappeared.

Oscar's problems had a social context. Wilson notes that power and social striving mark social life throughout the Caribbean. Upper class "respectability" is expressed in urbane speech, formal marriage, church attendance, and education. "Reputation" is indigenous and anticlass; it is expressed in fathering children and being a father, and in "a readiness to fight in defense of one's honor and a proficiency in the use of language, notably in sweet talk, word games, riddles, storytelling, punning, boasting, insults, curses – generally being verbally fluent" (ibid.: 116). English, the language of the slave holders, became in the dialect of the common people a device for deceiving and excluding slave holders, and a medium for competing for reputation. Wilson suggests that colonialism created a schizoid situation for the common people. They might aspire to respectability but, in practice, they had to settle for reputation. Oscar's desire for respectability was unusually strong, yet he gained neither respectability nor reputation. Instead, he tried to diminish the power of other people through his intrusive presence, thievery, and eccentric language. Wilson even ventured that madness is a label we apply to people who render us powerless (ibid.: 138).

Tuhami, a poor Moroccan tile-maker, imagined himself the husband of a camel-footed she-demon. His experience, while mediated through cultural symbols and understandings, was unique. He occupied a subjective space at the margins of the cultural norm. His sense of self was unsure and he was given to dissociation and dreamlike flights of imagination. His history included abandonment, rejection, disrupted relationships and unrealized ambitions, unresolved oedipal fantasies, and crushing guilt. Crapanzano suggests that Tuhami was thwarted in his passage to manhood by a culture that ritualized castration in the traumatic circumcision of young boys and relegated many men to dependency while allowing power and public voice to only a few. Tuhami was also affected by the death of his father (his hope for patrimony and legitimacy) and by the death of a friend in adolescence. Further, Crapanzano (1980: 86) suggests that Tuhami may have been hindered by his relationships with spirits, "frozen" in a traditional, and increasingly antiquated symbolic order.

The words of Tuhami and Oscar reflect their lack of attachment and powerlessness. Oscar's parody of upper-class speech improvises on the way in which poor people throughout the Caribbean adjust to their "schizoid" situation. Similarly, "[t]here was always something captivating about Tuhami's discourse. It was as though he wanted to entrap me, to enslave me *through the power of the word* in an intricate web of fantasy and reality – to reverse, if you will, the colonial relationship that I as a foreigner, a *nasrani*, must have suggested to him" (Crapanzano 1980: 140).

Schizophrenia

Cross-national and cross-cultural studies suggest that the risk of becoming schizophrenic during a lifetime is about 1 percent. Even so, it is often a devastating condition for its victims, and a major problem for mental-health care professionals. More than a mere symptom or condition, it alters entire personalities. The subjective experience and overt symptoms may include lack of insight, forethought, and self-control; gender-identity confusion; poor self-esteem; diffuse and unstable boundaries; depersonalization and derealization; deficits in language and narrative memory; and, paradoxically, exaggerated intellectualism.

Schizophrenia takes various forms. Although the *DSM-III-R* recognizes disorganized, catatonic, paranoid, undifferentiated, and residual schizophrenias, recent research suggests the disorder has two basic forms. Type I includes emotional instability, sensory disorders, hallucinations, delusions, and paranoia, whereas Type II appears as emotional flatness and deficits in intellectual functioning and communication. The two types can occur together or in succession, and they may reflect variations on a common pathological process (Crow et al. 1986).

Symptoms vary slightly from one society to another. A comparison of schizophrenic persons in Japan and the United States found that the Japanese patients were more assaulting but better at reality-testing than their American counterparts (Schooler and Caudill 1964). Irish-American men with schizophrenia in New York City have lower self-esteem and more guilt-feelings, apprehensions about females, and paranoia, whereas Italian-American patients are more impulsive, given to mood swings, and are hostile toward male authority figures (Opler 1957, 1959; Opler and Singer 1956; Singer and Opler 1956). Delusions and hallucinations vary with cultural and historical contexts. Horacio Fabrega, Jr. (1989) suggests that the symptoms and meanings of schizophrenia reflect cultural notions of the person and self. Since these notions vary considerably from one culture to another, according to Fabrega, the organization of schizophrenia can be expected to vary cross-culturally also. While it may, the evidence suggests that in broad outline schizophrenia does not vary much; the defining characteristics of schizophrenia are similar from one society to another.

Psychology

According to Freud, the ego's relation to external reality in schizophrenia is disturbed; perceptions and internal representations of others lose their significance. The libido is withdrawn from objects and reinvested in the self ([1917]1957: 244–245). The resulting narcissism, in Freud's formulation, accounts for the egocentricity and megalomania in schizophrenia, while hallucinations and delusions represent efforts to repair the "internal catastrophe."

The ego creates, automatically, a new external and internal world; and there can be no doubt of two facts – that this new world is constructed in accordance with the id's wishful impulses, and that the motive of this dissociation from the external world is some very serious frustration by reality of a wish – a frustration which seems intolerable. The close affinity of this psychosis to normal dreams is unmistakable. (Freud [1924]1961: 151)

The "delusion is found applied like a patch over the place where originally a rent had appeared in the ego's relation to the external world" (ibid.).

Milton Wexler (1971) related the withdrawal of libidinal investment in others and object representations to cognitive features of ego dysfunction in schizophrenia. The person has difficulty maintaining distance between one thing and another. Self and other, word and action, and perception and fantasy may seem to blend together (ibid.: 84–85). An inability or unwillingness to distinguish between supposition and reality also appears in unrealistic thinking, in lack of humor about the self and problems, and in confusion about personal identity and social roles. Empathy and an ability to develop new values, commitments, or more constructive ways of thinking about the self and others are usually impaired as well. Meanwhile, sexual and oral desires and fantasies may reflect a desire to cling to some familiar segment of reality. These features of the disorder, according to

Wexler, involve a deterioration of higher level object representations and a regressive effort to reconstitute the inner world with part-objects and symbolic substitutes for objects.

Lacan (1977) contended that the "rent" in the ego's relation to the world is a foreclosure or erasure of the signifying function, an absence of identification with the paternal metaphor and a failure to replace the mother with a symbol for desire. Actually, the speech of the person with schizophrenia is unusual. It may lack theme, narrative continuity, textual anchorage, and clear enunciation. Conspicuous instead are references to elusive, ill-defined "others" and odd uses of metaphor and metonymy (Rosenbaum and Sonne 1986). Persons with schizophrenia apply signifiers to concepts and referents willy-nilly, and thus fail, among other things, to make the usual connections between the existential *I*, the self, and subjective experience. Instead, they may identify fragments of the self with real or fantastic others. Hanna Segal (1991) comments on the concrete quality of the thinking of a psychotic patient. Words became objective objects. When the patient was psychotic he gave up playing the violin because he did not want to seem to masturbate in public. A nonpsychotic patient, in contrast, had similar erotic associations in dreams about violin playing but continued to play. In one instance the symbol was equated with the object whereas in the other it was merely associated with it, allowing for other, primary meanings.

Ego and superego deficits in schizophrenia may release drive. Disturbing increases of the libido are common in schizophrenia, especially during the early phases of the disorder. Clinical reports mention manialike increase in self-importance, genital sensations, lowered sensitivity to pain, increased heterosexual or homosexual activity, and compulsive masturbation. One American woman became psychotic when experiencing an intense orgasm for the first time. She imagined she was receiving telepathic messages from her partner (Arieti 1975: 278). Bizarre sexual delusions may include explicit oedipal fantasies and confused thinking about gender identity (Fenichel 1945: 437). Occasionally, persons with schizophrenia may seem as though they are courting others. "The picture is one of immensely brightened charisma" (Scheflen 1981: 62).

This increase in libido may promote anxieties about rejection, loss, or failure and these anxieties, in turn, may lead to defensive maneuvers (Freeman 1970: 411). Kempf (1917: 128) concluded that sexual motives produce conflict in schizophrenia, either because they are unproductive and require "censured forms of stimulation" or because they focus on "forbidden" or "unresponsive" objects.

Increased needs for attachment may provoke anxieties also. Patients may want love yet dread closeness. "The very excessiveness of his need for objects also makes them [i.e., the love objects] inordinately dangerous and fearsome since they can destroy him through abandonment" (Burnham et al. 1969: 28). "The patient may directly voice fears that the object will dominate, control, or enslave him and thereby deprive him of his separateness, independence, and identity" (ibid.: 31). Some male persons with schizophrenia prefer passive homosexuality as a way of receiving sustenance or "milk" from the other. One person with schizophrenia reported a disturbing fantasy in which he would be compelled to have intercourse with his mother and thus to "feed" her his penis (Karon and Rosberg 1958).

Social withdrawal and narcissistic preoccupations may be ways of coping with libidinal drive and a need for attachment (Freeman 1977: 384). Rather than trying to relate to others as objects of desire, the person may withdraw into fantasies about power and achievement. Yet such fantasies may arouse anxieties about competition and failure (Grotstein 1977: 421). One patient said, "I am a rabbit. I stay in my hole because every time I stick my head out, the world has a big role for me to play" (Scheflen 1981: 93).

Merging with others may be a way of managing ego-alien, anxiety-inducing surges of desire. The surplus libido is attributed to someone else or to a powerful alter ego. The imperfect self gains the support of the grandiose self or the imaginary ally. Alternatively, the other may be the target of a paranoid projection of the dangerous, unwanted sexual energy. In a brilliant paper, Victor Tausk ([1919]1948) theorized that the "influencing machines" in schizophrenic delusions are projections of the libido. The influx of narcissistic libido increases awareness of body parts and leads to defensive hypochondria and self-estrangement. Finally, the person projects his or her genitals and sexualized body into the dreaded machine or external agent.

Biology

It now seems likely that schizophrenia involves neurological dysfunction or deficits. Research is implicating the prefrontal cortex, cortical and sub-cortical structures of the temporal lobe, and abnormalities in neuro-transmission, especially in dopaminergic pathways (Buchsbaum 1990). Current thinking about how these abnormalities fit together resembles the ego–superego deficit theory in psychoanalysis. Ego–superego defects and dysregulation of the libido in the psychoanalytic model correspond with neurological lesions and abnormal neurotransmission in biological models.

Studies of brain functioning in schizophrenia are showing decreases in brain volume in the left temporal lobe, particularly in the amygdala and hippocampus (Crow 1990). Besides decreases in volume, autopsies have found increases in dopamine concentration in the left- or language-side amygdala (Reynolds 1992). Some schizophrenias are associated with increased activity in the dopaminergic pathways, particularly in the striatum and limbic system. Dopamine blockers inhibit the symptoms of acute schizophrenia, and psychotic behavior can be induced in animals and human beings with drugs that potentiate dopaminergic transmission. Activation of the striatum's nucleus accumbens is associated with stereotypy, a common symptom in schizophrenia (Robbins 1990). Some data also imply that glutamate pathways, which ordinarily inhibit dopaminergic systems, may be underactive in schizophrenia (Carlsson and Carlsson 1990). The nucleus accumbens, which is richly innervated with dopaminergic neurons, is a powerful reward center. An overactive nucleus accumbens may account for attention dysfunction in persons with acute schizophrenia (Carlson 1986: 693; Robbins 1990).

One theory relates the two sorts of biological anomalies to the difference between Type I (positive symptom) and Type II (negative symptom) schizophrenia. According to this view, Type I schizophrenia may reflect increased subcortical dopaminergic transmission, whereas the cognitive deficits in Type II may reflect neurological lesions, particularly in the amygdala and hippocampus of the temporal lobe (Crow et al. 1986).

Some symptoms of schizophrenia (e.g., abnormal eye movement, gait, and posture and deficits in planning and anticipation) imply that the underlying pathology may involve the prefrontal cortex. C.D. Frith (1987) implicates self-awareness, a prefrontal function; in his view, social action arises from external and internal stimuli. Appropriate social behavior requires continuous monitoring of external stimuli, willed intention, and behavior. An inability to monitor intentions of will might lead to the false attribution of action to external stimuli and thus to the ideas of reference, paranoia, and eccentric thinking seen in Type I schizophrenia. Type II schizophrenia may reflect a diminution of willed intention resulting from more severe frontal-lobe disorder. The changes in prefrontal metabolism are context dependent; they appear when the person is making and acting upon judgments and plans. In a series of studies Daniel R. Weinberger and his associates found reduced function in the dorsolateral prefrontal cortex when schizophrenic subjects were challenged with tasks requiring planning and self-monitoring while adjusting to shifting conditions. They theorize that this reduced function may result from too little dopaminergic transmission *in the prefrontal cortex* (Weinberger 1987; Weinberger and Berman 1988).

The neurological deficits and abnormalities in dopaminergic neurotransmission may be interrelated. The prefrontal cortex ordinarily modulates subcortical dopaminergic transmission. Thus, Daniel R. Weinberger (1987) theorizes that prefrontal lesions may encourage psychotic decompensation through disinhibition of dopamine neurons in the limbic system and striatum. Similarly, Robbins (1990) ventures that psychosocial stress may diminish dopaminergic firing in the frontal cortex and that this may in turn release dopaminergic activity in the striatum. Gray et al. (1991) theorize that schizophrenia involves a reduced ability to focus cognitive processes on selected stimuli on the basis of memories of past experience. Their experiments with animals have shown that such cognitive deficits can result from either the administration of dopamine agonists or damage to the amygdala and the septohippocampal system, especially that portion of the septohippocampal system that communicates with the nucleus accumbens through the subiculum. Presumably, the structures of the septohippocampal system and amygdala ordinarily mediate the modulation of attention or drive by past experience. Gray and his colleagues note that their theory may be fundamentally consistent with the ideas of Frith and Weinberger, since the prefrontal cortex acts to moderate subcortical dopamine through the septohippocampal system. Their theory is offered as an explanation for the symptoms of Type I or acute schizophrenia, although they suggest that the sorts of pathologies they postulate also may be related to Type II or chronic schizophrenia. The latter may represent the effects of coping with cognitive disorientation through withdrawal or the effects of limbic-system pathology without the presence of striatal dopaminine-mediated psychosis.

Some investigators now suspect that prefrontal disorder in schizophrenia is secondary to cortical and subcortical dysfunction in the temporal lobe, particularly on the dominant side (Weinberger 1988). Poor frontal-lobe function correlates with poor narrative recall in schizophrenic persons. This weakness may be a consequence of hippocampal dysfunction and defects in the language areas of the frontal and temporal lobes (Wood and Flowers 1990).

Weinberger, Berger, and Zec (1986) note the convergence between psychoanalytic thinking about schizophrenia and the emerging biological models. Our earlier discussions of the brain and human nature laid a basis for appreciating this convergence. As we have seen, there are rough parallels between the ego–superego and prefrontal cortex, and between the libido and subcortical dopamine. Abnormal dopaminergic transmission in the schizophrenic brain may explain reports of increased libido, grandiosity, and paranoia. A process of prefrontal defects with resulting disinhibition of subcortical dopamine pathways is congruent with the hypothesis of ego–superego defects: the prefrontal defects correspond to ego and superego defects and excessive dopaminergic transmission to the release of libido. Dopaminergic innervation of the amygdala, a structure that discriminates good and bad objects and associates them with emotion and behavioral response, may correspond to the need-fear and power-fear dilemmas in the phenomenology of schizophrenia. While the temporal-lobe pathology may underlie the disordered object relations in schizophrenia, the prefrontal defects are probably related to loss of will and desire and personality disorganization. The evidence for neurologically mediated language and memory deficits coheres with Lacan's contention that ego defects involve the signifying chain.[1]

Sass's revisionism

The classical psychoanalytic and recent biomedical models of schizophrenia cohere with long-standing western thinking about the psyche and body, sanity and madness. Beginning with pre-Socratic philosophers, there has been an inclination to see in madness a diminution of reason and a corresponding release of Dionysian intoxication. From Heraclitus to Freud, and from Freud to Lacan, Weinberger, and Gray, madness has been linked, explicitly or implicitly, with irrationality and disinhibition of passion or arousal.

In a provocative and ambitious book, Louis A. Sass (1992) questions this view of schizophrenia and theorizes instead that schizophrenia and various schizophrenialike personality disorders – he treats the different types of schizophrenia, schizotypal, and schizoid personality disorders as manifestations of the same tendencies – reflect a peculiar intensification of thought, what he calls "hyperobjectivism" and "hyperreflexivity" or self-observation. The problem in schizophrenia in some sense is not too little rationality but rather, in certain forms at least, too much. At the heart of this peculiar style of mentation is a "truth taking stare." The schizophrenic either stares at the world, seeing it as a desocialized aggregation of disconnected, literal objects or supplants it with abstract and reified philosophical preoccupations of a highly subjective nature. In either event, the result is a radical alienation from social reality and distortions of conventional orientations to time and space.

Sass agrees with psychoanalysis that schizophrenia involves estrangement from social others and an increased preoccupation with the self, but whereas psychoanalysis sees the latter as a consequence of the former, Sass relates both to an almost intentional excess of observation and cerebration. Accordingly, he questions the neurobiological findings insofar as they fit psychoanalytic thinking or reinterprets them to fit his own view; for example, he suggests that schizophrenia may involve overactivation of the dominant hemisphere.

Sass, however, may exaggerate the disparity between the two perspectives of schizophrenia. The psychoanalytic and Weinberger-type models of schizophrenia imply that intention and attention in schizophrenia are less organized by object-relations schemas, social intelligence, narratives about the self, and conventional associations between signifiers and referents than in normal personalities. The result of these defects might be a release of primitive psychosexual impulses (i.e., unmodulated activity of dopaminergic neurons in the nucleus accumbens), as in the psychoanalytic view, and an increase in post-frontal mechanisms of perception and association, as in Sass's view. Damasio's view of the prefrontal cortex is noteworthy here. It will be recalled that Damasio thinks that the prefrontal cortices – and especially the ventromedial portions of them – are critically important for socially appropriate emotion (see Chapter 2).

Etiology

The origins of schizophrenia are not well understood, although many researchers theorize that they involve both genetic-biological predisposition and environmental stresses. Biological predisposition may originate in chemical and physical trauma, viral infection, natural variation in brain-cell density, and psychological trauma and deprivation. It may then interact with changes in the body or brain resulting from normal maturation. It has been suggested that the tendency for schizophrenia to surface in late adolescence or the early twenties may reflect the late myelination of the frontal lobes and the peaking of brain dopamine metabolism during that period (Weinberger 1987).

Genetic disposition   Genetic disposition is a risk factor in schizophrenia. Concordance for schizophrenia among dizygotic twins is 5 to 16 percent, whereas in homozygotic twins – those who share identical genes – it ranges from 35 to more than 50 percent. One hypothesis traces the disorder to the gene that controls cerebral asymmetry. If the gene is defective, the result may be improper differentiation and development of the two hemispheres, and this in turn may result in additional neurological dysfunctions of the sort discussed earlier. This hypothesis suggests, in effect, that the human vulnerability to schizophrenia is an evolutionary by-product of the human capacity for spoken language (Crow 1990).

Cannon, Mednick, and Parnas (1990) consider genetic predisposition in a prospective longitudinal study of Danish children of schizophrenic mothers. They theorize that the genetic disposition to schizophrenia involves a susceptibility to perinatal damage to the temporal lobe and a tendency to emotional lability. Their data suggest that high-risk children may develop negative-symptom schizophrenia (Type II) when complications during pregnancy and birth damage temporal-lobe structures. High-risk children who develop positive-symptom schizophrenia (Type I) in their study tend to have had very disrupted childhoods (e.g., long periods of separation from the mother and institutionalization). Presumably, adverse developmental experiences interact with the disposition to increased autonomic reactivity to produce schizophrenia with a preponderance of positive symptoms.

Parenting and family dynamics   Some writers have theorized that schizophrenia begins in disordered early relationships with primary care-givers (Fromm-Reichmann 1948). Karon (1960) mentioned one mother who was angry with her infant after nursing him. More than thirty years later she still fought with her schizophrenic son after preparing food for him. Segal (1991) suggests that the psychotic proclivity for symbolic equation rather than symbolic association bespeaks a failure to move from the paranoid-schizoid position to the depressive position, that is, to a refusal to let go of the love object and to accept symbolic substitutes and displacements. We have already seen that object relations and their neurobiological substrates in the limbic system (especially in the septohippocampal system and amygdala) are disturbed in schizophrenia. Some animal experiments implicate the sorts of early social experiences that, in human beings, structure and inform unconscious object relations. According to Gray et al. (1991), a counterpart to the presumed defect in schizophrenic thought, namely, the failure to modulate attention or drive in terms of previous learning, can be found in experimental animals. The learning defects are aggravated by dopamine agonists and by injury to the hippocampus. They also result when the animals are not handled from birth to weaning.

Another line of thought traces the disorder to communication between parent and child in the formative years. Bateson, Jackson, Haley, and Weakland (1956) theorized that the disorder begins with faulty communication between parents and the young preschizophrenic child. Parents convey conflicting messages to the child and then suppress acknowledgment and criticism of the contradictions. Caught in a "double bind," the child's own communication and thought processes become evasive and illogical.

These ideas about the effects of early experience, however, have been difficult to corroborate. Studies of families have been marred by methodological problems. Among other things, there have been unresolved questions about cause and effect. Some studies detected peculiarities in the families of persons with schizophrenia, but since the studies were not prospective, they did not answer the question of whether the peculiarities of parents led to or resulted from schizophrenia in a child.[2] The evidence that parenting and the communication process may play some part in the etiology of schizophrenia has been getting stronger in recent years, however. Studies have found disordered communication in the families of persons with schizophrenia and elevated rates of personality disorder among their parents (Hirsch 1979; Liem 1980). A longitudinal-prospective study in the United States reexamined fifty-four mildly to moderately disturbed adolescents at five- and fifteen-year intervals. The communication deviance in the families before the onset of serious mental disorder was a significant predictor of schizophrenia and schizophrenia-spectrum disorders (Goldstein 1987). A large-sample study in Finland of children who had been adopted away from schizophrenic mothers found that several mental disorders, including schizophrenia, correlate with conflict, emotional problems, and communication abnormalities in the adopting families (Tienari et al. 1987). Many studies indicate that patients in remission are more likely to relapse when their parents are critical, rejecting, hostile, and excessively emotional (Lukoff et al. 1984). Emotional expression in families may vary cross-culturally with consequences for the prospects of recovery. Janis Hunter Jenkins (1991), for instance, finds that Mexican-American parents are less emotional and more accepting of their children than are Anglo-American parents.

Much discussion and controversy about family background in schizophrenia has focused on Paul Schreber, a nineteenth-century German judge. Schreber's late marriage remained childless, and when he ran for a seat in the Reichstag at age forty-two, he lost. After that he spent a short period in a mental hospital. At fifty-one, after accepting a promotion in the judiciary, he became delusional and paranoid. He believed that God and spirits of the dead were persecuting him, and that he was turning into a woman. During this period he wrote his memoirs, including a detailed account of his illness. After leaving the hospital and living with his wife and adopted daughter for four years, he again became severely psychotic and returned to the hospital where he died in 1911. Schreber claimed that God did not understand living persons and that He only had intercourse with corpses or with men who were asleep. Schreber combined this insubordinate attitude with respect for the deity and a notion that he was God's woman, the passive recipient of seminal sunshine and mother to a new race. Freud inferred from these ideas that God represented the father and that Schreber's paranoia was a defense against unconscious homoerotic attraction to the father.

The discussion of Schreber shifted to his childhood when Niederland (1959a, 1959b, 1974) examined the writings of the father, Moritz Schreber. The father, a medical doctor, had written about child-rearing. Niederland noticed that the father's writings contained advice that seemed to foreshadow the son's delusions. It is likely that the older Schreber probably followed many of his own recommendations in rearing his children. He oriented family life toward serving God, and was probably a godlike presence. He believed that children are ill or criminally oriented from an early age, demanded unquestioning obedience from them, and regarded their bad habits as "weeds." He did not allow eating between meals, expected self-denial even before the age of one, and promulgated harsh rules about play, toys, dramas, art, and baths. Especially bizarre were strictures on musical instruments, drawing, embroidery, and hair-plaiting intended to prevent "one-sidedness." The older Schreber also devised gadgets to prevent poor posture in growing children.

This suggested to Schatzman (1973) an alternative to the psychoanalytic interpretation, namely that Paul Schreber had been driven crazy by his father. The son's so-called "miracles" (i.e., ideas about what God was doing) often alluded to these strange notions, as did his comment that God did not know "how to treat a living human being" and his belief that God's ideas were "absurd" and "*contrary* to human nature" (ibid.: 77). Dr. Schreber believed that spirit should subdue nature, including sensual pleasure. To discourage masturbation, he recommended vigorous exercise before bed, cold baths, cold-water enemas, and the washing of the genitalia and perineum with cold water (ibid.: 83). He thought that children should be close to God, and that they should "reflect" the "pure rays of the concept of God." So the son's delusions included the idea that his "nervous system" was "illuminated" by God's "rays" (ibid.: 93). The father said that "true religion" should "penetrate" and "fill" children (ibid.: 95). The son thought that he had been "unmanned." The father phrased child-rearing in agricultural metaphors: "The soil of the field to be *cultivated* must be raised, receptive, penetrable, full of sap and strength for a grain of seed [*Samenkorn*] to implant and to rise up" (quoted in Schatzman 1973: 96).

Nothing has been settled by the dispute between Schatzman and the psychoanalysts, however. Following a detailed historical study of the Schreber family and a re-reading of Schreber's memoirs, Israëls (1989) notes that positive as well as negative features of the father's child-rearing appeared in the son's delusions, and he concluded that the father was probably less sadistic than Schatzman suggests. Israëls opines that Schatzman was ethnocentric in his evaluation of nineteenth-century child-rearing philosophy.[3]

It seems doubtful that parental behavior alone causes schizophrenia. But by failing to nurture self-esteem, social skills, impulse control, and effective defense mechanisms or by instilling anxiety through family conflict and divorce, some families may aggravate the conditions favoring schizophrenia. And once schizophrenia is present, families may tilt the balance toward recovery or relapse.

Social stress   As the Schreber case suggests, psychosis may surface during or immediately after stressful experiences. Many preschizophrenic persons become psychotic when leaving the family circle for college or marriage. Promotions, changes in occupation, the birth of a child, immigration, refugee status, and geographical mobility are also mentioned in case histories (Burnham et al. 1969; Lukoff et al. 1984). Harvey M. Brenner (1973) found a correlation between economic conditions and mental-hospital admissions in the United States throughout a 127-year period. Admissions for schizophrenia and other mental disorders increased following economic depression, particularly among persons who had more to lose in economic downturns.

Noting a correlation between lower socioeconomic status and the prevalence of schizophrenia, Kohn (1973) theorized that constricted and rigid conceptions of reality in lower-class families may encourage schizophrenia by interfering with flexible and resourceful coping with stressful situations. Warner (1994: 44–47) considers the alienation of workers in modern society to be a factor. Biological determinists, however, have argued that the greater prevalence of schizophrenia in lower socioeconomic groups results from persons with schizophrenia falling into the lower strata or failing to rise out of them. Yet matters may not be quite so simple. As Warner notes, some data suggest that social circumstances do make a difference. In India, for example, schizophrenia appears to be more common in the upper castes, perhaps because modernization is creating new stresses for them by undermining their traditional claims to power and privilege. Genetic drift cannot explain the Indian pattern because Hindus marry within their own castes.

Rural Ireland: A case study   In *Saints, scholars, and schizophrenics: Mental illness in rural Ireland*, Nancy Scheper-Hughes (1979) traced what she took to be a high prevalence of schizophrenia (as measured by first admissions to mental hospital) to child-rearing practices and social conditions. Scheper-Hughes found that schizophrenia in Ireland occurs more often among males than females and is associated with peripheral agriculture, celibacy, bachelorhood, and, inversely, with birth order, and she theorized that this pattern results from a combination of economic stress, harsh discipline and confusing communication patterns within the family, labeling, and a prudish morality that discourages intimacy between spouses. Since the potato famine (1845–1849), families in Ireland have suffered further economic setbacks. More recently, the fishing industry has declined, and entry into the European Common Market has subjected farmers to competition and shame, forcing them to measure their value in land, cattle, and money (1979: 42). Young women are leaving the countryside in large numbers. The young men who stay behind have little prospect of either marriage or economic success.

Asexuality and prudishness among the Irish reflect the Irish Catholic

Church's longstanding hostility toward physical pleasure and sexuality. In rural Ireland, sexuality is suppressed and shameful, even for married couples. Males and females are rigidly segregated – even husbands and wives do not walk together. Villagers were taught by the priests that celibacy was the purest form of existence and that sexual intercourse should be oriented toward having children. In addition, they were taught that sex for pleasure, departures from the "proper" position, and contraception were immoral, and women were counseled to resist their husbands as a "virgin threatened with rape" (ibid.: 119–120). Given this moral order and the choice between leaving home for menial work in the city and staying at home, caring for parents, and probable bachelorhood, some countrymen escape through identification with the company of "saints" in the asylum (ibid.: 80).

According to Scheper-Hughes, early life experiences also work against sensual relations and positive self-esteem. Oral gratification and other forms of pleasure are suppressed at an early age. Children do not learn that food is something to enjoy, and kissing and hugging are discouraged. Mothers often are overprotective, but they also express negative attitudes toward children and leave them alone for long periods. The father plays little part in caregiving during the first few years, except to administer punishment. The training of children is harsh, and even girls and young children receive severe beatings, particularly for "boldness." Children are expected to be obedient, and many are fearful and shy, especially with strangers. Because school teachers also beat children, many boys and girls fear attending school. Besides spanking children, parents manipulate them with lies and criticism.

The youngest son in particular is singled out for ridicule. "The parent can be observed belittling the runt for trying to put himself ahead, and then with the same breath chiding him for not being more aggressive and achievement-oriented like his older brothers" (ibid.: 185). Deception and ridicule in child-rearing is part of a broader pattern of skill with words, including teasing, flattery, the tall tale, and cracking, a type of verbal banter heard among men in which they "cut each other up." While the older sons are groomed for success in the city, later-born sons, the ones who will stay on the farm and, according to Scheper-Hughes, the ones who are at greatest risk for developing schizophrenia, are given much less encouragement.

These arguments about the schizophrenogenic character of Irish society and culture made sense as long as it seemed that the Irish were more prone to schizophrenia than other peoples. And, in fact, earlier studies had found that there were two to three times as many hospital admissions for schizophrenia in Ireland as in other countries. These statistics, however, may be an artifact of over-reporting first admissions in Ireland (i.e., two or more

hospitals claiming the same person as a first admittee); a survey of psychiatric facilities suggests that the prevalence of schizophrenia in Ireland is
actually comparable to that in other European countries (Ni Nuallain et al.
1987).

Scheper-Hughes's book is beautifully written, and it is full of insightful
description of the rural Irish and their way of life, but it may exaggerate the
extent to which social conditions and culture contribute to schizophrenia.
If so, it tells a cautionary tale about the dangers in overestimating psychological and cultural differences between societies.

Social labeling   The now commonly accepted view that schizophrenia results from a combination of biological risk or disposition and
social stress views the disorder as a substantive quality of the person.
Social-labeling theory holds instead that mental illness is a social construction, something imposed upon the person. Deviant behavior is labeled and
stigmatized. The person who is treated in this way – often someone lacking
power – is then encouraged to adopt the role of being mentally ill.

A strong form of labeling theory is not plausible, however, at least not
for schizophrenia. If severe mental illness is merely a social construction,
then prevalence and symptoms ought to vary greatly from one society to
another. The lifetime risk for schizophrenia, however, varies only slightly,
and the major symptoms of the disorder are everywhere similar. Social
behavior also may contradict labeling theory. The severely mentally ill are
not always stigmatized, nor are they always encouraged to play a role
(J. Murphy 1976). Stigmatizing and shunning the mentally ill can make
their lives more unpleasant, but it is unlikely that they cause mental disorder in the first place. Labeling theory, moreover, does not account for the
persistence of schizophrenia in the face of humane and caring efforts to
reincorporate the patient into the social fold, and it ignores the biological
components and psychological structure of the disorder.

Recovery

Many writers in cross-cultural psychiatry consider the chances of recovery
from schizophrenia to be greater in more traditional than in more complex
societies. The World Health Organization's "International Pilot Study of
Schizophrenia" (IPSS) and the follow-up World Health Organization
"Collaborative Study on Determinants of Outcome of Severe Mental
Disorders" found cross-cultural variations in prognosis and suggested that
these might be related to differences in social milieu, family, and treatment
(World Health Organization 1979; Sartorius et al. 1978). Murphy and
Raman (1971) found that less severely afflicted patients have a better

prognosis in Mauritius than Britain and speculated that the difference might be related to differing cultural beliefs about mental disorder. Richard Warner (1994) argues that recovery in traditional societies is facilitated by group membership and participation in productive activity and the resulting support for self-esteem. Waxler (1979) found a high rate of recovery among forty-four Sinhalese Buddhist individuals with schizophrenia in Sri Lanka in a five-year follow-up study. As many as 87 percent showed little or no maladjustment on various measures. According to Waxler, these results reflected supportive families, a positive treatment approach, and absences of stigmatization and a western-style sick-role for severe mental illness. Cohen (1992), however, notes that studies showing improved recovery in traditional societies are often impressionistic and may contain sampling biases and that the appearance of better prognosis in Third World countries may reflect incorrect diagnoses of people who are not truly schizophrenic and are therefore more likely to recover.

Mania

Mania is another form of madness, one that can resemble Type I schizophrenia. While it has received much less attention from anthropologists than schizophrenia, it deserves mention here. Like schizophrenia, mania is suggestive regarding the motivational bases of culture.

The characteristic features of manic episodes include inflation of self-esteem, delusions of grandeur, increased energy, drive, and sexual interest. The enhanced sense of pleasure gives way to increased irritability, perhaps because drive lowers thresholds for frustration. Along with the usual sense of euphoria and energy, there are changes in cognitive process and speech. The manic person speaks rapidly and is easily distracted (American Psychiatric Association 1987:214–215).

Mania seems to imply a diminution of the superego or a convergence of the senses of the ideal and actual selves and, also, an increase in narcissistic libido. Not only is there a powerful sense of actual or impending fulfillment, there is as well a greatly increased desire for objects (Fenichel 1945:407–411).

Madness, sanity, and culture

The line between madness and culture is fuzzy at best. Cultural beliefs can seem fanciful, even illusory. Religious dogmas and political ideologies in particular can resemble the delusions of psychotic individuals. Just as psychotic persons can be quite sensible in practical activities but become delusional when social relationships and reputations are at stake, cultures may take the greatest liberties with reality in beliefs and practices concerning social order and ingroup–outgroup relations. It is also interesting in this connection that highly creative persons can be seen as mad and that cultural creativity may make heavy use of primary process thinking. Culture and social life can also parallel the mood swings of manic-depressive persons. Freud ([1921]1955) noticed the similarity between mood swings in individuals and culturally constituted variations in mood. Whereas the collective mood is often somber, it may become more exuberant at festivals and carnivals; "That which is threatening and serious in tragedy and worship is play and fun in satyr plays and the fair" (Fenichel 1945: 409).

For their part, persons with schizophrenia and mania are often highly creative. Their speech may be poetic, witty, and rich in associations, and they may purport to have esoteric knowledge about unseen forces and beings and world-historical processes. The subjective experience of both schizophrenia and mania may afford mystical trancelike states that can seem to put the person in touch with a higher level of reality. In traditional societies, such experiences may affect shared knowledge about the cosmos. The mentation of the schizophrenic person is world-creating.

From the substrata archaic elements swell up, an intoxicating Dionysiac cosmic consciousness, a grandiose world phantasy; the person feels himself the center of the universe; he is the master of wonderful magic power; he expands into the cosmic whole; he becomes Mythos; he wars with the demons of his fate; in the mystical ecstacy [sic] of his introversion he attains to a knowledge of the infinite; he is God. (Storch 1924: 106)

David L. Beebe (1982) wrote eloquently of the poetic consciousness of persons with schizophrenia. They enter a mythic realm in which symbols are things and things are symbols. "He has gone to the space within the mind where dragons exist, where one is tempted by the devil, and where one collects the golden apples of the sun" (ibid.: 235).

Mania can involve a subjective sense of heightened perception; the world appears brighter, and there is a stronger sense of communion with the world and other people. John Custance (1951: 55; quoted in Lerner 1980: 78) mentioned a "heightened sense of reality" and "a sense of ineffable revelation" in mania. One patient reported that "during an exhilaration the mind penetrates infinitely more deeply into all things, and receives flashes of almost divine light and wisdom, which open to it, momentarily, regions of thought hitherto difficult or impossible of penetration" (MacCurdy 1925: 301; quoted in Lerner 1980: 80).

Mania may be the psychiatric equivalent of what Bucke ([1901]1946) called "cosmic consciousness." According to him, the person experiencing cosmic consciousness realizes and accepts the meaning and purpose of life, attains a sense of salvation, and overcomes the fear of death. Yet the most dramatic feature is sudden illumination: "It can be compared with nothing so well as with a dazzling flash of lightning in a dark night, bringing the landscape which had been hidden into clear view" (ibid.: 75). Bucke surmised that Buddha, Jesus, Paul, and many other religious leaders, poets, and philosophers have experienced cosmic consciousness.

Some older ethnographies suggest that the ranks of shamans number persons with epilepsy, hysterical personality, and schizophrenia and that many of them have been called to shamanism by severe personal crises. Ackerknecht (1943) thought that the shaman is not so much mentally ill as someone who has overcome an illness. Wallace (1970: 237–238) described "becoming a shaman" as a process of overcoming emotional crisis through reorganization of cognitive maps. Silverman (1967) suggested that acute schizophrenia may be the point of departure in shamanic careers. Shamans, he says, are schizophrenic persons who learn to comprehend their inner turmoil and to adjust themselves to society through the role of shaman. Similarly, Larry G. Peters (1982; see also Peters and Price-Williams 1980) showed that among the Tamang of Nepal the initiation and apprenticeship of the shaman provide a forum in which the shaman works through the precipitating crisis or madness. Through repeated trance experiences the novice shaman masters the once involuntary hallucinatory and emotional experiences in a manner not unlike the therapeutic use of "active imagination" and "waking dreams" described by various modern therapists.

Mania may be another entrée to shamanism. The metaphor of being struck by lightning in Bucke's description of cosmic consciousness parallels the significance of lightning in some shamanic traditions. In the Nahua region of central Mexico where I did research, shamans called "weather workers" perform rites to influence rain clouds and to drive away hail. They also cure illnesses, especially those related to spirits of the earth and weather. Weather workers are persons who have been struck by lightning. The lightning contains a weather spirit, and it is understood that it calls a person to serve the rain spirits. The victim may suffer from *susto* (see Chapter 5) until he or she agrees to serve the spirits as a weather worker and goes through a ceremony called a "coronation." Presumably, being struck by lightning can be either a real or figurative experience. Some persons are struck by lightning, or are almost struck by it, and live to become weather-working shamans. Others are perhaps affected by intrapsychic illumination (the occurrence of *susto* symptoms after a lightning experience is consistent with the observation that mania ordinarily precedes depression in bipolar disorders).

Richard Noll (1983) doubted that schizophrenic persons become shamans. He noted that shamans actively control their altered states of consciousness and that altered consciousness in shamanism is visionary, whereas hallucinations in schizophrenia are more often auditory. It seems unlikely that persons with Type II schizophrenia would be taken seriously as shamans; most of them are too disorganized for competent performance of an important social role. Some persons with Type I schizophrenia might manage this feat, however. They may not be continuously psychotic. During their psychotic episodes they may have ecstatic experiences and often, like the shaman, they are preoccupied with religious and cosmological issues. Even when they do not recover fully, they can have periods of relative sanity during which they can work on integrating their delusions and hallucinations with normative conceptions of reality.

Nonetheless, the evidence does not suggest that most shamans are severely or continuously psychotic (Peters and Price-Williams 1980). Fabrega and Silver (1973), for example, found little difference in social behavior between twenty shamans and twenty-three non-shamans in the highland Maya community of Zinacantan and only slightly more neurotic responses among the shamans' Holtzman Inkblots.[4] Noll (1983, 1985) thinks the essence of shamanism is a visionary consciousness that differs from ordinary consciousness but is not pathological. He suggests that "fantasy-prone persons" make good candidates for shamanism. Such persons hypnotize easily, hallucinate readily, and have rich fantasy lives and vivid memories.

A stronger case might be made for a connection between madness and modern cultures, however. Many poets and writers have been persons with bipolar personality disorder who have been at their most productive during manic and hypomanic phases of their mood swings. Roughly 4 percent of the US population exhibits cyclothymia or major bipolar disorder. The consequences for culture may be significant. Many persons with mood swings report increases in creativity, productivity, and sociability during hypomania (Jamison et al. 1980).

Devereux (1980) attributed schizophrenia to the cultural complexity and contradictions in modern life. He noted that in simpler traditional societies all adults have a working knowledge of their cultures whereas in industrialized society people master only part of the total cultural inventory. Even familiar neighborhoods may become strange with technological and social change. Persons with schizophrenia filter the influx of confusing information by withdrawing into simple, private worlds and by repeating religious and political nostrums (see also Diamond 1974). Murphy and Taumoepeau (1980) found a lower incidence of psychotic and nonpsychotic disorders in Tonga and speculated that the simplicity of life in traditional societies may be more conducive to mental health. Scheper-Hughes (1987) finds that religious themes pervade the delusions of Catholic persons with schizophrenia in South Bronx and that "panic-flight" responses are common whenever they leave the neighborhood. Similarly, Ellen E. Corin (1990) observes that schizophrenic persons who are less prone to rehospitalization seem to manage stress by avoiding employment and by remaining detached.

Warner (1994) suggests that the prevalence of schizophrenia may increase with modernization. For example, in 1934–1937 the anthropologist Meyer Fortes found only one psychotic person in a Tallensi population of about 5,000. In 1963, he and Mayer, a psychiatrist, located thirteen Tallensi with psychosis in a population of about 10,000. They surmised that economic and social change caused the increase (Fortes and Mayer 1969). Other studies imply that the prevalence of psychosis is similar in developing and developed areas. Jane M. Murphy (1976) found negligible differences among the Swedish, Inuit, Canadians, and Yoruba. The "Collaborative Study on Determinants of Outcome of Severe Mental Disorders" found comparable incidences of schizophrenia in different cultures (Sartorius et al. 1986). Sass (1992: 358–364), however, thinks that these results are inflated by the inclusion of cases of hysterical or brief reactive psychosis. He cites studies done in Papua New Guinea, Formosa, Sumatra, Oceania, Africa, and among the Hutterites and Amish of North America that show less prevalence than among peoples more involved in the modern economy.

Deleuze and Guattari (1983) contend that schizophrenia exemplifies the uncoded, unrestrained libidinal "flows" that energize productive activity. In their view, schizophrenia is the antithesis of the Oedipus complex and superego formation, which they see as bases for authoritarian social organization and as impediments to creative, productive activity. C.R. Badcock (1983) also discerns similarities between schizophrenia and contemporary culture, particularly, in art, literature, and music, but he is more critical. In his view, the psychosislike externalization of the unconscious in contemporary culture reflects a deterioration of superego and ego functions resulting from dislocations in modern society.

Sass (1992) suggests still another way of thinking about parallels and convergence between schizophrenia and modernity/postmodernity. As in schizophrenia, modern and postmodern art, literature, and academic thought evince a feeling that the world is unreal, feelings of "terror" and "wonder" about "mere being," "fragmentation," and "apophany" – an apperception of deeper, mysterious meaning behind the appearance of things. Sass is cautious about the implications of these parallels, although he implies that the alienation of modern life may form the matrix for both contemporary cultural trends and schizophrenia.

In fact, schizophrenic persons are often creative, and highly creative persons tend to score higher on measures of psychopathy and psychosis (Keefe and Magaro 1980). In a study of twins with schizophrenic mothers,

Heston (1966) found that the offspring who did not become schizophrenic were more likely to have creative hobbies and professions than were the control subjects who did not have schizophrenic mothers.

The use of schizophrenia as a metaphor for creativity and productivity, then, has some plausibility. Psychoanalysts have noted that creativity draws on the unconscious and makes use of primary process thinking. And, clearly, cultures can be renewed and energized by innovations that subvert established authority and ways of doing things. Deleuze and Guattari, however, romanticize schizophrenia when they make it a dominant metaphor for the psychological foundations of social life. There is madness in culture, but also sanity. Hallowell (1950) was perhaps closer to the truth when he pointed out that culture and sociality depend on people having coherent selves, moral centers, and willingness and ability to participate in meaningful and productive communicative interaction, traits that are lacking or seriously compromised in persons with schizophrenia.

7 Social psychology

So far, the focus of this book has been on human nature and individual personality; in the preceding chapters, social and cultural influences on the individual are considered, but we have not given much attention to sociality or culture. I now try to show how human nature and personality can illuminate social relations and cultural beliefs and practices. In this chapter, I consider how human nature and individual psychology subtend or inform common components of sociocultural systems (e.g., taboos, sacrifice, initiation rites, collective defenses, cultural artifacts, and social and political relations). In the following chapters, I take up two more general or encompassing phenomena, collective violence and religion.

The transformations of will and desire

In the social structuralism of Durkheim, the moral order constrains the egoistic inclinations of the individual; the moral sensibilities of the individual are produced and reproduced by group experience and collective symbols. The group exists merely by virtue of the signs that represent it; at the same time, the collective symbolic order does not exist apart from the moral life of the group it represents. Similarly, in Lacan and post-structuralism, the desires and moral thinking of the individual are artifacts of the social cultural milieu and discursive practices.

There is a good deal to be said in favor of these perspectives but in the end, I think, they are too simplistic, particularly as they portray subjectivity. Psychoanalysis enriches structuralist and post-structuralist views of social motivation with a more dialectic and biologically plausible understanding of the individual subject and his or her relation to the group. In the psychoanalytic perspective, the group and moral order involve transformations as well as suppression of individual will and desire. Social motives, that is, are often compromises between subjective needs and impulses, on the one hand, and moral reasoning and social expectations, on the other. The motives of individuals, even in the religious sphere and other highly refined cultural activities, may bear the traces of our primate heritage even as they reflect the human capacity for moral reasoning or abstract thought. Cultural symbols and discourse may shape and direct will and desire but they do not create them from scratch; they work with pre-existing, precultural motivational structures of the individual.[1]

In psychoanalytic terms, drives and needs are subject to sublimation and other defenses that bring drives, wishes, and unconscious fantasies into line with the mores and expectations of the group. Drive is transformed, and interest shifts from an original object or activity to a substitutive object or activity.

According to Freud, sublimation begins with the withdrawal of object libido into the self. As the libido is withdrawn from objects and reinvested in the ego, it becomes narcissistic libido, neutralized energy or desexualized libido ([1923a]1961: 45–46). This neutralized libido can then energize the pursuit of social status or attachments to persons, cultural artifacts, or supernatural beings. Sublimation can tap emotionally colored preoedipal and oedipal object-relations schemas or object- and power-seeking libido in a broad sense (Freud [1930]1961: 103–104). Power-seeking libido can merge with aggressive energy and destructive impulses, which are also subject to modulation and sublimation. "The instinct of destruction, moderated and tamed, and, as it were, inhibited in its aim, must, when it is directed towards objects, provide the ego with the satisfaction of its vital needs and with control over nature" (ibid.: 121). Sublimation can involve changes of object as well as of aim (Freud [1933a]1964: 97); the aim may shift from the satisfaction of sexual need to the satisfaction of some other purpose, and social ties and attachments to cultural objects and figures can substitute for earlier attachments.

Various ethnographic observations seem to lend support to the idea that culture involves transformations of will and desire. There are many traces of sexual and aggressive impulses in culture and social relations. Oral, scatological, and sexual imagery, metaphors, and symbols are ubiquitous in humor, folklore, myth, drama, and literature and in many rites and rituals (Bourke 1891). Eroticism is particularly evident in subversive humor, carnivals, and masquerades (Bakhtin 1984). Aggressive themes abound, often in combination with eroticism. Allusions to preoedipal mother figures and oedipal triangles are common, particularly in myth and ritual. Restrictions on sexual intercourse before or during hunting, war, work, and ceremonial activity suggest that culture depends on the suppression and, perhaps, the redirection of sexual energy.

The classical theory of sublimation, however, is too mechanistic. Aggressiveness and the libido are not constant forces nor are they independent from other mental processes. Aggressiveness and libidinal desire fluctuate with the play of imagination and with environmental stimulation, and their expression is organized by mental processes, including internal representations of cultural norms and social expectations. Freud's theorizing about sublimation can also be faulted for overemphasizing sexuality and for giving too little attention to other motives, especially the will-to-power and the need for attachment.

In earlier chapters I noted that drive and temperamental disposition are shaped and directed by object relations and cultural schemas. In human beings, drives and impulses are colored with emotion and anticipation, and infused with purpose and meaning. In short, they become wishes and desires. Because desire operates in the world of the symbolic, it is subject to symbolic manipulation.

The relation between sublimation and neurosis and perversion also needs rethinking. Freud viewed sublimation as one of several ways of organizing sexual and aggressive impulses. In sublimation, impulses are supposedly transformed into prosocial motives in keeping with the societal values and mores. In perversion, persons act out impulses whereas in neurosis, gratification is delayed or disguised under the pressure of guilt and anxiety (Freud [1905a]1953).

The suggestion that sublimation and collective defenses are alternatives to neurosis and perversion seems too schematic. It implies that neurosis and perversion are inherently unsocial but, as Freud himself realized, neurotic and perverse inclinations inform cultural beliefs and practice.

The mental processes in obsessive-compulsive disorder can be part of the psychology of socially normative behavior. Freud ([1907]1959) called attention, for example, to the similarities between the private rituals of persons with obsessive-compulsive disorder and religious practices and rituals; private and shared rituals alike are repetitive, performed under the rule of conscience, and associated with controlling impulses. Siri Dulaney and Alan Page Fiske (1994) have documented these and other similarities between the rituals of obsessive-compulsive personality disorder and cultural rituals in a cross-cultural study of ritual. They suggest that obsessive-compulsive behavior exaggerates a basic capacity for ritualistic behavior. Whereas obsessive-compulsive ritual may reflect brain dysfunction or emotional trauma, cultural rituals may be triggered by crises or stressful situations. Because they are shared, however, they are experienced as familiar rather than strange. Rituals become a way of making sense out of experience, and exerting agency. According to Dulaney and Fiske (1994: 275), "By concentrating many dimensions of significance into a few acts and concepts, rituals give these acts and concepts tremendous, mysterious power."

Hysterialike processes also inform the subjective motivation and organization of culture. We have already seen how dissociative disorders are subject to cultural shaping. Later in this chapter I note that identification and idealization – processes that are common in hysteria and dissociative disorders – are also part of normal social psychology.

The boundaries between perversion and sublimation are not always clear-cut. Perverse structures and sublimation may occur together (Fogel and Myers 1991). Chasseguet-Smirgel (1974) observed that the fetishist often shows unusual appreciation for cultural things. He may idealize artifacts and collect elegant knick-knacks, works of art, and furnishings along with leather, women's undergarments, shoes, and the like. He is "a man of good taste." The paraphiliac, threatened by exposure, embellishes the fetishistic lifestyle with the trappings of esthetic sensibility.

The difference between sublimation and perversion is further blurred by what contemporary psychoanalysts are calling "near-perversion," that is, perversion that occurs in fantasy but not behavior (Fogel and Myers 1991). Various forms of expressive culture can be seen as reflecting or nurturing perversion in collective fantasy or restricted social settings, particularly in modern societies. A large market exists for pornographic film and literature, and sadomasochistic and phallic ambisexual images abound in contemporary films and rock music (e.g., Alice Cooper and his pet python or Madonna in various poses). And, as Chasseguet-Smirgel (1984) has noted, there may be more subtle expressions of the perverse mentality in modern culture as well. She points, for example, to the perversionlike falsity and artificiality in contemporary society and culture.

Perverse strategies – or what may seem perverse to an outsider – have an affinity with power relations. Unregulated power can give vent to sadism. Resistance and subversion of power, meanwhile, may make use of perverse poetics. Bakhtin (1984) noticed how the imagery of the "grotesque" body in Carnival may express needs for empowerment and erotic gratification and resistance to a hegemonic political and cultural order. Ellen Handler Spitz (1991) perceptively traces the political entanglements of perverse imagery in Euripides' *The Bacchae*; the two protagonists, Dionysus and Pentheus, express their rage toward one another but it is Dionysus, the one who would usurp the power of the other, who personifies perversity.[2]

Perverse sexual acts focus on physical pleasure while depersonalizing or dehumanizing the self and the other. They often suggest pregenital and especially anal fixation. In men they also seem to involve denial of castration or, what may be the same thing, fantasies about phallic women. Chasseguet-Smirgel (1984) described perversion in men as a way of denying the differences between the genders and between the generations. Thus, it represents refusal to pass through the Oedipus complex. In both genders it is a rejection of identification with the father (including "father" as symbol for the social and moral order of adults). Instead of identifying with the father or moral order, persons with perverse inclinations fabricate a phallus – a grotesque substitute for the father and his values.[3] According to Chasseguet-Smirgel, they may only feign respect for the father in order to avoid unfavorable comparisons with him and submission to the demanding cultural standards he represents. Rather, they merely pretend to meet social standards with fabrication and artfulness. Similarly, Stoller (1991) describes how perverse persons seem oriented toward acting out a subversive posture vis-à-vis society, not simply for the pleasure it brings but, perhaps just as significantly, as a means of opposing authority.

Wherein, then, lies the difference between neurosis or perversion and sublimation? Obeyesekere (1990) contends that symbol systems may effect varying degrees of "remove" from unconscious fixations and conflicts, and he illustrates the point with an example from his research in Sri Lanka: the cult center of Kataragama where Abdin, the middle-aged Muslim, hangs himself on hooks every year. This religious practice began as penance after Abdin was accused of participating in a military coup. He was also, however, coping with childhood fears of his father. After the father's death, Abdin was free for a while from the need to hang from hooks but then resumed the practice and developed an hysterical paralysis. Abdin, says Obeyesekere, differs from the ecstatic priests and priestesses in the cult. The latter, feeling guilty about betraying a loved one, suffered debilitating spirit attacks yet they gradually managed to work through their guilt and to establish a more loving relationship with the once-hostile ancestor. In effect, sublimation may be neurotic or regressive in some persons and progressive in others.

Discerning what is progressive and what is regressive is not an easy matter, however. The difference between a progressive working through of unconscious issues and unproductive fixation on regressive fears or impulses is not simply a matter of distancing the self from childhood experiences and issues. Positive childhood experiences with love and attachment may lay an emotional, object relational basis for sociability in adulthood. Thus, there may be a sense in which emotional maturity involves not simply a transcendence of childhood conflicts and egocentricity but also conscious and unconscious memories of chilhood experience. Nor should we assume that the work of culture is always progressive for the individual. Some cultural practices may reinforce emotional conflicts and regressive tendencies in the individual. Fanatical religious sects and political movements, in particular, often seem to appeal to the most regressive inclinations in human beings. By the same token, some of the most productive forms of working through emotional conflicts may occur in creative cultural or political activities that set the individual in opposition to the group or received opinions and understandings.

Pragmatics, transference, and dialogue

Cultural beliefs and practices can be surprisingly "Freudian." Aggressive and sexual content, including allusions to incest and parricide, are common, particularly in humor, folktales, myths, and ritual. The real issue is not whether these qualities are present in expressive culture but rather how to interpret them. In the past, the working assumption in psychological anthropology was that expressive culture reflects individual wishes, desires, and anxieties, particularly those wishes, desires, and anxieties with origins in childhood experience.

A more plausible approach reworks this argument in terms of a constructivist theory of memory and with attention to the pragmatic functions of discourse. Current theory suggests that drive is inherently social. Moreover, it is organized by memory, cognitive processes, and social intelligence. These faculties transform drive into desire, purpose, intention. Evidence that memories are often reconstructed under the influence of current fantasy and experience, moreover, suggests that dialogue and discourse may affect not only the cultural content of desire but also its unconscious foundations. Through a process of "retranscription," cultural genres and tropes may affect how preoedipal and oedipal object relations influence desire and perhaps the very unconscious inscription of those object relations.

The bodily and familial figures in discursive practices and collective rituals are part of the pragmatics or rhetoric of social persuasion. When individuals try to influence each other in conversation, to maneuver in making claims to power and desiderata, or to amuse each other with humor, they use defense mechanisms and tropes. The symbolic content in such tactics may reflect the unconscious fantasies of the speaker and his or her intuitions about the conscious and unconscious motives of the interlocutor.

What psychoanalysts call "transference" – repeating early patterns of relating to others in current relationships – appears in the pragmatic functions of speech; the speaking subject may inject unconscious fantasy into dialogue and discourse where emotionally significant issues are at stake (Crapanzano 1981; Ewing 1987). Crapanzano (1992) in particular has reflected on the play of desire, power, and resistance as self and other – using rhetorical devices – seek to define themselves and each other for tactical and strategic advantage. Conversations also include negotiations about the social and political meanings of power, social statuses, and possessions. In conversation, then, pragmatics, transference, and social references intermingle. Social metaphors and symbols become more effective as they allude to the erotogenic body, and rituals become more influential when they represent preoedipal and oedipal object relations.

Ordinarily sublimation is a process of moving from regressive desires and fantasies to socially acceptable or productive work and social relations, of going from something crude or grotesque to something more refined, rational, or moral. It is a boot-strapping operation in which people lift each other through communicative interaction to shared understanding and emotional maturity. But the reverse is also possible. Social rhetoric may appeal to what is crude and egocentric in the individual. What is more, the retranscribable nature of memory suggests that discourse may reinforce regressive tendencies or even create them where they did not exist in the first place.

Such processes may be tactical and ephemeral. Grotesque or perverse images may be put in play in particular contexts and for specific purposes. The images do not necessarily affect entire personalities nor are their effects necessarily permanent. In carnivals, saturnalias, or spring festivals, for example, participants may identify with evil through masking and costuming, and they may relax their usual suppression of eroticism and aggression, but this need not mean that the participants are evil or perverse or that the festivities permanently rearrange the psychological organization of the individual.

This pragmatic aspect of social interaction puts the query about the boundaries between neurosis, perversion, and sublimation in another light. If cultures seem to have features of neurosis, perversion, or psychosis, it is not necessarily – or even likely – that the people of the culture are neurotic, perverse, or psychotic in a clinical sense. There is, though, similarity between neurosis and psychotic delusions, on the one hand, and cultural beliefs and practices, on the other. Social discourse can manipulate this continuity between normal psychology and neurosis or psychosis for pragmatic purposes. Whether such attempts to play on unconscious desires and fears or structural weaknesses in the ego and superego can permanently alter personality is an important but unsettled question. There is no doubt, however, that discourse and social context can affect desire, reality-testing, and moral reasoning over short periods of time.

Passionate attachments and substitutive objects

Heterosexual and homoerotic social relations may represent a working out of unconscious preoedipal and oedipal fantasies. Naomi Quinn (1991, 1992) suggests that the cultural schemas that inform American ideas about love and marriage have precursors in childhood experience, particularly experience with the nurturing mother. In his study of the Mehinaku of the Amazon, Gregor (1985) finds traces of preoedipal and oedipal fantasies in the language men and women use in passionate relationships. John Layard

(1959) suggested that homoeroticism in aboriginal Australia and Melanesia occurs in association with sister exchange. Brothers-in-law are the homosexual partners. Even when homosexual relations are more generalized, the boy-lover is called the "wife," the older male, the "sister's husband." Sister exchange itself has incestuous connotations, according to Layard; the brother-in-law stands for the self, and his sister – ego's actual or potential wife – is a substitute for one's own sister. In a study of the symbolic meaning of Dravidian kinship, Margaret Trawick (1990, 1992) shows that cross-cousin marriage is the culmination of a series of displacements of incestuous desire. The mother is the original object for boys and girls. Desire is then displaced, first into an idealized brother–sister relationship and then into the marital relationship; and since the marital relationship is riven with conflict, desire travels further, reaching vicarious satisfaction in cross-cousin marriage that joins the children of brother and sister.

Men and women may allude to the unconscious meanings of romance and marriage in order to achieve pragmatic effects. In *Enchanted maidens: Gender relations in Spanish folktales of courtship and marriage*, James M. Taggart (1990) finds that several well-known tales are concerned with freeing the enchanted maiden's sexuality for marriage, and he observes that the telling of the tales is part of dialogical processes in which men and women and parents and children negotiate the social contract. The tales Taggart examines reflect both the older generation's concerns with preserving family honor and the perspectives of young men and women, but variations in the actual telling of the tales indicate willingness to adjust to the wishes and concerns of others. Drawing on Bettelheim (1976), Taggart also observes that the tellers of tales may be working through unconscious preoedipal and oedipal issues: women affirm their willingness to turn from attachment to mothers to loving their husbands, whereas men admit their needs for love and their vulnerability to rejection while expressing willingness to subdue their masculine aggressiveness.

In Chapter 3, I noted that children often use cultural artifacts as substitutes for the maternal object. What the present examples suggest is that this inclination toward object substitution continues into adulthood. Cultural objects, however, can have various subjective meanings. Among other things, they can represent power and prestige. In a moment I will mention some examples of cultural objects that seem to represent both power and substitutes for the lost object or objects that represent a transitional space between a previous object and a new object. First, though, I want to call attention to the sublimation of the will-to-power. As noted earlier, the libido is power seeking as well as object seeking. In both respects, it undergoes displacement and symbolization.

Libido dominandi[4]

Psychoanalytically oriented writers have often commented on the oral, anal, and phallic content of expressive culture. Such content is seen as evidence for human needs for oral, anal, and genital gratification. From the perspective of a social or dialogical psychoanalytic anthropology, however, what is perhaps more noteworthy about such cultural expressions is how they evince close connections between eroticism and the will-to-power. Seen from this perspective, psychosexual imagery may express interest in power as well as in sexuality *per se*. At the same time, it may be part of a symbolic apparatus for asserting and maintaining power.

Power has varied associations with orality. Having plenty of food and sophisticated culinary tastes can express high status. In many cultures, power and prestige are enhanced by sharing food with others in feasts. The important personage may be the one who nurtures social others. In some societies, cannibalism symbolized power and terrorized actual and potential political subjects.

The anal connotations of power are apparent in beliefs and practices concerning money. Freud ([1908c]1959) mentioned the German *Dukantenscheisser* (shitter of ducats), a candy figure with a coin protruding from its rectum, and Freud and D.E. Oppenheim ([1911]1958) noted an association between excrement and buried treasure in German folklore. Dundes (1984) commented on this association as well as other anal associations of power in German culture.

Money illustrates how a cultural symbol or object can have both unconscious personal meanings and public social meanings. Explorations of feelings about money in psychotherapy have disclosed concerns with self-preservation, narcissistic motives, and anal erotic impulses (Fenichel [1938]1954).[5] The anal meanings of money may be related in part to its having exchange value but not use value. Money as such is worthless, like bodily waste; and since it passes through many hands, it may seem to transmit contamination from anonymous social others. Children may learn about these associations when they are told not to put money in their mouths. They may then associate money with other dirty things.

Ferenczi ([1914]1950) described the child's progression from an interest in playing with feces to playing with castoff epidermis from between the toes, nasal secretions, ear wax, mud, sand, pebbles, marbles, and, lastly, money. He mentioned one patient who ingested coins and then retrieved them from his feces, taking pleasure in the polish they got in transit. For children, the production of the smelly object may provide a sense of power, and this sense of power may later inform the sense of power that goes with making money. Yet, as Ferenczi's patient suggests, there is also something magical about money; while lacking use value, through exchange money can produce valuables and alter social relationships.

Phallic symbols represent power in many cultures. The phallus symbolized political and military power in many ancient European cultures (Vanggaard 1972). Throughout Africa, political power and male aggressiveness are associated with bulls, male birds, spears, arrows, or swords (Mazrui 1974). Power is also expressed in actual or symbolic sodomy in various societies. In parts of rural Mexico, for instance, young men use multilayered innuendo in verbal dueling to insinuate that they are penetrating each other sexually; to penetrate the interlocutor more than he penetrates you is a sign of superiority. When one man passes gas in front of another, the latter may say: "Te saludo buen anciano con el sombrero en la mano" (I salute you old man [*anciano* = *ano* = anus] with my hat [*sombrero* = penis] in my hand; Ingham 1986: 144–145). In Turkey, boys between the ages of eight and fourteen intimate with clever insults that they are penetrating each other. Each boy defends himself and asserts "his virile standing in his peer group by seeing to it that his phallus threatens the anus of any rival who may challenge him" (Dundes et al. 1970). The Sepik Arapesh say they "fight with food": they defeat and humiliate their adversaries by giving them long yams in a ritual substitute for war. As the skirmish lines approach, the aggressors lunge forward with their long yams attached to poles, a movement that humiliates their adversaries. Donald Tuzin showed that the yams represent the person, the penis, male narcissism, and pride. The presentation of yams thus symbolizes aggressive sodomy. The aggressors imply with gestures that their anuses will "skin" the penises of the enemies if the attack is returned (Tuzin 1972).

Some cultural objects may represent substitutive objects. Others may represent power. Still others may express both the power-seeking and object-seeking aspects of the libido. The Trobriand *kula* and the American automobile seem to combine representations of object and power in this way.

The *kula*

In the *kula* system of the Melanesian archipelago, red shell necklaces and white armshells circulate in opposite directions in a great, inter-island exchange system. Because a man may not receive armshells and necklaces from the same partner, he must have two or more partners. Ideally, partnerships last for life. In the Trobriands, *kula* trading is an aristocratic enterprise associated with virility, power, sexual prowess, monopoly of women, and rejuvenation. "*Kula*" means magic, and *kula* magic is likened to love magic. Red necklaces are "male" and white armshells are "female"; their exchange forms a "marriage." The last gift, the "clinching gift," is "the one that bites" – biting is part of lovemaking in the Trobriands (McDougall 1975: 63–65).

According to Lorna McDougall, the trading partners represent brother and sister. Trobrianders believe that they can test magic intended for *kula* rivals against a mother or sister; in myth, love magic causes a brother and sister to commit incest (McDougall 1975: 71, 87). Spiro (1982: 80–83) argued that the *kula* reflects oedipal fantasy; he cited among other things, a *kula* spell that Trobriand traders recite when they arrive on the beach at Dobu. The spell likens the wife and sister of the partner to the trader's own mother, and the partner, to his father. The implication is that the partner and his wife will take the trader to their breast as if the trader were a child and that the partner will feed him, not with a spoon but with his tongue. Another spell implies that the trader wants to seduce his partner with his beauty: "My head is made bright, my face flashes. I have acquired a beautiful shape, like that of a chief; I have acquired a shape that is good. I am the only one; my renown stands alone" (Malinowski [1922]1961: 339). In keeping with this imagery, there is also inter-male rivalry in *kula* trading.

Kula trading redirects hostility in intervillage and interlineage relations into relations with more distant trading partners, where it is more acceptable (Uberoi 1962). Interaction between trading partners includes ritualized displays of anger, and there are intimations that *kula* exchange is a symbolic commutation of headhunting. Before pacification, heads were exchanged in *kula* trading in some areas to the south of the Trobriands. In the Sudest-East Calvados area, the decorated head of a mutual enemy was given to allies along with shell necklaces and other valuables during feasts (Lepowsky 1983: 497).

In a story recorded by Malinowski ([1922]1961: 291–295) the Koya of Gabu treacherously killed the chief Toraya and other members of a Trobriand expedition. Later Toraya's younger brother, Tomakam, avenged the deaths. After exchanging *kula* valuables with the headman of the Koya, Tomakam cut off his head. Approaching the Trobriand shoreline, Tomakam signaled the conquest to his mother with blasts on a conch shell. The prose account of Tomakam's feat has the head of the defeated rival at one point on a "stick of the canoe," but the celebratory song leaves it unclear whether Tomakam has the head or the *kula* necklace in his basket as he greets his mother.

Consumerism and the American automobile

Images of social status, sex, love, and commercial products appear together in advertisements for consumer products in modern America. The enormous appetite for consumer goods may seem perfectly natural, or nearly so, but perhaps there is more to it than mere social expectations or cultural values. Consumerism may reflect needs for attachment, love, and empowerment. This in turn suggests that the feelings of alienation, loneliness, and frustration in social striving may help to motivate the ever-expanding circle of wants in the consumer economy. Kleptomania or compulsive shoplifting may be a revealing phenomenon in this respect. It seems to bespeak a deep craving for consumer goods. At least among patients in psychotherapy, kleptomania seems to be an attempt to counteract the loss, or lack, of power or love (Kaplan 1991).

The automobile deserves special attention in the study of modern consumerism. Its economic importance is obvious. Directly and indirectly, it accounts for a sizeable portion of modern economies. Yet the automobile also seems to have a great deal of emotional significance for many people, a significance that goes beyond its practical utility.

The automobile is a status symbol and, quite literally, an object that enhances a person's physical power. At the same time, it may function as a substitutive or transitional object. Interesting in this regard is a passage in Cuber and Haroff's ([1965]1970) book on work, marriage, and lifestyle among affluent Americans. Cuber and Haroff compared and contrasted two types of marriage: "intrinsic" marriage and "utilitarian." Couples with intrinsic marriages put less emphasis on their careers and more on their marriages and families. They devote more time to each other, to their children, and to their neighborhoods and communities. They are also less likely to have extramarital affairs. Men and women in utilitarian marriages, on the other hand, are less committed to their spouses and more likely to have affairs.

A remarkable passage shows how careerism, extramarital relations, and consumerism may replace commitment to spouses and children. A middle-aged woman describes her utilitarian marriage. There is no pleasure in her marriage, she says, and she is bored with her children. She rarely sees her husband – he travels on business – and when she does there is little passion or intimacy. After describing her marriage in these negative terms, she mentions that their careers are doing very well and that they now have a country home and horses. "And I have my new car – only mine is a hardtop. Bob likes a sports coupe. . ." (ibid.: 107–108).

The train of thought in her narrative implies that both husband and wife may be displacing needs for love and affection from each other into status-striving and consumerism in conformity with implicit cultural symbolism. Expensive automobiles in western culture symbolize personal empowerment, but they may also be surrogate love objects. Advertisements imply that cars are "sexy" and that Americans have "love affairs" with them. The

Toyota advertisement exclaims, "I love what you do for me!" The Toyota car here is an anthropomorphic subject, a self-object that promises both positive self-esteem and a relationship. Advertisements for sports cars often evoke the possibilities of a "passionate" relationship. Washing and waxing cars, an activity that resembles petting, is a common weekend ritual. Some avid collectors keep entire harems of expensive automobiles. Having a car also may help to attract a real lover (Marsh and Collett 1987). The fantasy, it seems, is social as well as subjective. The allure of having an automobile (the object/phallus) lies not merely in possession but in the knowledge that someone else might want it or one like it.

Pollution, abjection, and taboo

Cultures, among other things, are ways of organizing safe environments. They include subsistence systems, designs for shelter and clothing, methods for coping with illness, and weapons and fighting skills for group defense. In addition, they include magic and rituals for coping with real and imaginary dangers. David H. Spain (personal communication) observes that cultures provide what Sandler ([1960]1987) called a "background of safety."

The group itself can be a source of security and self-esteem. Thus, individual and collective defenses against insecurity may involve symbolic representations of social order and the boundaries between ingroup and outgroup. The sense of safety depends in part on ritual and discursive practices that discourage regressive, antisocial behavior. Such behavior may evoke anxiety, anger, and disgust. It may be taboo. The realm of the taboo is the "liminal," the space between social positions and beyond normative structure and order. The tabooed activity, in other words, represents temptation, a potential reversal of sublimation.

Social anthropologists consider the ways in which cultural ideas about pollution reinforce group boundaries and social order. Mary Douglas (1966) argued that ritual dirt represents an absence of order. Thus, dietary abominations may be associated with anomalous animals, themselves metaphors for social anomalies.

Psychoanalytic interpretations, meanwhile, point to the subjective underpinnings of ingroup/outgroup distinctions. Symbolization and ritualization of ingroup versus outgroup distinctions may correspond in the unconscious to defensive splitting of the self or object; the bad part of the self or object is attributed to the social or supernatural others. Outsiders and evil supernatural figures may represent unacceptable or disturbing aggressive and sexual impulses. Racist and ethnocentric stereotypes often attribute aggressive and illicit sexual impulses to the other (Kovel 1984).

Kristeva (1982: 57–58) wondered if social boundaries reflect preoedipal concerns with relatedness and differentiation as well as oedipal guilt. She saw in the feminine connotations of pollution and otherness, an inclination to establish individuation and separation of the self from the mother. Before the self develops desire for a separate object, it fashions an "abject" from the negative features of the early self-object unity. Ambiguous, the "abject" is a metaphor for the wanted object but, also, a token of negativity. Closely associated with perversion, it opposes morality, the sacred, the law. The perverse, then, may be seen in disrespect for social boundaries in contrast to the obsessive attitude, which reacts to the abject with censure and disgust. Kristeva suggests that anxiety about social boundaries reiterates the child's concerns with attachment and separation.

Her idea finds support in the way "primitive" defense mechanisms – splitting, projective identification, denial, and idealization – often seem to inform shared representations of the outgroup and ingroup. In clinical practice, these defenses are usually seen in persons with severe personality disorders, and yet many "normal" persons may lapse into these patterns of thought under the influence of political propaganda and social and racial stereotypes. A key element here may be the degree of identification with the leader or group. Individuals may identify with the group and project their superegos onto the group or leaders to protect and secure their individual identities, although in doing so they may reduce the group to the less mature, more sadistic features of superego functioning (Kernberg 1980: 219–220).

The causes of fear and anxiety include threats of loss and death. Funerary rituals and other beliefs and practices ease the pain of bereavement and temper the fear of death. Religion also may offer consolation for the universal human awareness of mortality and compensation for losses and separation, especially the primordial loss of the mother. Róheim (1943) concluded that cultures are elaborate systems of defense against anxiety, especially the anxiety occasioned by separation from the mother; culture restores the lost unity with the mother through symbolic substitutes. Spiro (1965) argued that religions may function as "culturally constituted defense systems." He examined, for example, collective psychological defenses in Buddhist monasteries in Burma. Rorschach protocols and interviews suggested that Burmese monks tended to have defensive personalities, while other evidence revealed or suggested aggressive and oral impulses, hypochondria, fear of women and mother-figures, and exaggerated narcissism. Spiro contended that these characteristics, which would be dysfunctional in lay society, find socially approved expression in spiritual self-absorption and monastic companionship.

Sacrifice

A system of taboos defines and safeguards the moral order or, more particularly, what might be called the "metonymical" order between social actors, groups, and strata. Taboos order contiguity *within* the group. Social relations are defined by things one may or may not touch, eat, approach, talk about. Ritual sacrifice, in contrast, restores order resulting from the violation of taboos by evoking the "metaphorical" similarities *between* the divinity and social body (Kristeva 1982: 111).

An enactment of death and rebirth, ritual sacrifice may celebrate both liminality and order. The sacrificial victim mediates the relation between society and the divine and thus restores the connection between them by returning to the divine what was first given to human beings by the divine (Zuesse 1974). Sacrificial rites thus carry a forceful message about the morality of order, social duty, and sublimation, but they may also express unconscious fantasies and impulses.

Earlier psychoanalytic writers discerned oedipal meanings and motives in sacrifice. R.E. Money-Kyrle ([1929]1965) theorized that for men sacrifice may represent, among other things, (a) hostility toward the father; (b) love for the father and a desire to preserve him through incorporation; and (c) guilt and propitiation.

Money-Kyrle's arguments now seem overly conjectural. They are based on second-hand accounts, they make little effort to consider local cultural meanings, and they virtually ignore social functions. Yet familial and erotic imagery inform ritual sacrifices in many cultural traditions.

Róheim ([1930]1972) discussed the oedipal symbolism in the divine kingships of ancient Egypt and some traditional African cultures (see p. 192 below). Layard (1955) argued that the sacrificial boar on Malekula in Melanesia is an ambisexual figure that represents an evil, devouring mother and a father. The sacrificial killing of the boar is a symbolic copulation in which the sacrificer separates from the mother and incorporates the libido-soul of the boar. With this sacrifice the men separate from the mothers – they can feed themselves – but they also, paradoxically, identify with the feminine qualities of the boar. Layard also suggested that the boar sacrifice resonates with marriage and cannibalism: pigs are given as bridewealth, and cannibal victims on Malekula are prepared in the same way as sacrificial boars.

More recently, Walter Burkert (1983) theorized that sacrifice forms the experiential core of religious experience and suggested that it began with paleolithic hunting, an activity that was analogous to killing and eating humans. The paleolithic society, according to Burkert, was a hunting society that reproduced itself through mimetic ritual, that is, by modeling hunting and its associated meanings and values in sacrificial ritual. Hunting, war, and sacrifice, then, composed a symbolic order. Because hunting resembled the male pursuit of females in certain respects, hunting, war, and sacrifice took on sexual meanings, at least for males. Finally, Burkert noted that the bloody initiations of pubescent boys have a sacrificial character, especially in agricultural and pastoral societies: "Deprived of its hunting quarry, the secret society makes the initiand himself into a victim" (ibid.: 46).

According to Burkert, sacrificial ritual combines violence and allusions to sexuality, including suggestions of parricide and incest. The sacrificial being becomes the god. The god/victim is killed, eaten, and, in the repetition of the ritual, forever resurrected. Variations are possible. The sacrificial victim may be the son of the father deity, and a mother goddess may be part of the pantheon:

Man, the paradigm of mankind in a male society, enters the permanent order as a young man, ritually and symbolically transformed into "his mother's bull," as we learn from one of the pharaonic epithets, and sooner or later he must die, just like the sacrificial animal. Thus, myth provides the Great Goddess with a chosen companion who is both her son and lover; he is known as "father" Attis, whom the goddess loves, emasculates, and kills. (Burkert 1983: 81)

Burkert implies that sacrifice encompasses sexuality, violence, and oedipal impulses.

In psychoanalytic interpretations of sacrifice oedipal themes reflect individual fantasy. There are other ways of interpreting oedipal imagery, however. René Girard (1977) saw oedipal symbolism in sacrifice as secondary to a social function of preserving the social order. Sacrifice, according to Girard, redirects violence toward a ritual victim, violence that might otherwise tear the social fabric apart. The impulse to violence arises in society from "mimesis," from wanting what someone else wants. Mimetic desire evokes envy, jealousy, and hostility, and, therefore, violence. Since human beings lack a biological mechanism for inhibiting violent urges, violence propagates violence. Sacrifice interrupts the cycle by focusing hostility on the sacrificial object. Any oedipal connotations of the sacrificial victim, according to Girard, are merely a *post hoc* rationale for ritualized victimization; the ritual murder is justified by associating the victim with incest and parricide, the worst of crimes.

Girard's argument is intriguing. Sacrifice is a social phenomenon and thus seems to call for sociological interpretation. The notion that shared hostility toward a third party may reinforce ingroup solidarity is plausible; there are many historical and ethnographic examples of formerly antagonistic groups and factions drawing together once they found some person or group for their collective hatred.

Girard's mimetic theory of desire, however, begs questions about how desire arises in the first place. The view that people simply want what social others have or want avoids the question of why people have particular desires and not others. It also avoids the question of where envy comes from, and why some individuals are more envious and aggressive than others. In addition, Girard's theory of sacrifice may construe the motives and meanings in sacrifice too narrowly. Sacrifice may channel aggressive impulses in some instances, but it may address the problem of order in other ways as well.

Sacrifice may provide not so much a release of aggression as a *model* for redirecting hostility in conformity with the social norms. At the same time, it may convey the necessity of self-control. The sacrificial victim mediates the relation between group and deity; it represents the members of the group, singly and together, and the deity. In symbolizing the social covenant in this way it also may allude to social duty, to the necessity of controlling impulses and meeting social obligations. The deity may depend on sacrifice, but insofar as the deity is a symbol of society, the implication is that society also depends on sacrifice, that is, on an inhibition of egoism and a willingness to work for the whole.

The sacrificial covenant, moreover, may bind the members of society together through guilt and expiation. Ritual murder implicates the members of society in a collective crime against an innocent victim, and it places the perpetrators in the debt of the victim whose sacrifice benefits society. Since guilt and the condition of being in debt are closely related, sacrifice may evoke memories of other transgressions and debts. And inasmuch as it includes imagery of parent–child relationships, it may arouse guilt about preoedipal and oedipal desires and emotions. Yet the ritual victim is a scapegoat who bears the guilt and sins of others. The victim reduces indebtedness to the divine and so reduces collective guilt. Hence sacrifice may reinforce the moral order while promoting a general sense of forgiveness.

It could be argued that moral order and forgiveness are just as important, if not more so, for the preservation of social peace as displacement of aggression. Moral order encourages self-control, whereas forgiveness may facilitate the acceptance of guilt and thus mitigate inclinations to blame others. If there is a sense of right and wrong, but no forgiveness, then blaming others and the externalization of aggression may become more likely.

Puberty rites

Many cultures mark the passages of young men and women to adulthood with special rites. Such rites often have a sacrificial character; like sacrifice, they may portray death and rebirth, in this case the death and rebirth of the self. The rites may occur before puberty or during adolescence. Such rites are more common in simpler societies, although the most complex rites are often found in tribal societies. The rites show the importance of gender as a social category in preindustrial societies, but they also may have other social and psychological meanings.[6]

Male rites

Many male rites celebrate the transition from boyhood to manhood and, more precisely, the transition to the status of warrior and marriageable man. They are concerned, in other words, with socializing aggression and sexuality as well as effecting change of status. They may involve genital operations (circumcision, subincision, or supercision) or some other painful ordeal (Schlegel and Barry 1979: 202).

Psychoanalytically oriented interpretations have seen genital mutilation as a key to understanding the meaning and functions of initiation rites. For Freud, circumcision was a symbolic castration and "an expression of submission to the father's will" ([1940]1964: 190n; see also [1913]1955: 153n). Reik (1931) interpreted male puberty rites as a retaliation against the sons for their rebellious feelings toward their fathers. Noting that in some cultures young men are not permitted to carry weapons until they have been initiated, he saw the rites as preserving society against the disruptive effects of oedipal hostility. The fathers invoke the gods or ancestors when justifying the rites, although in practice, according to Reik, the rites serve the purposes of the older men by encouraging the young men to identify with the fathers and to redirect their hostility toward enemies and their desire toward marriageable women.

Similarly, Whiting, Kluckhohn, and Anthony (1958) suggested that initiation rites suppress rebellion in boys and reinforce identification with their fathers. They found that male initiation ceremonies correlate cross-culturally with long periods of postpartum avoidance of sexual relations between husbands and wives and with exclusive mother–child sleeping arrangements, and they theorized that these customs intensify the son's resentment of the father when the latter eventually replaces the son in the mother's bed. Michio Kitahara (1976) also found a connection between initiation rites and close mother–child relationships in early childhood, but she emphasized the possible effects of paternal influence in the resolution of the Oedipus complex. She found that the relation between exclusive mother–child sleeping arrangements and initiation rites was stronger if the father slept in a separate domicile. Robert Bates Graber (1981) similarly regarded circumcision rites as ritual castration that discourages rebelliousness in sons. While tensions between fathers and sons develop in many societies, Graber theorized that they are especially troublesome where patrilocal residence and state formation confine fathers and mature sons to the same neighborhood or community. In his sample, genital mutilation occurs in 54 percent of the cultures having both patrilocal residence and state organization and in only 6 percent of the societies lacking these traits.

Initiation rites also may express concerns with gender and gender identity. Bettelheim (1954) inferred that ritualized bodily mutilation in some cultures may express male envy of female reproductive functions. Whiting, Kluckhohn, and Anthony (1958) theorized an alternative to their castration-anxiety hypothesis: that the boy may envy and identify with the mother if he sees her as responsible for ending the symbiotic mother–son relationship. Burton and Whiting (1961) saw the exclusive mother–son relationship as encouraging a primary identification with the mother. In patrilocal societies, where sons must identify with their fathers and agnates, initiation rites may replace the primary feminine identification with a secondary masculine identification.

Leora N. Rosen (1988) points out that preoedipal and oedipal conflicts tend to resurface during adolescence. Thus, initiation rites may encourage boys to separate themselves from internal representations of the object and to attach to extrafamilial objects. That is, they may deal with preoedipal conflicts around separation through bisexual symbolism and by offering older boys or adult men as maternal surrogates, and they may suppress oedipal conflicts through threats of castration. Rosen also notes that the rites inculcate culturally appropriate social identities.

Whatever the validity of these hypotheses, initiation rites also have social functions and meanings. Michael R. Allen (1967) argued that male cults and initiation rites in Melanesia express the division between the genders; the division itself reflects unilineal descent and unilocal residence. Yehudi A. Cohen (1964) saw the rites as separating youths from their families and incorporating them into unilineal descent groups. Frank W. Young (1965) argued that male initiation incorporates young men into male groups and dramatizes their masculine status.

Karen Eriksen Paige and Jeffery M. Paige (1981) theorized that circumcision rites mediate conflicting political agendas in societies with fraternal interest groups and kin-group control and defense of valuable resources. Patrilineal warlike societies tend to fragment into feuding factions. Building a strong lineage requires reproductive success. Successful men accomplish this by taking additional wives, both to increase the numbers of their offspring and to reduce those of their rivals. To preserve their power, they also must prevent junior or collateral lines from breaking away.

Circumcision symbolizes castration. Literal castration would be an effective strategy against political rivals but it would also undermine the power of the clan or tribe. Circumcision ritual, or symbolic castration, subordinates the young men to their elders and signals that the father does not intend to found a bigger and stronger lineage at the expense of other lineages. By acceding to the initiation of his son, the father in this way strengthens his ties with his consanguines in other lineages, but since the message is purely symbolic – the son is not actually castrated – he does not really give up the possibility of having many grandsons.

Paige and Paige argued that male puberty rites express the importance of male solidarity in the control of valuable resources. Consistent with their interpretation, they found circumcision to correlate with the presence of valuable resources and, especially, fraternal interest groups ($r = 0.53$), whereas it correlates only weakly with the postpartum sex taboo ($r = 0.18$) (1981: 162).

Paige and Paige preferred their political rhetoric argument to the psychological explanations mentioned earlier. Political rhetoric in ritual, however, may work with and on psychological dispositions. Simon Ottenberg (1988) uses both social and psychological interpretations in his study of circumcision and initiation rites for boys among the Afikpo, an Ibo people in southeast Nigeria. The Afikpo have localized patrilineal descent groups, dispersed matrilineal clans, age grades and sets, a preference for polygyny, a postpartum sex taboo, and elaborate secret societies and fertility rituals for men. Ottenberg infers that circumcision and initiation rites – presently the two are spread out over several years – express concerns of older men with suppressing rebellion among younger men. At the same time, he notes that the rites prepare young men for war and enhance social solidarity and male superiority. Fathers may resent being displaced by the nursing child during postpartum sexual avoidance. Young men may pose a threat to the older, polygynous men during these periods of sexual continence. There also are direct sources of conflict: sons may want their share of the father's land, and sons cannot receive more important titles than their fathers until the fathers die. The threats young men pose to the male gerontocracy may explain why fathers gain prestige by sponsoring elaborate initiation rites for their sons. Participation in the secret society represents a redirection and sublimation of men's libidinal interests.

The rites may be a form of discourse about political relations, but it seems reasonable to assume that the messages in myth and ritual are directed at the young as well as older men. A great deal of effort is expended in trying to communicate lore and values to the young men, evidently, it would seem, with the aim of encouraging a sense of male solidarity and pride as well as respect for elders. If the rites succeed in this purpose, it may be because the message that the boys have been too close to their mothers elicits or creates socially effective anxieties.

Female rites

Although less has been written about them, rites for young women are more common than male rites, particularly among simple foraging societies. Female rites often signal a change of status from girl to marriageable woman while calling attention to the value of female fertility. About one-third of the rites involve physical pain, and about 8 percent, genital mutilation (i.e., clitoridectomy, infibulation). Many rites seem concerned with encouraging domesticity and marital fidelity (Schlegel and Barry 1979, 1980).

Psychoanalytically oriented interpretations of female rites have considered the way in which menstruation may trigger anxiety for males. Along with suggesting bodily injury, it may stir up memories of parental intercourse and related oedipal anxieties. Folklore, it is pointed out, suggests that women may have teeth or a dangerous paternal phallus within the vagina. Stephens (1962) found a correlation between severity of menstrual taboos and several variables, including a long postpartum sex taboo which, in his view, may intensify the Oedipus complex in males.

Here again, however, social meanings and functions deserve consideration. Judith K. Brown (1963) noted that female initiation rites are more common in matrilocal or bilocal societies than in patrilocal societies, and hence she inferred that the rites mark a change of status when the change is not signaled by a change in residence. Ethnographers working in New Guinea have suggested that male fears of female pollution may be related to marriages between hostile, feuding agnatic groups (Meggitt 1964). Douglas (1966) contended that fears of female pollution may arise in societies in which men have difficulties dominating women. Paige and Paige (1981) argued that female initiation is a ritual strategy for recruiting political support to defend menarcheal daughters against seduction and preserve their marriageability. They found that the rites are less common where strong resource bases and fraternal interest groups make it easier for men to protect daughters' reputations.

The *tāli*-tying rites of the Nayar and Tiyyar of the Malabar coast of India illustrate the strengths and weaknesses of psychoanalytic and sociological interpretations. Traditionally, prepubescent girls went through mock-menstruation and then a ceremony in which they were "married" to someone who played the role of an appropriate husband. Among the Nayar of Southern Malabar, the groom was ideally of high status, perhaps a Nambudiri Brahman. After the ceremony, the young woman might never sleep with or even see her "husband" again; rather, she slept with lovers, who visited her in the house of her matrilineage.

Kathleen Gough (1955) showed that the *tāli* (a gold ornament) is a phallic symbol and that other aspects of the ritual refer to reproduction and fertility. The ceremonies, which occur before puberty, constitute a "symbolic defloration." The Nayar and Tiyyar believed that menstruating women are in a dangerous, polluting condition, and that if they disregard menstrual rules they can be raped by evil spirits, "appearing as hairy animals." This belief, in Gough's view, reflects fear of and fascination with paternal incest. She argued that the menstruating woman is unconsciously associated with the mother, which then sets up a fear of the father in association with the consummation of marital intercourse. It is thus necessary to have a mock menstruation and symbolic deflowering because of "the marked horror of incest in these castes, which makes it necessary for the natal kinsmen of a woman to renounce the rights in her mature sexuality before she is in fact mature" (ibid.: 64). The ritual husband represents the father, whereas the "bride" is strongly associated with the goddess Bhagavadi, who represents both mother and virgin. By having a "father-figure common to the whole society" symbolically deflower the young woman, her natal kinsmen become less threatening, and the relations with her are cleansed of their disturbing connotations; and she, for her part, is freed to have sexual relations (ibid.: 71). Before the deflowering, the girl is like the goddess who, having been subjected to a phallic attack by the male, becomes bloody but phallic and dangerous (ibid.: 75).

Yalman (1963) questioned these interpretations, contending instead that the *tāli*-tying ritual expresses a widespread South Asian concern with the preservation of caste standing. Since membership in a caste involves maternal and paternal descent, castes are endogamous. In practice, caste purity depends more on women than men because a man can reject his offspring whereas it is much more difficult for a woman to do so. Women, therefore, may have sexual relations with higher-status men, but never with lower-status men. In groups like the Nayar, where fatherhood has little importance and a woman takes lovers instead, the *tāli*-tying ritual affirms a marital connection with a higher-status male.

The sociological explanations seem more straightforward, but they tend to ignore symbolic details. The psychoanalytic explanations notice the symbolism but may disregard the pragmatic functions of ritual action. Perhaps, as with sacrifice and other social institutions, there is room for both types of interpretation. Ritual symbolism that associates a premarital daughter with the oedipal mother may indeed have the desired sociological effect of deterring unwanted suitors and thus preserving parental interests in the daughter. Formulated in this way, oedipality is not the primary motive. Rather, oedipal metaphors serve a pragmatic function in social discourse.

Identification and idealization

In *Group psychology and the analysis of the ego* Freud broadened his social psychology to include idealization, identification, and affectionate relationships. Love and identification are related phenomena. The infant identifies with its first love objects and so lays the basis for an ego-ideal. Later, identification may follow object loss. For example, "A child who was unhappy over the loss of a kitten declared straight out that now he himself was the kitten, and accordingly crawled about on all fours, would not eat at table, etc." ([1921]1955: 109). The members of a group, according to Freud, not only share mutual affection but, also, identify with each other in their egos and may substitute the leader for their ego-ideals (ibid.: 116). Identification in the ego refers to the actual self, and manifests itself in social behavior. Thus, for example, peers who identify with each other may dress alike. Identification in the ego-ideal is more a matter of sharing common values or ideals. Thus, identification with leaders may or may not involve obvious imitation. Soldiers take their commander as an ideal but do not imitate him. Christians, on the other hand, accept Jesus as their ideal and often try to emulate his example, although only psychotic Christians actually claim to be Jesus Christ.

Identification with the leader may involve idealization. In romantic love, for instance, the partners may exaggerate each other's positive qualities to a degree bordering on delusion. The virtues of leaders, culture heroes, and supernatural figures are similarly exaggerated. In either instance, idealization may involve an unconscious process of projecting childhood memories of wonderful and exciting parents onto the object.

Eroticized attachments, identification, and idealization may support social cohesion by giving the individual a stake in the group. Like romantic love, attachment to and identification with the leader provide narcissistic satisfaction, satisfaction which is enhanced by invidious comparisons with, and hostility toward, other groups. This identification with the ideal and the satisfaction associated with it serve to modulate the hostility that might otherwise divide society. People in lower social classes, according to Freud, identify with their social superiors; even though they may feel hostile towards them, they may see in them a manifestation of their cultural ideals ([1927a]1961: 13).

In romantic love and other instances of idealization the object replaces the ego-ideal. According to Freud, it may even provide "a substitute for some unattained ego ideal of our own" ([1921]1955: 112). In this way romantic love resembles the hypnotic trance, since in each case the other person replaces the ego-ideal. A hypnotist assumes the role of parent toward the subject (ibid.: 114–116, 127); at the same time, the interaction between the hypnotist and subject resembles leader–follower relations. While the hypnotist has special powers, the leader has charisma. The mysterious, magnetic power that leaders exert over their followers, in effect, resembles romantic enthrallment and hypnotists' control over their subjects.

Identification and idealization are reinforced and directed by culture and social practices. Rituals idealize cultural values, culture heroes, and supernatural figures. Accentuating positive qualities of the self is a common ploy in politics and social striving. Actual and would-be leaders dress and talk the part, convey and dramatize their credentials and exploits. In some societies, mystical affinities link elders, elites, and royalty to honored ancestors and deities.

Ulman and Abse (1983) applied these ideas about group dynamics in studies of group psychotherapy, political behavior, and religious sects. The followers of a charismatic leader substitute their ego-ideals for the ego-ideal of the leader. This identification is regressive because it repeats a process that began in childhood. The regressive tendencies strengthen as leader and follower react to each other's paranoia, passions, and fantasies. Fuzzy thinking, loss of self-awareness, and impulsive activity may be an expression of unquestioning, hypnoid attachment to and identification with an influential leader. Leaders themselves may partake of the emotional thinking they promote in their followers. According to Schiffer (1973), the charismatic leader is often a foreigner or a person who has an exotic quality. He has an imperfection or foible; he is called by a spirit or voice; he engages in an aggressive, romantic contest with a rival; he radiates a libidinal mystique; an actor, he can weave a spell and induce an almost willful suspension of judgment and critical reasoning in his followers. The charismatic leader is an innovator; his innovations reflect the charming, untarnished narcissism of childhood.

Schiffer also commented on the hypnoid quality of enthrallment to a charismatic leader. He contrasted the "uncanny," a dissociated presentiment about danger and death, with enthrallment: "Charismatic projections are an antithesis to the uncanny, for they allow idealized objects of rescue to appear in our outer world (in fields of entertainment, religion, or politics)" (Schiffer 1973: 76). Once spellbound, the followers of the charismatic leader banish cynics from their group and ignore anything that challenges their shared illusion.

Childhood, in Schiffer's view, inevitably leaves a residue of emotional vulnerability in supporters of the charismatic leader. The experience of being nurtured in infancy instills an expectation of similar relationships later. The child's fascination with the primal scene prefigures fascination with the erotic qualities of the charismatic leader, and the Oedipus complex lays a basis for idealization and political competition.

While childhood may lay psychological foundations for charisma, adverse or threatening social and economic conditions often seem to provide the immediate impetus. Identification or merging with the leader may counter the negative effects of adverse economic or social conditions on self-esteem (Lindholm 1988: 23). If a leader has some deficiency, this may merely reinforce the sense that there is hope for the disadvantaged follower.

Political influence does resemble hypnotism. Followers may let leaders make decisions for them, just as the subject of hypnosis relinquishes to the hypnotist some executive and monitoring functions of the ego and superego. It has been suggested that accepting direction from an authoritative, influential person is the essential feature of hypnotism (Hull 1933). Whereas reality-testing in hypnotism is impaired, one's imagination and access to childhood memories and feelings are enhanced. Thus, the followers of charismatic leaders are gullible and uncritical as they are caught up in their leaders' happy illusions and anxiety-provoking warnings of potential dangers.

In a study of Adolf Hitler, Charles Manson, and the Reverend Jones, Charles Lindholm (1990) reexamines Freud's ideas about love and group formation and relates them to sociological theorizing about charisma. Following Kohut, he emphasizes the difference between leader–follower relations based on identification and those based on idealization. Freud, he suggests, placed too much emphasis on the followers' submissive idealization of the leader and not enough on self-enhancing identification and infatuation with the leader. In particular, Lindholm calls attention to a sort of identification in which the self appears to merge or fuse with esteem-enhancing self-objects. Idealization, by contrast, regards the leader as a model but preserves the autonomy of the self (see also Lindholm 1988).

Both men and women may become focal points in these patterns of identification and idealization. In Freud's theory of social formation, the leader is a father figure; men identify with him much as they once identified with their own fathers. Maternal images, however, also figure in group psychodynamics. Hitler had both maternal and paternal characteristics for the German people (Lasswell 1933). In group therapy, the therapist may alternate between playing the oedipal father and the preoedipal mother (Ulman and Abse 1983). Schiffer (1973) suggested that leaders and public servants often have maternal qualities and that the real objective in male–male political rivalry is the primordial mother figure. Even in a patriarchal society the political father-figure may be a stand-in for the mother. Male leaders among the Murik of New Guinea emulate the loving, caring, and nurturing behavior of mothers (Meeker et al. 1986). The social-ization for this maternal style of leadership begins in childhood, as older male siblings are required to nurture younger siblings (Barlow 1990). In a comparative study of two groups of Kagwahiv Indians, Kracke (1978) showed that the emotional appeal of leaders and their wives to their follow-ers depends on the ability to function as parental surrogates. The leaders encourage dependency needs and incestuous fantasies by their presence and actions. They may satisfy these needs and longings by distributing food through a female figure, by giving women in marriage, and by helping to arrange marriages. Illicit relations with the women under their protection may be especially exciting because they have incestuous connotations. Simultaneously, leaders personify the group's ego-ideal by upholding tradi-tions and by approving legitimate marriages. They also model impulse control and the qualities of good leaders. Leaders do not display these qualities and serve these functions to the same measure, however. One type is unobtrusive, diplomatic, and generous and leads by example; the other is strong, belligerent, and suspicious. One is more like a nurturing mother and the other resembles a stern father.

In more complex societies chiefs and kings often are said to have divine powers and connections. They are the center of the world, and the well-being of their domain depends upon them. The death of the ruler clears the way for a younger successor. This set of ideas informed many polities in the ancient world. It was prominent in ancient Egypt and in kingdoms in east and west Africa.

In these African traditions the king had a special relation with his mother, and his passing was marked with ritual concern with rejuvenation. The king's virility was thought to influence rainfall, the fertility of the land and animals, and fortune in war. When the king's powers waned, depend-ing on local tradition, he might be expected to commit suicide or he was removed through ritual execution or armed insurrection. In addition to the king, there was a queen mother, the wife of the former king or her sister. The new king always had a special relationship with her. He might "marry" her or his half-sister (Seligman 1934).

Róheim ([1930]1972) argued that the divine king was associated with the life-giving phallus, incest, and patricide. He was deemed beneficent while the land remained fertile, but in famine or during royal succession the popular opinion could change and he could be subjected to actual or sym-bolic regicide. The king, Róheim speculated, served as a "scapegoat" for oedipal guilt.

Social explanations for divine kingship tend to see it as counteracting the divisive effects of stratification in societies where unilineal descent groups are still the primary locus of social solidarity. Cohen (1977), for example, saw the institution of the queen mother as a way to counteract the divisiveness associated with political succession following regicide. She represents the lineage that loses in the succession struggle, and so helps the king to retain the loyalty of de-royalized lineages. As a "social" mother for all other nonroyal lineages, she encourages their support for central authority also.

Paul (1982: 7) suggested that psychodynamic interpretations of divine kingship are congruent with these sociological approaches. Authority structures, he noted, often involve oedipal symbolism, perhaps because the Oedipus complex itself is political in the sense that it poses questions of power and succession. Paul found an oedipal structure in kingship and Buddhism in Tibet. The structure comprises four male roles. The paternal image is split into the king and usurper, and the son's image into avenger and innocent heir, thus concealing the oedipal nature of the conflict: the aggressive son (the avenger) attacks the usurper (the bad father), not the king (the good father).

These four roles appear in many contexts in Tibetan culture. The gods fit the scheme, as do the various religious practitioners (reincarnated lamas, monks, shamans, and lamas) and phases of the life cycle. Married life and monkhood are alternatives and, in certain respects, symbolic transformations of each other. The monk represents the presexual adolescent. The man who marries is like the shaman who takes on sexual and aggressive properties in worldly struggles. The senior male, having passed the ambiguous stage of being father and son, is like the lama. The senior male-lama and the junior male-monk enter on death into the other world, or womb of the mother goddess. Monkhood represents a homoerotic resolution of the successional crisis, whereas marriage realizes a facsimile of the oedipal relationship with the opposite-sex parent. Paul also found the scheme in myths about charismatic leaders, heroes, and saints and in royal succession.

Conclusions

In this chapter I have reviewed ideas about the psychological foundations of social relations and expressive culture. Following Freud, I have focused on two sets of phenomena: (a) sublimation and defense and (b) identification and idealization. The first set involves the way in which individuals express needs for pleasure and security in social relations and collective fantasy. The second involves emotional and mental foundations of social relations, especially relations between leaders and followers.

Much of the work I have considered implies that social relations and culture express individual psychology. According to this view, the individual mind is like a projector. Social relations and culture are a screen. The form and content of culture, the image on the screen, represents individual fantasies and anxieties. In anthropology, writers who have used this projection metaphor have often traced projected material to childhood experience. In relativistic versions of this thinking, local sociality and culture reflect local childhood experience as shaped by family organization and child-rearing. Childhood, in other words, accounts for the differences between cultures.

As I noted earlier, this approach is no longer credible. While the consequences of childhood experience are important for personality, they are too unpredictable to offer a reliable explanation for cultural differences. At the same time, social explanations for cultural beliefs and practices are often more convincing. Social anthropologists have long noted that cultures variously reflect, mystify, and legitimate social relations. Post-structuralists emphasize the way in which cultural symbols and idioms are used in social persuasion as individuals and groups contest and negotiate social relations.

Yet cultures clearly reflect the desiring, emotional nature of human beings. As we have seen, social relations and expressive culture reflect needs for attachment and security and power-and object-seeking libido. Myth, ritual, and politics often seem to reflect preoedipal object relations and oedipal fantasies.

My approach to this conundrum is to ask how psychoanalysis can help us to understand social meanings and motives. I think social actors negotiate unconscious as well as conscious objectives, and I think they mobilize unconscious fantasies and anxieties in each other for social purposes. Freud ([1916–1917]1963: 375–377) alludes to these processes in speculations about artistic production.

Artists, Freud says, wish for power, wealth, and love. Lacking these, they turn inward and seek pleasure in fantasy. Other people do this too but artists have a special genius for elaborating fantasy and putting it into a form that is pleasing to other people. The artist "understands how to work over his daydreams in such a way as to make them lose what is too personal about them and repels strangers, and to make it possible for others to share in the enjoyment of them" (ibid.: 376). Artists thus provide socially acceptable gratification for others as well as for themselves and so achieve in social life the very recognition, power, and love they were seeking in fantasy.

Freud's formulation is social and dialogical. Artists have social motives, and they refine their fantasies in accord with moral norms and aesthetic tastes. In these respects Freud's artists may be paradigmatic for a great deal of social interaction. Collective representations and cultural usages are not simply projective reflections of unconscious wishes, fears, and fantasies. They reflect compromises between different agencies or dispositions within the individual and compromises between the attitudes and fantasies of various individuals. More than mere expressions, they are rhetorical devices in pragmatic interaction; the blended, socialized fantasies that result from mediations (or dialogues) within and between individuals may affect the inscriptions of conscious and unconscious personal fantasies or at least the way which they motivate social activity.

War and religion are especially interesting in these terms. They evince a range of conscious and unconscious needs and motives, and yet they are social phenomena also. Both, moreover, involve social rhetoric. A war culture works against the inclinations of people to avoid the risks and dangers of actual hostilities. Religions must counteract skepticism and, in some cases, the contending claims of competing religions or sects. We may ask what sorts of individual fantasies and concerns are reflected in war and religion, but we may also try to see how these fantasies and concerns figure in social persuasion. We may consider how social actors mobilize desire in social others as they try to persuade them to participate in war or religion. Or, we may ask how militaristic and religious imagery mobilize the unconscious to produce social effects.

8   Collective violence

Enmity and violence between human groups are familiar – and troubling – features of the human scene. They have been so for a long time. Organized violence has occurred, and continues to occur, at every level of social complexity. Murder and feuding were frequent among hunter-gatherers, peoples sometimes thought to be relatively peaceful (Ember 1978). Headhunting and murderous retribution against suspected sorcerers were common among horticultural societies. Many tribal societies were warlike. Most preindustrial states were militaristic, and some even ritualized their hegemony with human sacrifice. And wars between states and, increasingly, terrorism and ethnic violence are commonplaces of the modern world.

Collective violence influences culture and society, sometimes profoundly. Preparations for war shape the way a society allocates resources, and they have far-reaching consequences for social relations and values. Gender roles and gender relations in particular may reflect a society's involvement in warmaking.

In this chapter I review ideas about the psychology of war. Then I present some ethnographic and historical examples. Both the review of the literature and the examples suggest that there is no single or simple explanation for war. The subjective motives for war interact in complicated ways with material and economic conditions and social practice.

The psychology of war

Various explanations have been offered for war. One psychological explanation attributes war to a violent streak in human nature or even to an instinct for war. Thinking along these lines, Freud dismissed the idea that human beings are gentle creatures who attack only in self-defense, and averred that "they are, on the contrary, creatures among whose instinctual endowments is to be reckoned a powerful share of aggressiveness" ([1930]1961:111). He concluded that a destructive "death instinct" is part of our evolutionary heritage; turned outward, it appears as aggressive

196

behavior; turned inward, it manifests itself as suicide and other forms of self-destructive behavior.

There appears to be a long-standing, phylogenetic disposition to violence in human beings. Chimpanzees, our closest relatives, can be quite violent in social interaction within the group, and they are aggressively territorial in relations with other groups (Ghiglieri 1987). The males of one colony have been observed to murder the males of another in a series of raids (Goodall 1986). Human cannibalism may have had early origins, although there is disagreement about how early. Some scholars trace it all the way back to *Homo erectus* whereas others would give it more recent origins. There is evidence that war and headhunting were fairly common in upper paleolithic and neolithic populations (La Barre 1984).

Human violence is an ethnographic and historical fact. The explanation for it is another matter. Freud's death-instinct hypothesis is widely rejected even within psychoanalysis. No one doubts that aggression occurs. The issue is whether it reflects an instinctual, constant drive. In Chapter 2 I noted that destructive aggression is an aversive reaction to threat or a learned response pattern. Some people have aggressive dispositions or even appetites for sadistic or destructive behavior, but in many other people such inclinations are much less noticeable; most individuals do not talk or behave as though they have a need to maim or kill other people. On the other hand, there is cold comfort in these observations for the idea that human beings are basically peaceful. Aggression may be reactive but, as a practical matter, it is so common as to seem like the manifestation of a constant disposition. Life is filled with frustration and provocation. Social life being what it is, people can experience a stream of hostility-nurturing threats to their self-interests.

The libido may be another source of motivation for war. The libido is drivelike and, as we have seen, it is assertive, aggressive, and power-seeking as well as sexual. Observations of chimpanzees suggest that the libido figures in territoriality and hostility toward the outgroup. Chimpanzee males tolerate sexually receptive females from adjacent colonies, but often attack nursing mothers and their infants. Young adult males patrolling territorial boundaries try to lure receptive females from adjacent colonies, and groups of male chimpanzees go on territorial patrols after bouts of copulation with females (Goodall 1986). This aggressive nature of male libido is evident in human beings also. In their research on homicide in North America, Daly and Wilson (1988), for example, observe that male–male homicide in human beings is far more common than female–female homicide and that young adult males are more violent than older males. They also note that most homicides within families are committed against wives by husbands who may be trying to preserve what they take to be their sexual prerogatives.[1]

Folklore and other verbal practices in many cultures also link aggressiveness with the libido. Abusive language and gestures often have sexual content, and competitive games and war also can have sexual meanings. Dundes (1978, 1985b) discerned eroticized dominance and submission and allusions to armed conflict in football humor and lore. Marcelo M. Suárez-Orozco (1993) has similarly described anal imagery in the highly aggressive expressions associated with Argentine soccer. Carol Cohn (1987) found procreative, homoerotic, and autoerotic imagery in the language of a defense-oriented think tank, and she observed that the intellectuals who worked there seemed to get a pleasurable sense of power from their knowledge of and discourse about weapons and military strategy.

A connection between the libido and war is also suggested by the way in which sexual frustration can provoke or reinforce irritable aggressiveness. Sexual prudishness, polygyny, postpartum sex avoidance, and female infanticide are all associated with warfare in many simple societies (Divale 1970; Divale and Harris 1976; Whiting and Whiting 1975). In some societies warriors are prohibited from having sexual relations before and during raids and campaigns.

Actually, Freud himself realized various motives may play a part in war. Writing to Albert Einstein, he suggested "that when human beings are incited to war they may have a whole number of motives for assenting – some noble and some base, some of which are openly declared and others which are never mentioned" ([1933b]1964: 210). Other early psychoanalysts agreed that war has various motives. Jones ([1915]1964: 70) discerned "the passions for cruelty, destruction, lust, and loot." Money-Kyrle (1937) mentioned various conscious and unconscious motives, including hostile and sexual impulses. Another motive for war may be altruistic impulses within the group. Warriors may sacrifice their lives out of devotion to their tribes or countries or simply out of affection for each other. (This may be one reason many warlike societies use initiation rites and secret societies to forge male solidarity.) Fears and anxieties about self-preservation also motivate violence. Such fears may reflect economic insecurity or threats posed by other groups. Ralph K. White (1984) concluded that fear has been perhaps the most important motive in twentieth-century wars.

Taken singly or together, these motives do not add up to a sufficient explanation for war, however. More important than drives and emotions *per se* may be mental structures and social relations that give them shape and direction. As we have seen, drives and emotions are organized by unconscious object relations and, at another level, by self-representations and cultural schemas and values. Whether impulses and emotions are expressed in destructive behavior, or a willingness to go along with collective violence, depends, therefore, on the whole personality and, beyond that, on cultural attitudes, political order, and public discourse.

The relevant mental structures may include preoedipal object relations, particularly as they structure social perceptions and reactions to loss. Splitting, denial, and projective identification – defense mechanisms thought to indicate preoedipal pathology in clinical patients – are often conspicuous in the group psychology of war. Like the young child who has yet to fully integrate good and bad aspects of the self and object, belligerents in intergroup conflict may externalize bad aspects of themselves or the ingroup while denying the good qualities of the enemy. Vamik D. Volkan (1979) explored these processes in the interethnic conflict on Cyprus, and noted how they may arise in child-rearing practices and family organization. Franco Fornari (1975) suggested that warfare is a defense against internal rage and fear. When evoked by loss, these feelings – Fornari called them "The Terrifier" – are managed through depression or paranoia, that is, either through internalizing – and accepting – the pain or through externalizing it. War is a "paranoid elaboration of mourning" in which negative feelings generated by loss are externalized.

Amok, a behavior mentioned in Chapter 5, illustrates the connection between paranoid mourning and a militaristic orientation in individual psychology. In *amok*, the perpetrator first goes into a depressive sulk after loss of love or a blow to self-esteem; later, he acts out his rage in public. John E. Carr (1978) noted that *amok* in Malaysia has historical roots in a military tradition of mass attacks with knives and fanatical religious attacks on infidels. In traditional Malay society *amok* attacks, or the threat of them, may have served to curtail the excesses of hereditary rulers. A more immediate precursor to the behavior may be a tendency in Malay culture to suppress inner feelings in social interaction. Emphases on hierarchical relations, etiquette, respect, moral appropriateness, and avoidance of shame in Malay social life ensure that some behavior will be offensive and inappropriate, but decorum requires that such behavior not be acknowledged. Inattention to inner feelings then encourages procrastination in resolving interpersonal difficulties. Parental indulgence and training for compliance and submissiveness, according to Carr, encourage subservience, impulsive expressions of anger, and fatalism. Carr and Vitaliano (1985) observe that *amok* resembles depression and that many *amok* patients respond favorably to antidepressant medications.

Explosive rage with destructive behavior occurs in other areas, for example, Papua New Guinea, Singapore, Indonesia, the Philippines, Laos, and Europe. In the United States, *amok*-like attacks have included tragic incidents in Austin, San Diego, Sacramento, and elsewhere. As in Southeast

Asia, these instances of *amok*-like behavior often have a militaristic quality; attackers may dress in military fatigues and carry assault rifles.

Status loss and loss of lovers and wives have been mentioned as triggering events (Westermeyer 1982: 183). An epidemic of *amok* in Thailand, the Philippines, and Laos in recent decades suggests that socioeconomic stress and political strife also encourage *amok* (ibid.: 185–186). Westermeyer (1985b) described eighteen cases of *amok* with grenades in Laos. In sixteen cases the outbreak of violence followed public humiliation or loss of love. Intoxication often reduced moral inhibition, while the use of a grenade – which affects people in a crowd at random – seemed to absolve the attacker of wanting to kill any one in particular. Burton-Bradley (1985: 243) suggested that shaming provokes *amok*-like behavior in New Guinea. The attacker is not a "big man" but he has his pride. When insulted or shamed, he tries to restore his reputation by killing others, even though he knows he may die in the effort. The similarity between one North American case and Southeast Asian *amok* suggested to Arboleda-Florez (1985) that *amok* is a universal response to alienation and need for self-assertion. Persons who go *amok*, feeling despair about failure and isolation, blame others or society as a whole for their problems. They often put on military clothing and carry military weapons, as if they were waging war, perhaps because war is seen as a legitimate way of expressing violent feelings. Fornari's work suggests that war mobilizes, psychodynamically, a collective version of *amok*.

For men, at least, another preoedipal issue in war may be gender identity and separation–individuation. In many cultures, hostility toward – and fear of – women is part of the warrior ethos. Where men are insecure about gender identity, an aggressive masculinity and hostility toward women may be a way of shoring up a sense of masculinity (Gilmore 1990).

War may also have oedipal meanings. According to oedipal theory, the son resents the father because he monopolizes the mother. To avoid rejection or castration, he relinquishes his libidinal interest in the mother and identifies with the father or, to be more precise, with the father's superego. Later, the love for the good father may be transferred to the leader of the ingroup, and the hostility toward the "bad" father, the leader of the outgroup (Money-Kyrle 1937: 221–222). In this way the unconscious remnants of the father–son component of oedipality are divided into idealization of the leader and hatred for the enemy. The love object may be either the homeland, which the enemy could violate, or the land or women of the enemy (Freud [1913]1955, [1933b]1964; Róheim 1945a).

The nature and role of moral reasoning, and the ambiguous relation between the moral reasoning of the individual and the orientation of society as a whole, add another layer of complexity to this picture of subjective meanings in collective violence. To some extent, the moral reasoning of the individual is closely linked with the shared understandings of the group. It represents and follows communal rules, taboos, and values. The group, moreover, constantly reinforces this internalization of collective norms in various ways, particularly through religious discourse and ritual. The community itself, however, consists of individuals who come to their moral orientations not only through socialization but, also, through the give-and-take of social life, first in the family and later with peers. The individuals who make up society are thus capable of forming their own moral judgments, of disagreeing with the standard morality or the received interpretation of it. The views of the majority or a hegemonic elite may or may not seem moral from the standpoint of the individual or a subaltern group. Conscientious thinking, then, may involve either conformity with what others are thinking and respect for authority or independent thinking and resistance to authority.

In matters of war and peace, moral dilemmas can be very complicated. Jones ([1915]1964) pointed out that war involves a socially sanctioned relaxation of ethical standards, whereas conscience and sublimation may involve individual resistance to group pressures. Yet in some situations independent moral reasoning and shared notions of justice may suggest that the group should meet moral outrage with collective violence. Lax moral reasoning may contribute to a readiness to engage in war in some situations and a reluctance in others. Matters are further complicated by the ambiguities of moral arguments; what seems sincere to a person on one side of a debate may seem hypocritical and self-serving to another.

Leadership and political discourse and dialogue can be crucial for the resolution of moral dilemmas. Freud ([1933b]1964: 212–213) noted that the decision for war or peace may turn on whether leaders are impulsive or reasonable. The lowering of ethical standards, or the failure or unwillingness to think through complicated moral issues, may be more likely where leaders are emotional and irrational and where, through charismatic influence, they succeed in substituting their own voices for reality-testing and ethical reasoning in their followers. If leaders are paranoid and destructive, followers may be drawn into immoral and emotionally regressive behavior. Moral slopes may be especially slippery in autocratic polities that discourage discussion and dissent. Leaders in such societies are often bellicose and warlike, perhaps, in part, because they find they can deflect criticism and reinforce social solidarity by directing hostile feelings toward an outgroup (Freud [1933b]1964: 212).

Leaders in some tribal societies use this tactic to promote wars to their own advantage (Sillitoe 1978). They may reinforce motivation for war by imposing sexual restrictions on young men, and they may appeal to group interest or to unconscious fantasies through symbolism and imagery. Still, the community may reserve some ability to curb the militaristic inclinations of its leaders. In small-scale societies, everyone is socially connected and leaders must engage their followers in face-to-face conversation. As a result, leaders may be less likely to develop unrealistic political fantasies or a special mystique. In more complex societies, in contrast, elites and leaders may be isolated and unresponsive to constituencies and thus insulated from the usual social checks on unrealistic thinking; bureaucratic power, then, may foster delusions of grandeur and errors in perception and judgment. Laura Nader describes what she calls "institutional insanity," an "inability of certain groups to distinguish delusions derived from ideology from reality based on empirical fact" (1986: 187). At the same time, social conditions in complex societies and their associated social psychology may undermine the psychological capacities of the masses to criticize and resist irrational leadership. Lindholm (1990) suggests that individualism, secularism, cynicism, and anomie in modern societies make charismatic leaders more appealing. The charismatic leader may become an idealized, imaginary love object for those who are feeling lonely and disconnected.

The ability of leaders to foment group narcissism and xenophobia may vary with economic conditions. Population pressure and scarce resources seem to play a role in conflicts among many preindustrial societies (Divale 1970), and disputes over scarce resources have often been in the background of wars in the twentieth century (Timberlake and Tinker 1984). Scarcity may promote warlike culture, which in turn perpetuates violence (Tefft 1975). Once a militaristic culture is established, people may tend to overreact to perceived threats and they may be less inclined to pursue peaceful solutions. Devereux (1955) drew a contrast between stressful situations in which people have the material and psychological resources to deal with their problems and a genuine *crisis* in which established coping mechanisms fail and fear gives way to chronic anxiety. In these conditions charismatic leaders become more appealing, and individuals may be less likely to do their own thinking about the morality of collective killing.

Social conditions and political discourse may reinforce or encourage the unconscious sources of hostility and militarism. In a comparison of the myths of two Amazonian societies, Orna Johnson and Allen Johnson (1988) found more violent oedipal myths in the more warlike society. Marvin Harris (1977) theorized that war actually encourages oedipal fantasies. He noted an association between polygyny and female infanticide and war in the cross-cultural record. Female infanticide maximizes the proportion of male warriors to women in a society, and polygyny is a way of rewarding the aggressive male. Both practices cause sexual scarcity for young males, thus reinforcing their aggressiveness. The young men envy and resent the older, polygynous males but also fear them, so they direct their rage and lust toward the men and women of other groups.[2] Girard's theory of sacrifice (see Chapter 7) also suggests that triangular social situations are an impetus for violence insofar as they stimulate desire and envy.

Ritual, myth, and discourse may stimulate and channel both preoedipal and oedipal structures and feelings about the frustrations, disappointments, and dangers of social life. Masculine myth and ritual and sexist and paranoid discourse may stir up preoedipal feelings of loss and rage or oedipal feelings of erotic frustration, envy, and resentment. Or, registering both preoedipal and oedipal structures, they may stimulate feelings of insecurity about masculinity, thereby motivating a defensive masculine aggressiveness.

Sorcery accusations

In simple societies, killing may represent vengeance against sorcerers: a person dies, supposedly of ensorcellment, and the victim's kin or allies may then kill the culprit. Every cycle of death, accusation, and retaliation may undermine public trust, sowing the seeds for another round of violence. Unchecked by authority or a system of justice, such cycles may permit and invite the expression of unconscious fears and impulses.

The Gebusi of western Papua New Guinea, as described by Bruce M. Knauft (1985), offer a fascinating example of these processes. The Gebusi live in a dozen or so scattered settlements on the Strickland Plain. Each settlement includes agnates, affines, and matrikin. Sister exchange is the ideal marriage arrangement, although romantic, common-law marriages also occur. The society lacks chiefs or big men. Gebusi children have a close relation with their mothers until they are displaced by the next lap child. Boys then turn to their fathers and other men for affection, a pattern repeated in later life when they deal with sexual frustration by turning to homoerotic encounters (Knauft 1987: 172–174).

The Gebusi are peaceful and friendly, yet they have a high rate of homicide or, since the victims are often putative sorcerers, a high rate of ritualized capital punishment. Traditionally, the victims were cooked and eaten. The accused are often affines who have not given a woman in return for one they received. The violence no doubt reflects resentment about the unfulfilled social contract, but fantasy exacerbates the resentment: asymmetrical marriages – ones where there has been no exchange of sisters – are thought to be more erotic than sister-exchange marriages.

According to Knauft, the Gebusi find "good company" in feasts and dances. During the festivities ritualized displays of anger give way to sharing tobacco, food, and drink, and to talk, sexual joking, and dances in which costumed transvestites represent spirit women. Women's songs intimate loneliness and sadness, although the men hear expressions of desire. Aroused by the jokes, dancing, and songs, some men enter the forest for homosexual relations. Feasts, remarkably, end with a public airing of grievances and accusations of sorcery. Sorcery inquests also involve sexual joking. In seances, the beautiful and lusty spirit women speak through the medium, describing their sexual and transparently incestuous affairs with men who transform back and forth between being nursing babies and sexual adults. Here, too, men become excited and seek out homosexual relations. In other words, the feasts or inquests allude to the sorts of spicy romantic relationships that provoke sorcery accusations.

The underlying issue may be whether society can allow individuals to realize selfish, incestuous fantasies at the expense of the group.[3] Knauft (1987: 174) notes that Gebusi men actively pursue adulterous relations and romantic unions, and he suggests that illicit sexuality and homoeroticism may represent oedipal gratification.

Headhunting

In some small-scale societies intergroup conflict takes the form of head-hunting. The practice involves cultural understandings about reproductive physiology. Ancient and widespread cultural associations link brain matter, spinal fluid, and bone marrow with semen and fertility. Eating the brain and bone marrow, then, may be a way of appropriating fertility, power, or virility. Headhunting is commonly understood to be a preliminary to marriage. The Asmat of New Guinea, for example, associate the womb with trees, skulls, and fruit and semen with brains and grubs. They place the brains of the headhunting victim in a bowl that seems to represent the female skull; male and female handle-figures represent coitus (La Barre 1984).

In this fertility logic, the death of the other or enemy may become the rebirth or regeneration of the ingroup. Images of reproduction and death are emotionally evocative, and for this reason they may be especially effective in mobilizing deep sources of motivation. The Marind of Irian Jaya (formerly Dutch New Guinea) illustrate this association between fertility ritual and headhunting. More particularly, they show how the ritual logic of war can employ a whole range of preoedipal and oedipal images. The description that follows is based on J. van Baal's reconstruction of how the Marind-anim lived in precontact times.[4]

The Marind-anim

The Marind people occupy some fifty villages. The men call themselves Marind-anim, "Marind men." They fight among themselves, often in disputes over women and sorcery, and they launch frequent headhunting expeditions against non-Marind peoples. Headhunting is thought to increase the supply of coconuts, group symbols of human heads and humanity. In fact, the kidnapping of children during raids may compensate for the Marind's low fertility (Baal 1984: 164). Given the many disputes and sorcery accusations among them, it is surprising that the Marind-anim do not fight among themselves more than they do. Headhunting may displace violent inclinations that originate within the ethnic group (Baal 1966: 695).

Each subtribe comprises various patrilineal clans and subclans. The clans are divided into four phratries, which are themselves grouped into two moieties which are responsible for supervising particular rites and ceremonies. The men have separate houses from the women. Marriages are stable and amicable for the most part, yet women are often treated as depersonalized objects of lust (e.g., they are subjected on various ritual occasions to sex with groups of men). Ritual involves a cycle of initiation, headhunting, and triumphal feasting. A boy sleeps with his mother in infancy, but then must sleep in his father's house until puberty, when he moves to the house of his mother's brother. Initiation follows several years during which a novice serves as a passive homosexual partner to a mentor, often his maternal uncle, and is compared to a "girl." The mentor addresses the boy as "son," and the boy addresses his mentor as "father" (Baal 1966: 118–119).

In the eastern section, initiation begins with the arrival of Sosom, or Anus-man, a castrated, headhunting giant who wears a necklace of human heads and is identified with the bull-roarer. During the rite a large, red phallus represents his detached penis. Sosom, according to the myth, was castrated by the mother of a young woman with whom he had sexual intercourse. The rite ends with the promiscuous sodomy of the youths. Sosom sodomizes the youth because he was castrated by the young woman's mother (Baal 1966: 268).

The rites of the Mayo and Imo subtribes dramatize the mythical passage of the sun from east to west and back again. Uaba (the sun, coconut spirit, initiate) follows his mother Ualiuamb (earth) to the west, where they copulate. They return to the east, where they separate; fire and the stork (symbol of initiates) spring from her vulva. Ualiuamb escapes to Imo country as a snake, where her son copulates with his foster mother. Sorcerers kill him and sever his head, which sprouts into a coconut. The Mayo rite dramatizes copulation between Uaba (the sun, brother of Sosom) and his wife Ualiuamb (mother earth, Mayo Woman), who gives birth to fire (the sun), the cassowary, and the stork (the initiate). In another myth, Imo men catch the mother and son, have sex with the mother, and kill and eat mother and son.

In contrast to the Mayo rites, which suggest rebirth, the Imo rites have nocturnal connotations and more explicit associations with headhunting. Here the woman is Bad Woman or Excrement Woman. In the second initiation the boys' faces are smeared with excrement and sperm. In the bangu portion of the ritual, which tells the story of the first Imo Woman, a pit is dug and surrounded with shields. Arrowheads are placed in holes in the shields to represent headhunting and the copulatory embrace of Ualiuamb and Uaba (Imo Woman and her son). The initiates wear black to impersonate the dead spirits. After a man drops coconuts from a tree, an act referring to the mythical killing of the woman and her son, the impersonators remove their costumes and climb out of the pit. The pit is then filled, with the understanding that the mother and son, locked in permanent coitus, begin an underground voyage to the east in imitation of the sun (Baal 1966: 624).

Headhunting evidently symbolizes copulation and procreation, perhaps in ways that mobilize preoedipal rage and patricidal, incestuous fantasies. According to myth, headhunting derived from Sobra, a Ualiuamb-like mother figure, and her husband, a vicious pig spirit and leader of mythical headhunting. In the myth she captures, kills, and eats children (Baal 1966: 411–412). She is, in a sense, the prototypical bad mother, the one who evokes rage. Among the Boadzi, a nearby people with a similar headhunting culture, the first headhunting spear was made by Anésaké, a giant. He told his older son to go to the river. The son returned first with nothing and then twice with a fish which he beheaded, serving the head to the father as a human head is served. But the father was not happy, so he gave the son a headhunting spear. That night the father sang the headhunter's song until dawn, and then told his son to place the stone disk on the shaft of the spear. The son immediately killed his father with it and cut off his father's head. The head then told him how to prepare a head. From the head worms appeared which turned into human beings (ibid.: 729). Another Boadzi myth implies that men must either take heads/coconuts or they will be killed and beheaded themselves (ibid.: 729–730).

The manner of killing and beheading has symbolic meaning. The leader of the hunt beats the victim's head or the ground with a ceremonial *pahui* or *bagwa* (spear). The spear has a fretwork blade from the point to two feet below it, where there is a disc that symbolizes the female genitalia. The spear itself represents a penis penetrating a vulva (Baal 1966: 740). The disc, which is not placed on the shaft until the last moment, slides up and down on the shaft. The victim's head is pounded with the spear until the fretwork falls off, leaving only a disc-headed club. Then the victim's head is severed from the body. A myth relates the disc-headed club to an arrow of a primordial headhunter; he aimed his arrow at a hen who watched him defecate, but the arrow landed in his own excrement and changed into a disc-headed club, apparently an allusion to Excrement Woman (ibid.: 739). Because heads are likened to coconuts and provide names for children, head-taking represents fertility, a transformation of death into life (Baal 1984: 150). The shields into which arrows are inserted in the Imo ritual, in allusion to the incestuous intercourse of Uaba and Ualiuamb, are called "*pahui*" (ibid.: 153).

Another clue to the meaning and purpose of Marind-anim ritual appears in the figure of Sosom. One mythical male after another suffers castration or emasculation in sexual relations with women. This theme is reflected in, and perhaps reinforced by, the ritual treatment of women. Ritual depersonalizes women and heterosexual intercourse and associates them with anality and castration. In the myths, the mother's vulva is huge and the boy's penis is small, which implies that the mother is the original castrating female, a supposition which finds support in the first stage of adolescence when the boy is regularly subjected to anal penetration by the maternal uncle. In the eastern area, the mythical character who seems responsible for the humiliation of the youths is Sosom, Anus-man, himself a male who has been castrated by a woman. In the Imo rites, Old Imo Woman, Ualiuamb, is also Excrement Woman, and the boys are smeared with excrement.

Myth implies that initiates (storks) are the sons of the incestuous union of Uaba and Ualiuamb. The mythical death of their son, Yawi, suggests that adulterous/incestuous unions produce heads, coconuts, and new life. Headhunting also has sexual connotations, but these reverse the meanings of sexuality in myth and ritual. Whereas the vulva is large and the penis is small in myth and ritual, in headhunting the phallus is more powerful, although here, too, there is at least an intimation of castration: the fretwork is crushed in the copulatory killing. Headhunting, in other words, follows a sacrificial logic in which regeneration requires death and castration.

Baal suggests that headhunting may express the rage of the Marind men about the infertility of their women which, ironically, may result from vaginal irritations caused by repeated instances of ritualized sexual intercourse with multiple partners.[5] But there is also a hint of turning victimization into triumph. By taking heads, the men may be working through their rage at being humiliated in ritual sodomy. Everything links this humiliation with excrement, anality, maternal incest, heterosexuality, and women. In the Imo rites the killing of Uaba and Ualiuamb, who remain locked in copulation, is associated with the production of coconuts, symbols of new life. In the Mayo ritual, the stork is the child of Uaba and Ualiuamb; the stork is a symbol of the initiates, and initiates go on headhunting expeditions. The relationship of Ualiuamb and Uaba has incestuous connotations. Taking heads must reenact the sacrificial, copulatory deaths of

Ualiuamb and Uaba. It is a symbolic killing of the parents, who are engaged in an incestuous embrace. Unconsciously, the killing may reverse the sexual humiliation of the initiate and, ultimately, that of the oedipal child.

The Murik

David Lipset's (n.d.) study of the Murik of Papua New Guinea offers another example of oedipal imagery in male ritual and a militant male ethos. Lipset has examined the world of men among the Murik in great detail. Here I merely focus on that part of it that bears on the childhood origins and erotic nature of aggression, particularly as they are manipulated by ritual processes.

Before pacification in 1918, Murik men were warriors; they took the heads of inland peoples as trophies for their war cults and waged war against each other to retaliate for rapes and the abduction of women. Today, war cults remain part of social life.

The cults center on the *kakar*, the ancestral spears (Meeker et al. 1986). The myth of Arakay describes the origin of *kakar* spears:

Their mother was a woman named Arakay, but their father was not a man. An axe-spirit, who was angry with Arakay's father, kidnapped and left her to die on an island in the middle of the Sepik. Turtle spirits raped her and she became pregnant. Arakay bore several baby eagle sons, all but one of whom died. She raised the lone survivor with special care. After her eagle son grew up, he flew his mother back to her father's village, where the Murik ancestors were living. But in the village, the eagle played badly with other children, scratching out their eyes with his talons. Everyone got angry. Arakay herself came forward and killed her son, pouring boiling water over his sleeping basket. She took the eagle's corpse to the edge of the Sepik and buried it. The corpse rotted. The *kakar* spears, lances (*mansareep*), cassowary bone daggers (*asor*), and fighting magic (*mwar*) arose from the stinking flesh and bones of the eagle. Arakay saw these things and hurried back to tell her father. Knowing that they were far too dangerous for women, he took a group of men to retrieve the powerful weapons. (Lipset n.d.: 182)

Another myth recounts the story of Sendam, the founder of the military organization. In the myth, Sendam's mother is a wild pig, his father, a villager. The men of the village hunt her, which prompts Sendam to kill all the men in the village, including his father. Sendam then travels to the coast where he introduces weapons and warrior organization to the men fighting there. He moves on to the mouth of the Sepik where two eagle spirits, husband and wife, prey on the village. Sendam kills them while they are having intercourse and the village offers him a great feast. He refuses to eat and demands the women instead (he has a treelike phallus and a voracious sexual appetite). When one woman refuses him, he enters a tree. When the men fell the tree with their axes, it only becomes light enough to move when he appears and again has intercourse with the women. Sendam crosses the river and sees a man and woman having sexual intercourse in their garden. After they leave, he rolls around on the ground where they made love and transforms himself into a crying baby. Hearing his cries, the woman returns to the garden and adopts him. When he cries through the night, his "mother" places him on her breast to nurse. He then turns back into a man and makes love with his "mother" (Lipset n.d.: 193–196).[6]

The Murik warriors are organized into two moieties or groups, each with a junior and senior age grade. The older grade is "father" to the younger grade. One moiety is said to be "big" and "male," the other, "small" and "female." Each grade possesses one of three weapons or war magic. Current holders of the *kakar* spears are fictive "elder brothers" to the junior age grade in the opposite moiety. The men of the latter get the spears by sending their wives to seduce their "elder brothers." One of these elder brothers, designated the "knot," is supposed to resist the temptation at all cost, but once he succumbs, the spears pass to the "younger brothers" in the opposite moiety. Wives of the younger brothers personify Arakay, the mother of the *kakar* weapons; older brothers personify the *kakar*.

The myth of Arakay underscores the separation of the community (women and children) from the war cult. Arakay's predator son is dangerous to the eyes of the community. The mother, through infanticide, chooses to protect the community while the war spears are in some sense the stinking remains of an extreme act of maternal rejection. The myth of Sendam continues to deal with the issue of men's desire to establish autonomy from women. Lipset thus notes the ironies in *kakar* myth and ritual; the men would like to assert their autonomy from feminine sexuality and nurture in war, but they feel dependent on women.

The men's house has a female spirit, and the bunting on the outside walls is likened to a woman's skirt. Thus the Murik say that when they enter the cult house they are "like children crawling underneath the skirts of their mothers." The images of the community's male gods and the *kakar* spears are kept within four "skirts" inside the building. The spears are like vessels or "canoes" of the *kakar* spirits. Cult leaders in a dissociated state can similarly serve as canoes for the spirits.

The spears may represent maternal rejection and separation from the world of women and children. Sendam, meanwhile, enjoys the nurturing of the preoedipal mother and the fulfillment of oedipal fantasy. He kills the fathers of his village, destroys the copulating couple, and copulates with his foster mother. The men who hold the *kakar* spears, then, play the role of Sendam and so enact an oedipal fantasy. In effect, ritual reverses the childhood experience of being frustrated by the father and having to nurture the younger sibling. In so doing, it may instill anger in the younger brothers by forcing them to part with their wives/mothers, much as the rape or abduction of their womenfolk arouses anger and provokes war. The anger stemming from one source may reinforce the anger of another; once aroused through ritual, the unconscious memories of childhood frustrations and angers may become a pragmatic resource in the social manipulation of aggression.

The Ilongot

The Ilongot are a hunting, fishing, and swidden agricultural people numbering 3,500 and living in hill country about ninety miles northeast of Manila. Marriage is uxorilocal and kin relations are bilateral. The largest social unit is a territorial descent group called the *bertan*. Ilongot raiders attack other Ilongot and non-Ilongot in lowland communities. After killing their victims, they sever their heads from their bodies and throw them on the ground.

Headhunting episodes have waxed and waned with fluctuations in population density. A period of population concentration between 1919 and 1923 was followed between 1924 and 1935 by a scattering of population toward the lowlands. Between 1936 and 1945 the population gradually reconcentrated at the center of Ilongot territory. Headhunting was common between 1919 and 1928, absent from 1929 and 1935, and common again between 1936 and 1945 (R. Rosaldo 1980: 48).

Insults, threats, thefts, killings, and conflicts over land provoke killings, but the Ilongot explain that *liget* (passion, anger) is a stronger motive than vengeance. Among older men, the issue is often attachment and loss. Older men explain that headhunting urges involve rage resulting from grief on losing a loved one through death or sexual rivalry (M. Rosaldo 1980: 138–139; R. Rosaldo 1984). Headhunting also helps older men recreate youthful energy and self-esteem. Among younger men the dynamics may involve loss but, also, reproductive politics and, perhaps, unconscious fantasies.

Young men feel frustration and shame before older men, whereas when they take heads they feel anger and a sense of lightness, vigor, and health (M. Rosaldo 1980, 1983). Headhunters say they want to equal the deeds of fathers, and add that headhunting transfers energy from aging men to young men. Headhunting may express rebellion against the fathers, for example, when the forays of youths disrupt the covenants arranged by fathers, but more often the elders direct the passions of the bachelors toward political ends. Relations between groups cycle from insults to headhunting and reprisal to peace, covenant, and intermarriage. The young men also want to maintain an equal footing with peers (R. Rosaldo 1980).

The meanings of red hornbill earrings reveal the eroticism in headhunting. A man wears the earrings because he has taken a head, and he takes a head to have an *amet*. An *amet* gives one the right to wear earrings. To get the earrings, the hunter courts the heart, or life-force, of the victim. If properly courted, the victim's life-force flies through the air and lands, birdlike, on the hunter's ear, precisely where the earring will be worn (live hornbills are regarded as omens). The spirit of the victim, identified with the earring, becomes an *amet* that stays with the headhunter. Ilongot liken the relationship between a headhunter and his victim or spirit to that between lovers, and the shape of the earrings represents concentrated anger (R. Rosaldo 1986).

A song associates the loss of the mother with the prospect of the bachelor-headhunter's desire for a wife:

Sadly, those who bore you, young bachelor, are no longer with us, and so, bachelor, bachelor, you go on hoping for someone who cares . . . Ah, it would have been fine if right off, when a babe in the care of one who bore you, you had died in her arms; since now she has wasted her pains . . . Ah, maybe a skirt, a blue skirt, will distract you; maybe you can turn to a woman. (M. Rosaldo 1980: 149–150)

Courtship, marriage, and reproduction are associated with headhunting in Ilongot cultural imagination. It is believed that headhunting victims are attracted to their killers. Young men want to enhance their status by taking heads and marrying. Having taken a head gives a young man more credibility as a suitor. Meanwhile, there is an understanding that marriage and reproduction involve a "cutting short" of vital energy similar to the cutting of heads or the clipping of plants by headhunters for decorating their armbands (ibid.: 151).

The erotic connotations of headhunting imply that the desire to equal the fathers and other men has oedipal meanings. For young men, headhunting is the preparation for marriage and a means to resolve their emotional and sexual frustrations. Headhunting is not a requirement for marriage, but successful headhunters gain the esteem of women. The wearing of red hornbill earrings, a sign that one has taken a head, deters the insults otherwise directed at novices who marry. The insults imply that husbands who have yet to take heads might take the heads of their wives (M. Rosaldo 1980: 140). In other words, headhunting may allow young men to vent the emotional turmoil they feel in not having a wife and in having to let go of their mothers (R. Rosaldo 1984: 191). Thus unsuccessful headhunters may be suspected of wanting to behead their wives because headhunting mimics coitus. Ilongot headhunting is a quest for power and love. In this respect, it resembles courtship. Marriage poses a challenge to the fathers and brothers of marriageable girls and women. When building a house, men carve maidens' breasts and knives into the roof beams to represent the presence of single women and the anger of their menfolks. Given these attitudes toward suitors and the parallel between headhunting and courtship, it is not surprising that suitors may try to placate potential in-laws by leading them on headhunting expeditions, or that headhunters may further assuage their anger by giving women in marriage in exchange for brides (M. Rosaldo 1980: 170). This tension in courtship and the affinity between courtship and headhunting are apparent when a suitor, after losing to a rival, takes out his anger by raiding his rival's relatives (ibid.: 171).

Tribal warfare

At the tribal level, fighting may involve large-scale battles as well as small-scale raiding. Studies of warfare in tribal-level societies have correlated warfare with demographic and economic conditions. They have also shown that warfare affects social organization, socialization practices, and social character.

Some tribal peoples have bilateral descent systems, but many have some form of unilineal descent. Typically, they combine patrilocal residence and patrilineal descent. Often unilineal societies are warlike and often they are found in areas of high population density or scarce resources or where protecting local resources is an issue. Agnatic societies in particular are often associated with high population densities and chronic fighting within the ethnic group. Under these conditions, keeping related males together and a warlike orientation are a way of protecting and defending vital resources (Ember et al. 1974). Among the Mae Enga of Highland New Guinea, for example, population pressure, agnation, and armed conflict are interrelated (Meggitt 1977). War occurs between phratries, clans of different phratries, clans of the same phratry, and between subclans, often over land or thefts of pigs. Frictions reach the flash point as populations increase. The Enga explain that they must have land to feed their pigs and themselves. What is more, without land to raise pigs for bridewealth, the male-centered clans cannot obtain wives to reproduce themselves.

War and preparation for war can affect relations between the genders and even the entire orientation of a society. As men put more time and effort into preparing for war and less into subsistence, women may work more at subsistence activities in addition to the labor they already devote to domestic chores and childcare. When this happens, social values may become more patriarchal and militaristic (Sanday 1974). Men in warlike societies value aggressive masculinity and look down on feminine passivity. Women often are seen as polluting, and customs may severely limit amorous heterosexual relations. The rationale for this aloofness between husbands and wives may be social and political. Men may view wives as dangerous because they come from other groups, which may be actual or potential enemies, or, alternatively, merely because the attractions of male–female relations can interfere with bonding between males.

Some writers theorized that male–female aloofness and close mother–son relationships promote belligerent, narcissistic personalities in tribal societies. In a cross-cultural study, Slater and Slater (1965) found significant correlations between measures of narcissistic-aggressive behavior and postpartum sexual avoidance and polygyny, low indulgence of children, and estrangement of the sexes (see also Russell 1972).

Many of these same societies have initiation rites for boys, which, as I note earlier, may suppress rebellious impulses and reinforce masculine identity and male bonding. These same rites may organize young men into cohesive fighting groups.

Male circumcision is common in Africa whereas supercision and subincision are typical of Australia–Oceania (Harrington 1968). In both Africa and Australia–Oceania genital mutilation may inhibit the inclination of boys to act out oedipal fantasies while reinforcing identification with the agnatic group. The meanings of the rites in the two areas seem to differ in other respects, however.

In Australia–New Guinea the rites may remove unwanted maternal influence and encourage loyalty to agnates. In marginal areas of New Guinea and Eastern Melanesia, where war occurs with other tribes, the emphasis is on masculinizing the boys through insemination. In Australia, the Eastern Highlands of New Guinea, and other regions where people marry their enemies, ritual emphasizes masculinizing the boys through removal of maternal blood and female influence. Bisexual symbolism (i.e., symbols that represent both male and female genitalia or reproductive capacities) may be part of a strategy for getting boys to identify with males. The effects are a graphic removal of female influence even as it mimics female functions.

In Africa initiation rites seem directed more to subordinating potentially rebellious youths to the elders and to their political projects. The traditional Nuer are a classic example of warfare and male initiation in an African society (see next chapter).

War, power, and the state

Under conditions of chronic warfare, leaders tend to become more powerful. In unilineal societies lineage heads and clan leaders control and organize the young warriors. Continued growth in population and violence may lead to the formation of chiefdoms. In Amazonia, for instance, intergroup violence and the power of community leaders increase with population density despite a general reluctance to yield power to local leaders (Clastres 1987).

State formation may be a continuation of this process. Carneiro (1970) argued that preindustrial states usually emerged under conditions of population pressure, warfare, and environmental obstacles to social fission and migration. Where the environment prevents dispersal, communities coalesce and develop professional military strata, elite leadership, and centralized bureaucracies as the way to compete more effectively with their enemies.

War has also figured in the rise of modern states. In Europe, warlords and state makers were aggressive, self-serving entrepreneurs, and the war-making state resembled modern organized crime. Cities and city-states in Europe regularly employed pirates, bandits, and mercenaries in pursuit of their political and economic aims; like modern-day organized criminals, the state makers expanded their operations by eliminating rivals and selling protection to their constituents (Tilly 1985).

A South African kingdom

The rise of the early nineteenth-century Zulu kingdom under Shaka illustrates the way in which resource scarcity may favor state formation and an escalation of violence. The Zulu had moved into southern Africa as part of the Bantu expansion, displacing the pastoral San peoples of the area. During migration, the tribes divided along kinship lines. Chiefs established wives of varying status in different parts of their territories. The rightful heir to the tribal throne was an elder son of the woman the tribal chief married after he assumed chieftainship. Princes who were not in line for chieftainship often set up rival principalities. The result was chronic conflict between tribes and tribal segments and political disunity.

Max Gluckman (1960) suggested that tribal splitting, petty warfare, and migration after 1500 were responses to the growing populations of the Bantu tribes and deteriorating soils. By the late eighteenth century, tribal splitting was no longer solving the problem of land shortage (ibid.: 166). At this point Dingiswayo, a Mtetwa chief, introduced wars of conquest. After he was killed, Shaka, the Zulu leader, seized control of the Mtetwa kingdom, avenged Dingiswayo's death, and waged wars that made devastating use of a short jabbing spear, long shield, and flanking movements.

Fearing that a son would kill him for the throne, Shaka avoided marriage and had his concubines killed when they became pregnant. He quartered his men in all-male barracks and denied them permission to marry or to have sexual relations until middle age. Shaka's father had rejected Shaka, an illegitimate son, and his mother. In turn, Shaka killed those who had ill-treated him and his mother in earlier years. When his mother died, he had thousands of people executed for displaying too little grief, prohibited sexual intercourse for a year, suspended milking and planting, and sent his armies on one campaign after another.

Nazi Germany

One of the most destructive political movements in human history, the Nazis killed people by the tens of millions with their war machine, and the Nazi SS murdered more than 6,000,000 Jews and thousands of Gypsies, disabled persons, and political adversaries.

Nazi anti-Semitism expressed lower middle-class hostility toward communist workers and modern corporate capitalists (Lasswell 1933). Fromm (1941) observed that lower middle-class artisans and shopkeepers had been threatened by the socialist revolution of 1918 and devastated by high inflation in 1923. They suffered further from the economic depression of 1929–1932 that put nearly one-third of the labor force out of work. The position of the lower middle class was always precarious but under the conditions that prevailed prior to World War I, the monarchy was a source of security and a symbol of group pride (ibid.: 213). The humiliating defeat of World War I, the downfall of the Kaiser, the socialist revolution, and communist agitation all seemed to threaten the lower middle class. Fromm concluded that the social character of the lower middle class made it especially sensitive to these stresses and, consequently, receptive to Nazi ideology and promises. Part of this social character was a valuation of hard work and frugality. Economic conditions undermined confidence in hard work and saving and reinforced the traditional longing for a strong leader.

More recent research suggests, however, that the Nazis took advantage of the social ambitions, economic insecurity, and patriotic sentiments among many segments of the population (Childers 1983; Gordon 1984; Merkl 1975). The character traits of the lower middle class, moreover, were widespread in the German population. In interviews with German prisoners of war, Henry V. Dicks found that the typical German soldier was "tense, earnest, industrious, meticulous, over respectful to authority and anxious to impress" (1950: 137). Orderly and self-constrained, he also wanted emotional release. Dicks attributed these characteristics to dominant, strict fathers and indulgent mothers who, especially in the early years of children's lives, offered "furtive" rewards without the father's knowledge. Hostility toward the father was denied by idealizing the father and father-figures and by redirecting hostility toward other personages and symbols.

Narcissism and exaggerated patriotism offered defenses against the stern superego.

Some writers have tried to refine psychodynamic understandings of Nazism by focusing on the personality characteristics of the cohort that came of age with Nazism and gave it much of its political energy. Martin Wangh (1964) saw Nazi anti-Semitism as a regressive projection of oedipal and preoedipal sexuality and aggression. He argued that the stresses of 1930–1933 rekindled in the young generation of German voters memories of traumatic childhood experiences during 1917–1920. The poverty and downward social mobility aroused anxieties associated with hunger and absent fathers, incestuous mother–child closeness, and masculinity. Because fathers were away at war (and often did not return), according to Wangh, boys were deprived of realistic masculine role models and mother–son relationships were intensified. The absence of the father intensified hostility toward him. The failure of the fathers to win the war encouraged cynicism about established authority and morality. Conscious admiration for the father was a defense against the increased closeness to the mother, while conscious love for the father reinforced the denial of pleasure in the defeat of the fathers in war. The Nazi movement, according to Wangh, provided a collective defense for men's insecure gender identity by encouraging a hard masculinity, depreciation of women, male bonding, and hero worship. Anti-Semitism, meanwhile, provided an idiom for projecting repressed desire.[7]

Dicks's (1950) evaluations of the most pro-Nazi prisoners revealed identification with harsh father-figures and redirected aggression, depreciation of women and emphasis on ties to state and Fuhrer, "vague deistic mumbo-jumbo," sadomasochistic impulses, and masculine protest against feminine softness. In another study, Dicks (1973) described prominent SS personalities, evaluated sixty-one autobiographical statements by Nazi Party members, and reported on his interviews with eight Nazi war criminals. In the most violent Nazis he found the same personality traits he had discerned in his earlier study but with more paranoia and less depression. The superegos of this group were weak and merged with images of their SS superiors; even after years of incarceration, they blamed others for their failings. He also found that they had vivid memories of their mothers and of the hardships caused by the absence, deaths, or postwar difficulties of their fathers.

Richard A. Köenigsberg (1975) traced major themes in Hitler's speeches to the trauma of his mother's death from cancer when he was eighteen years old. Excerpts from his speeches show that Hitler likened Germany to an "organism," "national body," and "living substance." The enemies of the organism caused "disintegration," "decay," "decomposition," and "ferment." Hitler's aim was to prevent decomposition through "union" and by combating and isolating Jews and communists, the sources of "pestilence," "cancerous ulcer," "tumor," or "ulcer" in the body social. Relations with other nations were phrased in similar terms. Hitler wanted to protect Germany from "submission" and attack from the "rear."

On a deeper level these idioms may have reflected unresolved oedipal issues. The relation between Germany and the Hapsburg rulers of Austria was characterized as an "unholy alliance" in which Germany was the "mother" and the Hapsburg rulers represented the father. A reunion between Germany and Austria was likened to a reunion of the "mother" and her "sons." Hitler's anti-Semitism and pursuit of war, then, were attempts to undo the mother–father relationship and to protect the mother from the sexual assaults of the father while recreating the lost intimacy between mother and son.

Robert G.L. Waite (1977) also traced Hitler's personality and fascist mentality to formative experiences. Hitler's paternal grandmother gave birth to his father out of wedlock, and his paternal grandfather may have been a Jew – at least Hitler worried that he was. Hitler's mother, according to Waite, had adulterous relations with Hitler's father during his two previous marriages. She was twenty-two and four months pregnant when she married; the groom was forty-six and twice widowed. The father's previous wives had died, and Hitler's mother, a devoted Catholic, probably felt guilty. The deaths of her first three children added to her dysphoria and may have caused her to be too protective of Adolf.

Hitler's father was a strict disciplinarian. He was a heavy smoker and may have been an alcoholic and abusive. He was an obedient civil servant. He demanded silence from his children. Hitler's own style revealed a mixture of identification with and hostility toward his father. He had a life-long aversion to tobacco smoking, a penchant for aggressive speech, and a curious mixture of laziness and grandiose ambition. From an early age he imagined himself the leader; and he rose much higher in public employment than his father.

Waite maintained that Hitler projected his Oedipus complex in political and racial idioms. Hitler associated Germany with his mother, and the despised Hapsburg rulers of Austria with his father. A concurrent projection of negative paternal imagery onto Jews may have reflected his worry that he had received Jewish blood from his paternal grandfather.

Hitler was enthralled with German folktales and the cowboy adventure stories of Karl May. What captured his imagination even more were the pornographic paintings of Franz von Stuck and the music and operas of Richard Wagner. Von Stuck's themes included alluring nudes entwined with gigantic black snakes and Wotan, the Wild Hunter, the personification of death and destruction. Yet nothing moved Hitler as much as the anti-Semitic Wagner. Incestuous and oedipal themes abound in Wagner's operas, as do evocations of German nationalism and the medieval warrior-knight.

There are indications, however, that preoedipal issues may have been more significant for Hitler's personality and political attitudes than his oedipal fantasies. Bromberg and Small (1983) viewed Hitler as a narcissistic, borderline personality with paranoid trends. Among other things, they commented on his anxiety, impulsiveness, poor ego strength, destructiveness, grandiosity, risk-taking, hunger for praise, inability to love, hypochondria, phobias and obsessions, envy, lack of humor, perverse sexuality, and his penchant for splitting, denial, and projective identification. They also discussed his castration anxiety, insecure masculinity, and fear and hatred of women, traits they attributed to an overprotective mother, to anxieties about monorchism (absence of one testicle) and physical sickliness as a child, and to his father's physical and psychological absence during much of Hitler's childhood. Hitler's preoccupation with appearing masculine, hard, and brutal and his fascination, beginning in childhood, with cowboys, Indians, and war may have been a defense against insecure masculine identity. His anti-Semitism may have reflected his misogyny and sexual perversity.

More recent psychoanalytic studies emphasize preoedipal bases of Nazism in general. Chasseguet-Smirgel (1986) discerns in German romanticism – including themes of merging with nature, a fascination with death, transcending social, temporal, and spatial divisions, and a valuation of mystical ecstasy – a desire for return to a maternal womb free of obstructing interference from the father, his penis, or siblings – a desire she characterized as the archaic matrix of the Oedipus complex. It bespeaks, she wrote, "a primary desire to discover a universe without obstacles, without roughness or differences, entirely smooth, identified with the mother's belly stripped of its contents, an interior to which one has free access" (ibid.: 134). She theorized that Nazi anti-Semitism may have involved, among other things, hostility toward the monotheistic, paternalistic deity of the Jews who stood in the way of incestuous regression.

Klaus Theweleit (1987, 1989) has explored the preoedipal foundations of Nazism in his massive two-volume study, *Male fantasies*, the most thorough study of the psychology of Nazism to date. Theweleit examines the novels and memoirs of 250 *Freicorps* soldiers, veterans of World War I who helped the socialist government to suppress communist agitation in the working class. The *Freicorps* soldiers were proto-Nazis. Indeed, many of them later became leaders in the SA and SS.

Theweleit finds sexism at the core of the Nazi mentality. The narratives he examines reveal, again and again, fear of and hatred for women. Being a Nazi soldier is a way of establishing a male identity in opposition to women, who are split into negative images of femininity associated with fluids, floods, sexuality, pestilence, on the one hand, and good, asexual women, on the other. The masculine identity is a way of maintaining ego organization and fending off dissolution; the soldier fashions a coherent ego by forming a body of steel and by melding with the totalizing machine of the military unit. Everything seems aimed at suppressing pleasure, although the soldier finds an explosive gratification in battle. The female, associated with liquidity and weakness, represents just what the soldier fears in himself. The enemy, then, is a projected part of the disavowed self.

Theweleit thinks that oedipal issues have been overemphasized in discussions of Nazism. The writings he has analyzed suggest that the men in question had not reached a stage of ego organization based on resolution of oedipality and identification with the father. The secret of fascism's success was that it afforded a resurgence of desire in the eroticized images of violence, a resurgence of blood, at the front. "The arena of war is first and foremost his own body [the fascist writer's]; a body poised to penetrate other bodies and mangle them in its embrace" (Theweleit 1989: 191).

According to Theweleit, the psychic structure is more "psychotic" than oedipal. The psychic strategies evidenced in the fascist narratives remind Theweleit of the mechanisms that psychotic children use to maintain ego integration and a basic sense of safety. "What this child seeks (its whole life long, if need be) is unification with maternal bodies, within which it can become 'whole,' born to completion" (ibid.: 213). The relationship with the missing mother, however, is shaped by a need for revenge. In the violent explosion of battle, then, the soldier seeks fusion with the mother and, perhaps, annihilation of the father. The-enemy-as-father is the target of aggression because he inhabited the mother's body. Beneath these seemingly oedipal themes, however, is hostility toward the mother for her failings and for permitting the father's access to her body (ibid.: 279).

Anson Rabinbach and Jessica Benjamin (1989) point out that "psychosis" may not be quite the right word. What Theweleit describes, they observe, has more in common with perversion, especially as described by Chasseguet-Smirgel, than with psychosis. Yet they suggest that Theweleit goes beyond Chasseguet-Smirgel in showing that the rabid Nazi soldier wanted not only to return to a mother, to ravage her body, and to escape the law of the father, but also to "rid himself and the earth of all those maternal qualities of warmth and sensuality that could be called mother. It is a frantic repudiation of her" (ibid.: xxii).

The *Freicorps* soldiers were extremists but they may have epitomized tendencies that were widespread among German males. Authoritarianism, sexism, and militarism were deeply rooted in pre-Nazi German culture (Willems 1986). The fear and depreciation of women and the readiness to solve problems through collective violence were part of this tradition. They were mobilized, however, under specific political and economic conditions. Military defeat and economic and social stresses created a climate in which political discourse could evoke not only longstanding themes in German culture but also latent structures of personality.

Hitler and other Nazi leaders may have had personality disorders, and German culture and history may have placed the German people at greater risk of fascism, but it would be a mistake to assume that most of the Germans who followed Hitler were inherently evil or perverse. The truth about German Nazism may be more complicated and far more disturbing.

Psychopathic individuals are prone to evil behavior, but what is true of individuals may not be true of groups. Studies in social psychology and historical examples suggest that the pressures and influences of the group can result in a general lowering of moral standards, even among persons who show no signs of emotional or mental disorder (Darley 1992). Many of the most reprehensible acts in the Nazi regime were committed by the physicians who worked in the concentration camps. They were intelligent, well educated, and law-abiding. Since intelligence and education correlate with moral development in Kohlberg's sense, we can presume that many of those physicians were capable of higher stages of moral reasoning. And yet they were unspeakably immoral. They seem to have dissociated immoral activity in work from family, community, and church, domains in which they continued to exercise moral judgment (Lifton 1986).

Most of the Nazi physicians probably did not have noticeable personality disorders. Thus they may illustrate how a mass psychology of evil can operate in a group even when more people than not in the group are psychologically normal. The studies of German Nazism suggest that given the right cultural background and social conditions, charismatic leaders and their discourse can effect virtual transformations of personality in their followers, creating thereby a facsimile of shared psychosis and collective perversion.

Conclusions

Collective violence deserves anthropological study and discussion. In addition to being a matter of serious human concern, it can have ramifications for the whole of social life. Preparations for war, and the attitudes that are nurtured by war itself, can affect gender relations, socialization practices, and the entire moral order.

War is clearly a complex, over-determined phenomenon, and there are, accordingly, different ways of looking at it. Seen from the perspectives of culturalism, war may express a local, culturally constructed militaristic ethos. The militaristic orientation is reproduced through socialization for aggressiveness.

Psychoanalysis, in contrast, suggests that various motives may inform collective violence. Desire, the will-to-power, and needs for attachment and security may all in different ways provide an impetus for intergroup conflict. These basic drives and needs are organized by preoedipal and oedipal object relations and modulated and directed by ego and superego structures.

The two approaches are complimentary; from a psychoanalytic perspective, at least, cultural schemas, values, symbols, and meanings are part of the ego and superego. Still, the matter is somewhat more complicated than this. The motivation for war may vary depending on how emotional disposition and moral reasoning are affected by socioeconomic conditions, life experiences, discursive practices, and political leadership.

Material conditions and life experiences may lower the threshold for violence. Economic adversity can arouse anxieties about security, and losses and humiliations can fill a person with shame and rage. We have seen that both economic insecurity and rage resulting from losses of love or social status are fertile sources of aggression. A paranoid mourning process seemed to motivate Shaka and Hitler and may have in some sense informed the entire Nazi movement. The Gebusi, Marind-anim, and Ilongot offer other examples.

Social discourse may promote war by idealizing aggressiveness but, also, by stirring up conscious and unconscious feelings of insecurity and rage. More particularly, it may allude to social and economic misfortunes and dangers on one level and to childhood fears and fantasies on another. Myth, ritual, and discursive practices may activate the anger and rage in preoedipal and oedipal structures and link them with feelings about actual social events and relations. What may be decisive, in other words, is not the mere fact of drives and emotions or unconscious object relations, since these can motivate various social activities but, rather, how they are construed and channeled by cultural practices and persuasive speech. Even in societies or groups with a cultural inclination toward violence, it may take a worsening of material conditions and provocative discourse to tilt the balance toward actual hostilities.

9   Religion

Religious belief and practice offer a fertile field for studies of the relation between personality and culture and society. For believers, religions can be emotionally evocative and personally meaningful. The stories individuals tell about their lives may be in some measure stories about the tribulations and progress of their spiritual selves. Religions, as Geertz (1966) noted, formulate the general nature of the world, a moral vision of society, and a sense of what it means to be a person. They inform the mood of a people and their most enduring motives. Yet religions are also social phenomena. They are the work of groups and societies. As such, they tend to give symbolic expression to social relations and group boundaries, imbuing them in the process with mystery and legitimacy. They are, in other words, forms of social discourse and persuasion. These psychological and social dimensions of religion are probably interconnected. Religious discourse and practice may have social effects precisely because they are meaningful and emotional for individuals.

In this chapter I review what scholars have been saying about the subjective foundations of religion. Examples of religion in several different societies will then suggest how the underlying motives for religion are emphasized and configured in different ways under different historical and social conditions.

Mysterium tremendum et fascinans

In an often-cited work, Rudolf Otto (1925) related religious sentiment to an apprehension of *mysterium tremendum*: a feeling of awe and foreboding, a sensation of tremendous power and energy; and to feelings of being powerless, sinful, and in need of atonement. In addition, he found that religious sensibility may entail ecstasy and fascination and identification with the deity. The idea of the deity, he stated,

> may appear to the mind an object of horror and dread, but at the same time it is no less something that allures with a potent charm, and the creature, who trembles before it, utterly cowed and cast down, has always at the same time the impulse to turn to it, nay even to make it somehow his own. (Otto 1925: 31)

Otto, in other words, attributed religious sentiment to fear and foreboding on the one hand and to feelings of ecstatic communion and empowerment on the other. This may not be a complete enumeration of religious motives, and it may not fit every society, but it remains a useful formulation; fear, foreboding, communion, fascination, empowerment, and ecstasy are common themes in the religions of many different societies.

Thunder, fear, and the father

In a paper on fear and foreboding in religion, Donald Tuzin (1984) proposed that thunder and other infrasonic sounds provoke anxiety and a sense of religious mystery. Large drums, bull-roarers, flutes, and pipe organs figure in religious ritual in many societies, according to Tuzin, because they recreate mysterious natural sounds. Noting a connection between temporal-lobe epilepsy and religiosity, he observed that the temporal lobe is the locus of auditory processing in the brain and that it overlies the emotional brain. He noted that bull-roarers are associated with thunder, spirits, and supernatural power in many cultures (see Dundes 1976), and he cited Freeman (1968) who suggested that thunder-gods symbolize the threatening authority and voice of the father in childhood. Thus, Tuzin traced religious awe and foreboding to hearing the paternal voice.

Empowerment, euphoria, and visions

Experiences of a more positive kind are also sources of religious sentiment. Visionaries, mystics, and prophets often ascribe their religious convictions to mystical experiences. Ecstatic trance is part of shamanism; in trance states shamans take magical flight or become possessed by spirits (Peters and Price-Williams 1980).

Trance may involve mixtures of anxiety and pleasure with erotic connotations. Spiritual ecstasy and sexual orgasm resemble one another, and symbolic expressions of concerns with power, eroticism, and procreation appear in shamanic beliefs and practices. The shaman descends into the underworld through a tunnel; he flies, or climbs a magic ladder, to the sky-world. He has empowering animal companion spirits, fights cosmic battles with other shamans or spirits, recovers and fortifies souls, administers plant power, protects his community, and dazzles his followers with tricks and magic. Shamans may marry spirits; in some traditions religious ecstasy is clearly erotic. Róheim (1952: 154–258) argued that shamanism incorporates a "basic dream" involving tension between a return to the womb and libidinal relations. Fighting or killing beings of the underworld, according to Róheim, recreates the primal scene and occasions the rebirth of the self.[1]

Attachment and covenant

Religious groups may address the needs of individuals for attachment and community. At a deeper level, they may recreate the experience of being safely attached to parents (Freud [1927a]1961). Consider the image of Our Lady of Guadalupe in Mexico, an invocation of the Virgin Mary. The patron saint of Mexico, she is the focus of pilgrimages and fiestas, and her picture graces millions of family altars and street-side shrines throughout the country. She is also a model for actual mothers. In a study of the cult of Our Lady of Guadalupe in San Juan Atzingo, Bushnell (1958) suggested that she is a "surrogate mother."

Following the model of the Virgin, village mothers are loving and attentive to each child – but primarily during the first few years of its life. Everything changes with weaning and the arrival of the next child. Diet deteriorates, and the child receives less affection. Within a few years children must work, and boys are subjected to physical punishment. Interpersonal relations, meanwhile, are fraught with mistrust. The imaginary relationship with the Virgin may offer compensation for the sense of loss and for disappointing social relations. Her image restores the maternal presence and celebrations in her honor encourage sociability. Men refer to *pulque*, the maguey beer they consume during her fiesta, as "the milk of the Virgin" (ibid.: 261).

Preserving the good self and good object

People like to feel good about themselves and each other; indeed, to some extent, a sense of well-being and sociability depend on positive self-regard and positive sentiments toward social others. Yet, in fact, people and societies are not perfect. Individuals have illicit and subversive impulses and thoughts, and they do not always achieve their ideals or live up to expectations. There is conflict in social interaction and society generally. Relations with people one loves the most can be seedbeds of the strongest feelings of ambivalence. Parents, to use Winnicott's language, can be "good enough" but they are rarely perfect.

Individuals cope with ambivalence in various ways. One is through splitting and projection. They may split the bad aspects of the self or object off from the good and project them onto social others. Versions of this strategy are common in collective representations. Pantheons of supernatural figures often comprise good figures and bad figures. In rural Mexico, for example, the good figures include Our Lady of Guadalupe; negative figures include The Weeper and witches. Whereas the Virgin of Guadalupe is asexual and nurturing, the Weeper is a loose woman who killed her own children; witches are similarly sexual and dangerous to children (Ingham 1986).

Spiro (1952) found that the Ifaluk valued nonaggression, yet he also detected concealed aggression in projective test data and folklore (1952). The Ifaluk recognized deities and ghosts. The former were deemed remote but the latter were part of people's lives. Some ghosts were benevolent, others malevolent. The malevolent ghosts were both feared and hated. Spiro concluded that ghosts supplied an outlet for hostility and so preserved the nonaggressive ethos in Ifaluk social life.

Both positive and negative supernatural figures may have developmental origins in images and representations of parents. In a study of records of a case of seventeenth-century demonic possession, Freud ([1923b]1961) suggested that both the deity and the Devil in Christianity represent the father of childhood. The victim of the possession was a painter who had become melancholic after the death of his father. The pact the man signed with the Devil to exorcise the demonic spirit implied that the man would give his soul to the Devil after nine years if in the meantime the Devil would serve as a father-substitute. Jones ([1951]1959) suggested that the various witches, demons, and devils of European folklore all reflect disturbing aspects of parental representations.

The psychoanalyst Ana-Maria Rizzuto (1979) showed how individual ideas about God among her patients indeed vary with representations of the self and the parents. Rizzuto noted that the idea of God may derive from representations of the self and mother as well as the father, and she emphasized that it adjusts to a person's changing circumstances. For some persons, the God representation supports psychic equilibrium in the face of psychosocial crises. Religion in her view operates in the transitional, illusionary space between representations of primary objects and reality. The deity is a transitional object that can, when it is vital and meaningful, help to sustain a positive self-representation. Following Winnicott, she suggests that this relationship with the deity takes the form of "silent communication," of an inner dialogue (Rizzuto 1979: 205).

Guilt, depression, and expiation

Religious beliefs and practices can also support positive self-representation by helping individuals to manage guilt and shame. Insofar as religions entail moral and ethical codes, they may encourage shame and guilt about moral lapses and transgressions. But they also may offer relief from the feelings of shame and guilt through ritual cleansing, penitence, atonement, or casting out of demons. Guilt about current transgressions may, through the retranscription of unconscious memory, tie in with childhood memories of illicit desires and related anxieties. Some religions – Roman Catholicism, for example – may, therefore, use subtle oedipal imagery as a trope in both the representation of sin and its amelioration. Alternatively, evil supernatural figures and nonbelievers may represent projections of negative facets of the self or object. The members of a religious group may tolerate deviants within the group because they lend themselves as targets for projection in this way and, also, because they offer vicarious enjoyment of surreptitious pleasure (Forsyth 1988).

Religious belief and practice also may help individuals to cope with depression. Obeyesekere (1985) observed that a somber outlook is part of the Buddhist world view in Sri Lanka. Suffering and sadness are accepted as inherent in human life, and salvation is said to depend on letting go of attachment and desire. Ordinarily, people are more hopeful about life than these ideas would suggest, but in moments of personal crisis Buddhist beliefs may become more relevant. At these moments people may meditate on the body's putrescence and fecal connotations with the aims of realizing the shortness of life and of letting go of desire. In this way negative affects are resolved by working them into cultural meanings and symbols. Obeyesekere describes the "work of culture" as "the process whereby painful motives and affects such as those occurring in depression are transformed into publically accepted sets of meanings and symbols" (ibid.: 147; see also Obeyesekere 1990).

Obeyesekere ventures in passing that depression in western culture lacks cultural meaning. In his view, western rationalism and secularism leave little room for a religious understanding of dysphoria or for a religious approach to therapy. Instead, difficulties in living get labeled and appropriated by the mental-health establishment.

While this comparison between Sri Lanka and western approaches to depression may have some merit, it also seems overdrawn. Western culture is more religious than Obeyesekere suggests, and psychotherapy has deep roots in western religious practice. Indeed, it can be argued that traditional and contemporary Christianity is very much concerned with preventing and treating depression.

Christianity portrays human beings as alienated from paradise, tainted with original sin, and subject to evil. That is, Christianity recognizes the existential origins of depression as central points of theology. The desert fathers attributed depression to the "noonday demon"; in early and medieval Christianity depression was included among the seven or eight vices or cardinal sins under the headings of "acedia," a negative sorrow about the world, and "tristesia," a positive remorse about one's sins that can lead to salvation through penance.

If Christians believe that their faith is redemptive, then they also believe by implication that it is an answer to depression. There is a long tradition in the west of "working through" depression in terms of cultural values and meanings. Cassian (ca. AD 360–435) recommended manual labor as a remedy for acedia. After the Fourth Lateran Council (1215–1216), confession and penitence were seen as treatments for the disorder (Jackson 1985). And contemporary Christian discourse and practice counsel against despair and encourage instead forgiveness, fellowship, communion, and hope, that is, they promote the very sorts of relationships and attitudes that protect people from depression.

Western psychotherapy incorporates these religious themes and reworks them in secular terms. Haynal (1985), noting that depression is a nearly ubiquitous presence in psychotherapy, contends that psychotherapy exemplifies a practice in western society of overcoming depression and grieving through creative, productive work. The practice and theory of secular psychotherapy are very much a part of western culture. As Obeyesekere himself notes, the idea of the work of culture comes from Marx and Freud, western thinkers. I would only note – ironically, given Obeyesekere's view of the west – that the notions of work in Marx and Freud resonate with religious and secular meanings and values in the west.

Hunter-gatherers

Shamanism, a religious complex involving trance and direct knowledge of the supernatural, may have been the first religion of humanity. It is universal or nearly universal among hunter-gatherers, and elements of it occur in cultures everywhere. The roles of healer, medium, and priest in more complex societies probably derived from the role of shaman in hunter-gatherer societies. It has been suggested that trance states may give greater access to the unconscious while heightening sensory awareness. Thus, trance may help emotional problem-solving while seeming to empower people for divination (Winkelman 1990).

While shamanism forms the core of religion in hunter-gatherer societies, religious beliefs and practices vary considerably. Where conditions (e.g., water supply, game migration, etc.) require intergroup cooperation, religion may consist of shamanism and belief in nature spirits and one or more major deities. Where conditions favor territoriality in defense of scarce resources, it may ritualize agnatic solidarity through secret societies, fertility cults, and male initiation rites. The San of South Africa and the natives of Central Australia illustrate these two modes of adaptation. These two examples illustrate two different elaborations of the shamanic complex; the first is open, pragmatic, and egalitarian; the second is secretive, mysterious, and patriarchal.

The Kalahari !Kung San

Among the San hunter-gatherers of the Kalahari Desert the men hunt and the women gather. Meat is shared throughout the camp but especially with in-laws. Food-sharing is highly valued, and people gossip about those who seem reluctant to share.

Gender relations tend to be egalitarian. Apart from the distribution of food, sexuality is the only significant source of tension. Since having a wife is a man's main claim to social standing, adultery can lead to fighting. Homicides are fairly common, but the San are not warlike and they lack the institutions that are often found in more warlike societies. Kinship is bilateral, and male initiation rites are either absent or minimal. Traditionally, circumcision was practiced by only one marginal group. The northern San had special communal dancing for boys in late adolescence, but it did not differ much from other forms of communal dancing (Schapera 1930: 69–71, 122–126). Nor do the San have male fertility cults or secret societies.

!Kung San religion is communal, shamanic, and oriented toward healing and strengthening social ties. !Kung recognize a great god and a lesser god and ancestral spirits. Each god has a wife and children, and both are anthropomorphic to the point of earthiness – the lesser god represents cannibalism and incest, the worst of sins. All the supernatural figures live in the sky. The !Kung pray to these gods for water and food with unabashed utilitarianism.

Healing dances, the most important religious events, are held roughly four times a month. Usually open to everyone (some dances are exclusively for women) and lasting through the night, they stir *num* (spiritual energy) in the participants and so provoke *kia*, a trancelike altered state of consciousness. An energy that heats up and cools down, *num* is associated with fire (Katz 1982: 120). The ceremony begins with the lighting of a fire at sunset. "The women who are to sing and clap the healing songs come together informally and gradually. They sit together in intimate physical contact, legs intertwined, shoulder to shoulder, forming a circle around the fire. The dancers, both men and women, circle the fire" (ibid.: 40). As *num* begins to boil, the dancers may go into *kia*. *Kia* is experienced as death and rebirth; there is fear and foreboding, followed by heightened consciousness and exhilaration, sometimes with the experience of traveling to the spirit world. Everyone who dances receives healing, and to heal, !Kung go into *kia.* By adulthood 50 percent of the men and 10 percent of the women are healers, and many more have experienced *num* and *kia.* "Boiling" *num* is itself healing; it seems to give the !Kung a sense of empowerment and communion.

Aborigines of Central Australia

The peoples of Central Australia traditionally were hunter-gatherers who lived in patrilocal bands. Communities were organized by cross-cousin marriage, marriage classes, and clanship. Society was a gerontocracy, with the mature men forming one stratum, women and children another. War and feuding between groups were common. Since natural deaths were blamed on sorcery, provocations for armed conflict were plentiful. Wife-stealing also evoked punitive raiding. The men initiated boys and staged fertility rituals. Male rituals recreated the "dream time," the moment when the rainbow serpent, rain spirits, and totemic ancestors roamed the earth (Spencer and Gillen 1899).

Initiation rites had four parts: painting and tossing the boys in the air, circumcision, subincision, and the fire ceremony. The boys were taken away from the women to a ceremonial ground. There, after they heard the bull-roarers, they were circumcised and told that the bull-roarers are sacred *tjurungas* (oblong-shaped boards decorated with iconographic representations). The boys' foreskins were given to the younger brothers to eat or to sisters to wear on necklaces (ibid.: 250–251). The next phase was a ceremonial "roasting" of the initiate by women, which was then followed by a long series of totemic rituals ending with another ordeal by fire.

In pioneering contributions to psychoanalytic anthropology, Róheim (1945b, 1950) viewed Aboriginal culture as a projection of the individual unconscious. He paid little attention to how culture is grounded in social relations, and many of his interpretations of unconscious motives have a mechanistic, cookbook quality about them. Nonetheless, some of his insights seem suggestive even now.

Róheim detected oedipal themes in myths about the Dual Heroes among the tribes to the west of the Aranda. A Primal Father kills everyone or takes all the women until he is killed by his sons. The sons introduce circumcision, which modifies the hostility. The heroes, father and son or penis and testicles, replace the mother–child unity with a phallic, father–son unity. The foreskin symbolizes the child and the vagina or the womb that was around the child. Circumcision thus represents the separation from the mother. In return, according to Róheim, the initiate gets a wife and a *tjurunga.* Like the bull-roarer, the *tjurunga* is a bisexual object, a phallus covered with concentric circles, a narcissistic symbol and an erotic object that compensates the initiate for the loss of the mother and symbolizes the self, the phallus, and identification with the ancestors (Róheim 1945b: 99–101). The subincision wound, a "vagina," adds to the boy's symbolic accouterments (ibid.: 164). In the final phase of the rites, the boys are reborn from a male "womb."

The fire ordeal recalls the ritual smoking of babies after birth. The rebirth symbolism completes the transition to manhood and returns the youths to society (Róheim 1945b: 116–117). The boys are killed and then reborn from the men (ibid.: 198). By giving boys the *tjurunga* and marking their bodies with bisexuality, according to Róheim, the rite also equips them for fertility rituals. The men smear bird's-down on designs made with red ocher and blood drawn from the subincised penis and arm wounds. The fertility rituals end with the quivering of the decorated actors, which sends the bloody bird's-down flying. The quivering resembles intercourse, and the down is said to fertilize plants, animals, and women. Spirits emanating from bull-roarers and *tjurungas* can cause pregnancy (ibid.: 90–91, 155).

Róheim observed a close relationship between mother and child. Mothers are very nurturing with infants and toddlers, and they sleep with the young children. Male dominance, then, reverses symbiosis with the mother by replacing it with a superior, vaginal male: "When the men represent their own penes as bleeding vaginas," according to Róheim, "they again are overcoming the separation plus the castration trauma by identification" (ibid.: 177). Male ritual assuages separation: mimicry of female reproduction compensates men for the loss of their mothers and helps them to deal with Mother Nature, which can be less than nurturing (ibid.: 223). The ambisexual symbolism is present in the rainbow serpent, a phallus and a vagina–uterus (ibid.: 196). Blood from the subincised penis is said to represent "milk." The men drink blood from hands and arms to symbolize solidarity (Spencer and Gillen 1899: 461–462). Boys begin their lives in a milk-covenant with their mothers but mature into a bloodletting covenant with men (Róheim 1945b: 233–234).

Róheim's interpretations of religion in Central Australia anticipate Mahler's ideas about mother–child symbiosis and the related theories of Stoller, Greenson, Chodorow, and others about gender-identity insecurity in males. In the chapter on war and elsewhere in this book we have seen other examples suggesting that male solidarity may be grounded in fear of merging with, and hostility toward, women.

Róheim implied that the initiation-rite complex is required by the peculiar character of the mother–child relationship among the Aborigines. This seems unlikely, given the nurturing infants and toddlers receive. If anything, the kind of maternal care children receive would encourage secure attachment. A more likely hypothesis is that ritual is a rhetorical practice aimed at rekindling or reinforcing castration anxiety and separation anxiety. Even when childcare is very good, children may experience some separation anxiety, and male children especially may have insecurities about core gender identity. By reinforcing such anxieties and insecurities, male ritual may then offer compensation in the form of male companionship and a masculinity-building warrior ethos.

The Sambia

In many tribal-level societies the initiation of males in late childhood or at puberty was associated with fertility cults, and warfare and male dominance were emphasized, much as in Central Australia. In the cults, men used *sacra* – often flutes – to increase human and natural fertility. Male initiations incorporated young men into the cults or into the ranks of warriors.

Many cultures of precontact New Guinea were warlike. Many were agnatic and polygynous, and many had postpartum sex taboos and exclusive mother–child sleeping arrangements. And many had puberty rites for boys and male secret societies, fertility cults, and magical flutes. Throughout the region there was a close connection between male violence and fertility cults. The cults may have appropriated the productive and reproductive powers of women on the symbolic plane in order to legitimize and mystify the power and solidarity of adult males. The cults were the idiom through which men entered intercommunal exchange relationships that were phases in cycles of war and peace (Whitehead 1986a, 1986b).

Regional variations existed. In the coastal areas of New Guinea and in parts of Eastern Melanesia, population density was usually low and ritual male homosexuality was common. Fathers were more apt to sleep in the same huts with their wives. Traditionally, violence often took the form of headhunting (Herdt 1981, 1989). In the northern lowlands and eastern highlands male solidarity was phrased in terms of removing female blood. The secret flutes and fertility rites mystified the power of senior men over boys and women. Women produced children for the clans and tended the gardens and the pigs, while men were busy with warfare and politics. Male insecurity over their actual economic contributions may have motivated men's assertions that they had magical influence on the fertility of pigs, plants, and people (Langness 1974). Initiation rites, by contrast, were less elaborate or absent in the western highlands, where big-man politics and bridewealth supported male power.

Lindenbaum (1984) regarded the eastern highlands as a transitional area between the lowlands and central and western highlands. She theorized that egalitarian sister exchange in the lowlands and the dominance of wife-givers in the highlands are transformations of a single system: semen in the lowlands is equivalent to bride-price valuables (pigs and shells) in the western highlands.

The Sambia are a geographically and culturally transitional people between the lowlands and the eastern highlands. Herdt (1981, 1982) described the Sambia's ritual use of fellatio and semen ingestion to reinforce boys' identification with men and male ideology and purposes. The Sambia associate the secret flutes with penes and the maternal breast, and they liken semen to breast milk (Herdt 1982, 1984: 173). A myth told about the origins of fellatio suggests that it prevents incest. If youths were not having sexual relations with older initiated boys, they might want sex with their mothers (Herdt 1981: 256–260). The myth implies that initiation rites discourage oedipal inclinations while promoting identification with adult males and adult solidarity (Lidz and Lidz 1984, 1986). Among the Sambia, semen is secretly associated with shells and other exchange valuables. In various New Guinea cultures, coconuts, semen, human heads, and penis heads have overlapping meanings (Herdt 1984: 59–60).

Headhunting and male homoeroticism may be substitutes for the oedipal object and for marriage and ways of easing the threat that bachelor males pose to older polygynous males. Moreover, the homoerotic relationship seems to establish a relationship with a surrogate father in which the younger recipient of male substance is identifying physically and spiritually with the social world of fathers (Herdt 1989). Why this should happen in the lowlands, where husbands sleep with wives and the father is more available to his children than in the highlands, is curious. Herdt (ibid.) opined that this lowland paternal presence is inconsistent and ambivalent and therefore requires homosexual "resocialization."

Herdt's interpretations of the Sambia, like Róheim's interpretations of the central Australians, assume that the child's early relation with the mother sets up a necessity for some sort of resocialization. This necessity, however, is never firmly established.

Following the discussion in Chapter 7 of initiation rites, it may be more apt to emphasize how Sambia initiation resocializes boys for *social* purposes. A psychoanalytic view of the desiring, speaking subject helps us to understand the content of social rhetoric. In most cases, it does not take us very far in trying to explain the differences between cultures. A cogent example of how psychoanalytic understanding enhances a basically sociological perspective can be found in T.O. Beidelman's (1966) interpretation of the Nuer. Evans-Pritchard's classic monographs on traditional Nuer society were published many years ago, and the Nuer have certainly changed in the meantime. Beidelman's reading of the Nuer ethnography shows, however, that the traditional Nuer are still instructive for thinking about the psychology of religion.

The Nuer

Among the Nuer of the Sudan, traditional culture centers on cattle. The Nuer fight over cattle and pasture lands, they drink milk from cows and blood from oxen, and they give cattle as bridewealth. Men take the names of their oxen. The most powerful men are known as *gaat twot*, the children of bulls. A powerful man is usually an eldest son, the master of his hamlet, and the owner of many cattle. Clustered around him are the homesteads of his sons and perhaps those of his sisters' and daughters' husbands (Evans-Pritchard 1940: 179). The Nuer blame fights between bulls for the splitting and movements of lineages (ibid.: 34). Related but separate lineages are traced to the different co-wives of the founding male (ibid.: 247); similarly, herds are traced through and identified with cows, not bulls (Evans-Pritchard 1956: 260). According to Beidelman (1966), Nuer social life and ritual reflect tension between idealized agnatic solidarity, on the one hand, and uterine loyalties and the divisive effects of men trying to become "bulls," on the other.

A man's first ox name is taken from the ox that his father gives to him after initiation. Boys are initiated in age-sets. The "man of cattle" opens and closes the age-sets. The initiate receives six cuts across the forehead, perhaps symbolizing the dominance of the five or six more senior sets. Besides his first ox, he also gets a spear from his father, thus becoming eligible for warfare.

The age-sets, which extend across the villages and tribal segments, subordinate younger men to older men. Initiation into an age-set resembles castration and likens a youth to an ox. Bull calves are not only castrated but, also, their horns are slashed. The reason, Nuer explain, is so that the resulting deformations of the horns will please the owners; the Nuer compare this procedure to the cutting of the forehead in initiation. The initiation dances are called *ruath*; the word refers to a bull-calf that has been weaned and will later be castrated. The wearing of metal bracelets on the left arms of the initiates, moreover, duplicates the deformations of the oxen's left horns (Evans-Pritchard 1956: 256–257). Since the left side connotes femininity and evil (ibid.: 233–234) and the bracelets hinder the left arm, the rite also connotes separation from the mother and the suppression of femininity.

Initiations imply castration and sacrifice. Oxen are objects of sacrifice in offerings to Spirit. Spirit is said to take the blood and, perhaps, the souls of oxen. Bulls are rarely sacrificed, and then only to end a blood-feud. Sacrifices occur at various times, including initiation (Evans-Pritchard 1956: 197–230). The oxen are smeared with ashes in preparation for sacrifice, a parallel to smearing the boys' foreheads with ashes before they are cut (ibid.: 261–262). Since young men become warriors upon initiation, it is precisely as warriors who may die in battle that they are most like sacrificial oxen. Sacrificial offerings are made before wars to the spirits of the air, who give victory in war. The air spirits are manifestations of *kwoth* or Spirit (ibid.: 45, 51). These air spirits are distinct from the spirits of the earth, which are related to particular lineages, especially those thought to have Dinka or alien origins. The Nuer say that the spirits of the air are superior to totemic spirits of particular lineages (ibid.: 93). The religious metaphors, in other words, idealize the subordination of self and lineage loyalties to Spirit, to broader kin-groups, and even to the Nuer people as a whole.

In Beidelman's analysis, the castrated sacrificial ox represents socialized sexuality, whereas the bull symbolizes unrestrained libido, selfishness, and political ambition. The ox is associated with idealized agnatic organization, sharing, enduring social relations, whereas the bull represents divisiveness, uterine divisions, and local settlements. The spear, the instrument of castration and sacrifice, represents agnatic solidarity. Thus the initiation-rite–sacrifice complex is a system for inhibiting and sublimating sexuality within an agnatic moral order.

Roman Catholicism

Dundes (1981) showed that the life of Jesus fits the hero pattern identified by von Hahn, Rank, and Raglan. Although he is the Son of God, Jesus had humble parents and, in conformity with actual incest in other hero stories, there are hints of an incestuous closeness between Jesus and Mary. The Pieta is not unlike the Greek tradition of portraying a dying hero in his lover's arms. After he is risen, Christ shakes off the effort of Mary Magdalene to touch him and goes to be with his father. The pattern, Dundes noted, has elements of the initiation-rite complex in tribal societies in which boys are separated from women and incorporated into the world of men. Dundes likened the Holy Family to the Mediterranean family in which sons often have difficulty freeing themselves from the symbiotic relation with the mother.

Michael P. Carroll (1986) regards the bleeding image of the crucified Christ and the adoration of the Virgin Mary as setting Catholicism apart from Protestantism. For Catholics, Mary is a virgin in several senses: she conceived without sexual intercourse, her maidenhead was never ruptured, and she abstained from sexual intercourse after giving birth to Jesus. Carroll argues that the emphasis on virginity is a defense against the Oedipus complex, and concerns with the Crucifixion and penitence in Catholicism reflect a need to punish the self for oedipal inclinations.

In Carroll's interpretation, the two themes were grounded in father-absent families. Before the fourth or fifth centuries when the themes became prominent, Christianity had been a middle-class religion. Subsequently, it began to attract urban and rural poor in increasing numbers. Father-absent families may have been common among the poor, and they may have encouraged oedipal ties between mothers and sons. Carroll theorizes that the father-absent family may also have intensified oedipal fantasies in the father–daughter relationship, and that Mariolatry may reflect a daughter's desire to have a baby by her father (Mary conceived Jesus through her mystical relation with God). The hypermasculinity of fathers encourages oedipal fantasies in daughters. Carroll finds support for these arguments in the Cybele cult that preceded the development of the cult of Mary. Many of Cybele's supporters may have belonged to the lower social strata. She represented chastity and, in fact, some of her priests castrated themselves. A passage in Lucretius even implies an understanding that Cybele's priests castrated themselves as punishment for violating their mothers sexually and for showing disrespect to their fathers (Carroll 1986: 102–103).[2]

Nancy Breuner (1992) wonders if Carroll's argument about the Marian cult focuses too much on men and not enough on women. In a fine example of how attention to social meanings and social relations promotes more discriminating uses of psychoanalytic interpretation in anthropology, she draws on the ethnographic, psychologically oriented studies of Spain and Italy by Brandes (1980), Gilmore and Gilmore (1979), and others to suggest a somewhat different and definitely more nuanced view of the meaning and motivation of Marian devotion. She shows, contrary to what we should expect from Carroll's argument, that men from absent-father families are not necessarily more devoted to Mary than other men, and that men in general are less devoted to her than women. She notes the paradoxical mixtures of weakness and strength associated with men's and women's roles, and relates the concerns of adult men and women to preoedipal problems with gender identity, attachment, and individuation. While she does not reject the oedipal interpretation – she feels that at some level it may still have merit – more salient in her view is how the symbol of Mary helps men and women shore up power in gender relations: by justifying men's control of women's sexuality and by associating women with both "strength and tranquility" (ibid.: 90).

A difficulty in Carroll's argument is that it does not address the fact that believing Catholics come from various family backgrounds and social settings. While his reconstruction of psychological motivation in early Roman Catholicism seems plausible, it cannot explain why Catholicism has managed over time to appeal to people in different social classes and in many different societies. Breuner's analysis is more plausible here. To understand the widespread appeal of Catholicism, it is necessary to consider not simply or primarily the psychological issues of a particular culture or region but, also, issues of general human concern. The images of the Virgin Mary and the story of the Crucifixion may speak to common human needs for nurture, to unconscious memories of common remnants of childhood oedipal desires, or to common human needs for atonement and expiation.

In my own writing about Roman Catholicism, I have considered both theology and iconography and the way in which folk Catholics think about and experience their religion (Ingham 1986, 1989, 1992). I notice that Adam, Eve, and the Tree in Eden are replicated and transmuted in Christ (the Second Adam), Mary (the Second Eve), and the Tree of the Cross. There are textual and iconographic intimations of incest as well as disobedience of the father in original sin. In keeping with the unity of the opposites in the dualism of the Garden and Golgotha, the allusion to mother–son closeness is repeated in the Crucifixion, but with a refinement that coheres with the message of expiation and redemption. Viewed in this way, Catholicism is a social psychological discourse that can, among other things, minister to people's internal struggles with failure and transgression.

Hindu India

Psychological studies of Hindu culture in South Asia illustrate further the limitations of psychological determinism and, at the same time, that it may be more illuminating to consider the psychology of religion within a broader discussion of social relations and cultural discourse. Hindu myth and ritual are replete with parental figures and erotic imagery. Various authors have seen these figures and imagery as reiterations of childhood experience, especially the boy's relation with his mother; the idea, it would seem, is that Hinduism is essentially a male fantasy.

Caste distinctions are expressed in ideas about food, sexuality, pollution, and health. Caste members preserve their caste purity by eating together, never with persons of other castes. Light-colored foods (e.g., rice, sugar, milk, butter, honey) are thought to enhance the production of semen, and the production and conservation of semen in the male are thought to correlate with health. This seminal vitality increases with caste power, whereas pollution reduces caste power. High castes are associated with lightness and purity, lower castes with darkness and pollution.

Marriage in village India is patrilocal and between young men and women from different villages. Thus brides find themselves in alien villages and under the rule of mothers-in-law who can be strict and less than friendly. Sexual intimacy is discouraged by the extended family and concerns about semen-loss. The bride's rise in status depends on motherhood.

The Hindu pantheon includes many variants of several principal gods and goddesses. A common form of the goddess is Kali, the naked, black demon who wears a garland of giant heads and dances upon her male partner, Shiva. The sacred cow is one manifestation of the goddess. Nandi or Bull, her consort and invocation of Shiva, is passive and submissive. He is associated with the erect phallus or Lingam, though he represents self-castration and asceticism. Vishnu-Krishna, another major deity, is the youthful lover.

G. Morris Carstairs (1957) traced major themes in Hindu religion to the close mother–child relationship in the first several years of life and, in the son's case, to the sudden subjugation of the son to the father's authority around age five or six. The mother is very good to her young child but, when menstruating, withdraws for reasons the child cannot understand. The alternating experience of gratification and frustration, according to Carstairs, lays the basis for splitting the maternal figure into benevolent and malevolent deities. Even the blissful relation to the mother comes to a traumatic end when, at the age of five or six, the boy is subjugated to the will of the father. The oedipal trauma, according to Carstairs, is resolved in a passive orientation to authority figures.

In this same vein, Sudhir Kakar (1978), an Indian psychoanalyst, suggested that the altruistic yearnings and desire for oneness with God derive from this close mother–child relationship. The young mother turns her attentions on her infant and finds in him or her a "savior," the object of her unfulfilled wishes and fantasies. Along with images of the good mother, there is also the bad mother who is aggressive and sexual. The latter corresponds to the experience of the male child who, aware of the mother's frustration, feels threatened by her neediness and sexuality, and to that of the husband who, similarly, may feel threatened by the erotic needs of his wife. The little boy's transition from the ideal and comforting world of women to that of men may be a blow to childhood narcissism that "tends to foster both regression to an earlier 'happier' era and a tendency to consolidate one's identification with the mother in order to compensate for her loss" (Kakar 1978: 130). Meanwhile, the boy's many emotional ties within the extended family may militate against his identification with his father (ibid.: 131).

Kurtz (1992) also tries to account for important elements of Hindu culture in terms of child-rearing, but he argues that Hindu child development is radically different from anything we are familiar with in the west. In his view, the interpretations of Carstairs, Kakar, and others who have used psychoanalysis to understand India have been colored by western preconceptions. Western and Hindu child development, he opines, are quite different and must be seen, if they are to be understood, through rather different frameworks. In the west, according to Kurtz, development begins with separation–individuation and then progresses through the oedipal phase. In India, the boy – Kurtz has almost nothing to say about girls – moves from separation from the mother to integration into the group (the extended family). The mother is said to push the child away by withholding affection (but not physical care). The other women of the extended family serve as alternate mothers. Simultaneously, they pose the danger of "castration," because they, not the father, are the ones who pull the boy away from the mother and into the group. Fear of castration by the father is secondary to, and assimilated to, the specter of castration posed by the other mothers: "the male child's incestuous strivings are played out, especially at the start, not in a triangle of father, mother, and son but in a triangle of in-law mothers, natural mother, and son" (Kurtz 1992: 160).

Kurtz finds support for his separation from the mother–integration into the group hypothesis in a film about the goddess Santoshi Ma as well as in several myths and tales. The film supposedly portrays the tension between a daughter-in-law's devotion to one divine mother (Santoshi Ma) and devotion to all the goddesses, a tension that is resolved in favor of group unity at the end of the film.

In the tale of Krishna, the hero steals butter from the *gopīs* (milkmaids). When Yashoda, Krishna's foster mother, keeps him at home by binding him to a mortar, the *gopīs* visit Krishna and chastise Yashoda for being too harsh. According to Kurtz, they are claiming to be better mothers than Yashoda. In the circle dance, Krishna splits into many images so he can dance with all the *gopīs*, including his principal lover, Radha. The dance supposedly depicts the transfer of love from the mother to the other mothers (Kurtz 1992: 144–149).

My view of Hinduism gives less weight to early life experiences while, at the same time, relating them to social discourse. Hinduism, like other religions, is a philosophical perspective, a guide to moral action, and a gloss on social life. It appeals to women as well as men. Hinduism may resonate with unconscious fantasies but this is not all it is about and, in any case, what is more interesting is the way in which Hindu epics, lore, and practice may have rhetorical effects on socially germane unconscious motivation. That is to say, religious belief and practice may, through their tactical and strategic deployment in actual social relations, bring about a *retranscription* of desire or inhibition in ways that fit the interests or desires of one or another individual, gender, or group. In the Indian family, rhetorical maneuver and retranscription may favor the elders of the extended family or, in subversive genres, the young wife.

The presence of aunts and uncles may complicate the object relations of the Hindu child, but there is ample reason to think that the nuclear family forms the core of the child's fantasy; the child's relationship with the mother is close and intimate, and young children usually sleep close to their mothers and thus are aware of the sexual relations between their mothers and fathers. In fact, Indian myth and folklore are permeated with oedipal themes and allusions to the primal scene (Devereux 1951b; Goldman 1978; Ramanujan 1984).

Kurtz has argued that the extended family gives a very different twist to Indian child development. In a critique of his work, I suggest that many of the materials he adduces in support of his argument are better understood as commentaries about gender relations in which oedipal allusions exert the pragmatic effect of either inhibiting husband–wife eroticism while reinforcing mother–son attachment or promoting eroticism in the husband–wife relationship (Ingham, in press).

Psychoanalysts have noticed that triangular fantasies either promote or inhibit erotic attachment in marital relationships. Triangular structures in which the self defeats a rival or becomes the object of two suitors may imbue the relationship with excitement, but if the early oedipal origins of these fantasies become too explicit they may provoke anxiety and thus an inhibition of desire (Kernberg 1988, 1991).

Epic myths and tales in India may reinforce the patriarchal extended family and the suppression of husband–wife intimacy. This trend is especially evident in the mythic tales about Shiva, Parvati, and their sons Ganesha and Skanda. Shiva is a phallic god, brimming with erotic energy, but he is essentially ascetic. Parvati is his frustrated but dutiful wife. The sons, Ganesha and Skanda, are strongly attached to their mother.

Ganesha has a pot belly, an elephant's head and limp trunk, a broken tusk which he carries in his hand, and a rat for a mount. In one story, Shiva goes hunting with all his servants. Parvati, not having anyone to guard the entrance to her bath, makes Ganesha from the dirt of her body. When Shiva returns he is angry at being prevented by Ganesha from entering his own house so he cuts off Ganesha's head. Parvati then becomes angry; to placate her, Shiva replaces Ganesha's head with that of an elephant. In another tale, Skanda kills the demon enemy of the gods; he then veers out of control and makes love to the wives of the gods. To stop him, Parvati takes the form of all the women Skanda desires. Seeing his mother everywhere, Skanda loses desire and becomes celibate (O'Flaherty 1973: 204). Skanda, like his father, becomes an ascetic. At Kataragama in Sri Lanka, Skanda can only have sex with a mistress, evidently because his wife reminds him of his mother (Obeyesekere 1990: 120). In short, the Shiva–Ganesha cycle de-emphasizes the husband–wife relationship while subordinating the son to the father and highlighting the son's erotic attachment to his mother.

Various writers have noted that Indian women have suppressed or unsatisfied needs for empowerment, erotic gratification, and intimacy resulting from their subordinate position within the extended family (Kakar 1990; Raheja and Gold 1994; Trawick 1990, 1992). In her study of Bengali women, Roy (1975a, 1975b) shows how a woman's needs in the marital relation are shaped by a very affectionate and affirming father–daughter relationship in childhood. As the girl matures, she is taught to idealize Shiva as the ideal husband figure. Gradually she finds Krishna a more appealing figure. After she marries, her husband may not fulfill these earlier idealizations of the male object, and she may turn instead to her child and, eventually, to a guru to satisfy her needs for intimacy.

The need for intimacy is expressed in spring festivals, in the figures of Krishna and Radha, and in women's songs and tales. In his classic paper about the festival *Holī*, McKim Marriott (1968) noticed a carnavalesque opposition to caste hierarchy and the usual subordination of women. The festival celebrates the spiritual liberation of a goddess who opposed proper paternal authority and favored her own demon father instead. The festival also invokes the spirit of Krishna, who encourages love between husbands and wives.

Krishna is a boy deity who has a fondness for butter. In the tales, he steals butter from the milkmaids. His mother tries to keep him at home by tying him down. In the end, he loves and marries Radha, one of the milkmaids. Radha in the tales is variously a mother figure for Krishna or a lover (Doniger 1993).

Krishna may register women's desires for a relationship with their husbands that has the same qualities of intimacy and sensuality women experience with their babies. Following Roy, we can also discern in the stories a displacement of desire running from father, to Shiva, to Krishna, to husband, to baby. For men, the figures of Krishna and Radha may imbue the marital relationship with eroticism by exciting its oedipal undercurrents.

Songs also express women's desires for more intimate relationships with their husbands, sometimes with implied criticism of the mother-in-law's role as rival for the husband's attentions (Raheja and Gold 1994). Women's tales discussed by Ramanujan (1991) offer other examples of their concerns with improving marriages. The tales portray fate: the woman endures until she can tell her story, until she can become a speaking subject. Typically stories move from a marital union, to separation, to reunion and a closer husband–wife relationship. In the tale of the "Serpent Lover," a woman has an unfaithful husband. She decides to give him a love potion but when, in the mixing, it turns blood red, she discards it in a snake hole. The snake falls in love with her and comes to her at night as her husband. She becomes pregnant. The snake helps her to prove her virtue before the raja's court. Instructed by the snake, she says she will hold the cobra in Shiva's temple with impunity. The five-headed cobra that is wrapped around the Shiva-phallus is actually the king of snakes. In the end, the woman reunites with her husband, they enjoy their beautiful son, and the husband's concubine becomes the wife's maid. Since the wife is now totally devoted to her husband, and he to her, the snake, still in love with the woman, hangs himself to death one night by her tresses (Ramanujan 1991: 47–51). Notice the triangles: two women and the husband, two males and the wife. The snake is not only a lover but, also, a father figure: he is a king, and he is associated with Shiva.

Cults

Religious cults are common in complex societies. Occupying niches at the margins of orthodoxy, they appeal particularly to women or other oppressed classes and groups. They may be enduring "peripheral cults," or they may be "crisis cults" that reflect temporary conditions. The two types may be interrelated. Crisis cults may emerge out of peripheral cults or develop into them (Bourguignon 1973, 1976; Crapanzano 1973; Crapanzano and Garrison 1977; Finkler 1985; La Barre 1970; I.M. Lewis 1971).

Peripheral cults

Stable religious cults often form around a shaman or spirit medium, and often center on ancestor or weather spirits or pagan deities. Although they may be concerned with controlling the weather and ensuring a good harvest, their main interests are usually physical health and spiritual well-being. Potential recruits come to the cults seeking relief from affliction. Often, it seems that they suffer from dissociative, somatoform, or depressive disorders. Once in the cult, devotees learn to have ecstatic relations with the supernatural. The cults thrive in peasant and tribal societies with strict, patriarchal values. They tend to recruit more women than men. It seems likely, therefore, that the cults address the emotional suffering and stress women experience in traditional, patriarchal societies.

Obeyesekere (1981) offered a detailed picture of the subjective concomitants of a religious cult in his study of Kataragama. The devotees of the cult grow matted locks, walk on fire, and hang from hooks. The main pageant of the cult celebrates the god's ecstatic sexual union with his mistress; however, the cult also embraces ascetic Buddhist values. Taking issue with the notion that religious symbols are exclusively social in meaning, Obeyesekere showed that matted locks, which identify the devotee with the god, are phallic symbols with deep personal significance: for women devotees who have withdrawn from unhappy marriages, matted locks may represent a sublimated sexual reunion, and ritual dancing an orgasmic experience. Some of Obeyesekere's female informants lost fathers in childhood or had close relationships with them. In other words, the cult may have represented a quest for an alternative to the marital relationship on the model of the happier father–daughter relationship, although Obeyesekere also shows that the devotees were working through guilt resulting from unsatisfactory marital relationships.

Peripheral cults occur in modern societies as well. Protestant snake-handling cults have taken hold in certain areas of the southern United States. Faith healing, trance, and ecstatic displays of emotion are part of the service: men kiss men and women kiss women and, of course, the minister and members of the congregation handle deadly snakes.

In his study of snake-handling, La Barre (1962) considered the biblical account of Adam and Eve and the ethnographic literature to educe the snake's associations with the phallus, fertility, rain, and death and rebirth. He also examined the personality of Barefoot, a cult leader, and the motivations of his followers. Barefoot tempted God and Fate and beguiled his congregation, especially the women. Handling the snakes may have been a collective compromise formation for the devotees: while perhaps expressing autoerotic and oedipal impulses, it gave them a medium for conquering evil. Barefoot's wife was, like his mother, ascetic and self-denying, as were his female communicants. But the serpents allowed him to eroticize his relationship with them and to offer them relief from otherwise dreary lives. By flouting conventional religion, Barefoot exemplified the Southerner's identification with the rebel. Many of his followers were mill workers. Economically marginal and socially alienated, they lived by an ethos that was "repressive and compulsive, joyless and denying, economically as well as libidinally" (ibid.: 169). Barefoot "performs the functions of the Snake in the Garden of Eden and seduces the hysteric from her repressions" (ibid.: 159).

There is currently growing interest in the occult, paganism, and magic in western societies. In a study of modern magicians in Britain, T.M. Luhrmann (1989) shows how secrecy and esoteric knowledge enhance a sense of personal power in an uncertain world:

Esoteric knowledge allows them to identify and label irrational fears and other emotions so that these emotions can be redescribed. One experiences death, labels it symbolically as the horned god, and redescribes it as life. The redescription of the

label, and the labeling process itself, may give the magician a sense of personal volition within the sometimes terrifying turmoil of his inner life. (Lurhman
1989: 161–162)

The secrecy and fellowship of the cult, and the mythic symbolism, provide
a medium for working through emotional issues and conflicts and, perhaps,
attaining a greater sense of personal control or power. Luhrmann, however,
says little about the psychological characteristics of cult participants.

More informative in this regard is Edward J. Moody's (1971) study of
participants in a Satanic cult in San Francisco. Satanists redefine the seven
cardinal sins as virtues, and in their rituals they mock the Holy Eucharist.
Observation, psychological testing, and interviews revealed anxiety and
poor self-esteem. Sexual perversion was also common among Moody's
informants, and 85 percent of them reported unhappy childhoods in families marked by divorce or other problems. Many had experienced a succession of failures in love, sex, and work, and many had experimented with
other cults and superstitious practices. As in Southern snake-handling and
British white-magic cults, a motive seems to have been a wish for empowerment. The difference lies in symbolic strategy. The snake-handlers and
devotees of white magic may be unconsciously attracted to death and evil
but they identify with good. The Satanists, feeling defeated by evil in their
lives, and concluding that evil is generally stronger than good, seek the
power of evil by identifying with it. It may also be that Satan, the image of
evil, reflects their own rage and perverse inclinations.

Crisis cults

Wallace described revitalization movements as "organized attempts by
some members of a society to construct a more satisfying culture by rapid
acceptance of a pattern of multiple innovations" (1970: 188). Among the
traditional Seneca, "the good hunter," "the brave warrior," and the "forest
statesman" were the stereotypes of manly success (ibid.: 189). After the
Indian War the Seneca had only small, mostly isolated reservations, and
their ideals were no longer practical. They could neither hunt nor fight.
White men treated them with disrespect, and Indian allies saw them as
cowards for having agreed to get along with whites (ibid.: 190).

Drunkenness, witchcraft accusations, and social bickering increased.
Then in 1799 a revitalization movement began. It was inspired by
Handsome Lake, who preached religious and ethical reform. He proscribed
drinking, witchcraft, other objectionable behaviors, and traditional rituals,
and he admonished the Seneca to take up agriculture and to focus their
attentions on the nuclear family instead of the clan or lineage. Within a few
years, "A group of sober, devout, partly literate, and technologically up-to-

date farming communities suddenly replaced the demoralized slums in the wilderness" (ibid.: 190).

Wallace discerned two psychological processes in revitalization: cognitive reorganization among the charismatic prophets and, among the followers, hysterialike dissociation and emotionality. Following conversion, the devotee's behavior might conform to social expectations.

But his behavior has changed not because of a radical resynthesis, but because of the adoption under suggestion of an additional social personality which temporarily replaces, but does not destroy, the earlier. He remains, in a sense, a case of multiple personality and is liable, if removed from reinforcing symbols, to lapse into an earlier social personality. (Wallace 1970: 197)

The trancelike state, according to Wallace, can be sustained for years, yet the followers' proneness to revert to the old ways contrasts with the "almost paranoid intensity and stability of the resynthesized prophet." A successful movement depends on gradually reprogramming the followers as well so the fate of the movement does not rest solely on the magnetism of the leader (ibid.: 198).

La Barre (1970) found that revitalization movements usually occur in times of stress or acculturation. Their leaders are charismatic shamans who are also politicians. "Perhaps," La Barre considered, "every political leader is in some sense a charisma-laden savior . . . Perhaps charisma comes merely from awe before a leader's functional fatherhood" (ibid.: 303). "Stress, trauma, and wounded narcissism invariably thrust both individuals and societies back onto autistic preoccupation with the old and intimate" (ibid.: 305). The shamans work their magic by conjuring up timely and compelling fantasies. La Barre concluded that religion originates in crisis cults.

Devotees of cargo cults in Melanesia believed that the ancestors would return bearing European goods and wealth. Cult prophets, having communicated with God, Jesus, or the ancestors, explained what must be done to secure the arrival of the cargo. The belief that the Second Coming was approaching was common, and hysterical seizures, speaking in tongues, and visitations spread like contagion as the fateful arrival of cargo seemed to draw near. Theodore Schwartz (1973, 1976) attributed the form and frequency of cargo cults to Melanesian culture and social organization. While allowing for the influence of colonial domination, racism, and exploitation, he found the immediate impetus for the cults in psychological processes. Given that traditional Melanesian culture was highly materialistic, contact with Europeans was stressful, for it made even powerful Melanesians feel poor and powerless. Schwartz doubted that cult behavior was pathological or that it was always symptomatic of acute stress. Instead, he saw cult behavior as role-playing. Cult members were often euphoric and highly suggestible. He also speculated that a cultural orientation toward suspicion and suggestibility may have predisposed Melanesians to cult participation.

In a comparative study of twenty-one cargo cults, Knauft (1978) found that the strength of cult expression correlated strongly with "relational separation," that is, with a decrease in administrative, commercial, military, and religious contact with Europeans and decrease in employment opportunities. He theorized that the loss of contact with the Europeans threw the natives back on discredited traditional cultural patterns and insufficient resources. The result was a feeling of loss. The expectation of magical cargo was like searching for the lost object following bereavement.

John W. Connor (1989) argued that German Nazism was a revitalization movement or crisis cult. It began in a period of economic and social stress occasioned by the harsh demands of the Versailles treaty, postwar inflation and economic chaos, and dislocations to the lower middle class caused by a large influx of Russian Jewish immigrants. Hitler was a charismatic leader who encouraged the sort of euphoria, sense of renewal, and ritualism seen in other crisis cults. Nazi culture, Connor noted, seemed to mimic Christianity, though it was radically unchristian.

Connor's implication that Germans did what many other peoples might have done in similar circumstances ignores Hitler's personality and the peculiarities of German culture and history. Yet, it may be that modern societies are generally susceptible to crisis cults. After considering Nazism, Jonestown, and the Manson cult, Lindholm (1990) wondered why industrialized societies are susceptible to cults and charismatic fanaticism. Traditionally, romantic love and the family provided a haven of relatedness, but they are under stress. Increasingly, an ideal of self-fulfillment undermines the willingness of individuals to make commitments to and sacrifices for long-term relationships. Under these conditions, enthrallment with the charismatic leader may serve as a substitute for a romantic relationship or the secure attachment of family ties.

Charisma, mystery, and evil

Charismatic leadership, religious mystery, and demonization of the other are often interconnected. The charismatic leader excites interest in religious mysteries, and the same mixture of foreboding and ecstatic longing that attends the deity can attend the leader (Balter 1985). The demonization of the other is a common corollary of charismatic leadership and group narcissism (Devereux 1955). The invidious splitting of the ingroup and outgroup in the discourse of charismatic leaders and their followers may derive emotional energy from unconscious object relations. Unconscious associations between images of primary objects and social others may infuse social others with qualities of the bad mother, the frustrating oedipal object, the oedipal rival, or unwanted parts of the self. Together, conscious and unconscious splitting and projection may, by dehumanizing the other, promote real evil.

Alternatively, religions may reassure believers that disappointment, losses, frustration, and imperfection, while inevitable, are bearable. They may compensate for losses by fostering community and self-esteem, and they may dampen the inclination toward splitting and projection by encouraging conscientiousness and forgiveness. Much may depend on real events and objective conditions, however. Human nature being what it is, the alternative to irrational charisma and paranoid process is more likely where economic security and social justice lay real foundations for trust and optimism.

10   Conclusion

I began this book by observing the interplay in self–other relations: while individuals are shaped by their social experience, they also create and recreate their social milieu. Rather than privileging either the passive or active side of this interplay, I have tried to give each its due by recasting the question in dialogical terms: in dialogue and discourse subjects express themselves and they influence each other.

Much of the book has focused on work in psychoanalysis and anthropology. While various disciplines are contributing to our understanding of the mind, psychoanalysis offers what is arguably the most comprehensive and anthropologically relevant perspective on human psychology. It provides a framework for integrating work in neuroscience, psychiatry, and psychology in a way that enriches observations of social relations and cultural practice.

Anthropology provides an intellectual space in which to link this psychoanalytic view of the individual with the sociocultural milieu in the broadest possible terms. It puts personality in evolutionary perspective and it allows us to evaluate its relevance to social life in many different types of society. The ethnographic record in anthropology shows that social relations are suffused with passion, and everyday discourse, folklore, myth, and ritual, with dreamlike poetics and fantasy. It thus makes a case for paying attention to psychodynamic processes in the study of society and culture.

In this book, discussions of human nature and childhood set the stage for chapters on personality and mental disorder. The result is a picture of the emotional and mental components of personality. We saw how personality is grounded in a phylogenetic nature and shaped by formative social and cultural experiences. We also saw how the mental and emotional orientations of the individual are shaped by social expectations and cultural norms.

In the second part of the book I turned to the psychological foundations of social relations and cultural beliefs and practices. Emotion and passion are obviously a part of social relations and, just as obviously, individuals and groups often take their beliefs and opinions very seriously. Where such affect and seriousness come from is often not so obvious, however. To outsiders, the passion individuals bring to social life can seem irrational, and it can even seem perplexing to the individuals themselves. I drew on the discussions of human nature, childhood, and normal and abnormal personality in trying to illuminate the enigmatic, affective dimensions of social life and cultural practice.

The basic emotional and mental characteristics of human beings run, like connecting threads, through the various chapters. Some involve archaic instinctual and emotional elements in human nature. Perhaps the most important among these is attachment. I discussed the importance of attachment in early childhood, where it lays the experiential ground for all subsequent object relations. I noted that attachment is a basic disposition in human personality. And I showed that attachment and its corollary, separation anxiety, are issues in personality disorders and serious mental disorders as well. Conflict and anxiety around attachment are especially prominent in borderline personality.

The theme of attachment surfaces again in social relations and culture. It is present in the sections of the book that deal with love, idealization, and identification. Mixed with libidinal impulses, it is found in leader–follower relations also. It is a major theme in religiously structured community, and it may be part of what holds warriors together and inspires them to fight for each other and the group.

The libido is another theme. I noted that the libido is a driving force in human affairs, and that it takes various forms. Psychological theory and neurobiology imply that the libido is object-seeking and power-seeking. Indeed, we came across many ethnographic examples of the melding of eroticism and power.

The object-seeking libido combines with attachment in human beings to produce infatuation, passion, hero worship, religious ecstasy and devotion, and binding attraction between lovers and spouses. Power-seeking libido is nearly everywhere in human affairs. We see it in competition for power and wealth, sports and games, and war. Religions, we noticed, may among other things minister to felt needs for empowerment. Unusual and exaggerated manifestations of the will-to-power, sometimes mixed with eroticism, are evident in narcissistic personality disorder, sensation-seeking personalities, mania, and schizophrenia.

Another theme running through various topics was the principle of self-preservation and the need for a background of safety. Irritable aggression, fear and anxiety, hypnoid relaxation, and depressive withdrawal are phylogenetically old mechanisms for dealing with dangers to the self. We noticed how personalities and cultures alike are organized to modulate danger, or at least the perception of danger. Some personality styles and all the serious mental disorders we discussed are in some degree modes of coping with danger or conscious or unconscious memories of previous traumas. We noticed that threats to human needs for attachment, passionate attachment, and power (or at least positive self-esteem) figure frequently in negative emotional reactions and the etiologies of serious mental and emotional disorders.

In addition to discussing the basic drives and emotions of human beings, I reviewed their mental characteristics. Drawing on both psychoanalysis and neuroscience, I suggested that mental processes occur on various levels and in various agencies. The mind/brain, I noted, comprises various parts and functions. Contrary to what culturalists and postmodernists imply, it is definitely not an undifferentiated serial symbolic computer and learning machine. Language, general intelligence, and memory, of course, are exceedingly important components of human psychology, and they are prerequisites for human forms of life, but they are not the whole story. Personality also includes drives, emotions, or social intelligence. These functions, we noted, are central to the organization of the self and appear to underlie language and general intelligence.

Drives and emotions are organized in the first instance in the limbic system. At this level, phylogenetic dispositions are schematized by early learning in what psychoanalysts call "object relations." The drives and emotions are further organized by the cerebral cortex and, especially, by the prefrontal context, the seat of social intelligence. Social intelligence comprises judgment, planning, and the ability to structure past, present, and anticipated experience in a coherent narrative around a subjective self. It also includes the ability to control, modulate, and transform instincts, drives, and primary emotions into more differentiated, socially appropriate, and subtle affects and inclinations. It can also simulate emotion in actual and imaginary realities. In the prefrontal cortex, the basic mammalian values of the self are filtered through anticipation and transmuted into feelings and desires.

It is not simply that the prefrontal cortex modulates the brain stem and limbic system. Through a process which Damasio (1994) calls "somatic marking," basic drives and emotions cue social intelligence to what is important. That is to say, social intelligence is grounded in the body. There is reason to think that language and other cognitive processes are also grounded in embodied, subjective experience.

This view of the mind/brain involves actual and potential conflict. A mind/brain that is differentiated vertically and horizontally and which by its very nature is constantly weighing the utility of impulses and values, and various short- and long-run goals, is not always at peace with itself. Through as-if simulation of emotion and intention, it may displace actual or primary emotion from the conscious agendas of the self. And it can also read articulate purpose of the conscious self back into an inarticulate, semiotic language of the body. Some brain structures and processes are geared to maintaining an adaptive level of unity in the fractious mind/brain. I have suggested that a general background of safety and feeling of well-being, coordinated bodily movement and balance during the day, and dreaming at night may be especially important for integrating impulses, purposes, and varied elements of experience.

This picture of the mind/brain has been developing during the last thirty years in the work of many neuroscientists. It will no doubt undergo emendation and elaboration, but its main outline now seems well established. In various ways current thinking about the mind/brain is congruent with Freudian and post-Freudian thinking about the mental apparatus. The contemporary view of human nature also has a good deal in common with theories that would situate embodied, speaking subjects in dialogical interaction with social others. I think, however, that the current view of the brain should prompt all theorists to recognize a more social, lively, imaginative, and agentic human subject.

I used these impressions of the mental nature of human beings to elaborate a picture of both the individual personality and the psychological foundations of society and culture. What was said earlier about the importance of attachment, object- and power-seeking libido, the need for a background of safety, and self-preservation took us some distance toward formulating a picture of individual psychology. By emphasizing the role of separation anxiety and object relations, moral reasoning, and the social and cultural structuring of emotion and desire, we added nuance and complexity to our view of the willful, desiring subject.

The direction I have been taking here also emphasizes notions of dialogue, discourse, and pragmatics. Following contributions by Abu-Lughod, Crapanzano, Ewing, Maranhão, Taggart, Trawick, and others, I have suggested that these terms are important to understand how the links between self and other, subjectivity and intersubjectivity, and personality and culture, are actually realized. The nexus of emotion, desire, social relation, and cultural idiom is created and recreated in dialogue and discourse, particularly in poetic practices with rhetorical effects.

In pursuing a dialogical framework I have suggested that the self comprises internalized voices. Lacan says something similar, but I want to emphasize that the subject speaks as well as listens, that the subject converses with others. I noted that we can consider psychic defense mechanisms as processes that mute, expurgate, and rescript internal voices. These internal voices may represent morality, various social selves, or fears, wants, wishes, and desires. What goes on within the self is interrelated with interpersonal discourse. Thus, the defense mechanisms inform not only intrapsychic communication but also impression management in social interaction.

This psychoanalytic, dialogical view of the subject underpinned the discussions of personality disorder, hysteria, depression, and schizophrenia. We saw how these conditions involve distinctive configurations of drive, affect, and cognitive processes, but we also noted how they can involve particular styles of communication. Hysteria may involve cryptic communication, perhaps as resistance to dominant discourse. Depression can involve asymbolia, a withdrawal from dialogical interaction. In schizophrenia, disturbances of drive, affect, and mentation radically disrupt a person's capacity for meaningful communication with social others.

Personality disorders and emotional and mental disorders are interesting phenomena for anthropology in their own right, but they have significant implications for understanding normal social relations and the production and reproduction of culture. Mental disorders imbricate social life and culture in various ways and may influence them. Beyond that, they can serve as models for how emotional and mental processes shape the form and content of social relations and cultural beliefs and practices. Object substitution, employment of archaic self-objects, displacement, splitting, projection, identification, and idealization seem to inform both personality disorders, on the one hand, and the normal psychology of social life, on the other. Culture also evinces sublimation and uses of transitional objects and self-objects. It is an arena in which people express their needs for creative expression, empowerment, attachment, love, and community.

Figurative usages in dialogue and discourse appeal to either regressive or progressive motives and mental structures in individuals. Lurking in a great deal of discourse and many social situations is a choice between a paranoid-schizoid position and a depressive position, that is, a choice between denying pain and blaming others, on the one hand, and working through pain, accepting responsibility, and making reparations, on the other hand.

Charismatic leadership, economic and social insecurity, and humiliation tend to weight the odds toward the paranoid-schizoid end of the continuum. Even so, individual subjects are not without personal resources for dealing with regressive rhetoric or destructive, dehumanizing cultural forms. They can resist, and they can imagine alternatives. Their internal resources for doing so include memories of satisfying relationships in family and community, and the spiritual self, not to mention mere social intelligence. Here, too, others are important. It is one of the paradoxes of human personality that people are often more in touch with their true selves and inner strengths, and more able to find moral adjustments to the pain of being human, when they share their stories with each other.

Notes

1: INTRODUCTION

1. For a systematic critique of the basic premises of psychological determinism in culture-and-personality studies, see Shweder (1979a, 1979b).
2. I use the word "postmodernism" somewhat loosely as a rubric for post-structuralism (social constructionism and deconstruction, especially) as well as cultural relativism and aversion to theory and deep interpretation.
3. For example, "Accountability (and criticism) is perhaps the most human and most social of all activities. It presupposes that which is most distinctive of our species, language and a *super*-ego" (Shweder 1980: 86).
4. See also papers by Spiro in Kilbourne and Langness (1987).
5. The story of the origins of psychoanalysis often has been told. It is the subject of an increasing number of psychologically and historically sophisticated interpretations. For a contemporary retelling as well as an entrée to the growing body of Freud scholarship, see Gay (1988).
6. Schizophrenia and personality disorders pose difficulties for the often-expressed view in postmodernist writing that fragmentation is a common and desirable feature of the psyche. In these conditions, at least, intrapsychic fragmentation is almost always painful and dysfunctional (see Flax 1990: 218–219; Glass 1993; and Chapters 5 and 6 in this book).
7. See Ingham (1982) and Johnson (1992) for further discussions of materialism in psychoanalytic anthropology.
8. For a review of psychoanalytically oriented work in psychological anthropology, see Paul (1989).
9. For an intriguing example of an implicit psychoanalytic orientation in the work of a social anthropologist, see Oring (1993) on Victor Turner.

2: HUMAN NATURE

1. For discussions of the parallels between psychoanalysis and work in evolutionary biology, neurobiology, and cognitive neuroscience, see Badcock (1990, 1991), Erdelyi (1985, 1992), Glymour (1991), La Barre (1954, 1991), Modell (1993), Rancour-Laferriere (1985), and Reiser (1984, 1990).
2. Psychoanalytic writers prefer the word "unconscious" to "subconscious."
3. Strachey translated *Trieb* in Freud's writings as "instinct." In most places, "drive" is a better translation.

4. On the relation between the limbic system and object relations, see Kernberg (1976).
5. On dopamine as a basis of the libido, see Hartmann (1982) and Vincent (1990).
6. For papers on evolutionary, biological, and cultural aspects of fatherhood, see Hewlett (1992).
7. It has been theorized that a capacity for paternal feeling may have evolved as part of mating strategy (Smuts and Gubernick 1992).
8. Fox (1983) doubts that there is a human inclination to pair-bonding and suggests that the human male particularly is strongly inclined toward promiscuity and polygyny. To be sure, most human societies (roughly, 84 percent) permit or favor polygyny, and extramarital relationships are common in many human societies (Ghiglieri 1987: 341). Fox's arguments, however, are based on a dubious use of a baboon model of early hominid social organization. Most human marriages are monogamous, and even human polygyny involves a sort of pair-bonding that is missing from the promiscuous "polygyny" of baboons. Fox's arguments also ignore the capacities of human men for parental feelings, self-control, and moral commitment.

   A chimpanzee model for early hominid social behavior is more plausible. Genetic and molecular evidence shows that human beings and chimpanzees are very closely related (Hasegawa et al. 1985; Sibley and Ahlquist 1984). Evidence that early hominids remained adapted to a forest environment or moved in a mixed environment also supports a chimpanzee model and, more precisely, a bonobos model (Susman 1987).

   Biological evidence suggests that selection pressures during human evolution favored stable male–female relationships (monogamy and polygyny). Comparison of chromosomal variations (gene flow) and mating patterns among primate species implies that chimpanzees and gorillas provide the best models of early hominid social organization and mating; more precisely, the early hominids probably evinced more pair-bonding than baboons and less than gibbons (Marks 1987). Comparative sexual physiology, body size, and neuroanatomy all imply that hominid mating patterns gradually diverged from chimpanzeelike promiscuity toward a preference for more stable relationships. Among gorillas large size and dominance correlate strongly with male reproductive success. Since dominance does not ensure reproductive success among the promiscuous chimpanzees, large testes evolved in males in order to maximize effective insemination. Human testes are midway in relative size between those of chimpanzees and gorillas, which suggests that promiscuity among early hominids may have been less than among chimpanzees but greater than among gorillas (Badcock 1991: 147–149). Sexual dimorphism (i.e., a pattern of sex differences in which males are consistently larger and/or stronger than females) is a corollary of polygyny among primates; where males compete for multiple partners, selection favors larger size in the male. It is significant, therefore, that the fossil record suggests a gradual reduction in sexual dimorphism from the time of the australopithecines to *Homo erectus* or the pithecantropines. The large anterior thalamic nucleus in human brains, meanwhile, implies that hominids began evolving early toward family stability and less promiscuity. Among primates, large anterior thalamic nuclei are positively correlated with stable male–female relationships (i.e., pair-bonding in single-male monogamy or polygyny) and negatively associated with multi-male social organizations (Armstrong et al. 1987).

9. These studies are especially intriguing because they were done before awareness of Freudian symbolism became part of popular culture.

10. This course of events, incidentally, matches Freud's speculations about the origin of the family. Freud conjectured that families made their first appearance during the "ape-like prehistory" of human beings when the disappearance of sexual cycling gave males a motive for permanent association with their mates (Freud [1930]1961: 99–100).

11. Although it does not seem reasonable to speak, as Freud did, of a destructive instinct or drive, there is a connection between anxiety, psychophysiological stress, and depression on the one hand and various disease processes on the other. Interestingly, this morbid side of negative affect and stress resembles Freud's much-criticized death instinct (see Bakan 1968).

12. This opposition between self-preservation and reproduction is regulated in part by the limbic system (MacLean 1990). In a classic experiment, Klüver and Bucy (1939) removed the frontotemporal lobes of rhesus monkeys, including the amygdala. The monkeys became unusually docile and fearless, and they copulated and masturbated frequently. Surgical amygdalectomies in humans seldom result in a complete Klüver–Bucy syndrome, yet evidence suggests that self-preservation and reproduction are mutually inhibiting in the human limbic system also. After removal of both temporal lobes, a murderous patient became less aggressive and more sexual; he was sexually aroused by an anatomical chart, masturbated frequently, and made sexual advances toward his physicians (Terzian and Ore 1955). Some temporal-lobe epilepsy patients exhibit the Klüver–Bucy syndrome in reverse. Between seizures they are suspicious, irritable, aggressive, and lacking in sexual drive (Bear 1979).

13. The fossil evidence shows that upright posture was present about 4.3 million years BP. Six million years ago the average cranial capacity among the hominids was probably about 300 cc. Between four to two million years ago it grew from about 475 cc. to about 670 cc. In *Homo sapiens*, the average cranial capacity is 1,330 cc. The evidence suggests that it increased continuously from the time of separation from the early chimpanzees, with the pace of expansion accelerating as the process continued (Falk 1987). This expansion of the brain in human evolution was very rapid in comparison with average rates of evolutionary change.

14. Whether the language areas are more or less localized is still under discussion. Gender may be a factor. Some evidence suggests that language is more evenly distributed between the two hemispheres in women than in men (Moir and Jessel 1989).

15. Hallowell was ahead of his time on this point. Various writers now think that selection for social intelligence was a major factor in the evolutionary expansion of the hominid brain (Alexander 1989; Byrne and Whiten 1988; Dunbar 1988; Fox 1983).

16. Some evidence links limbic system and especially amygdala dysfunction to self-fragmentation and experiences of derealization and world dehumanization in schizophrenia (see Chapter 7).

17. For a lucid discussion of unconscious representation in dreams and their relation to tropes, see Spiro (1993a).
18. Some research suggests that activity in the amygdala figures in the aversive quality of dreams (Calvo et al. 1987).
19. According to Winson, the dream mechanism, especially that portion of it concerned with linking short-term and long-term memories, depends on the hippocampus, a part of the limbic system that functions as a gateway between the emotional brain and cerebral cortex. For a recent psychoanalytic synthesis of the dream research, including Winson's work, similar to the one I suggest, see Reiser (1990).
20. For a review of Roheim's dream theory as well as a discussion of the history of psychoanalytic thinking about the connection between dreams and folklore, myth, and ritual, see Morales Caldwell (1988).
21. D'Andrade (1991) makes this point.

3: CHILDHOOD

1. I am following a suggestion by David H. Spain (personal communication) that we use "oedipality" to refer to normal oedipal phenomena. It avoids the connotations of pathology in the notion of the Oedipus complex.
2. For reviews of separation–individuation theory, see Nachman (1991) and other papers in the same volume.
3. These longitudinal continuities with early attachment do not seem to be mere artifacts of temperament, as some writers have suggested (Sroufe 1985).
4. For appraisals of Bowlby's work and attachment theory, see Sroufe (1986) and Karen (1994).
5. Kirschner (1992) has discussed the possible influence of Anglo-American individualism in the work of Mahler and other psychoanalysts.
6. For a review of Freud's thinking about gender, see Fliegel (1986).
7. The *DSM III-R* replaces "perversion" with "paraphilia" in an attempt to seem less judgmental, although the new term literally means "deviant attraction." Many psychoanalysts, however, still use the term "perversion." In their view, the hint of disapproval in the traditional term is not without warrant; there is an element of hostility and destructiveness in perversions, in many cases with women and children as targets. Female perversions may be less sexual and more concerned with attachment and loss than male perversions (Kaplan 1991).

   Homosexuality in either males or females, it should be noted, is *not* perversity according to contemporary psychiatric and most psychoanalytic understandings. There is no correlation between homosexuality and perversion or, for that matter, any form of psychopathology. Various attempts to explain homosexuality in terms of early learning and psychodynamic factors are now seen as unconvincing (Friedman 1986; O'Connor and Ryan 1994).
8. See p. 65. Socialization practices do not necessarily predict individual behaviour.
9. Whatever the proper interpretation may be, there appears to be a moderate but significant connection between father-absence for boys and stereotypical expressions of masculinity (Stevenson and Black 1988).
10. While I find these two studies interesting for my purposes, I wonder how valid

they are. Specifically, there is a question about whether the low transitional object groups (the rural Italians and the Seoul Koreans) had as much access to potential transitional objects. Perhaps they did. The Seoul Koreans were the children of hospital residents in Seoul and the rural Italian children were living in an area not far from Rome, raising questions about how economically disadvantaged they were. Unfortunately, the researchers did not control for socioeconomic status.

11. There is empirical evidence that some mothers in fact relate to their children in this way. In observations of 173 low socioeconomic-status mothers, Sroufe and Ward (1980) found that about 10 percent were seductive toward their sons. These mothers kissed their toddler sons on the lips and rubbed their buttocks and genitals, sometimes in response to disobedience. They were also less affectionate and less able to control their sons' behavior.

   Freud ([1927c]1961) thought that perversion in males is an expression of castration anxiety. While the phallic preoccupations of men with paraphilias suggests that this may be the case, many clinicians now think that preoedipal issues of attachment, separation, and loss are more fundamental.

12. Among primates, sexual politics involves the use of sexual postures and display to express dominance and submission. It has been suggested that the so-called negative Oedipus complex – same-sex attachment – in the boy may have evolutionary roots in the display of sexual submission to ward off an attack by a dominant animal (Maslow et al. 1960).

13. These remarks concern the child's motivation. The incest taboo applies to both parents and children. For discussions of psychological aspects of the taboo, see Spain (1987, 1988) and Willner (1983).

14. Lacan is difficult reading. For summaries, see Bowie (1991) and Lemaire (1977).

4: PERSONALITY

1. Eysenck and Gray draw heavily on research with rodents in their discussions of the biological foundations of personality factors. It is perhaps not surprising, therefore, that they tend to collapse rewarding behavior into a single system. The attachment system, a more recent addition to the limbic system, is far more developed in higher primates than in rodents.

2. Cloninger (1987) hypothesizes three personality components: novelty-seeking, harm avoidance, and reward dependency. Novelty-seeking is dopamine-mediated and comprises power-seeking and object-seeking appetitive behavior in other schemes. Harm avoidance and reward dependency are modulated, respectively, by serotoninergic and noradrenergic systems. This formulation suggests that attachment (which seems to be the main component of reward dependence in this scheme) is motivated by separation anxiety. Cloninger's scheme thus does not actually address the positive motivation for attachment.

3. See papers in D'Andrade and Strauss (1992).

4. Both Mead and Winnicott in this respect anticipate Damasio's view that the self is grounded in drive, emotion, and embodied experience (see Chapter 2).

5. The division of the personality into three parts in James and Freud may have roots in philosophical notions of body, soul, and spirit (Ellenberger 1970: 206).

6. There is debate about whether repression in the psychoanalytic sense exists.

While some clinical evidence seems to require a notion of repression, the empirical research is open to varying interpretation. For different views and discussions of the evidence in this debate, see Singer (1990).

7. For a review of psychoanalytic ideas about conscience and the ego-ideal, see Chasseguet-Smirgel (1985).

8. See also Alpert and Spencer (1986).

9. Spiro (1993a), however, notes that there are serious, perhaps fatal, methodological flaws in this study.

10. Freud thought that paranoia involves projection and transformation of homosexual thoughts: "I love him" is turned into "I hate him" which is then turned into "He hates me." Actually, there is evidence that some cases of paranoia may involve homophobia and gender-identity conflict (Fisher and Greenberg 1985: 255–270).

11. "Borderline personality" is one form of what Kernberg calls "borderline personality organization." People with borderline personalities show the characteristics of borderline personality organization, but so do people with other personality disorders, particularly if they are at the impulsive end of the spectrum being discussed here.

12. Murray (1993) thoroughly refutes the notion that there is a single western philosophical notion of the self. Spiro (1993a) effectively critiques empirical typifications of the western self.

13. Discontinuity in longitudinal studies may reflect poor methodology and unreasonable attempts to predict specific behaviors from personality variables. Epstein (1984) concluded that correlations across situations weaker than 0.2 to 0.3 may be artifacts of the use of single measures of behavior. Correlations between 0.8 and 0.9 emerged in his research when different ratings were aggregated. Personality effects are also more apparent in situations that are emotionally significant for individuals. Relations between psychological traits and behavior are often stronger when individuals choose situations (Snyder 1987: 208).

5: DEPRESSION AND HYSTERIA

1. According to H.B.M. Murphy (1976), *latah* reflects dispositions toward dissociation and suggestibility in Malay personality. These dispositions may derive from parental affection for children (or, rather, a specific manner of expressing affection), from eroticism in the parent–child relationship, and from training for obedience and self-control. Murphy also suggested that teasing, tickling, and touching the genitals of young children by parents may promote fragmented body images. Being tickled in adulthood, then, may be experienced as a sexual attack. *Latah*, Murphy theorized, occurs in situations that seem to arouse unconscious oedipal conflicts. Simons (1980, 1983) theorized that *latah* is a local cultural elaboration of an exaggerated startle reflex, something that can be observed in many cultures, and that anxiety may potentiate the startle reflex. H.B.M. Murphy (1983) replied that *latah* may combine a startle reflex and hysterialike processes.

   Another possibility is that *latah* is a variant of Gilles de la Tourette's disease, a syndrome that involves multiple tics, spasmodic movements, and compulsive swearing. Tourette's disorder, however, usually begins before puberty and affects males more often than females (American Psychiatric Association 1987: 79–80), whereas *latah* seems to be more common among older women.

2. For the nineteenth-century background of psychoanalysis, see Ellenberger (1970), Gay (1988), or MacMillan (1991).

3. On the similarity between euphoric trance and the psychobiology of sexual orgasm, see Davidson (1980).

4. Freud has been criticized for abandoning the "seduction" or sexual-trauma theory of neurosis. In fact, he continued to recognize that actual trauma, including sexual abuse, often figures in the etiology of neurosis ([1940]1964: 187; see also Lothane 1987 and Paul 1985). The development of self psychology and object-relations theory in psychoanalysis has sensitized many psychoanalysts to actual abuse (see, especially, Shengold 1989). US estimates and findings for incest in the backgrounds of people with dissociative and somatoform disorders vary, but many fall in the 15 to 65 percent range (Loewenstein 1990).

5. Anthony F.C. Wallace (1961) proposed that hypocalcemia (low levels of ionized calcium in the blood) may be a causal factor in *piblokto* and other hysterical conditions. Calcium deficiency produces emotional and cognitive disorganization and motor symptoms that resemble those of hysterical conversion. He noted that there is evidence for calcium deficiency in Polar Inuit. The arctic environment does not provide rich sources of calcium, and the lack of light during winter months and full body clothing during most of the year may interfere with the body's production of vitamin D3. Wallace noted also that tetany was common in the late nineteenth century, a time when hysteria was getting the attention of Freud and other physicians. Wallace thus suggested that calcium deficiency may have been a factor in nineteenth-century hysteria along with situation, individual history, and biological constitution. A comparison between ten Inuit with a history of *piblokto* attacks and twenty-one normal Inuit by Foulks and Katz (1975), however, did not reveal either a history of hypocalcemia or lower blood calcium levels in the former. They proposed instead a multifactorial explanation: chronic low calcium and magnesium levels in the blood, and/or a disposition to temporal lobe-seizures, and stress, anxiety, and hyperventilation (which temporarily reduces serum calcium ion concentration) could bring on the attacks.

6: ECCENTRICITY AND MADNESS

1. Arlow and Brenner (1969) argued that psychosis makes more sense in terms of drive and preexisting psychic conflict, especially conflicts around rage and aggression. Psychotic decompensation is triggered by rage, and delusions and hallucinations assume regressive expression because of the ego's impaired reality testing. The classical or ego–superego deficit model of schizophrenia, however, is more congruent with the biomedical research.

2. For a review of psychoanalytically oriented family studies in schizophrenia research, see Howells and Guirguis (1985).

3. For additional discussion of the case, see Allison, Oliveira, Roberts, and Weiss (1988).

4. Some shamans may have hysterical character structures, however. Peters and Price-Williams (1980) observed the presence of dissociation in shamanism. A

comparison of the Rorschach protocols of fifty-two normal persons, twelve shamans, and seven "pseudoshamans" among the Mescalero Apache disclosed hysterical tendencies and greater capacity for reality-testing and regression in service of the ego among the shamans and psychological impoverishment and imposture among the pseudoshamans, shamans whose powers were discounted either by themselves or by others (Boyer et al. 1964).

7: SOCIAL PSYCHOLOGY

1. For a comparison of Durkheim and Freud on subjectivity and religion, see Meeker (1990).
2. It is interesting, given what was said earlier about the possible childhood origins of perversion, to note that the rage of the two protanganists in *The Bacchae* begins with the loss of the mother (Spitz 1991).
3. For example, guns, knives, mannikins, high-heeled shoes, silk stockings.
4. An old Augustinian notion. According to Pascal, "the drive/desire to dominate and control"; also, "pride" (see Friedrich 1986:294). In psychoanalytic usage, the narcissistic libido.
5. For psychoanalytic writings on money, see Borneman (1976).
6. When the rites simply mark the passage from childhood to adulthood, they are best referred to as "rites of passage" or as puberty ceremonies. When they induct the child into a social group, they are best called initiation rites. Much of the literature, however, does not make this distinction.

8: COLLECTIVE VIOLENCE

1. Evidently, androgens play a part in male aggressiveness. Serum androgens in adolescent boys correlate with lack of frustration tolerance, verbal and physical aggression, acting out, and delinquent behavior (Susman et al. 1987; Olweus et al. 1980). The studies show conflicting results, however, and a link between androgens and female aggressiveness is uncertain. Serum androgen levels may not be so much a cause of aggression as a by-product, along with assertiveness, of central nervous system libido.
2. Harris simply ignores the evidence for oedipal fantasies in children. It may be more apt to say that various customs create triangular structures that can encourage envy and rage and that such structures may resonate with unconscious memories of the oedipal situation. For a critique of Harris's Oedipus theory, see Spain (1992).
3. The Gebusi situation is a variant of a common theme in human sociality. Kernberg (1988:79) observes that there is always tension between the group and the romantic inclinations of a couple. The wish to destroy the couple, he points out, may derive from both preoedipal envy and oedipal rivalry.
4. The traditional ritual system was largely suppressed by the colonial government in an attempt to control venereal disease.
5. Krauft (1993:165–166) has since shown that the cause of the infertility is almost certainly pelvic inflammatory disease.
6. For another discussion of the Sendam myth, see Meeker, Barlow, and Lipset (1986:61–62).

7. Loewenberg (1971), building upon Wangh's paper, argued in his cohort analysis of the youth element in Nazi party strength that 1917-1920 was a stressful time for German youth. Famine was widespread, and mothers entered the work force in large numbers.

9: RELIGION

1. For an example of a shamanic pilgrimage with these and related symbolic elements, see Furst (1972) and Myerhoff (1974).
2. Family psychodynamics and Catholicism may be similarly entwined in rural Ireland. Here too, the remoteness of God and the bond between Mary and Christ may reflect actual role relationships within the family. The father, a distant figure, has little part in child-rearing whereas the mother has an ambiguous role: she is solicitous of the child's instrumental needs and inclined to encourage dependency but, simultaneously, she is likely to frustrate the child's emotional need for affection. Russell (1984) argued that these parental roles encourage both the Oedipus complex and the longing for a nurturing maternal figure.

References

Aberle, David F. 1952. "Arctic hysteria" and latah in Mongolia. *Transactions of the New York Academy of Sciences* 14: 291–297.

Abse, D. Wilfred. 1950. *The diagnosis of hysteria*. Bristol: John Wright.

——— 1966. *Hysteria and related disorders: An approach to psychological medicine.* Bristol: John Wright.

Abu-Lughod, Lila. 1986. *Veiled sentiments: Honor and poetry in a Bedouin society.* Berkeley: University of California Press.

——— 1993. *Writing women's worlds: Bedouin stories.* Berkeley: University of California Press.

Ackerknecht, Erwin H. 1943. Psychopathology, primitive medicine, and primitive culture. *Bulletin of History of Medicine* 14: 30–67.

Adityanjee, G.S.P. Raju and S.K. Khandelwal. 1989. Current status of multiple personality disorder in India. *American Journal of Psychiatry* 146: 1607–1610.

Adler, Alfred. [1929]1969. *The science of living.* Ed. H.L. Ansbacher. Garden City, N.Y.: Anchor, Doubleday.

——— [1931]1979. The differences between individual psychology and psychoanalysis. In *Superiority and the social interest: A collection of later writings,* ed. H.L. Ansbacher and R.R. Ansbacher, 205–218. New York: Norton.

Aguilar, John L. 1982. Shame, acculturation and ethnic relations: A psychological "process of domination" in Southern Mexico. *Journal of Psychoanalytic Anthropology* 5: 155–171.

Ainsworth, Mary D. Salter. 1982. Attachment: Retrospect and prospect. In *The place of attachment in human behavior,* ed. C.M. Parkes and J. Stevenson-Hinde, 3–30. New York: Basic Books.

Alexander, Richard D. 1989. Evolution of the human psyche. In *The human revolution: Behavioural and biological perspectives on the origins of modern humans,* ed. P. Mellars and C. Stringer, 455–513. Princeton, N.J.: Princeton University Press.

Allen, Michael R. 1967. *Male cults and secret initiations in Melanesia.* London: Melbourne University Press.

Allison, David B., Prado de Oliveira, Mark S. Roberts, and Allen S. Weiss, eds. 1988. *Psychosis and sexual identity: Toward a post-analytic view of the Schreber case.* Albany: State University of New York Press.

Alpert, Judith L. and Jody Boghossian Spencer. 1986. Morality, gender, and analysis. In *Psychoanalysis and women: Contemporary reappraisals,* ed. J.L. Alpert, 83–111. Hillsdale, N.J.: Analytic Press.

American Psychiatric Association. 1987. *Diagnostic and statistical manual of mental disorders, third edition, revised.* Washington, D.C.: American Psychiatric Association.

Antelman, Seymour M. and Anthony R. Caggiula. 1980. Stress-induced behavior: Chemotherapy without drugs. In *The psychobiology of consciousness,* ed. J.M. Davidson and R.J. Davidson, 65–104. New York: Plenum Press.

Anthony, E.J. 1957. An experimental approach to the psychopathology of childhood: Encopresis. *British Journal of Medical Psychology* 30: 146–175.

Arboleda-Florez, J. 1985. Amok. In *The culture-bound syndromes: Folk illnesses of psychiatric and anthropological interest,* ed. R.C. Simons and C.C. Hughes, 251–262. Dordrecht: Reidel.

Arieti, Silvano. 1975. Sexual problems of the schizophrenic and preschizophrenics. In *Sexual behavior: Pharmacology and biochemistry,* ed. M. Sandler and G.L. Gessa, 277–282. New York: Raven.

Arlow, Jacob A. and Charles Brenner. 1969. The psychopathology of the psychoses: A proposed revision. *International Journal of Psycho-Analysis* 50: 5–14.

Armstrong, Este. 1990a. Evolution of the brain. In *The human nervous system,* ed. G. Paxinos, 1–16. San Diego: Academic Press.

1990b. Limbic thalamus: Anterior and mediodorsal nuclei. In *The human nervous system,* ed. G. Paxinos, 469–481. San Diego: Academic Press.

1991. The limbic system and culture: An allometric analysis of the neocortex and limbic nuclei. *Human Nature* 2: 117–136.

Armstrong, Este, Margaret R. Clarke, and Elizabeth Hill. 1987. Relative size of the anterior thalamic nuclei differentiates anthropoids by social system. *Brain, Behavior and Evolution* 30: 263–271.

Auerbach, Carl. 1985. What is a self?: A constructivist theory. *Psychotherapy* 22: 743–746.

Baal, J. van. 1966. *Dema: Description and analysis of Marind-anim culture (South New Guinea).* The Hague: Martinus Nijhoff.

1984. The dialectics of sex in Marind-anim culture. In *Ritualized homosexuality in Melanesia,* ed. G.H. Herdt, 128–166. Berkeley: University of California Press.

Bachofen, Johann Jacob. 1861. *Das mutterecht.* Stuttgart: Krais & Hoffman.

Bacon, Margaret K., Irvin L. Child, and Herbert Barry III. 1963. A cross-cultural study of correlates of crime. *Journal of Abnormal and Social Psychology* 66: 291–300.

Badcock, Christopher R. 1983. *Madness and modernity: A study in social psychoanalysis.* Oxford: Basil Blackwell.

1990. *Oedipus in evolution: A new theory of sex.* Oxford: Basil Blackwell.

1991. *Evolution and individual behavior: An introduction to human sociobiology.* Oxford: Basil Blackwell.

Badrian, Alison and Noel Badrian. 1984. Social organization of *Pan paniscus* in Lomako Forest, Zaire. In *The pygmy chimpanzee: Evolutionary biology and behavior,* ed. R.L. Susman, 325–346. New York: Plenum Press.

Badrian, Noel and Richard K. Malenky. 1984. Feeding ecology of *Pan paniscus* in the Lomako Forest, Zaire. In *The pygmy chimpanzee, evolutionary biology and behavior,* ed. R.L. Susman, 275–299. New York: Plenum Press.

Bak, Robert C. 1974. Distortions of the concept of fetishism. *Psychoanalytic Study of the Child* 29: 191–214.

Bakan, David. 1966. *The duality of human existence: Isolation and communion in western man*. Boston: Beacon Press.

1968. *Disease, pain, and sacrifice: Toward a psychology of suffering*. Chicago: University of Chicago Press.

Bakan, Paul. 1969. Hypnotizability, laterality of eye movements and functional brain asymmetry. *Perceptual and Motor Skills* 28: 927–932.

Bakhtin, Mikhail. 1984. *Rabelais and his world*. Trans. H. Iswolsky. Bloomington, Ind.: Indiana University Press.

Balter, Leon. 1985. The charismatically led group: The mental processes of its members. In *The psychoanalytic study of society*, vol. XI, ed. L.B. Boyer and S.A. Grolnick, 173–215. Hillsdale, N.J.: Analytic Press.

Bandlamudi, Lakshmi. 1994. Dialogics of understanding self/culture. *Ethos* 22: 460–493.

Barlow, David H. 1988. *Anxiety and its disorders: The nature and treatment of anxiety and panic*. New York: Guilford Press.

Barlow, Kathleen. 1985. Learning cultural meanings through social relationships: An ethnography of childhood in Murik society, Papua New Guinea. Ph.D. dissertation, University of California, San Diego.

1990. The dynamics of siblingship: Nurturance and authority in Murik society. In *Sepik heritage: Tradition and change in Papua New Guinea*, ed. N. Lutkehaus, C. Kaufman, W.E. Mitchell, D. Newton, L. Osmundsen, and M. Schuster, 325–336. Durham, N.C.: Carolina Academic Press.

Barry, Herbert, III, Irvin L. Child, and Margaret K. Bacon. 1959. Relation of child training to subsistence economy. *American Anthropologist* 61: 51–63.

Bartholomew, Robert E. 1990. Ethnocentricity and the social construction of "mass hysteria." *Culture, Medicine and Psychiatry* 14: 455–494.

Basso, Ellen B. 1992. The implications of a progressive theory of dreaming. In *Dreaming: Anthropological and psychological interpretations*, ed. B. Tedlock, 86–104. Santa Fe, New Mexico: School of American Research Press.

Bateson, Gregory, Don D. Jackson, Jay Haley, and John Weakland. 1956. Toward a theory of schizophrenia. *Behavioral Science* 1: 251–264.

Bear, David M. 1979. Temporal lobe epilepsy – a syndrome of sensory-limbic hyperconnection. *Cortex* 15: 357–384.

Beck, Aaron T. [1967]1972. *Depression: Causes and treatment*. Philadelphia: University of Pennsylvania Press.

Beebe, David L. 1982. Notes on psychosis. *Archetypal Psychology and Jungian Thought* (Spring): 233–252.

Beidelman, T.O. 1966. The ox and Nuer sacrifice: Some Freudian hypotheses about Nuer symbolism. *Man* 1: 453–467.

Bem, Sandra Lipsitz. 1989. Genital knowledge and gender constancy in preschool children. *Child Development* 60: 649–662.

Benaim, Silvio, John Horder, and Jennifer Anderson. 1973. Hysterical epidemic in a classroom. *Psychological Medicine* 3: 366–373.

Benedict, Ruth. 1934. *Patterns of culture*. Boston: Houghton Mifflin.

Benson, D. Frank and Donald T. Stuss. 1990. Frontal lobe influence on delusions: A clinical perspective. *Schizophrenia Bulletin* 16: 403–411.

Bernstein, Irving C., William A. Callahan, and James M. Jaranson. 1975. Lobotomy in private practice: Long-term follow-up. *Archives of General Psychiatry* 32: 1041–1047.

Bettelheim, Bruno. 1954. *Symbolic wounds: Puberty rites and the envious male.* Glencoe, Ill.: Free Press.

1976. *The uses of enchantment: The meaning and importance of fairy tales.* New York: Knopf.

Block, Jack. 1981. Some enduring and consequential structures of personality. In *Further explorations in personality*, ed. A.I. Rabin, J. Arnoff, A.M. Barclay and R.A. Zucker, 27–43. New York: Wiley.

Bollas, Christopher. 1987. *The shadow of the object: Psychoanalysis of the unthought known.* New York: Columbia University Press.

Borneman, Ernest, ed. 1976. *The psychoanalysis of money.* New York: Urizen Books.

Bourdieu, Pierre. 1977. *Outline of a theory of practice.* Trans. R. Nice. Cambridge: Cambridge University Press.

1991. *Language and symbolic power.* Trans. G. Raymond and M. Adamson; ed. J.B. Thompson. Cambridge, Mass.: Harvard University Press.

Bourguignon, Erika. 1973. Introduction: A framework for the comparative study of altered states of consciousness. In *Religion, altered states of consciousness, and social change*, ed. E. Bourguignon, 3–35. Columbus: Ohio State University Press.

1976. *Possession.* San Francisco: Chandler & Sharp.

1979. *Psychological anthropology: An introduction to human nature and cultural differences.* New York: Holt, Rinehart & Winston.

1989. Multiple personality, possession trance, and the psychic unity of mankind. *Ethos* 17: 371–384.

Bourke, John G. 1891. *Scatalogic rites of all nations. A dissertation upon the employment of excrementitious remedial agents in religion, therapeutics, divination, witchcraft, love-philters, etc. in all parts of the globe.* Washington, D.C.: W.H. Lowdermilk.

Bower, Gordon H. 1990. Awareness, the unconscious, and repression: An experimental psychologist's perspective. In *Repression and dissociation: Implications for personality theory, psychopathology, and health*, ed. J.L. Singer, 209–231. Chicago: University of Chicago Press.

Bowie, Malcolm. 1991. *Lacan.* Cambridge, Mass.: Harvard University Press.

Bowlby, John. 1969. *Attachment and loss. Vol. I: Attachment.* New York: Basic.

1973. *Attachment and loss. Vol. II: Separation: Anxiety and anger.* New York: Basic.

1980. *Attachment and loss. Vol. III: Loss, sadness, and depression.* New York: Basic.

Boyer, L. Bryce, Bruno Klopfer, Florence B. Brawer, and Hayao Kawai. 1964. Comparisons of the shamans and pseudoshamans of the Apaches of the Mescalero Indian reservation: A Rorschach study. *Journal of Projective Techniques & Personality Assessment* 28: 173–180.

Brain, James L. 1977. Sex, incest, and death: Initiation rites reconsidered. *Current Anthropology* 18: 191–208.

Brandes, Stanley. 1980. *Metaphors of masculinity: Sex and status in Andalusian folklore.* Philadelphia: University of Pennsylvania Press.

Brenner, Charles. 1955. *An elementary textbook of psychoanalysis.* New York: International Universities Press.

1982. The concept of the superego: A reformulation. *Psychoanalytic Quarterly* 51: 501–525.

Brenner, Harvey M. 1973. *Mental illness and the economy*. Cambridge, Mass.: Harvard University Press.

Breuer, Josef and Sigmund Freud. [1893–1895]1955. *Studies in hysteria*. In *The standard edition of the complete psychological works of Sigmund Freud*. Ed. and trans. J. Strachey, vol. II. London: Hogarth.

Breuner, Nancy Frey. 1992. The cult of the Virgin Mary in southern Italy and Spain. *Ethos* 20: 66–95.

Brill, A.A. 1913. Piblokto or hysteria among Peary's Eskimos. *Journal of Nervous and Mental Disease* 40: 514–520.

Bromberg, Norbert and Verna Volz Small. 1983. *Hitler's psychopathology*. New York: International Universities Press.

Broude, Gwen J. 1988. Rethinking the couvade: Cross-cultural evidence. *American Anthropologist* 90: 902–911.

1990. Protest masculinity: A further look at the causes and the concept. *Ethos* 18: 103–122.

Brown, George W. 1982. Early loss and depression. In *The place of attachment in human behavior*, ed. C.M. Parkes and J. Stevenson-Hinde, 232–268. New York: Basic.

Brown, George W. and Tirril Harris. 1978. *Social origins of depression: A study of psychiatric disorder in women*. New York: Free Press.

Brown, Judith K. 1963. A cross-cultural study of female initiation rites. *American Anthropologist* 65: 837–853.

Bruner, Jerome. 1990. *Acts of meaning*. Cambridge, Mass.: Harvard University Press.

Buchsbaum, Monte S. 1990. The frontal lobes, basal ganglia, and temporal lobes as sites for schizophrenia. *Schizophrenia Bulletin* 16: 379–389.

Bucke, Richard M. [1901]1946. *Cosmic consciousness: A study in the evolution of the human mind*. 12th edn. New York: Dutton.

Burkert, Walter. 1983. *Homo necans: The anthropology of ancient Greek sacrificial ritual and myth*. Trans. P. Bing. Berkeley: University of California Press.

Burnham, Donald L., Arthur I. Gladstone, and Robert W. Gibson. 1969. *Schizophrenia and the need–fear dilemma*. New York: International Universities Press.

Burton-Bradley, B.G. 1985. The *amok* syndrome in Papua and New Guinea. In *The culture-bound syndromes: Folk illnesses of psychiatric and anthropological interest*, ed. R.C. Simons and C.C. Hughes, 237–249. Dordrecht: Reidel.

Burton, Roger V. and John W.M. Whiting. 1961. The absent father and cross-sex identity. *Merrill-Palmer Quarterly* 7: 85–95.

Bushnell, John. 1958. La Virgen de Guadalupe as surrogate mother in San Juan Atzingo. *American Anthropologist* 60: 261–265.

Byrne, Richard W. and Andrew Whiten, eds. 1988. *Machiavellian intelligence: Social expertise and the evolution of intellect in monkeys, apes, and humans*. Oxford: Clarendon.

Calvo, J.M., S. Badillo, M. Morales-Ramirez, and P. Palacios-Salas. 1987. The role of the temporal lobe amygdala in ponto-geniculo-occipital activity and sleep organization in cats. *Brain Research* 403: 22–30.

Cannon, Tyrone D., Sarnoff A. Mednick, and Josef Parnas. 1990. Two pathways to schizophrenia in children at risk. In *Straight and devious pathways from childhood to adulthood*, ed. L.N. Robins and M. Rutter, 328–350. Cambridge: Cambridge University Press.

Cantlie, Audrey. 1993. The non-lover: Desire and discourse in the psychoanalytic session. *Free Associations* 4: 210–240.

Carlson, Neil R. 1986. *The physiology of behavior*. 3rd edn. Boston: Allyn.

Carlsson, Maria and Arvid Carlsson. 1990. Schizophrenia: A subcortical neurotransmitter imbalance syndrome? *Schizophrenia Bulletin* 16: 425–432.

Carneiro, Robert. 1970. A theory of the origin of the state. *Science* 169: 733–738.

Carr, John E. 1978. Ethno-behaviorism and the culture-bound syndromes: The case of *amok*. *Culture, Medicine and Psychiatry* 2: 269–293.

Carr, John E. and Peter P. Vitaliano. 1985. The theoretical implications of converging research on depression and the culture-bound syndromes. In *Culture and depression: Studies in the anthropology and cross-cultural psychiatry of affect and disorder*, ed. A. Kleinman and B. Good, 244–266. Berkeley: University of California Press.

Carroll, Michael P. 1986. *The cult of the Virgin Mary: Psychological origins*. Princeton, N.J.: Princeton University Press.

Carstairs, G. Morris. 1957. *The twice-born: A study of a community of high-caste Hindus*. London: Hogarth.

Caspi, Avshalom, Glen H. Elder Jr., and Ellen S. Herbener. 1990. Childhood personality and the prediction of life-course patterns. In *Straight and devious pathways from childhood to adulthood*, ed. L.N. Robins and M. Rutter, 13–35. Cambridge: Cambridge University Press.

Castillo, Richard J. 1994a. Spirit possession in South Asia, dissociation or hysteria? Part 1: Theoretical background. *Culture, Medicine and Psychiatry* 18: 1–21.

    1994b. Spirit possession in South Asia, dissociation or hysteria? Part 2: Case histories. *Culture, Medicine and Psychiatry* 18: 141–162.

Cath, Stanley. 1986. Fathering from infancy to old age: A selective overview of recent psychoanalytic contributions. *Psychoanalytic Review* 73: 469–479.

Chasseguet-Smirgel, Janine. 1974. Perversion, idealization and sublimation. *International Journal of Psycho-Analysis* 55: 349–357.

    1984. *Creativity and perversion*. New York: Norton.

    1985. *The ego ideal: A psychoanalytic essay on the malady of the ideal*. Trans. P. Barrows. New York: Norton.

    1986. *Sexuality and mind: The role of the father and the mother in the psyche*. New York: University Press.

Chernela, Janet M. 1991. Symbolic inaction in rituals of gender and procreation among the Garifuna (Black Caribs) of Honduras. *Ethos* 19: 52–67.

Childers, Thomas. 1983. *The Nazi voter: The social foundations of fascism in Germany, 1919–1933*. Chapel Hill: University of North Carolina Press.

Chiu, T.L., J.E. Tong, and K.E. Schmidt. 1972. A clinical and survey study of latah in Sarawak, Malaysia. *Psychological Medicine* 2: 155–165.

Chodoff, Paul and Henry Lyons. 1958. Hysteria, the hysterical personality and "hysterical" conversion. *American Journal of Psychiatry* 114: 734–740.

Chodorow, Nancy J. 1978. *The reproduction of mothering: Psychoanalysis and the sociology of gender*. Berkeley: University of California Press.

1989. *Feminism and psychoanalytic theory*. New Haven: Yale University Press.

Claridge, Gordon. 1985. *Origins of mental illness: Temperament, deviance and disorder*. Oxford: Basil Blackwell.

Clark, Katerina and Michael Holquist. 1984. *Mikhail Bakhtin*. Cambridge, Mass.: Belknap Press, Harvard University Press.

Clastres, Pierre. 1987. *Society against the state: Essays in political anthropology*. Trans. R. Hurley and A. Stein. New York: Zone Books.

Cloninger, C. Robert. 1987. A systematic method for clinical description and classification of personality variants: A proposal. *Archives of General Psychiatry* 44: 573–588.

Cohen, Alex. 1992. Prognosis for schizophrenia in the third world: A reevaluation of cross-cultural research. *Culture, Medicine and Psychiatry* 16: 53–75.

Cohen, Ronald. 1977. Oedipus rex and regina: The queen mother in Africa. *Africa* 47: 14–30.

Cohen, Yehudi A. 1964. *The transition from childhood to adolescence: Cross-cultural studies of initiation ceremonies, legal systems, and incest taboos*. Chicago: Aldine Publishing Company.

Cohn, Carol. 1987. Sex and death in the rational world of defense intellectuals. *Signs* 12: 687–718.

Colapietro, Vincent M. 1990. The vanishing subject of contemporary discourse: A pragmatic response. *Journal of Philosophy* 8711: 644–655.

Colby, Anne and Lawrence Kohlberg. 1987. *The measurement of moral judgement. Vol. I: Theoretical foundations and research validation*. Cambridge: Cambridge University Press.

Colby, Benjamin N. 1987. Well-being: A theoretical program. *American Anthropologist* 89: 879–895.

1991. The Japanese tea ceremony: Coherence and metaphor in social adaptation. In *Beyond metaphor: The theory of tropes in anthropology*, ed. J.W. Fernandez, 244–260. Stanford: Stanford University Press.

Colligan, Michael J. and Lawrence R. Murphy. 1979. Mass psychogenic illness in organizations: An overview. *Journal of Occupational Psychology* 52: 77–90.

Cone, Cynthia A. 1979. Personality and subsistence: Is the child the parent of the person? *Ethnology* 18: 291–301.

Connor, John W. 1989. From ghost dance to death camps: Nazi Germany as a crisis cult. *Ethos* 17: 259–288.

Corin, Ellen E. 1990. Facts and meaning in psychiatry: An anthropological approach to the lifeworld of schizophrenics. *Culture, Medicine and Psychiatry* 14: 153–188.

Crapanzano, Vincent. 1973. *The Hamadsha: A study of Moroccan ethnopsychiatry*. Berkeley: University of California Press.

1980. *Tuhami, portrait of a Moroccan*. Chicago: Chicago University Press.

1981. Text, transference, and indexicality. *Ethos* 9: 122–148.

1982. The self, the third, and desire. In *Psychosocial theories of the self*, ed. B. Lee and K. Smith, 179–206. New York: Plenum Press.

1990. On self characterization. In *Cultural psychology: Essays on comparative human development*, ed. J.W. Stigler, R.A. Shweder, and G. Herdt, 401–423. Cambridge: Cambridge University Press.

1992. *Hermes' dilemma and Hamlet's Desire: On the epistemology of interpretation*. Cambridge, Mass.: Harvard University Press.

Crapanzano, Vincent and Vivian Garrison, eds. 1977. *Case studies in spirit possession*. New York: Wiley.

Crawford, C. Joanne. 1994. Parenting practices in the Basque country: Implications of infant and childhood sleeping location for personality development. *Ethos* 22: 42–82.

Cronin, John E. 1986. Molecular insights into the nature and timing of ancient speciation events: Correlates with palaeoclimate and palaeobiogeography. *South African Journal of Science* 82: 83–85.

Crow, Timothy J. 1990. Temporal lobe asymmetries as the key to the etiology of schizophrenia. *Schizophrenia Bulletin* 16: 433–443.

Crow, T.J., I.N. Ferrier, and Eve C. Johnstone. 1986. The two-syndrome concept and neuroendocrinology of schizophrenia. *Psychiatric Clinics of North America* 9: 99–113.

Csordas, Thomas J. 1990. Embodiment as a paradigm for anthropology. *Ethos* 18: 5–47.

Cuber, John F. and Peggy B. Haroff. [1965]1970. *Sex and the significant Americans: A study of sexual behavior among the affluent*. Reprint. Baltimore: Penguin Books.

Curtis, James L. 1955. A psychiatric study of 55 expectant fathers. *United States Armed Forces Medical Journal* 6: 937–950.

Custance, John. 1951. *Wisdom, madness and folly: The philosophy of a lunatic*. London: Gollancz.

Daelemans, Sven and Tullio Maranhão. 1990. Psychoanalytic dialogue and the dialogical principle. In *The interpretation of dialogue*, ed. T. Maranhão, 219–241. Chicago: University of Chicago Press.

Daly, Martin and Margo Wilson. 1988. *Homicide*. New York: Aldine de Gruyter.

Damasio, Antonio R. 1994. *Descartes' error: Emotion, reason, and the human brain*. New York: Putnam.

Damasio, Antonio R. and Hanna Damasio. 1992. Brain and language. *Scientific American* 267 (September): 88–95.

D'Andrade, Roy G. 1990. Some propositions about the relations between culture and human cognition. In *Cultural psychology: Essays on comparative human development*, ed. J.W. Stigler, R.A. Shweder and G. Herdt, 65–129. New York: Cambridge University Press.

1991. Connectionism and culture, or some implications of a new model of cognition with respect to anthropological theory. Paper presented at meeting of the Society for Psychological Anthropology. Second bi-annual conference on current thinking and research, October 11–13, at Chicago, Illinois.

1992. Schemas and motivation. In *Human motives and cultural models*, ed. R.G. D'Andrade and C. Strauss, 23–44. Cambridge: Cambridge University Press.

D'Andrade, Roy G. and Claudia Strauss, eds. 1992. *Human motives and cultural models*. Cambridge: Cambridge University Press.

Darley, John M. 1992. Social organization for the production of evil. *Psychological Inquiry* 3: 199–218.

David-Ménard, Monique. 1989. *Hysteria from Freud to Lacan: Body and language in psychoanalysis*. Trans. C. Porter. Ithaca: Cornell University Press.

Davidson, Julian M. 1980. The psychobiology of sexual experience. In *The psychobiology of consciousness*, ed. J.M. Davidson and R.J. Davidson, 271–332. New York: Plenum Press.

de Certeau, Michel. 1984. *The practice of everyday life*. Trans. S. Rendall. Berkeley: University of California Press.

Deleuze, Gilles and Félix Guattari. 1983. *Anti-Oedipus: Capitalism and schizophrenia*. Trans. R. Hurley, M. Seem, and H.R. Lane. Minneapolis: University of Minnesota Press.

deMause, Lloyd. 1991. The universality of incest. *Journal of Psychohistory* 19: 123–164.

Dennett, Daniel C. 1991. *Consciousness explained*. Boston: Little.

Derné, Steve. 1992. Beyond institutional and impulsive conceptions of self: Family structure and the socially anchored real self. *Ethos* 20: 259–288.

Dervin, Daniel. 1987. *Roland Barthes*: The text as self; the self as text. *Psychoanalytic Review* 74: 281–292.

Deutsch, Helen. 1942. Some forms of emotional disturbance and their relationship to schizophrenia. *Psychoanalytic Quarterly* 11: 301–321.

Devereux, George. 1951a. *Reality and dream: Psychotherapy of a Plains Indian*. New York: International Universities Press.

1951b. The oedipal situation and its consequences in the epics of ancient India. *Samīksa* 5: 5–13.

1953. Why Oedipus killed Laius: A note on the complementary Oedipus complex in Greek drama. *International Journal of Psycho-Analysis* 34: 132–141.

1955. Charismatic leadership and crisis. In *Psychoanalysis and the Social Sciences*, vol. IV, ed. W. Muensterberger and S. Axelrad, 145–157. New York: International Universities Press.

1961. Two types of modal personality models. In *Studying personality cross-culturally*, ed. B. Kaplan, 227–241. Evanston, Ill.: Row, Peterson.

1966. Pathogenic dreams in non-western societies. In *The dream and human societies*, ed. G.E. von Grunebaum and R. Caillois, 213–228. Berkeley: University of California Press.

1980. A sociological theory of schizophrenia (1939). Trans. B. Miller Gulati and G. Devereux. In *Basic problems of ethnopsychiatry*, 185–213. Chicago: University of Chicago Press.

De Vos, George. 1973a. Some observations of guilt in relation to achievement and arranged marriage. In his *Socialization for achievement: Essays on the cultural psychology of the Japanese*, 144–164. Berkeley: University of California Press.

1973b. Role narcissism and the etiology of Japanese suicide. In his *Socialization for achievement: Essays on the cultural psychology of the Japanese*, 438–485. Berkeley: University of California Press.

Diamond, Michael J. 1986. Becoming a father: A psychoanalytic perspective of the forgotten parent. *Psychoanalytic Review* 73: 445–468.

Diamond, Stanley. 1974. Schizophrenia and civilization. In his *Search of the primitive: A critique of civilization*, 227–254. New Brunswick, N.J.: Transaction.

Dicks, Henry V. 1950. Personality traits and national socialist ideology: A war-time study of German prisoners of war. *Human Relations* 3: 111–154.

1973. *Licensed mass murder: A socio-psychological study of some SS killers*. New York: Basic.

Divale, William T. 1970. An explanation for primitive warfare: Population control and the significance of primitive sex ratios. *New Scholar* 2: 173–192.

Divale, William Tulio and Marvin Harris. 1976. Population, warfare, and the male supremacist complex. *American Anthropologist* 78: 521–538.

Dominguez, Virginia R. 1989. *People as subject, people as object: Selfhood and peoplehood in contemporary Israel.* Madison: University of Wisconsin Press.

Donald, Merlin. 1991. *Origins of the modern mind: Three stages in the evolution of culture and cognition.* Cambridge, Mass.: Harvard University Press.

Doniger, Wendy. 1993. When a lingam is just a good cigar: Psychoanalysis and Hindu sexual fantasies. In *The Psychoanalytic Study of Society*, vol. XVIII, ed. L.B. Boyer, R.M. Boyer, and S.M. Sonnenberg, 81–103. Hillsdale, N.J.: Analytic Press.

Douglas, Mary. 1966. *Purity and danger: An analysis of concepts of pollution and taboo.* London: Pelican.

Draper, Patricia and Henry Harpending. 1982. Father absence and reproductive strategy: An evolutionary perspective. *Journal of Anthropological Research* 38: 225–273.

Dulaney, Siri and Alan Page Fiske. 1994. Cultural rituals and obsessive-compulsive disorder: Is there a common psychological mechanism? *Ethos* 22: 243–283.

Dunbar, R.I.M. 1988. *Primate social systems.* Ithaca, N.Y.: Comstock Associates, Cornell University Press.

Dundes, Alan. 1976. A psychoanalytic study of the bullroarer. *Man* 11: 220–238.

1978. Into the endzone for a touchdown: A psychoanalytic consideration of American football. *Western Folklore* 37: 75–88.

1981. The hero pattern and the life of Jesus. In *The psychoanalytic study of society*, vol. IX, ed. W. Muensterberger and L.B. Boyer, 49–83. New York: Psychohistory Press.

1984. *Life is like a chicken coop ladder: A portrait of German culture through folklore.* New York: Columbia University Press.

1985a. The psychoanalytic study of folklore. *Annals of Scholarship* 3 (3): 1–42.

1985b. The American game of "smear the queer" and the homosexual component of male competitive sport and warfare. *Journal of Psychoanalytic Anthropology* 8: 115–129.

Dundes, Alan, Jerry W. Leach, and Bora Özkök. 1970. The strategy of Turkish boys' verbal dueling rhymes. *Journal of American Folklore* 83: 325–349.

Dunn, Judy. 1988. *The beginnings of social understanding.* Cambridge, Mass.: Harvard University Press.

Dunn, Judy and Robert Plomin. 1990. *Separate lives: Why siblings are so different.* New York: Basic.

Eagle, Morris N. 1984. *Recent developments in psychoanalysis: A critical evaluation.* New York: McGraw.

Edelman, Gerald M. 1992. *Bright air, brilliant fire: On the matter of the mind.* New York: Basic.

Edmunds, Lowell. 1985. *Oedipus: The ancient legend and its later analogues.* Baltimore: Johns Hopkins University Press.

Edmunds, Lowell and Alan Dundes, eds. 1983. *Oedipus: A folklore casebook.* New York: Garland.

Edwards, James W. 1985. Indigenous *koro*, a genital retraction syndrome of insular Southeast Asia: A critical review. In *The culture-bound syndromes: Folk ill-*

nesses of psychiatric and anthropological interest, ed. R.C. Simons and C.C. Hughes, 169–191. Dordrecht: Reidel.

Eigen, Michael. 1986. *The psychotic core*. Northvale, N.J.: Aronson.

Ekman, Paul. 1980. *Face of man: Universal expression in a New Guinea village*. New York: Garland.

Ellenberger, Henri F. 1970. *The discovery of the unconscious: The history and evolution of dynamic psychiatry*. New York: Basic.

Ellman, Steven J. 1985. Toward a psychoanalytic theory of drive: REM sleep, a CNS self-stimulation system. *Clinical Psychology Review* 5: 185–198.

Ember, Carol R. 1974. An evaluation of alternative theories of matrilocal versus patrilocal residence. *Behavior Science Research* 9: 135–149.

1978. Myths about hunter-gatherers. *Ethnology* 17: 439–448.

Ember, Carol R., Melvin Ember, and Burton Pasternak. 1974. On the development of unilineal descent. *Journal of Anthropological Research* 30: 69–94.

Engel, George L. and Arthur H. Schmale. 1972. Conservation-withdrawal: A primary regulatory process for organismic homeostasis. In *Physiology, emotion & psychosomatic illness*, 57–75. Amsterdam: Elsevier.

Epstein, Seymour. 1984. The stability of behavior across time and situations. In *Personality and the prediction of behavior*, ed. R.A. Zucker, J. Aronoff, and A.I. Rabin, 209–268. Orlando, Florida: Academic Press.

Erdelyi, Matthew Hugh. 1985. *Psychoanalysis: Freud's cognitive psychology*. New York: W.H. Freeman.

1992. Psychodynamics and the unconscious. *American Psychologist* 47: 784–787.

Evans-Pritchard, E.E. 1940. *The Nuer: A description of the modes of livelihood and political institutions of a Nilotic people*. Oxford: Clarendon Press, Oxford University Press.

1956. *Nuer religion*. Oxford: Clarendon Press, Oxford University Press.

Everett, Guy M. 1975. Role of biogenic amines in the modulation of aggression and sexual behavior in animals and man. In *Sexual behavior: Pharmacology and biochemistry*, ed. M. Sandler and G.L. Gessa, 81–84. New York: Raven.

Ewing, Katherine P. 1987. Clinical psychoanalysis as an ethnographic tool. *Ethos* 15: 16–39.

1990. The illusion of wholeness: Culture, self, and the experience of inconsistency. *Ethos* 18: 251–278.

1991. Can psychoanalytic theories explain the Pakistani woman? Intrapsychic autonomy and interpersonal engagement in the extended family. *Ethos* 19: 131–160.

Eysenck, H.J. 1967. *The biological basis of personality*. Springfield, Ill.: Thomas.

1982. A psychological theory of hysteria. In *Hysteria*, ed. A. Roy, 57–80. Chichester: Wiley.

Fabrega, Horacio, Jr. 1989. On the significance of an anthropological approach to schizophrenia. *Psychiatry* 52: 45–65.

Fabrega, Horacio, Jr. and Daniel B. Silver. 1973. *Illness and shamanistic curing in Zinacantan: An ethnomedical analysis*. Stanford: Stanford University Press.

Fairbairn, W.R. 1952. *Psychoanalytic studies of the personality*. London: Routledge & Kegan Paul.

Falk, Dean. 1987. Hominid paleoneurology. *Annual Review of Anthropology* 16: 13–30.

Farrington, David P., Rolf Loeber, Delbert S. Elliott, J. David Hawkins, Denise B.

Kandel, Malcolm W. Klein, Joan McCord, David C. Rowe, and Richard E. Tremblay. 1990. Advancing knowledge about the onset of delinquency and crime. In *Advances in clinical child psychology*, vol. XIII, ed. B.B. Lahey and A.E. Kazdin, 283–342. New York: Plenum Press.

Fast, Irene. 1974. Multiple identities in borderline personality organization. *British Journal of Medical Psychology* 47: 291–300.

—— 1984. *Gender identity; A differentiation model*. Hillsdale, N.J.: Analytic Press.

Fenichel, Otto. [1938]1954. The drive to amass wealth. In *The collected papers of Otto Fenichel*, vol. II, 89–108. New York: Norton.

—— 1945. *The psychoanalytic theory of neurosis*. New York: Norton.

Ferenczi, Sandor. [1914]1950. The ontogenesis of the interest in money. Trans. E. Jones. In his *Sex in psychoanalysis*, 319–331. New York: Basic.

Fernando, S.J.M. 1969. Cultural differences in the hostility of depressed patients. *British Journal of Medical Psychology* 42: 67–74.

Finkler, Kaja. 1985. *Spiritualist healers in Mexico: Successes and failures of alternative therapeutics*. New York: Praeger Publishers; So. Hadley, Mass.: Bergin & Garvey.

Fischer, Kurt W. and Malcolm W. Watson. 1981. Explaining the Oedipus conflict. *New Directions for Child Development* 12: 79–92.

Fischman, Lawrence G. 1983. Dreams, hallucinogenic drug states, and schizophrenia: A psychological and biological comparison. *Schizophrenia Bulletin* 9: 73–94.

Fisher, Charles. 1965a. Psychoanalytic implications of recent research on sleep and dreaming. Part I: Empirical findings. *Journal of the American Psychoanalytic Association* 13: 197–270.

—— 1965b. Psychoanalytic implications of recent research on sleep and dreaming. Part II: Implications for psychoanalytic theory. *Journal of the American Psychoanalytic Association* 13: 271–303.

Fisher, Helen E. 1982. *The sex contract: The evolution of human behavior*. New York: William Morrow.

—— 1992. *Anatomy of love: The natural history of monogamy, adultery, and divorce*. New York: Norton.

Fisher, Seymour and Roger P. Greenberg. 1985. *The scientific credibility of Freud's theories and therapy*. New York: Columbia University Press.

Flax, Jane. 1990. *Thinking fragments: Psychoanalysis, feminism, and postmodernism in the contemporary west*. Berkeley: University of California Press.

Fliegel, Zenia Odes. 1986. Women's development in analytic theory: Six decades of controversy. In *Psychoanalysis and women: Contemporary reappraisals*, ed. J.L. Alpert, 3–31. Hillsdale, N.J.: Analytic Press.

Flor-Henry, P., D. Fromm-Auch, M. Tapper, and D. Schopflocher. 1981. A neuropsychological study of the stable syndrome of hysteria. *Biological Psychiatry* 16: 601–626.

Fogel, Gerald I. and Wayne A. Myers, eds. 1991. *Perversions and near-perversions in clinical practice: New psychoanalytic perspectives*. New Haven: Yale University Press.

Fogelson, Raymond D. 1982. Person, self, and identity: Some anthropological retrospects, circumspects, and prospects. In *Psychosocial theories of the self*, ed. B. Lee and K. Smith, 67–109. New York: Plenum Press.

Fornari, Franco. 1975. *The psychoanalysis of war*. Trans. A. Pfeifer. Bloomington, Ind.: Indiana University Press.

Forsyth, Dan W. 1988. Tolerated deviance and small group solidarity. *Ethos* 16: 398–420.

Fortes, Meyer. 1987. *Religion, morality, and the person: Essays on Tallensi religion.* Ed. J. Goody. Cambridge: Cambridge University Press.

Fortes, Meyer and Doris Y. Mayer. 1969. Psychosis and social change among the Tallensi of Northern Ghana. In *Psychiatry in a changing society*, ed. S.H. Foulkes and G.S. Prince, 33–73. London: Tavistock.

Foster, George M. 1972. The anatomy of envy: A study in symbolic behavior. *Current Anthropology* 13: 165–202.

Foulks, Edward F. 1972. *The arctic hysterias of the north Alaskan Eskimo.* Washington, D.C.: American Anthropological Association.

Foulks, Edward F. and Solomon H. Katz. 1975. Biobehavioral adaptation in the Arctic. In *Biosocial interrelations in population adaptation*, ed. E.S. Watts, F.E. Johnston, and G.W. Lasker, 183–193. The Hague: Mouton.

Fox, Robin. 1983. *The red lamp of incest: An enquiry into the origins of mind and society*. Notre Dame, Ind.: University of Notre Dame Press.

Frank, Jan. 1950. Some aspects of lobotomy (prefrontal leucotomy) under psychoanalytic scrutiny. *Psychiatry* 13: 35–42.

Freed, Stanley A. and Ruth S. Freed. 1964. Spirit possession as illness in a north Indian village. *Ethnology* 3: 152–171.

Freeman, Daniel M.A., Edward F. Foulks, and Patricia A. Freeman. 1978. Child development and arctic hysteria in the north Alaskan Eskimo male. *Journal of Psychological Anthropology* 1: 203–210.

Freeman, Derek. 1967. Shaman and incubus. In *The psychoanalytic study of society*, vol. IV, ed. W. Muensterberger and S. Axelrad, 315–343. New York: International Universities Press.

1968. Thunder, blood, and the nicknaming of God's creatures. *Psychoanalytic Quarterly* 37: 353–399.

Freeman, Thomas. 1970. The psychopathology of the psychoses: A reply to Arlow and Brenner. *International Journal of Psycho-Analysis* 51: 407–415.

1977. On Freud's theory of schizophrenia. *International Journal of Psycho-Analysis* 58: 383–401.

French, Thomas M. and Erika Fromm. 1964. *Dream interpretation: A new approach*. New York: Basic.

Freud, Anna. 1946. *The ego and the mechanisms of defense*. New York: International Universities Press.

Freud, Sigmund. [1892–1893]1966. A case of successful treatment by hypnotism, with some remarks on the origin of hysterical symptoms through "counterwill." In *The Standard Edition of the Complete Psychological Works of Sigmund Freud* (trans. and ed. J. Strachey in 24 volumes), vol. I. London: Hogarth [hereafter *S.E.*].

[1896]1962. The aetiology of hysteria. In *S.E.*, vol. III.

[1900]1953. *The interpretation of dreams*. In *S.E.*, vols. IV and V.

[1905a]1953. *Three essays on the theory of sexuality*. In *S.E.*, vol. VII.

[1905b]1953. Fragment of an analysis of a case of hysteria. In *S.E.*, vol. VII.

[1907]1959. Obsessive actions and religious practices. In *S.E.*, vol. IX.

[1908a]1959. "Civilized" sexual moraiity and modern nervous illness. In *S.E.*, vol. IX.

[1908b]1959. Hysterical phantasies and their relation to bisexuality. In *S.E.*, vol. IX.

[1908c]1959. Character and anal eroticism. In *S.E.*, vol. IX.

[1909]1959. Some general remarks on hysterical attacks. In *S.E.*, vol. IX.

[1910]1957. The psycho-analytic view of psychogenic disturbance of vision. In *S.E.*, vol. XI.

[1911]1958. Psycho-analytical notes on an autobiographical account of a case of paranoia (dementia paranoides). In *S.E.*, vol. XII.

[1912]1958. A note on the unconscious in psycho-analysis. In *S.E.*, vol. XII.

[1913]1955. *Totem and taboo: Some points of agreement between the mental lives of savages and neurotics*. In *S.E.*, vol. XIII.

[1914]1957. On narcissism: An introduction. In *S.E.*, vol. XIV.

[1916–1917]1963. *Introductory lectures on psycho-analysis*. In *S.E.*, vols. XV and XVI.

[1917]1957. Mourning and melancholia. In *S.E.*, vol. XIV.

[1920]1955. *Beyond the pleasure principle*. In *S.E.*, vol. XVIII.

[1921]1955. *Group psychology and the analysis of the ego*. In *S.E.*, vol. XVIII.

[1923a]1961. *The ego and the id*. In *S.E.*, vol. XIX.

[1923b]1961. A seventeenth-century demonological neurosis. In *S.E.*, vol. XIX.

[1924]1961. Neurosis and psychosis. In *S.E.*, vol. XIX.

[1926]1959. *Inhibitions, symptoms, and anxiety*. In *S.E.*, vol. XX.

[1927a]1961. *The future of an illusion*. In *S.E.*, vol. XXI.

[1927b]1961. Humour. In *S.E.*, vol. XXI.

[1927c]1961. Fetishism. In *S.E.*, vol. XXI.

[1930]1961. *Civilization and its discontents*. In *S.E.*, vol. XXI.

[1931]1961. Libidinal types. In *S.E.*, vol. XXI.

[1933a]1964. *New introductory lectures on psycho-analysis*. In *S.E.*, vol. XXII.

[1933b]1964. Why war? In *S.E.*, vol. XXII.

[1940]1964. *An outline of psycho-analysis*. In *S.E.*, vol. XXIII.

Freud, Sigmund and Daniel Ernest Oppenheim. [1911]1958. Dreams in folklore. In *S.E.*, vol. XII.

Frick, Robert B. 1982. The ego and the vestibulocerebellar system: Some theoretical perspectives. *Psychoanalytic Quarterly* 51:93–122.

Friedman, Robert M. 1986. The psychoanalytic model of male homosexuality: A historical and theoretical critique. *Psychoanalytic Review* 73:483–519.

Friedrich, Paul. 1986. *The princes of Naranja: An essay in ethnohistorical method*. Austin: University of Texas Press.

Frith, C.D. 1987. The positive and negative symptoms of schizophrenia reflect impairments in the perception and initiation of action. *Psychological Medicine* 17:631–648.

Fromm, Erich. 1941. *Escape from freedom*. New York: Farrar & Rinehart.

1947. *Man for himself: An inquiry into the psychology of ethics*. New York: Farrar & Rinehart.

Fromm-Reichmann, Frieda. 1948. Notes on the development of treatment of schizophrenics by psychoanalytic psychotherapy. *Psychiatry* 11:263–273.

Furst, Peter T. 1972. To find our life: Peyote among the Huichol Indians of Mexico.

In *Flesh of the gods: The ritual use of hallucinogens*, ed. P.T. Furst, 136–184. New York: Praeger Publishers.

Fuster, Joaquin M. 1988. *The prefrontal cortex: Anatomy, physiology, and neuro-psychology of the frontal lobe.* 2nd edn. New York: Raven.

Gaddini, Renata. 1970. Transitional objects and the process of individuation: A study in three different social groups. *Journal of American Academy of Child Psychiatry* 9: 347–365.

Gay, Peter. 1988. *Freud: A life for our time.* New York: Norton.

Gaylin, Willard and Ethel S. Person, eds. 1988. *Passionate attachments: Thinking about love.* New York: Free Press.

Geertz, Clifford. 1966. Religion as a cultural system. In *Anthropological approaches to the study of religion*, ed. M. Banton, 1–46. London: Tavistock.

1973. *The interpretation of cultures: Selected essays.* New York: Basic.

1983. "From the native's point of view": On the nature of anthropological understanding. In his *Local knowledge: Further essays in interpretive anthropology*, 55–70. New York: Basic.

Geertz, Hildred. 1968. Latah in Java: A theoretical paradox. *Indonesia* 5 (April): 93–104.

Gellhorn, Ernst. 1967. *Principles of autonomic-somatic integrations: Physiological basis and psychological and clinical implications.* Minneapolis: University of Minnesota Press.

Gergen, Kenneth J. 1972. Multiple identity: The healthy, happy human being wears many masks. *Psychology Today* 5: 31–35, 64–66.

1985. The social constructionist movement in modern psychology. *American Psychologist* 40: 266–275.

1990. Social understanding and the inscription of self. In *Cultural psychology: Essays on comparative human development*, ed. J.W. Stigler, R.A. Shweder and G. Herdt, 569–606. Cambridge: Cambridge University Press.

1991. *The saturated self: Dilemmas of identity in contemporary life.* New York: Basic.

Ghiglieri, Michael P. 1987. Sociobiology of the great apes and the hominid ancestor. *Journal of Human Evolution* 16: 319–357.

Giddens, Anthony. 1991. *Modernity and self-identity: Self and society in the late modern age.* Stanford: Stanford University Press.

Gilligan, Carol. 1982. *In a different voice: Psychological theory and women's development.* Cambridge, Mass.: Harvard University Press.

Gilmore, David D. 1990. *Manhood in the making: Cultural concepts of masculinity.* New Haven: Yale University Press.

Gilmore, Margaret M. and David D. Gilmore. 1979. "Machismo": A psycho-dynamic approach (Spain). *Journal of Psychological Anthropology* 2: 281–299.

Girard, René. 1977. *Violence and the sacred.* Trans. P. Gregory. Baltimore: Johns Hopkins University Press.

Glass, James M. 1985. *Delusion: Internal dimensions of political life.* Chicago: University of Chicago Press.

1993. *Shattered selves: Multiple personality in a postmodern world.* Ithaca: Cornell University Press.

Gloor, Pierre. 1975. Electrophysiological studies of the amygdala (stimulation and recording): Their possible contribution to the understanding of neural mechanisms of aggression. In *Neural bases of violence and aggression*, ed. W.S. Fields and W.H. Sweet, 5–36. St. Louis, Missouri: Warren H. Green.

1992. Role of the amygdala in temporal lobe epilepsy. In *The amygdala: Neurobiological aspects of emotion, memory, and mental dysfunction*, ed. J.P. Aggleton, 505–538. New York: Wiley-Liss, Wiley.

Gluckman, Max. 1960. The rise of a Zulu empire. *Scientific American* 202 (4): 157–168.

Glymour, Clark. 1991. Freud's androids. In *The Cambridge companion to Freud*, ed. J. Neu, 44–85. Cambridge Companions to Philosophers. Cambridge: Cambridge University Press.

Goffman, Erving. 1959. *The presentation of self in everyday life*. Garden City, N.Y.: Doubleday.

Goldberg, Evelyn L. 1973. Crowd hysteria in a junior high school. *Journal of School Health* 43: 362–366.

Goldberg, Lewis R. 1993. The structure of phenotypic personality traits. *American Psychologist* 48: 26–34.

Goldman, R.P. 1978. Fathers, sons and gurus: Oedipal conflict in the Sanskrit epics. *Journal of Indian Philosophy* 6: 325–392.

Goldstein, Jeffrey H. 1986. *Aggression and crimes of violence*. 2nd edn. Oxford: Oxford University Press.

Goldstein, Michael J. 1987. Family interaction patterns that antedate the onset of schizophrenia and related disorders: A further analysis of data from a longitudinal, prospective study. In *Understanding major mental disorder: The contribution of family interaction research*, ed. K. Hahlweg and M.J. Goldstein, 11–32. New York: Family Process Press.

Goodall, Jane. 1986. *The chimpanzees of Gombe: Patterns of behavior*. Cambridge, Mass.: Belknap Press, Harvard University Press.

Goodwin, Jean, Mary Simms, and Robert Bergman. 1979. Hysterical seizures: A sequel to incest. *American Journal of Orthopsychiatry* 49: 698–703.

Gordon, Sarah. 1984. *Hitler, Germans, and the "Jewish question."* Princeton, N.J.: Princeton University Press.

Gough, E. Kathleen. 1955. Female initiation rites on the Malabar coast. *The Journal of the Royal Anthropological Institute of Great Britain and Ireland* 85: 45–80.

Graber, Robert Bates. 1981. A psychocultural theory of male genital mutilation. *Journal of Psychoanalytic Anthropology* 4: 413–434.

Gray, Jeffrey Alan. 1987. *The psychology of fear and stress*. 2nd edn. Cambridge: Cambridge University Press.

Gray, J.A., J. Feldon, J.N.P. Rawlins, D.R. Hemsley, and A.D. Smith. 1991. The neuropsychology of schizophrenia. *Behavioral and Brain Sciences* 14: 1–84.

Gray, Jeffrey A., Susan Owen, Nicola Davis, and Eleftheria Tsaltas. 1983. Psychological and physiological relations between anxiety and impulsivity. In *Biological bases of sensation seeking, impulsivity, and anxiety*, ed. M. Zuckerman, 181–217. Hillsdale, N.J.: L. Erlbaum Associates.

Greenacre, Phyllis. [1958]1971. The impostor. In her *Emotional growth: Psychoanalytic studies of the gifted and a great variety of other individuals*, vol. I, 93–112. II vols. New York: International Universities Press.

Greenberg, Jay R. 1991. *Oedipus and beyond: A clinical theory*. Cambridge, Mass.: Harvard University Press.

Greenberg, Ramon and Chester Pearlman. 1974. Cutting the REM nerve: An approach to the adaptive role of REM sleep. *Perspectives in Biology and Medicine* 17: 513–521.

Greenson, Ralph R. 1968. Dis-identifying from mother: Its special importance for the boy. *International Journal of Psycho-Analysis* 49: 370–374.

Gregor, Thomas. 1985. *Anxious pleasures – the sexual lives of an Amazonian people*. Chicago: University of Chicago Press.

Groos, Karl. 1911. *The play of animals*. Trans. E.L. Baldwin. New York: D. Appleton.

Grotstein, James S. 1977. The psychoanalytic concept of schizophrenia: I. The dilemma. *International Journal of Psycho-Analysis* 58: 403–425.

Gunderson, John G. 1984. *Borderline personality disorder*. Washington, D.C.: American Psychiatric Press.

Gussow, Zachary. 1960. *Pibloktoq* (hysteria) among the polar Eskimo: An ethnopsychiatric study. In *The psychoanalytic study of society*, vol. I, ed. W. Muensterberger and S. Axelrad, 218–236. New York: International Universities Press.

Guze, Samuel B. 1975. The validity and significance of the clinical diagnosis of hysteria (Briquet's syndrome). *American Journal of Psychiatry* 132: 138–141.

Gwee, Ah Leng. 1985. *Koro* – a cultural disease. In *The culture-bound syndromes: Folk illnesses of psychiatric and anthropological interest*, ed. R.C. Simons and C.C. Hughes, 155–159. Dordrecht: Reidel.

Habermas, Jürgen. 1992. Individuation through socialization: On Mead's theory of subjectivity. In *Postmetaphysical thinking: Philosophical essays*, trans. W.M. Hohengarten, 149–204. Cambridge, Mass.: MIT Press.

Halgren, Eric. 1992. Emotional neurophysiology of the amygdala within the context of human cognition. In *The amygdala: Neurobiological aspects of emotion, memory, and mental dysfunction*, ed. J.P. Aggleton, 191–228. New York: Wiley-Liss, Wiley.

Hallowell, A. Irving. 1950. Personality structure and the evolution of man. *American Anthropologist* 52: 159–173.

Harland, Richard. 1987. *Superstructuralism: The philosophy of structuralism and post-structuralism*. London: Methuen.

Harlow, Harry F. 1971. *Learning to love*. New York: Ballantine, Albion.

Harrington, Charles. 1968. Sexual differentiation in socialization and some male genital mutilations. *American Anthropologist* 70: 951–956.

Harris, Grace Gredys. 1957. Possession "hysteria" in a Kenya tribe. *American Anthropologist* 59: 1046–1066.

1989. Concepts of individual, self, and person in description and analysis. *American Anthropologist* 91: 599–612.

Harris, Helena. 1987. Subjectivity and symbolization. *Psychoanalytic Review* 74: 1–17.

Harris, Marvin. 1977. *Cannibals and kings: The origins of cultures*. New York: Random House.

Hartmann, Ernest. 1982. From the biology of dreaming to the biology of the mind. *Psychoanalytic Study of the Child* 37: 303–335.

1984. *The nightmare: The psychology and biology of terrifying dreams.* New York: Basic.

Hartmann, Heinz. 1964. *Essays on ego psychology: Selected problems in psychoanalytic theory.* New York: International Universities Press.

Hasegawa, Masami, Hirohisa Kishino, and Taka-aki Yano. 1985. Dating of the human–ape splitting by a molecular clock of mitochondrial DNA. *Journal of Molecular Evolution* 22: 160–174.

Haynal, Andre. 1985. *Depression and creativity.* New York: International Universities Press.

Herdt, Gilbert H. 1981. *Guardians of the flutes: Idioms of masculinity.* New York: McGraw.

1982. Fetish and fantasy in Sambia initiation. In *Rituals of manhood: Male initiation in Papua New Guinea*, ed. G.H. Herdt, 44–98. Berkeley: University of California Press.

1984. Ritualized homosexual behavior in the male cults of Melanesia, 1862–1983: An introduction. In *Ritualized homosexuality in Melanesia*, ed. G.H. Herdt, 1–81. Berkeley: University of California Press.

1989. Father presence and ritual homosexuality: Paternal deprivation and masculine development in Melanesia reconsidered. *Ethos* 17: 326–370.

1992. Selfhood and discourse in Sambia dream sharing. In *Dreaming: Anthropological and psychological interpretations*, ed. B. Tedlock, 55–85. Santa Fe, New Mexico: School of American Research Press.

Hermans, Hubert J.M. and Harry J.G. Kempen. 1993. *The dialogical self: Meaning as movement.* San Diego: Academic Press.

Hermans, Hubert J.M., Harry J.G. Kempen, and Rens J.P. van Loon. 1992. The dialogical self: Beyond individualism and rationalism. *American Psychologist* 47: 23–33.

Heston, Leonard L. 1966. Psychiatric disorders in foster home reared children of schizophrenic mothers. *British Journal of Psychiatry* 112: 819–825.

Hewlett, Barry S., ed. 1992. *Father-child relations: Cultural and biosocial contexts.* New York: Aldine de Gruyter.

Hiatt, L.R. 1984. Your mother-in-law is poison. *Man* 19: 183–198.

Hilgard, Ernest R. 1986. *Divided consciousness: Multiple controls in human thought and action.* Expanded edn. New York: Wiley.

Hirsch, Steven R. 1979. Do parents cause schizophrenia? *Trends in Neurosciences* 2: 49–52.

Hobson, J. Allan. 1988. *The dreaming brain.* New York: Basic.

Hoffman, Louise E. 1981. War, revolution, and psychoanalysis: Freudian thought begins to grapple with social reality. *Journal of the History of the Behavioral Sciences* 17: 251–269.

Holland, Dorothy C. 1992. How cultural systems become desire: A case study of American romance. In *Human motives and cultural models*, ed. R.G. D'Andrade and C. Strauss, 61–89. Cambridge: Cambridge University Press.

Holman, S.D. and R.W. Goy. 1980. Behavioral and mammary responses of adult female rhesus to strange infants. *Hormones and Behavior* 14: 348–357.

Holquist, Michael. 1990. *Diologism: Bakhtin and his world.* London: Routledge.

Holt, Robert R. 1989. *Freud reappraised: A fresh look at psychoanalytic theory.* New York: Guilford Press.

Hong, K. Michael and Brenda D. Townes. 1976. Infants' attachment to inanimate objects: A cross-cultural study. *Journal of the American Academy of Child Psychiatry* 15: 49–61.

Horney, Karen. 1937. *The neurotic personality of our time.* New York: Norton.

Howells, John G. and Waguih R. Guirguis. 1985. *The family and schizophrenia.* New York: International Universities Press.

Hull, Clark L. 1933. *Hypnosis and suggestibility: An experimental approach.* New York: Appleton-Century.

Humphrey, Nicholas. 1986. *The inner eye.* Boston: Faber & Faber.

    1992. *A history of the mind.* New York: Simon & Schuster.

Hunter, Mic. 1990. *Abused boys: The neglected victims of sexual abuse.* Lexington: Lexington Books.

Ingham, John M. 1982. Toward a psychoanalytic materialism in anthropology. In *Crisis in anthropology: View from Spring Hill, 1980,* ed. E.A. Hoebel, R. Currier, and S. Kaiser, 301–319. New York: Garland.

    1986. *Mary, Michael, and Lucifer: Folk Catholicism in Central Mexico.* Austin: University of Texas Press.

    1989. Chalma and Tepoztecatl: Further reflections on religious syncretism in Central Mexico. *L'Uomo* 2: 61–83.

    1992. Freud in a forest of symbols: The religious background of psychoanalytic anthropology. In *Psychoanalytic anthropology after Freud: Essays marking the fiftieth anniversary of Freud's death,* ed. D.H. Spain, 139–161. New York: Psyche Press.

    In press. Oedipality in pragmatic discourse: The Trobriands and Hindu India. *Ethos.*

Insel, Thomas R. 1992. Oxytocin – a neuropeptide for affliation: Evidence from behavioral, receptor autoradiographic, and comparative studies. *Psychoneuroendocrinology* 17: 3–35.

Isabella, Russell A. and Jay Belsky. 1991. Interactional synchrony and the origins of infant-mother attachment: A replication study. *Child Development* 62: 373–384.

Israëls, Han. 1989. *Schreber: Father and son.* Madison, Conn.: International Universities Press.

Jackson, Stanley W. 1985. Acedia the sin and its relationship to sorrow and melancholia. In *Culture and depression: Studies in the anthropology and cross-cultural psychiatry of affect and disorder,* ed. A. Kleinman and B. Good, 43–62. Berkeley: University of California Press.

Jacobson, Edith. 1965. *The self and the object world.* London: Hogarth and the Institute of Psycho-Analysis.

James, William. [1892]1985. *Psychology: The briefer course,* ed. G. Allport. Notre Dame, Ind.: Notre Dame University Press.

Jamison, Kay R., Robert H. Gerner, Constance Hammen, and Christine Padesky. 1980. Clouds and silver linings: Positive experiences associated with primary affective disorders. *American Journal of Psychiatry* 137: 198–202.

Jankowiak, William R. and Edward F. Fischer. 1992. A cross-cultural perspective on romantic love. *Ethnology* 31: 149–155.

Jenkins, Janis Hunter. 1991. Anthropology, expressed emotion, and schizophrenia. *Ethos* 19:387–431.

Johnson, Allen. 1992. Psychoanalysis and materialism: Do they mix? In *Psychoanalytic anthropology after Freud: Essays marking the fiftieth anniversary of Freud's death*, ed. D.H. Spain, 225–249. New York: Psyche Press.

Johnson, Allen and Douglass Price-Williams. 1996 *Oedipus ubiquitous: The family complex in world folk literature*. Stanford: Stanford University Press.

Johnson, Mark. 1987. *The body in the mind: The bodily basis of meaning, imagination, and reason*. Chicago: University of Chicago Press.

Johnson, Orna R. and Allen Johnson. 1988. Oedipus in the political economy: Theme and variations in Amazonia. In *Dialectics and gender: Anthropological approaches*, ed. R.R. Randolph, D.M. Schneider, and M.N. Diaz, 38–56. Boulder, Col.: Westview.

Jones, Ernest. [1913]1964. The god complex. In his *Essays in applied psycho-analysis*, vol. II, 244–265. New York: International Universities Press.

[1915]1964. War and individual psychology. In his *Essays in applied psycho-analysis*, vol. I, 55–76. New York: International Universities Press.

[1951]1959. *On the nightmare*. New York: Grove, Evergreen.

Joseph, Rhawn. 1982. The neuropsychology of development: Hemispheric laterality, limbic language, and the origin of thought. *Journal of Clinical Psychology* 38:4–33.

Jung, Carl G. 1948. General aspects of dream psychology. Trans. R.F.C. Hull. In *The collected works of C.G. Jung*, vol. VIII. Princeton, N.J.: Princeton University Press.

Kakar, Sudhir. 1978. *The inner world: A psycho-analytic study of childhood and society in India*. Delhi: Oxford University Press.

1990. *Intimate relations: Exploring Indian sexuality*. Chicago: University of Chicago Press.

Kano, Takayoshi. 1980. Social behavior of wild pygmy chimpanzees (*Pan paniscus*) of Wamba: A preliminary report. *Journal of Human Evolution* 9:243–260.

Kaplan, Bert. 1954. A study of Rorschach responses in four cultures. *Papers of the Peabody Museum of American Archaeology and Ethnology, Harvard University* 42:2.

Kaplan, Louise J. 1991. *Female perversions: The temptations of Emma Bovary*. New York: Doubleday.

Kardiner, Abram. 1939. *The individual and his society: The psychodynamics of primitive social organization*. New York: Columbia University Press.

Karen, Robert. 1994. *Becoming attached: Unfolding the mystery of the infant-mother bond and its impact on later life*. New York: Warner Books.

Karon, Bertram P. 1960. A clinical note on the specific nature of an "oral" trauma. *Journal of Abnormal and Social Psychology* 61:480–481.

Karon, Bertram P. and Jack Rosberg. 1958. The homosexual urges in schizophrenia. *Psychoanalysis and Psychoanalytic Review* 45 (4):50–56.

Katz, Richard. 1982. *Boiling energy: Community healing among the Kalahari Kung*. Cambridge, Mass.: Harvard University Press.

Keefe, Jack A. and Peter A. Magaro. 1980. Creativity and schizophrenia: An equivalence of cognitive processing. *Journal of Abnormal Psychology* 89:390–398.

Kemper, Theodore D. 1978. *A social interactional theory of emotions.* New York: Wiley.

  1984. Power, status, and emotions: A sociological contribution to a psychophysiological domain. In *Approaches to emotion*, ed. K.R. Scherer and P. Ekman, 369–383. Hillsdale, N.J.: L. Erlbaum Associates.

Kempf, Edward J. 1917. The social and sexual behavior of infrahuman primates with some comparable facts in human behavior. *Psychoanalytic Review* 4: 127–154.

Kendall, Robert E. 1970. Relationship between aggression and depression: Epidemiological implications of a hypothesis. *Archives of General Psychiatry* 22: 308–318.

Kenny, Michael G. 1983. Paradox lost: The latah problem revisited. *Journal of Nervous and Mental Disease* 171: 159–167.

  1986. *The passion of Ansel Bourne: Multiple personality in American culture.* Washington, D.C.: Smithsonian Institution Press.

Kernberg, Otto F. 1972. Early ego integration and object relations. *Annals of the New York Academy of Sciences* 193: 233–247.

  1976. *Object-relations theory and clinical psychoanalysis.* New York: Aronson.

  1980. *Internal world and external reality.* New York: Aronson.

  1985. *Borderline conditions of pathological narcissism.* Northvale, N.J.: Aronson.

  1988. Between conventionality and aggression: The boundaries of passion. In *Passionate attachments: Thinking about love*, ed. W. Gaylin and E.S. Person, 63–83. New York: Free Press.

  1991. Aggression and love in the relationship of the couple. In *Perversions and near-perversions in clinical practice: New psychoanalytic perspectives*, ed. G.I. Fogel and W.A. Myers, 153–175. New Haven: Princeton University Press.

Khan, M. Masud. 1979. *Alienation in perversions.* London: Hogarth and The Institute of Psycho-Analysis.

Kiefer, Christie W. and Jonathan Cowan. 1979. State/context dependence and theories of ritual. *Journal of Psychological Anthropology* 2: 53–83.

Kilborne, Benjamin and L.L. Langness, eds. 1987. *Culture and human nature: Theoretical papers of Melford E. Spiro.* Chicago: University of Chicago Press.

Kirkpatrick, John and Geoffrey M. White. 1985. Exploring ethnopsychologies. In *Person, self, and experience: Exploring Pacific ethnopsychologies*, ed. G.M. White and J. Kirkpatrick, 3–32. Berkeley: University of California Press.

Kirschner, Suzanne R. 1992. Anglo-American values in post-Freudian psychoanalysis. In *Psychoanalytic anthropology after Freud: Essays marking the fiftieth anniversary of Freud's death*, ed. D.H. Spain, 162–197. New York: Psyche Press.

Kitahara, Michio. 1976. A cross-cultural test of the Freudian theory of circumcision. *International Journal of Psychoanalytic Psychotherapy* 5: 535–546.

Klein, Melanie. 1975a. *Love, guilt and reparation; & other works, 1921–1945.* London: Hogarth and The Institute of Psycho-Analysis.

  1975b. *Envy and gratitude; & and other works.* London: Hogarth and The Institute of Psycho-Analysis.

Kleinman, Arthur and Joan Kleinman. 1985. Somatization: The interconnections in Chinese society among culture, depressive experiences, and the meanings of pain. In *Culture and depression: Studies in anthropology and cross-cultural psychiatry of affect and disorder*, ed. A. Kleinman and B. Good, 429–490. Berkeley: University of California Press.

Klerman, Gerald L. 1982. Hysteria and depression. In *Hysteria*, ed. A. Roy, 211–228. Chichester: Wiley.

Kling, Arthur S. and Leslie A. Brothers. 1992. The amygdala and social behavior. In *The amygdala: Neurobiological aspects of emotion, memory, and mental dysfunction*, ed. J.P. Aggleton, 353–377. New York: Wiley-Liss, Wiley.

Klüver, Heinrich and Paul C. Bucy. 1939. Preliminary analysis of functions of the temporal lobes in monkeys. *Archives of Neurology and Psychiatry* 42:979–1000.

Knauft, Bruce M. 1978. Cargo cults and relational separation. *Behavior Science Research* 13:185–240.

1985. *Good company and violence: Sorcery and social action in a lowland New Guinea society*. Berkeley: University of California Press.

1987. Review essay: Homosexuality in Melanesia. *Journal of Psychoanalytic Anthropology* 10:155–191.

1993. *South coast New Guinea cultures: History, comparison, dialetic*. Cambridge: Cambridge University Press.

Knight, James A., Theodore I. Friedman, and Julie Sulianti. 1965. Epidemic hysteria: A field study. *American Journal of Public Health* 55:858–865.

Knowles, John B., Eugene J. Beaumaster, and Alistair W. MacLean. 1973. The function of rapid eye movement sleep and of dreaming in the adult. In *A triune concept of the brain and behaviour*, ed. T.J. Boag and D. Campbell, 146–155. Toronto: Published for the Ontario Mental Health Foundation by University of Toronto Press.

Köenigsberg, Richard A. 1975. *Hitler's ideology: A study in psychoanalytic sociology*. New York: Library of Social Science.

Kohn, Melvin L. 1973. Social class and schizophrenia: A critical review and a reformulation. *Schizophrenia Bulletin* 7:60–79.

Kohut, Heinz. 1966. Forms and transformations of narcissism. *Journal of the American Psychoanalytic Association* 14:243–272.

1971. *The analysis of the self: A systematic approach to the psychoanalytic treatment of narcissistic personality disorders*. New York: International Universities Press.

1972. Thoughts on narcissism and narcissistic rage. *Psychoanalytic Study of the Child* 27:360–400.

1977. *The restoration of the self*. New York: International Universities Press.

Kondo, Dorinne K. 1990. *Crafting selves: Power, gender, and discourses of identity in a Japanese workplace*. Chicago: University of Chicago Press.

Konner, Melvin J. 1976. Maternal care, infant behavior and development among the !Kung. In *Kalahari hunter-gatherers: Studies of the !Kung San and their neighbors*, ed. R.B. Lee and I. DeVore, 218–245. Cambridge, Mass.: Harvard University Press.

Kosslyn, Stephen M. and Olivier Koenig. 1992. *Wet mind: The new cognitive neuroscience*. New York: Free Press.

Kovel, Joel. 1984. *White racism: A psychohistory*. New York: Columbia University Press.

Kracke, Waud H. 1978. *Force and persuasion: Leadership in an Amazonian society*. Chicago: University of Chicago Press.

1992. Myths in dreams, thought in images: an Amazonian contribution to the psychoanalytic theory of primary process. In *Dreaming: Anthropological and psychological interpretations*, ed. B. Tedlock, 31–54. Santa Fe, New Mexico: School of American Research Press.

Kretschmer, Ernst. 1960. *Hysteria, reflex, and instinct*. Trans. V. Baskin and W. Baskin. New York: Philosophical Library.

Kristeva, Julia. 1982. *Powers of horror: An essay on abjection*. Trans. L.S. Roudiez. New York: Columbia University Press.

1986. Revolution in poetic language. In *The Kristeva reader*, ed. T. Moi, 89–136. New York: Columbia University Press.

1989. *Black sun: Depression and melancholia*. Trans. L.S. Roudiez. New York: Columbia University Press.

Krohn, Alan. 1978. *Hysteria: The elusive neurosis*. Psychological Issues, Monograph 45/46. New York: International Universities Press.

Kuroda, Suehisa. 1980. Social behavior of the pygmy chimpanzee. *Primates* 21: 181–197.

Kurtz, Stanley N. 1991. Polysexualization: A new approach to Oedipus in the Trobriands. *Ethos* 19: 68–101.

1992. *All the mothers are one: Hindu India and the cultural reshaping of psychoanalysis*. New York: Columbia University Press.

La Barre, Weston. 1954. *The human animal*. Chicago: University of Chicago Press.

1962. *They shall take up serpents: Psychology of the southern snake-handling cult*. Minneapolis: University of Minnesota Press.

1966. The dream, charisma, and the culture-hero. In *The dream and human societies*, ed. G.E. von Grunebaum and R. Caillois, 229–235. Berkeley: University of California Press.

1970. *The ghost dance: Origins of religion*. Garden City, N.Y.: Doubleday.

1984. *Muelos: A stone age superstition about sexuality*. New York: Columbia University Press.

1991. *Shadow of childhood: Neoteny and the biology of religion*. Norman, Okla.: University of Oklahoma Press.

LaBerge, Stephen. 1985. *Lucid dreaming*. Los Angeles: JP Tarcher.

Lacan, Jacques. 1977. On a question preliminary to any possible treatment of psychosis. Trans. A. Sheridan. In *Ecrits: A selection*, 179–225. New York: Norton.

1978. *The four fundamental concepts of psycho-analysis*. Trans. A. Sheridan, ed. J.-A. Miller. New York: Norton.

La Fontaine, J.S. 1985. Person and individual: Some anthropological reflections. In *The category of the person: Anthropology, philosophy, history*, ed. M. Carrithers, S. Collins, and S. Lukes, 123–140. Cambridge: Cambridge University Press.

Lakoff, George. 1987. *Women, fire, and dangerous things: What categories reveal about the mind*. Chicago: University of Chicago Press.

Langacker, Ronald W. 1990. *Concept, image, and symbol: The cognitive basis of grammar*. Berlin and New York: Mouton de Gruyter.

Langness, L.L. 1965. Hysterical psychosis in the New Guinea Highlands: A Bena Bena example. *Psychiatry* 28: 258–277.

　　1967. Hysterical psychosis: The cross-cultural evidence. *American Journal of Psychiatry* 124: 143–152.

　　1974. Ritual, power, and male dominance in the New Guinea Highlands. *Ethos* 2: 189–212.

Lasch, Christopher. 1978. *The culture of narcissism: American life in an age of diminishing expectations*. New York: Norton.

Lasswell, Harold D. 1933. The psychology of Hitlerism. *Political Quarterly* 4: 373–384.

Layard, John. 1955. Boar-sacrifice. *Journal of Analytical Psychology* 1: 7–31.

　　1959. Homo-eroticism in primitive society as a function of the self. *Journal of Analytical Psychology* 4: 101–115.

Lebra, Takie Sugiyama. 1971. The social mechanism of guilt and shame: The Japanese case. *Anthropological Quarterly* 44: 241–255.

　　1983. Shame and guilt: A psychosexual view of the Japanese self. *Ethos* 11: 192–209.

Leff, Julian. 1981. *Psychiatry around the globe: A transcultural view*. New York: Dekker.

Lehmann, Heinz E. 1985. Unusual psychiatric disorders, atypical psychoses, and brief reactive psychoses. In *Comprehensive textbook of psychiatry/IV.*, 4th edn, ed. H.I. Kaplan and B.J. Sadock, 1224–1238. Baltimore: Williams & Wilkins.

Lemaire, Anika. 1977. *Jacques Lacan*. Trans. D. Macey. London: Routledge & Kegan Paul.

Lepowsky, Maria. 1983. Sudest Island and the Louisiade Archipelago in Massim exchange. In *The kula: New perspectives on Massim exchange*, ed. J.W. Leach and E. Leach, 467–501. Cambridge: Cambridge University Press.

Lerner, Yakov. 1980. The subjective experience of mania. In *Mania: An evolving concept*, ed. R.H. Belmaker and H.M. van Praag, 77–88. Jamaica, N.Y.: Spectrum.

Lesser, Ira M. 1981. A review of the alexithymia concept. *Psychosomatic Medicine* 43: 531–543.

LeVine, Robert A. 1982. The self and its development in an African society: A preliminary analysis. In *Psychosocial theories of the self*, ed. B. Lee and K. Smith, 43–65. New York: Plenum Press.

　　1990. Infant environments in psychoanalysis: A cross-cultural view. In *Cultural psychology: Essays on comparative human development*, ed. J.W. Stigler, R.A. Shweder and G. Herdt, 454–474. Cambridge: Cambridge University Press.

Levy, Robert Isaac. 1973. *Tahitians: Mind and experience in the Society Islands*. Chicago: University of Chicago Press.

Lewis, Helen B. 1971. *Shame and guilt in neurosis*. New York: International Universities Press.

　　1986. The role of shame in depression. In *Depression in young people: Developmental and clinical perspectives*, ed. M. Rutter, C.E. Izard and P.B. Read, 325–339. New York: Guilford Press.

Lewis, I.M. 1971. *Ecstatic religion: An anthropological study of spirit possession and shamanism*. Harmondsworth, England: Penguin Books.

Lichtenberg, Joseph D. 1989. *Psychoanalysis and motivation*. Hillsdale, N.J.: Analytic Press.

Lidz, Theodore and Ruth W. Lidz. 1984. Oedipus in the stone age. *Journal of American Psychoanalytic Association* 32: 507–527.

1986. Turning women things into men: Masculinization in Papua New Guinea. *Psychoanalytic Review* 73: 521–539.

Liebowitz, Michael R. 1983. *The chemistry of love*. Boston: Little.

Liem, Joan Huser. 1980. Family studies of schizophrenia: An update and commentary. *Schizophrenia Bulletin* 6: 429–455.

Lifton, Robert Jay. 1986. *The Nazi doctors: Medical killing and the psychology of genocide*. New York: Basic.

1993. *The protean self: Human resilience in an age of fragmentation*. New York: Basic.

Lindenbaum, Shirley. 1984. Variations on a sociosexual theme in Melanesia. In *Ritualized homosexuality in Melanesia*, ed. G.H. Herdt, 337–361. Berkeley: University of California Press.

Lindholm, Charles. 1988. Lovers and leaders: A comparison of social and psychological models of romance and charisma. *Social Science Information* 27: 3–45.

1990. *Charisma*. Oxford: Basil Blackwell.

Lipset, David M. n.d. Mangrove man: The embodiment of society in the Sepik estuary. Department of Anthropology, University of Minnesota. Typescript.

Loewenberg, Peter. 1971. The psychohistorical origins of the Nazi youth cohort. *American Historical Review* 76: 1457–1502.

Loewenstein, Richard J. 1990. Somatoform disorders in victims of incest and child abuse. In *Incest-related syndromes of adult psychopathology*, ed. R.P. Kluft, 75–111. Washington, D.C.: American Psychiatric Press.

Lothane, Zvi. 1987. Love, seduction, and trauma. *Psychoanalytic Review* 74: 83–105.

Lotto, David. 1994. On witches and witch hunts: Ritual and satanic cult abuse. *Journal of Psychohistory* 21: 373–396.

Lovejoy, C. Owen. 1981. The origin of man. *Science* 211: 341–350.

Ludolph, Pamela S., Drew Westen, Barbara Misle, Anne Jackson. Jean Wixom, and F. Charles Wiss. 1990. The borderline diagnosis in adolescents: Symptoms and developmental history. *American Journal of Psychiatry* 147: 470–476.

Ludwig, Arnold M. 1972. Hysteria: A neurobiological theory. *Archives of General Psychology* 27: 771–777.

Luhrmann, T.M. 1989. The magic of secrecy. *Ethos* 17: 131–165.

Lukoff, David, Karen Snyder, Joseph Ventura, and Keith H. Nuechterlein. 1984. Life events, familial stress, and coping in the developmental course of schizophrenia. *Schizophrenia Bulletin* 10: 258–292.

Lutz, Catherine and Geoffrey M. White. 1986. The anthropology of emotions. *Annual Reviews in Anthropology* 15: 405–436.

MacCurdy, J.T. 1925. *The psychology of emotion, morbid and normal*. London: K. Paul, Trench, Trubner.

MacLean, Paul D. 1990. *The triune brain in evolution: Role in paleocerebral functions*. New York: Plenum Press.

MacMillan, Malcolm. 1991. *Freud evaluated: The completed arc*. Amsterdam: Elsevier.

Maeder, A. 1912. Über die Funktion des Traumes. *Jahrbuch für psychoanalytische und psychopathologische Forschungen* 4: 692–707.

Mahler, Margaret, Fred Pine, and Anni Bergman. 1975. *Psychological birth of the human infant: Symbiosis and individuation*. New York: Basic.

Mahoney, Maureen A. and Barbara Yngvesson. 1992. The construction of subjectivity and the paradox of resistance: Reintegrating feminist anthropology and psychology. *Signs* 18: 44–73.

Malinowski, Bronislaw. [1922]1961. *Argonauts of the western Pacific: An account of native enterprise and adventure in the archipelagoes of Melanesian New Guinea*. New York: Dutton.

1927. *Sex and repression in savage society*. New York: HarBrace.

Manson, Spero M., James H. Shore, and Joseph D. Bloom. 1985. The depressive experience in American Indian communities: A challenge for psychiatric theory and diagnosis. In *Culture and depression: Studies in the anthropology and cross-cultural psychiatry of affect and disorder*, ed. A. Kleinman and B. Good, 331–368. Berkeley: University of California Press.

Maranhão, Tullio. 1986. *Therapeutic discourse and Socratic dialogue*. Madison: University of Wisconsin Press.

Marks, Jon. 1987. Cytogenetic methods: Social and ecological aspects of primate cytogenetics. In *The evolution of behavior: Primate models*, ed. W.G. Kinzey, 139–150. Albany, N.Y.: State University of New York Press.

Markus, Hazel and Paula Nurius. 1986. Possible selves. *American Psychologist* 41: 954–969.

Marmer, Stephen S. 1991. Multiple personality disorder: A psychoanalytic perspective. *Psychiatric Clinics of North America* 14: 677–693.

Marriott, McKim. 1968. The feast of love. In *Krishna: Myths, rites, and attitudes*, ed. M. Singer, 200–213. Chicago: University of Chicago Press.

Marsella, Anthony J., Norman Sartorius, Assen Jablensky, and Fred R. Fenton. 1985. Cross-cultural studies of depressive disorders: An overview. In *Culture and depression: Studies in the anthropology and cross-cultural psychiatry of affect and disorder*, ed. A. Kleinman and B. Good, 299–324. Berkeley: University of California Press.

Marsh, Peter E. and Peter Collett. 1987. *Driving passion: The psychology of the car*. Boston: Faber & Faber.

Maslow, A.H., H. Rand, and S. Newman. 1960. Some parallels between sexual and dominance behavior of infra-human primates and the fantasies of patients in psychotherapy. *Journal of Nervous and Mental Disease* 131: 202–212.

Mathews, Holly F. 1992. The directive force of morality tales in a Mexican community. In *Human motives and cultural models*, ed. R.G. D'Andrade and C. Strauss, 127–162. Cambridge: Cambridge University Press.

Mauss, Marcel. [1938]1985. A category of the human mind: The notion of person; the notion of self. In *The category of the person: Anthropology, philosophy, history*, ed. M. Carrithers, S. Collins and S. Lukes, 1–25. Cambridge: Cambridge University Press.

Mazrui, Ali A. 1974. Phallic symbols in politics and war: An African perspective. *Journal of African Studies* 1: 40–69.

Mazur, Allan. 1976. Effects of testosterone on status in primate groups. *Folia primatologia* 26: 214–226.

McDougall, Lorna. 1975. The quest of the argonauts. In *Psychological anthropology*, ed. T.R. Williams, 59–101. The Hague: Mouton.

McEvedy, Colin P., Alwyn Griffith, and Thomas Hall. 1966. Two school epidemics. *British Medical Journal* (ii): 1300–1302.

Mead, George Herbert. 1934. *Mind, self & society from the standpoint of a social behaviorist*. Ed. C.W. Morris. Chicago: University of Chicago Press.

Mead, Margaret. 1928. *Coming of age in Samoa*. New York: W. Morrow.

Meeker, Michael E. 1990. Natural objects and substitutive acts: The symbolic process in the anthropologies of Durkheim and Freud. In *Personality and the cultural construction of society: Papers in honor of Melford E. Spiro*, ed. D.K. Jordan and M.J. Swartz, 60–79. Tuscaloosa: University of Alabama Press.

Meeker, Michael E., Kathleen Barlow, and David M. Lipset. 1986. Culture, exchange, and gender: Lessons from the Murik. *Cultural Anthropology* 1: 6–73.

Meggitt, M.J. 1964. Male–female relationships in the highlands of Australian New Guinea. *American Anthropologist* 66: 204–224.

1977. *Blood is their argument: Warfare among the Mae Enga tribesmen of the New Guinea Highlands*. Palo Alto, Calif.: Mayfield Publishing.

Merkl, Peter H. 1975. *Political violence under the swastika: 581 early Nazis*. Princeton, N.J.: Princeton University Press.

Merrill, William. 1992. The Rarámuri stereotype of dreams. In *Dreaming: Anthropological and psychological interpretations*, ed. B. Tedlock, 194–219. Santa Fe, New Mexico: School of American Research Press.

Miller, Joan G. 1994. Cultural psychology: Bridging disciplinary boundaries in understanding the cultural grounding of self. In *Psychological anthropology*, ed. P.K. Bock, 139–170. Westport, Con.: Praeger Publishers.

Miller, Peggy J. and Barbara Byhouwer Moore. 1989. Narrative conjunctions of caregiver and child: A comparative perspective on socialization through stories. *Ethos* 17: 428–449.

Millon, Theodore. 1981. *Disorders of personality: DSM-III, Axis II*. New York: Wiley.

Mischel, Walter, Yuichi Shoda, and Monica L. Rodriguez. 1989. Delay of gratification in children. *Science* 244: 933–938.

Modell, Arnold H. 1971. The origin of certain forms of pre-oedipal guilt and the implications for a psychoanalytic theory of affects. *International Journal of Psycho-Analysis* 52: 337–346.

1990. *Other times, other realities: Toward a theory of psychoanalytic treatment*. Cambridge, Mass.: Harvard University Press.

1993. *The private self*. Cambridge, Mass.: Harvard University Press.

Moir, Anne and David Jessel. 1989. *Brain sex: The real difference between men and women*. New York: Dell, Doubleday.

Money, John. 1988. *Gay, straight, and in-between: The sexology of erotic orientation*. New York: Oxford University Press.

Money, John and Anke A. Ehrhardt. 1972. *Man & woman, boy & girl: The differentiation and dimorphism of gender identity from conception to maturity*. Baltimore: Johns Hopkins University Press.

Money-Kyrle, R.E. [1929]1965. *The meaning of sacrifice.* New York: Johnson Reprint Corporation.

1937. The development of war: A psychological approach. *British Journal of Medical Psychology* 16: 219–236.

Moody, Edward J. 1971. Urban witches. In *Conformity and conflict: Readings in cultural anthropology*, 5th edn, ed. J.P. Spradley and D.W. McCurdy, 328–338. Boston: Little.

Morales Caldwell, Sarah. 1988. Géza Róheim's theory of the dream origin of myth. In *The psychoanalytic study of society*, vol. XIII, ed. L.B. Boyer and S.A. Grolnick, 7–28. Hillsdale, N.J.: Analytic Press.

Moran, Frances M. 1993. *Subject and agency in psychoanalysis: Which is to be master?* New York: New York University Press.

Moss, Peter D. and Colin P. McEvedy. 1966. An epidemic of overbreathing among schoolgirls. *British Medical Journal* (ii): 1295–1300.

Munroe, Robert L., Ruth H. Munroe, and John W.M. Whiting. 1973. The couvade: A psychological analysis. *Ethos* 1: 30–74.

Munroe, Ruth H. and Robert L. Munroe. 1980. Infants' experience and childhood affect among the Logoli: A longitudinal study. *Ethos* 8: 295–315.

Murphy, H.B.M. 1976. Notes for a theory on *latah*. In *Culture-bound syndromes, ethnopsychiatry, and alternate therapies*, ed. W.P. Lebra, 3–21. Honolulu: East–West Center, University Press of Hawaii.

1983. Commentary on "The resolution of the latah paradox." *Journal of Nervous and Mental Disease* 171: 176–177.

Murphy, H.B.M. and A.C. Raman. 1971. The chronicity of schizophrenia in indigenous tropical peoples: Results of a twelve-year follow-up survey in Mauritius. *British Journal of Psychiatry* 118: 489–497.

Murphy, H.B.M. and B.M. Taumoepeau. 1980. Traditionalism and mental health in the South Pacific: A re-examination of an old hypothesis. *Psychological Medicine* 10: 471–482.

Murphy, Jane M. 1976. Psychiatric labeling in cross-cultural perspective. *Science* 191 (12 March): 1019–1028.

Murray, D.W. 1993. What is the western concept of the self? On forgetting David Hume. *Ethos* 21: 3–23.

Murray, Henry A. 1955. American Icarus. In *Clinical studies of personality*, vol. II, ed. A. Burton and R.E. Harris, 615–641. New York: Harper & Row.

Myerhoff, Barbara G. 1974. *Peyote hunt: The sacred journey of the Huichol Indians.* Ithaca: Cornell University Press.

Nachman, Patricia A. 1991. Contemporary infant research and the separation–individuation theory of Margaret S. Mahler. In *Beyond the symbiotic orbit: Advances in separation–individuation theory*, ed. S. Akhtar and H. Parens, 121–149. Hillsdale, N.J.: Analytic Press.

Nachman, Steven R. 1984. Shame and moral aggression on a Melanesian atoll. *Journal of Psychoanalytic Anthropology* 7: 335–365.

Nader, Laura. 1986. The drift to war. In *Peace and war: Cross-cultural perspectives*, ed. M.L. Foster and R.A. Rubinstein, 185–192. New Brunswick, N.J.: Transaction.

Nathanson, Donald L. 1992. *Shame and pride: Affect, sex, and the birth of the self.* New York: Norton.

Newman, Philip L. 1964. "Wild man" behavior in a New Guinea Highlands community. *American Anthropologist* 66: 1–19.

Newton, Niles. 1973. Interrelationships between sexual responsiveness, birth, and breast feeding. In *Contemporary sexual behavior: Critical issues in the 1970s*, ed. J. Zubin and J. Money, 77–98. Baltimore: Johns Hopkins University Press.

Niederland, William G. 1959a. Schreber: Father and son. *Psychoanalytic Quarterly* 28: 151–169.

1959b. The "Miracled-up" world of Schreber's childhood. *Psychoanalytic Study of the Child* 14: 383–413.

1974. *The Schreber case: The psychoanalytic profile of a paranoid personality.* New York: Quadrangle Res, New York Times Book Co.

Ni Nuallain, Mairin, Aileen O'Hare, and Dermot Walsh. 1987. Incidence of schizophrenia in Ireland. *Psychological Medicine* 17: 943–948.

Noll, Richard. 1983. Shamanism and schizophrenia: A state-specific approach to the "schizophrenia metaphor" of shamanic states. *American Ethnologist* 10: 443–459.

1985. Mental imagery cultivation as a cultural phenomenon: The role of visions in shamanism. *Current Anthropology* 26: 443–461.

Nuckolls, Charles W. 1992. Toward a culture history of the personality disorders. *Social Science and Medicine* 35: 37–47.

Obeyesekere, Gananath. 1981. *Medusa's hair: An essay on personal symbols and religious experience.* Chicago: University of Chicago Press.

1985. Depression, Buddhism, and the work of culture in Sri Lanka. In *Culture and depression: Studies in the anthropology and cross-cultural psychiatry of affect and disorder*, ed. A.. Kleinman and B. Good, 134–152. Berkeley: University of California Press.

1990. *The work of culture: Symbolic transformation in psychoanalysis and anthropology.* Chicago: University of Chicago Press.

O'Connor, Noreen and Joanna Ryan. 1994. "Truth" and "reality": Joyce McDougall and gender identity. *Free Associations* 4: 338–368.

O'Flaherty, Wendy Doniger. 1973. *Asceticism and eroticism in the mythology of Siva.* Delhi: Oxford University Press.

1984. *Dreams, illusion, and other realities.* Chicago: University of Chicago Press.

Olczak, Paul V., Edward Donnerstein, Thomas J. Hershberger, and Irwin Kahn. 1971. Group hysteria and the MMPI. *Psychological Reports* 28: 413–414.

Olweus, Dan, Ake Mattsson, Daisy Schalling, and Hans Löw. 1980. Testosterone, aggression, physical, and personality dimensions in normal adolescent males. *Psychosomatic Medicine* 42: 253–269.

O'Nell, Carl W. and Henry A. Selby. 1968. Sex differences in the incidence of susto in two Zapotec pueblos: An analysis of the relationships between sex role expectations and a folk illness. *Ethnology* 7: 95–111.

Ong, Aihwa. 1987. *Spirits of resistance and capitalist discipline: Factory women in Malaysia.* Albany: State University of New York Press.

Opler, Marvin K. 1957. Schizophrenia and culture. *Scientific American* 97: 103–110.

1959. Cultural perspectives in research on schizophrenias: A history with examples. *Psychiatric Quarterly* 33: 506–524.

Opler, Marvin K. and Jerome L. Singer. 1956. Ethnic differences in behavior and psychopathology in the Italian and Irish. *International Journal of Social Psychiatry* 2: 11–23.

Oring, Elliott. 1993. Victor Turner, Sigmund Freud, and the return of the repressed. *Ethos* 21: 273–294.

Ottenberg, Simon. 1988. Oedipus, gender and social solidarity: A case study of male childhood and initiation. *Ethos* 16: 326–352.

Otto, Rudolf. 1925. *The idea of the holy: An inquiry into the non-rational factor in the idea of the divine and its relation to the rational.* Trans. J.W. Harvey. London: Milford; Oxford University Press.

Paige, Karen Ericksen and Jeffery M. Paige. 1981. *The politics of reproductive ritual.* Berkeley: University of California Press.

Paley, Ann-Marie N. 1988. Growing up in chaos: The dissociative response. *American Journal of Psychoanalysis* 48: 72–83.

Parsons, Anne. 1964. Is the Oedipus complex universal? The Jones–Malinowski debate revisited and a south Italian "nuclear complex." In *The psychoanalytic study of society*, vol. III, ed. W. Muensterberger and S. Axelrad, 278–328. New York: International Universities Press.

Paul, Robert A. 1982. *The Tibetan symbolic world: Psychoanalytic explorations.* Chicago: University of Chicago Press.

    1985. Freud and the seduction theory: A critical examination of Masson's The Assault on Truth. *Journal of Psychoanalytic Anthropology* 8: 161–187.

    1987. The question of applied psychoanalysis and the interpretation of cultural symbolism. *Ethos* 15: 82–103.

    1989. Psychoanalytic anthropology. *Annual Review of Anthropology* 18: 177–202.

    1990. What does anybody want? Desire, purpose, and the acting subject in the study of culture. *Cultural Anthropology* 5: 431–451.

    1991. Freud's anthropology: A reading of the "cultural books." In *The Cambridge companion to Freud*, ed. J. Neu, 267–286. Cambridge: Cambridge University Press.

Peacock, James L. and Dorothy C. Holland. 1993. The narrated self: Life stories in process. *Ethos* 21: 367–383.

Person, Ethel S. 1988. *Dreams of love and fateful encounters: The power of romantic passion.* New York: Norton.

Person, Ethel S. and Lionel Ovesey. 1983. Psychoanalytic theories of gender identity. *Journal of the American Academy of Psychoanalysis* 11: 203–226.

Peters, Larry G. 1982. Trance, initiation, and psychotherapy in Tamang shamanism. *American Ethnologist* 9: 21–46.

    1988. Borderline personality disorder and the possession syndrome: An ethnopsychoanalytic perspective. *Transcultural Psychiatric Research Review* 25: 5–46.

Peters, Larry G. and Douglass Price-Williams. 1980. Towards an experiential analysis of shamanism. *American Ethnologist* 7: 397–413.

Piers, Gerhart and Milton B. Singer. 1953. *Shame and guilt: A psychoanalytic and a cultural study.* Springfield, Ill.: Charles C. Thomas.

Pine, Fred. 1990. *Drive, ego, object, and self: A synthesis for clinical work.* New York: Basic.

Poole, Fitz John Porter. 1982a. Couvade and clinic in a New Guinea society: Birth among the Bimin-Kuskusmin. In *The use and abuse of medicine*, ed. M.W. de Vries, R.L. Berg, and M. Lipkin, Jr., 54–95. New York: Praeger Publishers.

1982b. The ritual forging of identity: Aspects of person and self in Bimin-Kuskusmin male initiation. In *Rituals of manhood: Male initiation in Papua New Guinea*, ed. G.H. Herdt and R.M. Keesing, 99–154. Berkeley: University of California Press.

1987. Personal experience and cultural representation in children's "personal symbols" among Bimin-Kuskusmin. *Ethos* 15: 104–135.

1991. Cultural schemas and experiences of the self among the Bimin-Kuskusmin of Papua New Guinea. In *The psychoanalytic study of society*, vol. XVI, ed. L.B. Boyer and R.M. Boyer, 55–85. Hillsdale, N.J.: Analytic Press.

Post, Robert M. 1980. Biochemical theories of mania. In *Mania: An evolving concept*, ed. R.H. Belmaker and H.M. van Praag, 217–265. Jamaica, N.Y.: Spectrum.

Proskauer, Stephen. 1980. Oedipal equivalents in a clan culture: Reflections on Navajo ways. *Psychiatry* 43: 43–50.

Quinn, Naomi. 1991. The cultural basis of metaphor. In *Beyond metaphor: The theory of tropes in anthropology*, ed. J.W. Fernandez, 56–93. Stanford: Stanford University Press.

1992. The motivational force of self-understanding: Evidence from wives' inner conflicts. In *Human motives and cultural models*, ed. R.G. D'Andrade and C. Strauss, 90–126. Cambridge: Cambridge University Press.

Rabinbach, Anson and Jessica Benjamin. 1989. Foreword to *Male fantasies. Vol II: Male bodies: Psychoanalyzing the white terror*, by Klaus Theweleit. 2 vols. Minneapolis: University of Minnesota Press.

Raheja, Gloria Goodwin and Ann Grodzins Gold. 1994. *Listen to the Heron's words: Reimagining gender and kinship in North India*. Berkeley: University of California Press.

Ramanujan, A.K. 1984. The Indian Oedipus. In *Oedipus: A folklore casebook*, ed. L. Edmunds and A. Dundes, 234–261. New York: Garland.

1991. Toward a counter-system: Women's tales. In *Gender, genre, and power in South Asian expressive traditions*, ed. A.. Appadurai, F.J. Korom and M.A. Mills, 33–55. Philadelphia: University of Pennsylvania Press.

Rancour-Laferriere, Daniel. 1985. *Signs of the flesh: An essay on the evolution of hominid sexuality*. New York: Mouton.

Redmond, D.E., Jr. 1979. New and old evidence for the involvement of a brain nor-epinephrine system in anxiety. In *Phenomenology and treatment of anxiety*, ed. W.E. Fann, I. Karacan, and A.D. Porkorny, 153–203. Jamaica, N.Y.: Spectrum.

Reid, Barbara V. 1990. Weighing up the factors: Moral reasoning and culture change in a Samoan community. *Ethos* 18: 48–70.

Reik, Theodor. 1931. *Ritual: Psycho-analytic studies*. London: Hogarth and Institute of Psycho-Analysis.

[1941]1962. *Masochism in sex and society*. Trans. M.H. Beigel and G.M. Kurth. New York: Grove.

Reiser, Morton F. 1984. *Mind, brain, body: Toward a convergence of psychoanalysis and neurobiology*. New York: Basic.

1990. *Memory in mind and brain: What dream imagery reveals*. New York: Basic.

Reynolds, Gavin P. 1992. The amygdala and the neurochemistry of schizophrenia.

In *The amygdala: Neurobiological aspects of emotion, memory, and mental dysfunction*, ed. J.P. Aggleton, 561–574. New York: Wiley-Liss, Wiley.

Reynolds, Peter C. 1976. Play, language and human evolution. In *Play – its role in development and evolution*, ed. J.S. Bruner, A. Jolly and K. Sylva, 621–635. New York: Basic.

Richardson, J. Steven. 1973. The amygdala: Historical and functional analysis. *Acta Neurobiolgiae Experimentalis* 33: 623–648.

Riesman, David with Reuel Denney and Nathan Glazer. [1950]1962. *The lonely crowd: A study of the changing American character*. New Haven: Yale University Press.

Riesman, Paul. 1983. On the irrelevance of child-rearing practices for the formation of personality. *Culture, Medicine and Psychiatry* 7: 103–129.

Rivers, W.H.R. 1923. *Conflict and dream*. London: K. Paul, Trench, Trubner.

Rizzuto, Ana-Maria. 1979. *The birth of the living god: A psychoanalytic study*. Chicago: University of Chicago Press.

Robbins, Trevor W. 1990. The case for frontostriatal dysfunction in schizophrenia. *Schizophrenia Bulletin* 16: 391–402.

Rochlin, Gregory. 1953. Loss and restitution. *Psychoanalytic Study of the Child* 8: 288–309.

——— 1973. *Man's aggression: The defense of the self*. Boston: Gambit.

Roffenstein, Gaston. [1924]1951. Experiments on symbolization in dreams. In *Organization and pathology of thought: Selected sources*, ed. D. Rapaport, 249–256. New York: Columbia University Press.

Róheim, Géza. [1930]1972. *Animism, magic, and the divine king*. New York: International Universities Press.

——— 1943. *The origin and function of culture*. New York: Nervous and Mental Disease Monographs.

——— 1945a. *War, crime and the covenant*. Monticello, N.Y.: Medical Journal Press.

——— 1945b. *The eternal ones of the dream: A psychoanalytic interpretation of Australian myth and ritual*. New York: International Universities Press.

——— 1950. *Psychoanalysis and anthropology: Culture, personality and the unconscious*. New York: International Universities Press.

——— 1952. *The gates of the dream*. New York: International Universities Press.

Rohner, Ronald P. 1975. *They love me, they love me not: A worldwide study of the effects of parental acceptance and rejection*. New Haven: HRAF Press.

——— 1986. *The warmth dimension: Foundations of parental acceptance-rejection theory*. Beverly Hills: Sage.

Roiphe, Herman and Eleanor Galenson. 1981. *Infantile origins of sexual identity*. New York: International Universities Press.

Roland, Alan. 1988. *In search of self in India and Japan: Toward a cross-cultural psychology*. Princeton, N.J.: Princeton University Press.

Rosaldo, Michelle Z. 1980. *Knowledge and passion: Ilongot notions of self and social life*. Cambridge: Cambridge University Press.

——— 1983. The shame of headhunters and the autonomy of self. *Ethos* 11: 135–151.

——— 1984. Toward an anthropology of self and feeling. In *Culture theory: Essays on mind, self, and emotion*, ed. R.A. Shweder and R.A. LeVine, 137–157. Cambridge: Cambridge University Press.

Rosaldo, Renato. 1980. *Ilongot headhunting, 1883–1974: A study in society and history*. Stanford: Stanford University Press.

1984. Grief and a headhunter's rage: On the cultural force of emotions. In *Text, play, and story: The construction and reconstruction of self and society*, ed. E.M. Bruner, 178–195. Prospect Heights, Ill.: Waveland.

1986. Red hornbill earrings: Ilongot ideas of self, beauty, and health. *Cultural Anthropology* 1: 310–316.

1993. *Culture & truth: The remaking of social analysis*. Boston: Beacon Press.

Roseman, Marina. 1990. Head, heart, ordor, and shadow: The structure of the self, the emotional world, and ritual performance among Senoi Temiar. *Ethos* 18: 227–250.

Rosen, Leora N. 1988. Male adolescent initiation rituals: Whiting's hypothesis revisited. In *Psychoanalytic study of society*, vol. XII, ed. L.B. Boyer and S.A. Grolnick, 131–155. Hillsdale, N.J.: Analytic Press.

Rosenbaum, Bent and Harly Sonne. 1986. *The language of psychosis*. New York: New York University Press.

Rosenberger, Nancy R. 1989. Dialectic balance in the polar model of the self: The Japan case. *Ethos* 17: 88–113.

Rothstein, Arnold. 1984. *The narcissistic pursuit of perfection*. 2nd rev. edn. New York: International Universities Press.

Roy, Manisha. 1975a. *Bengali women*. Chicago: University of Chicago Press.

1975b. The Oedipus complex and the Bengali family in India (a study of father–daughter relations in Bengal). In *Psychological anthropology*, ed. T.R. Williams, 123–134. The Hague: Mouton.

Rozin, Paul and Carol Nemeroff. 1990. The laws of sympathetic magic: A psychological analysis of similarity and contagion. In *Cultural psychology: Essays on comparative human development*, ed. J.W. Stigler, R.A. Shweder and G. Herdt, 205–232. Cambridge: Cambridge University Press.

Rubel, Arthur J., Carl W. O'Nell, and Rolando Collado-Ardón. 1984. *Susto, a folk illness*. Berkeley: University of California Press.

Rubel, Arthur J. and Joseph Spielberg. 1966. Aspects of couvade in Texas and Northeast Mexico. In *Summa anthropologica: en homenaje a Roberto J. Weitlaner*, 299–307. Mexico City: Instituto Nacional de Antropología e Historia, Secretaria de Educación Publica.

Rubin, Robert T. 1982. Koro (shook yang): A culture-bound psychogenic syndrome. In *Extraordinary disorders of human behavior*, ed. C.T.H. Friedmann and R.A. Faguet, 155–172. New York: Plenum Press.

Russell, Elbert W. 1972. Factors of human aggression: A cross-cultural factor analysis of characteristics related to warfare and crime. *Behavior Science Notes* 7: 275–312.

Russell, John C. 1984. Family experience and folk Catholicism in rural Ireland. *Journal of Psychoanalytic Anthropology* 7: 141–170.

Sacks, Oliver. 1970. *The man who mistook his wife for a hat, and other clinical tales*. New York: Simon & Schuster.

[1973]1983. *Awakenings*. New York: Dutton.

Salzman, Leon. 1968. *The obsessive personality: Origins, dynamics, and therapy*. New York: Science House.

Sampson, Edward E. 1989. The deconstruction of the self. In *Texts of identity*, ed. J. Shotter and K.J. Gergen, 1–19. Newbury Park, Calif.: Sage.

Sanday, Peggy R. 1974. Female status in the public domain. In *Woman, culture, and society*, ed. M.Z. Rosaldo and L. Lamphere, 189–206. Stanford: Stanford University Press.

Sandler, Joseph. [1960]1987. The background of safety. In *From safety to superego: Selected papers of Joseph Sandler*, 1–8. New York: Guilford Press.

Sandler, Joseph, Alex Holder, and Dale Meers. [1963]1987. Ego ideal and ideal self. In *From safety to superego: Selected papers of Joseph Sandler*, ed. J. Sandler, 73–89. New York: Guilford Press.

Sandler, Joseph and Bernard Rosenblatt. [1962]1987. The representational world. In *From safety to superego: Selected papers of Joseph Sandler*, ed. J. Sandler, 58–72. New York: Guilford Press.

Sapir, Edward. [1939]1963. Psychiatric and cultural pitfalls in the business of getting a living. In *Selected writings of Edward Sapir in language, culture and personality*, ed. D.G. Mandelbaum, 578–589. Berkeley: University of California Press.

Sarbin, Theodore R. 1986. The narrative as a root metaphor for psychology. In *Narrative psychology: The storied nature of human conduct*, ed. T.R. Sarbin, 3–21. New York: Praeger Publishers.

Sarbin, Theodore R. and William C. Coe. 1972. *Hypnosis: A social psychological analysis of influence communication*. New York: Holt, Rinehart & Winston.

Sartorius, N.A., A. Jablensky, A. Korten, G. Ernberg, M. Anker, J.E. Cooper, and R. Day. 1986. Early manifestations and first-contact incidence of schizophrenia in different cultures: A preliminary report on the initial evaluation phase of the WHO Collaborative Study on Determinants of Outcome of Severe Mental Disorders. *Psychological Medicine* 16: 909–928.

Sartorius, Norman, Assen Jablensky, and Robert Shapiro. 1978. Cross-cultural differences in the short-term prognosis of schizophrenic psychoses. *Schizophrenia Bulletin* 4: 102–113.

Sass, Louis A. 1992. *Madness and modernism: Insanity in the light of modern art, literature, and thought*. New York: Basic.

Savage-Rumbaugh, E. Sue and Beverly J. Wilkerson. 1978. Socio-sexual behavior in *Pan paniscus* and *Pan troglodytes*: A comparative study. *Journal of Human Evolution* 7: 327–344.

Schafer, Roy. 1978. *Language and insight*. New Haven: Yale University Press.

Schapera, Isaac. 1930. *The Khoisan peoples of South Africa: Bushmen and Hottentots*. London: Routledge.

Schatzman, Morton. 1973. *Soul murder: Persecution in the family*. New York: Random.

Scheflen, Albert E. 1981. *Levels of schizophrenia*. New York: Bruner/Mazel.

Scheper-Hughes, Nancy. 1979. *Saints, scholars, and schizophrenics: Mental illness in rural Ireland*. Berkeley: University of California Press.

1985. Culture, scarcity, and maternal thinking: Maternal detachment and infant survival in a Brazilian shantytown. *Ethos* 13: 291–317.

1987. "Mental" in "Southie": Individual, family, and community responses to psychosis in South Boston. *Culture, Medicine and Psychiatry* 11: 53–78.

Schieffelin, Bambi B. 1990. *The give and take of everyday life: Language socialization of Kaluli children.* Cambridge: Cambridge University Press.

Schieffelin, Edward L. 1985. The cultural analysis of depressive affect: An example from New Guinea. In *Culture and depression: Studies in the anthropology and cross-cultural psychiatry of affect and disorder,* ed. A. Kleinman and B. Good, 101–133. Berkeley: University of California Press.

Schiffer, Irvine. 1962. The psycho-analytic study of the development of a conversion symptom. *International Journal of Psycho-Analysis* 43: 169–174.

1973. *Charisma: A psychoanalytic look at mass society.* Toronto: University of Toronto Press.

Schilder, Paul. 1950. *The image and appearance of the human body: Studies in the constructive energies of the psyche.* New York: International Universities Press.

Schlegel, Alice and Herbert Barry, III. 1979. Adolescent initiation ceremonies: A cross-cultural code. *Ethnology* 18: 199–210.

1980. The evolutionary significance of adolescent initiation ceremonies. *American Ethnologist* 7: 696–715.

Schooler, Carmi and William Caudill. 1964. Symptomatology in Japanese and American schizophrenics. *Ethnology* 3: 172–178.

Schwalbe, Michael L. 1991. The autogenesis of the self. *Journal of the Theory of Social Behaviour* 21: 269–295.

Schwartz, Theodore. 1973. Cult and context: The paranoid ethos in Melanesia. *Ethos* 1: 153–174.

1976. The cargo cult: A Melanesian type-response to change. In *Responses to change: Society, culture, and personality,* ed. G.A. De Vos, 157–206. New York: D. Van Nostrand.

Scott, James C. 1990. *Domination and the arts of resistance: Hidden transcripts.* New Haven: Yale University Press.

Segal, Hanna. 1991. *Dream, phantasy, and art.* London: Tavistock, Routledge.

Seligman, C.G. 1934. *Egypt and negro Africa: A study in divine kingship.* London: G. Routledge & Sons.

Shapiro, David. 1965. *Neurotic styles.* New York: Basic.

Shengold, Leonard. 1988. *Halo in the sky: Observations on anality and defense.* New York: Guilford Press.

1989. *Soul murder: The effects of childhood abuse and deprivation.* New Haven: Yale University Press.

Shweder, Richard A. 1979a. Rethinking culture and personality theory. Part I: A critical examination of two classical postulates. *Ethos* 7: 255–278.

1979b. Rethinking culture and personality theory. Part II: A critical examination of two more classical postulates. *Ethos* 7: 279–311.

1980. Rethinking culture and personality theory. Part III: From genesis and typology to hermeneutics and dynamics. *Ethos* 8: 60–94.

1985. Menstrual pollution, soul loss, and the comparative study of emotions. In *Culture and depression: Studies in the anthropology and cross-cultural psychiatry of affect and disorder,* ed. A. Kleinman and B. Good, 182–215. Berkeley: University of California Press.

1991. *Thinking through cultures: Expeditions in cultural psychology.* Cambridge, Mass.: Harvard University Press.

Shweder, Richard A. and Edmund J. Bourne. [1982]1991. Does the concept of the person vary cross-culturally? In *Thinking through cultures: Expeditions in cultural psychology*, 113–155. Cambridge, Mass.: Harvard University Press.

Shweder, Richard A., Manamohan Mahapatra, and Joan G. Miller. 1990. Culture and moral development. In *Cultural psychology: Essays on comparative human development*, ed. J.W. Stigler, R.A. Shweder, and G. Herdt, 130–204. Cambridge, Mass.: Cambridge University Press.

Shweder, Richard A. and Nancy C. Much. 1991. Determinations of meaning: Discourse and moral socialization. In *Thinking through cultures: Expeditions in cultural psychology*, 186–240. Cambridge, Mass.: Harvard University Press.

Sibley, Charles G. and Jon E. Ahlquist. 1984. The phylogeny of the hominoid primates, as indicated by DNA–DNA hybridization. *Journal of Molecular Evolution* 20: 2–15.

Siever, Larry J. and Kenneth L. Davis. 1985. Overview: Toward a dysregulation hypothesis of depression. *American Journal of Psychiatry* 142: 1017–1031.

Sillitoe, Paul. 1978. Big men and war in New Guinea. *Man* 13: 252–271.

Silverman, Doris K. 1987. Female bonding: Some supportive findings for Melanie Klein's views. *Psychoanalytic Review* 74: 201–215.

Silverman, Julian. 1967. Shamans and acute schizophrenia. *American Anthropologist* 69: 21–31.

Simons, Ronald C. 1980. The resolution of the latah paradox. *Journal of Nervous and Mental Disease* 168: 195–206.

  1983. Latah III – how compelling is the evidence for a psychoanalytic interpretation? A reply to H.B.M. Murphy. *Journal of Nervous and Mental Disease* 171: 178–181.

Singer, Jerome L., ed. 1990. *Repression and dissociation: Implications for personality theory, psychopathology, and health*. Chicago: University of Chicago Press.

Singer, Jerome L. and Marvin K. Opler. 1956. Contrasting patterns of fantasy and motility in Irish and Italian schizophrenics. *Journal of Abnormal and Social Psychology* 53: 42–47.

Singer, Milton B. 1984. *Man's glassy essence: Explorations in semiotic anthropology*. Bloomington: Indiana University Press.

Sirois, François. 1982. Perspectives on epidemic hysteria. In *Mass psychogenic illness: A social psychological analysis*, ed. M.J. Colligan, J.W. Pennebaker, and L.R. Murphy, 217–236. Hillsdale, N.J.: L Erlbaum Associates.

Siskind, Janet. 1973. Tropical forest hunters and the economy of sex. In *Peoples and cultures of native South America*, ed. D.R. Gross, 226–240. Garden City, N.Y.: Doubleday, Natural History Press.

Slater, Philip E. and Dori A. Slater. 1965. Maternal ambivalence and narcissism: A cross-cultural study. *Merrill-Palmer Quarterly* 11: 241–259.

Small, Gary W. and Jonathan F. Borus. 1983. Outbreak of illness in a school chorus: Toxic poisoning or mass hysteria? *New England Journal of Medicine* 308: 632–635.

Small, Gary W. and Armand M. Nicholi. 1982. Mass hysteria among schoolchildren. *Archives of General Psychiatry* 39: 721–724.

Smith, M. Brewster. 1985. The metaphorical basis of selfhood. In *Culture and self: Asian and western perspectives*, ed. A.J. Marsella, G. De Vos, and F.L.K. Hsu, 56–88. New York: Tavistock.

Smith, Paul. 1988. *Discerning the subject*. Minneapolis: University of Minnesota Press.

Smuts, Barbara B. and David J. Gubernick. 1992. Male–infant relationships in non-human primates: Paternal investment or mating effort? In *Father–child relations: Cultural and biosocial contexts*, ed. B.S. Hewlett, 1–30. New York: Aldine de Gruyter.

Snarey, John R. 1985. Cross-cultural universality of social-moral development: A critical review of Kohlbergian research. *Psychological Bulletin* 97: 202–232.

Snyder, Mark. 1987. *Public appearances/private realities: The psychology of self-monitoring*. New York: W.H. Freeman.

Spain, David H. 1987. The Westermarck–Freud debate: An evaluation and reformulation. *Current Anthropology* 28: 623–645.

1988. Taboo or not taboo: Is that the question? *Ethos* 16: 285–301.

1992. Oedipus Rex or edifice wrecked? Some comments on the universality of oedipality and on the cultural limitations of Freud's thought. In *Psychoanalytic anthropology after Freud: Essays marking the fiftieth anniversary of Freud's death*, ed. D.H. Spain, 198–224. New York: Psyche Press.

Spence, Donald P. 1982. *Narrative truth and historical truth*. New York: Norton.

1987. *The Freudian metaphor: Toward paradigm change in psychoanalysis*. New York: Norton.

Spencer, Baldwin and F.J. Gillen. 1899. *The native tribes of Central Australia*. London: Macmillan.

Sperling, Melitta. 1973. Conversion hysteria and conversion symptoms: A revision of classification and concepts. *Journal of the American Psychoanalytic Association* 21: 745–771.

Spiro, Melford E. 1952. Ghosts, Ifaluk, and teleological functionalism. *American Anthropologist* 54: 497–503.

1965. Religious systems as culturally constituted defense mechanisms. In *Context and meaning in cultural anthropology*, ed. M.E. Spiro, 100–113. New York: Free Press.

1982. *Oedipus in the Trobriands*. Chicago: University of Chicago Press.

1984. Some reflections on cultural determinism and relativism with special reference to emotion and reason. In *Culture theory: Essays on mind, self, and emotion*, ed. R.A. Shweder and R.A. LeVine, 323–346. Cambridge: Cambridge University Press.

1986. Cultural relativism and the future of anthropology. *Cultural Anthropology* 1: 259–286.

1992. Oedipus redux. *Ethos* 20: 358–376.

1993a. Is the western conception of the self "peculiar" within the context of the world cultures? *Ethos* 21: 107–153.

1993b. Tropes, defenses, and unconscious mental representation: Some critical reflections on the "primary process." *Psychoanalysis and Contemporary Thought* 16: 155–196.

Spitz, Ellen Handler. 1991. Reflections on the smile of Dionysus: Theatricality, specularity, and the perverse. In *Perversions and near-perversions in clinical practice: New psychoanalytic perspectives*, ed. G.I. Fogel and W.A. Myers, 207–231. New Haven: Yale University Press.

Spitz, René A. 1945. Hospitalism: An inquiry into the genesis of psychiatric conditions in early childhood. *Psychoanalytic Study of the Child* 1: 53–74.

Spitz, René A. and Katherine M. Wolf. 1946. Anaclitic depression: An inquiry into the genesis of psychiatric conditions in early childhood, II. *Psychoanalytic Study of the Child* 2: 313–342.

Sroufe, L. Alan. 1983. Infant-caregiver attachment and patterns of adaptation in preschool: The roots of maladaptation and competence. In *Minnesota symposium in child psychology*, ed. M. Perlmutter, 41–81. Hillsdale, N.J.: L Erlbaum Associates.

  1985. Attachment classification from the perspective of infant-caregiver relationships and infant temperament. *Child Development* 56: 1–14.

  1986. Appraisal: Bowlby's contribution to psychoanalytic theory and developmental psychology; attachment: separation: loss. *Journal of Child Psychology and Psychiatry* 27: 841–849.

Sroufe, L. Alan, Byron Egeland, and Terri Kreutzer. 1990. The fate of early experience following developmental change: Longitudinal approaches to individual adaptation in childhood. *Child Development* 61: 1363–1373.

Sroufe, L. Alan, Elizabeth Carlson, and Shmuel Shulman. 1993. Individuals in relationships: Development from infancy through adolescence. In *Studying lives through time*, ed. D. Funder, R. Parke, C. Tomlinson-Keesey and K. Widaman, 315–342. Washington, D.C.: American Psychological Association.

Sroufe, L. Alan and Mary J. Ward. 1980. Seductive behavior of mothers of toddlers: Occurrence, correlates, and family origins. *Child Development* 51: 1222–1229.

Steiner, Solomon S. and Steven J. Ellman. 1972. Relation between REM sleep and intracranial self-stimulation. *Science* 177: 1122–1124.

Stepansky, Paul E. 1977. *A history of aggression in Freud.* New York: International Universities Press.

Stephens, William N. 1962. *The Oedipus complex: Cross-cultural evidence.* Glencoe, Ill.: Free Press.

Stern, Daniel N. 1985. *The interpersonal world of the infant: A view from psychoanalysis and developmental psychology.* New York: Basic.

Stevenson, Michael R. and Kathryn N. Black. 1988. Paternal absence and sex-role development: A meta-analysis. *Child Development* 59: 793–814.

Stoller, Robert J. 1968. *Sex and gender: On the development of masculinity and femininity.* New York: Science House.

  1975. *Perversion: The erotic form of hatred.* New York: Pantheon.

  1991. The term perversion. In *Perversions and near-perversions: New psychoanalytic perspectives*, ed. G.I. Fogel and W.A. Myers, 36–56. New Haven: Yale University Press.

Stone, Michael H. 1980. *The borderline syndromes: Constitution, personality, and adaptation.* New York: McGraw.

Storch, Alfred. 1924. *The primitive archaic forms of inner experiences and thought in schizophrenia: A genetic and clinical study of schizophrenia.* New York: Nervous and Mental Disease Publishing Co.

Straus, Erwin W. 1948. *On obsession: A clinical and methodological study.* New York: Nervous and Mental Disease Monographs.

Strauss, Claudia. 1992a. Models and motives. In *Human motives and cultural models*, ed. R. D'Andrade and C. Strauss, 1–20. Cambridge: Cambridge University Press.

  1992b. What makes Tony run? Schemas as motives reconsidered. In *Human motives and cultural models*, ed. R.G. D'Andrade and C. Strauss, 197–224. Cambridge: Cambridge University Press.

Suárez-Orozco, Marcelo M. 1993. A psychoanalytic study of Argentine soccer. In *The psychoanalytic study of society*, vol. XVIII, ed. L.B. Boyer, R.M. Boyer, and S. Sonnenberg, 211–234. Hillsdale, N.J.: Analytic Press.

Susman, Elizabeth J., Gale Inoff-Germain, Editha D. Nottelmann, D. Lynn Loriaux, Gordon B. Cutler, Jr., and George P. Chrousos. 1987. Hormones, emotional dispositions, and aggressive attributes in young adolescents. *Child Development* 58: 1114–1134.

Susman, Randall L. 1987. Pygmy chimpanzees and common chimpanzees: Models for the behavioral ecology of the earliest hominids. In *The evolution of human behavior: Primate models*, ed. W.G. Kinzey, 72–86. Albany, N.Y.: State University of New York Press.

Svrakic, Dragan M., Kimberli McCallum, and Popovic Milan. 1991. Developmental, structural, and clinical approach to narcissistic and antisocial personalities. *American Journal of Psychoanalysis* 51: 413–432.

Swanson, Guy E. 1988. *Ego defenses and the legitimation of behavior*. Cambridge: Cambridge University Press.

Szasz, Thomas S. 1961. *The myth of mental illness: Foundations of a theory of personal conduct*. New York: Harper & Row.

Taggart, James M. 1990. *Enchanted maidens: Gender relations in Spanish folktales of courtship and marriage*. Princeton, N.J.: Princeton University Press.

———. 1992. Gender segregation and cultural constructions of sexuality in two Hispanic societies. *American Ethnologist* 19: 75–96.

Tam, Y.K., M.M. Tsoi, B. Kwong, and S.W. Wong. 1982. Psychological epidemic in Hong Kong. Part II: Psychological and physiological characteristics of children who were affected. *Acta Psychiatric Scandinavica* 65: 437–449.

Tausk, Victor. [1919]1948. On the origin of the "influencing machine" in schizophrenia. In *The psychoanalytic reader: An anthology of essential papers with critical introductions*, ed. R. Fliess, 52–85. New York: International Universities Press.

Tefft, Stanton K. 1975. Warfare regulation: A cross-cultural test of hypotheses. In *War, its causes and correlates*, ed. M.A. Nettleship, R.D. Givens, and A. Nettleship, 693–712. World Anthropology. The Hague: Mouton.

Terzian, Hrayr and Giuseppe Dalle Ore. 1955. Syndrome of Klüver and Bucy: Reproduced in man by bilateral removal of the temporal lobes. *Neurology* 5: 373–380.

Theweleit, Klaus. 1987. *Male fantasies. Vol I: Women, floods, bodies, history*. Trans. S. Conway. 2 vols. Minneapolis: University of Minnesota Press.

———. 1989. *Male fantasies. Vol II: Male bodies: Psychoanalyzing the white terror*. Trans. E. Carter and C. Turner. 2 vols. Minneapolis: University of Minnesota Press.

Thomas, Alexander and Stella Chess. 1984. Genesis and evolution of behavioral disorders: From infancy to early adult life. *American Journal of Psychiatry* 141: 1–9.

Tienari, Pekka, Anneli Sorri, Mikko Naarala, Karl-Erik Wahlberg, Tuula Rönkkö, and Lyman C. Wynne. 1987. The Finnish adoptive family study of schizophrenia: Possible joint effects of genetic vulnerability and family interaction. In *Understanding major mental disorder: The contribution of family interaction research*, ed. K. Hahlweg and M.J. Goldstein, 33–54. New York: Family Process Press.

Tilly, Charles. 1985. War making and state making as organized crime. In *Bringing the state back in*, ed. P.B. Evans, D. Rueschemeyer and T. Skocpol, 169–191. Cambridge: Cambridge University Press.

Timberlake, Lloyd and Jon Tinker. 1984. *Environment and conflict*. Washington, D.C.: Earthscan.

Trawick, Margaret. 1988. Spirits and voices in Tamil songs. *American Ethnologist* 15: 193–215.

   1990. *Notes on love in a Tamil family*. Berkeley: University of California Press.

   1992. Desire in kinship: A Lacanian view of the South Indian familial self. In *Psychoanalytic Anthropology after Freud: Essays Marking the Fiftieth Anniversary of Freud's Death*, ed. D.H. Spain, 49–62. New York: Psyche Press.

Trethowan, W.H. 1968. The couvade syndrome – some further observations. *Journal of Psychosomatic Research* 12: 107–115.

Trethowan, W.H. and M.F. Conlon. 1965. The couvade syndrome. *British Journal of Psychiatry* 111: 57–66.

Tuzin, Donald. 1972. Yam symbolism in the Sepik: An interpretative account. *Southwestern Journal of Anthropology* 28: 230–254.

   1984. Miraculous voices: The auditory experience of numinous objects. *Current Anthropology* 25: 579–596.

Tylor, Edward B. 1889. On a method of investigating the development of institutions: Applied to laws of marriage and descent. *Journal of the Royal Anthropological Institute* 18: 245–272.

Uberoi, J.P. Singh. 1962. *Politics of the kula ring: An analysis of the findings of Bronislaw Malinowski*. Manchester: Manchester University Press.

Ulman, Richard Barrett and D. Wilfred Abse. 1983. The group psychology of mass madness: Jonestown. *Political Psychology* 4: 637–661.

Vanggaard, Thorkil. 1972. *Phallos: A symbol and its history in the male world*. New York: International Universities Press.

van Ginneken, Jaap. 1984. The killing of the father: The background of Freud's group psychology. *Political Psychology* 5: 391–414.

van IJzendoorn, Marinus H., and Pieter M. Kroonenberg. 1988. Cross-cultural patterns of attachment: A meta-analysis of the strange situation. *Child Development* 59: 147–156.

Vincent, Jean-Didier. 1990. *The biology of the emotions*. Trans. J. Hughes. Oxford: Basil Blackwell.

Volgyesi, Ferenc Andras. 1966. *Hypnosis of man and animals, with special reference to the development of the brain in the species and in the individual*. 2nd edn, rev. with Gerhard Klumbies. Trans. M.W. Hamilton. London: Bailliere, Tindall, & Cassell.

Volkan, Vamik D. 1979. *Cyprus – war and adaptation: A psychoanalytic history of two ethnic groups in conflict*. Charlottesville: University Press of Virginia.

Waal, F.B.M. de. 1982. *Chimpanzee politics: Power and sex among apes*. New York: Harper & Row.

Waite, Robert G.L. 1977. *The psychopathic god: Adolf Hitler*. New York: New American Library.

Wallace, Anthony F.C. 1961. Mental illness, biology, and culture. In *Psychological anthropology: Approaches to culture and personality*, ed. F.L.K. Hsu, 255–295. Homewood, Ill.: Dorsey.

1970. *Culture and personality*. 2nd edn. New York: Random.

Wangh, Martin. 1964. National socialism and the genocide of the Jews: A psychoanalytic study of a historical event. *International Journal of Psycho-Analysis* 45: 386–395.

Warner, Richard. 1994. *Recovery from schizophrenia: Psychiatry and political economy*. 2nd edn. London: Routledge.

Watson, Malcolm W. and Kenneth Getz. 1990. The relationship between oedipal behaviors and children's family role concepts. *Merrill-Palmer Quarterly* 36: 487–505.

Waxenberg, Sheldon E. 1969. Psychotherapeutic and dynamic implications of recent research on female sexual functioning. In *Modern woman, her psychology and sexuality*, ed. G.D. Goldman and D.S. Milman, 3–24. Springfield, Ill.: Charles C. Thomas.

Waxler, Nancy E. 1979. Is outcome from schizophrenia better in nonindustrial societies? The case of Sri Lanka. *Journal of Nervous and Mental Diseases* 167: 144–158.

Weinberger, Daniel R. 1987. Implications of normal brain development for the pathogenesis of schizophrenia. *Archives of General Psychiatry* 44: 660–669.

1988. Schizophrenia and the frontal lobe. *Trends in Neurosciences* 11: 367–370.

Weinberger, Daniel R. and Karen Faith Berman. 1988. Speculation on the meaning of cerebral metabolic hypofrontality in schizophrenia. *Schizophrenia Bulletin* 14: 157–168.

Weinberger, Daniel R., Karen Faith Berman, and Ronald F. Zec. 1986. Physiologic dysfunction of dorsolateral prefrontal cortex in schizophrenia. Part I: Regional cerebral blood flow evidence. *Archives of General Psychiatry* 43: 114–124.

Weiss, Robert S. 1982. Attachment in adult life. In *The place of attachment in human behavior*, ed. C.M. Parkes and J. Stevenson-Hinde, 171–184. New York: Basic.

Wessely, Simon. 1987. Mass hysteria: Two syndromes? *Psychological Medicine* 17: 109–120.

Westermeyer, Joseph. 1982. Amok. In *Extraordinary disorders of human behavior*, ed. C.T.H. Friedmann and R.A. Faguet, 173–190. New York: Plenum Press.

1985a. Psychiatric diagnosis across cultural boundaries. *American Journal of Psychiatry* 142: 798–805.

1985b. Sudden mass assault with grenade: An epidemic *amok* form from Laos. In *The culture-bound syndromes: Folk illnesses of psychiatric and anthropological interest*, ed. R.C. Simons and C.C. Hughes, 225–235. Dordrecht: Reidel.

Wexler, Milton. 1971. Schizophrenia: Conflict and deficiency. *Psychoanalytic Quarterly* 40: 83–99.

White, Ralph K. 1984. *Fearful warriors: A psychological profile of U.S.–Soviet relations*. New York: Free Press.

Whitehead, Harriet. 1986a. The varieties of fertility cultism in New Guinea: Part I. *American Ethnologist* 13: 80–99.

1986b. The varieties of fertility cultism in New Guinea: Part II. *American Ethnologist* 13: 271–289.

Whiting, Beatrice B. 1965. Sex identity conflict and physical violence: A comparative study. *American Anthropologist* 67: 123–140.

Whiting, Beatrice Blyth and Carolyn Pope Edwards. 1988. *Children of different worlds: The formation of social behavior*. Cambridge, Mass.: Harvard University Press.

Whiting, John W.M. and Irvin L. Child. 1953. *Child training and personality: A cross-cultural study*. New Haven: Yale University Press.

Whiting, John W.M., Richard Kluckhohn, and Albert Anthony. 1958. The function of male initiation ceremonies at puberty. In *Readings in social psychology*, ed. E.E. Maccoby, T.M. Newcomb and E.L. Hartley, 359–370. New York: Holt, Rinehart, & Winston.

Whiting, John W.M. and Beatrice B. Whiting. 1975. Aloofness and intimacy of husbands and wives: A cross-cultural study. *Ethos* 3: 183–207.

Wikan, Unni. 1987. Public grace and private fears: Gaity, offense, and sorcery in northern Bali. *Ethos* 15: 337–365.

Willems, Emilio. 1986. *A way of life and death: Three centuries of Prussian–German militarism, an anthropological approach*. Nashville: Vanderbilt University Press.

Williams, A. Hyatt. 1950. A psychiatric study of Indian soldiers in the Arakan. *British Journal of Medical Psychology* 23: 130–181.

Willner, Dorothy. 1983. Definition and violation: Incest and the incest taboos. *Man* 18: 134–159.

Wilson, Peter J. [1974]1992. *Oscar: An inquiry into the nature of sanity?* Prospect Heights, Ill.: Waveland.

Winkelman, Michael James. 1990. Shamans and other "magico-religious" healers: A cross-cultural study of their origins, nature, and social transformations. *Ethos* 18: 308–352.

Winnicott, D.W. 1953. Transitional objects and transitional phenomena: A study of the first not-me possession. *International Journal of Psycho-Analysis* 34: 89–97.

1965. *The maturational processes and the facilitating environment: Studies in the theory of emotional development*. London: Hogarth.

Winson, Jonathan. 1985. *Brain and psyche: The biology of the unconscious*. Garden City, N.Y.: Anchor, Doubleday.

Winzeler, Robert. 1984. The study of Malayan latah. *Indonesia* 37: 77–104.

Wolf, Ernest S. 1988. *Treating the self: Elements of clinical self psychology*. New York: Guilford Press.

Wood, Frank B. and D. Lynn Flowers. 1990. Hypofrontal vs. hypo-sylvian blood flow in schizophrenia. *Schizophrenia Bulletin* 16: 413–424.

World Health Organization. 1979. *Schizophrenia: An international follow-up study*. Chichester: Wiley.

Wrong, Dennis H. 1961. The oversocialized conception of man in modern sociology. *American Sociological Review* 26: 183–193.

Wulff, M. 1946. Fetishism and object choice in early childhood. *Psychoanalytic Quarterly* 15: 450–471.

Yalman, Nur. 1963. On the purity of women in the castes of Ceylon and Malabar. *The Journal of the Royal Anthropological Institute of Great Britain and Ireland* 93: 25–58.

Yap, Pow Meng. 1951. Mental diseases peculiar to certain cultures: A survey of comparative psychiatry. *Journal of Mental Science* 97: 313–327.

1969. The culture-bound reactive syndromes. In *Mental health research in Asia and the Pacific*, ed. W.A. Caudill and T. Lin, 33–53. Honolulu: East–West Center Press.

Yengoyan, Aram. 1990. Cloths of heaven: Freud, language, and the negation in Pitjantjatjara dreams. In *Personality and the cultural construction of society: Papers in honor of Melford E. Spiro*, ed. D.K. Jordan and M.J. Swartz, 201–221. Tuscaloosa: The University of Alabama Press.

Young, Frank W. 1965. *Initiation ceremonies: A cross-cultural study of status dramatization*. Indianapolis: Bobbs-Merrill.

Zihlman, Adrienne L. 1984. Body build and tissue composition in *Pan paniscus* and *Pan troglodytes*, with comparisons to other hominoids. In *The pygmy chimpanzee: Evolutionary biology and behavior*, ed. R.L. Susman, 179–200. New York: Plenum Press.

Zihlman, Adrienne L., John E. Cronin, Douglas L. Cramer, and Vincent M. Sarich. 1978. Pygmy chimpanzee as a possible prototype for common ancestor of humans, chimpanzees and gorillas. *Nature* 275: 744–746.

Žižek, Slavoj. 1989. *The sublime object of ideology*. London: Verso.

Zuckerman, Marvin. 1991. *Psychobiology of personality*. Cambridge: Cambridge University Press.

1992. What is a basic factor and which factors are basic? Turtles all the way down. *Personality and Individual Differences* 13: 675–681.

Zuesse, Evan M. 1974. Taboo and the divine order. *Journal of the American Academy of Religion* 42: 482–504.

Index